# Lecture Notes in Computer Science 774

Edited by G. Goos and J. Hartmanis

Advisory Board: W. Brauer  D. Gries  J. Stoer

Michel Banâtre  Peter A. Lee (Ed.)

# Hardware and Software Architectures for Fault Tolerance

Experiences and Perspectives

Springer-Verlag

Berlin Heidelberg New York
London Paris Tokyo
Hong Kong Barcelona
Budapest

Michel Banâtre   Peter A. Lee   (Ed.)

# Hardware and Software Architectures for Fault Tolerance

## Experiences and Perspectives

Springer-Verlag

Berlin Heidelberg NewYork
London Paris Tokyo
Hong Kong Barcelona
Budapest

Series Editors

Gerhard Goos
Universität Karlsruhe
Postfach 69 80
Vincenz-Priessnitz-Straße 1
D-76131 Karlsruhe, Germany

Juris Hartmanis
Cornell University
Department of Computer Science
4130 Upson Hall
Ithaca, NY 14853, USA


Volume Editors

Michel Banâtre
INRIA-IRISA
Campus de Beaulieu, F-35042 Rennes Cedex, France

Peter A. Lee
Department of Computing Science, University of Newcastle upon Tyne
NE1 7RU Newcastle upon Tyne, United Kingdom

CR Subject Classification (1991): C.3, D.4.5, H.2.7, E.5, B.4.5, D.4.7


ISBN 3-540-57767-X Springer-Verlag Berlin Heidelberg New York
ISBN 0-387-57767-X Springer-Verlag New York Berlin Heidelberg


CIP data applied for

© Springer-Verlag Berlin Heidelberg 1994
Printed in Germany

Typesetting: Camera-ready by author
SPIN: 10131918      45/3140-543210 - Printed on acid-free paper

# Preface

For many years now, fault tolerance has been a very active research area, and there are many conferences and workshops at which fault tolerance research papers and results are presented. However, in 1992 we felt that the time was ripe for a different, yet complementary, workshop on fault tolerance where a small number of key researchers and practitioners in the area could get together for more "intimate" discussions and presentations. The kinds of issues we wished such a workshop to consider included:

- There seem to have been relatively few major advances in fault tolerant architectures over the last few years; is this true, and if so is this because the subject is becoming mature or stale?
- Or is it the case that fault tolerance has become a mature topic for some applications (e.g. transaction processing) but still requires research to be undertaken in other application areas (e.g. safety-critical or real-time)?
- What are the present-day causes of system failures which require fault tolerance in our systems? Are hardware faults as relevant today as the amount of literature on hardware fault tolerance techniques might suggest?
- What operating system work is relevant to fault tolerant architectures?
- What is the application experience - that is, what do applications like transaction processing and database systems or real-time systems now require in terms of support from the hardware and operating systems, to enable them to provide an efficient and reliable service?
- What can we learn from the experiences so far, and hence what will be the hot topics for research in the coming years?

With questions such as these in mind, we approached a number of experts in the field, and formed a Program Committee consisting of Michel Banâtre, Pete Lee, Ken Birman, W. Kent Fuchs, Farnam Jahanian, David Powell and Jack Stiffler. The committee decided upon the technical topics to be covered in the workshop and selected a final set of approximately 25 speakers to present invited papers. The committee were also responsible for selecting the attendees of the workshop, and we were very happy with the enthusiastic responses of speakers and participants to our personal invitations. Organisation of the workshop was undertaken by INRIA-IRISA, Rennes and the University of Newcastle upon Tyne, and was held in June 1993, at Le Mont Saint Michel in France. Approximately 40 experts eventually attended the workshop, and by all accounts, the workshop was a great success, well received and commended by those who attended.

This volume of Lecture Notes contains the papers presented at the workshop, but revised after the workshop to take account of some of the issues that the workshop raised. We have organised the papers into five sections: Field Experiences with Fault Tolerant Systems; Hardware Architectures for Fault Tolerance; Software Architectures for Fault Tolerance; Embedded and Real-Time Systems; and finally Data and Databases. Within each section there is a mixture of papers from academia and from industry, with technical presentations as well as position papers addressing some of the issues mentioned earlier. Indeed, it is these position papers, presenting the views of people in the computer industry on fault tolerance and its future, which make this book unique. (The papers are discussed below with respect to the author who presented the paper at the workshop, although some of the papers have multiple authors.)

The section on "Field Experiences with Fault Tolerant Systems" contains three papers from authors working in industry, discussing different aspects of their experiences of real fault tolerant systems. There are papers from Ram Chillarege of IBM TJ Watson Research Center, Ytzhak Levendel of AT&T and Doug Locke from IBM Federal Systems. Chillarege's paper presents his view of the top challenges facing the practice of fault tolerance. Reliability experiences from AT&T's Electronic Switching Systems (ESS) are the subject of Levendel's paper, which also discusses the fault tolerance approaches that future systems might take. Locke's paper, derived from many years experience of specifying and constructing high reliability applications, addresses the fault tolerance requirements from the perspective of applications, noting the increasing dependence upon software for fault tolerant behaviour and hence the growing importance of software-fault tolerance techniques.

The section on "Hardware Architectures for Fault Tolerance" contains papers presented by Michel Banâtre (IRISA-INRIA), W. Kent Fuchs (University of Illinois), Barry Gleeson (Unisys Corporation), Jeremy Jones (Trinity College Dublin), David Liddell (IMP Ltd.), Dhiraj Pradham (Texas A&M University) and Jack Stiffler (Sequoia Systems Inc.). The papers are a mixture of technical topics and position papers on the way ahead. Banâtre's paper addresses some on-going research into the provision of fault tolerant scalable shared memory multiprocessor architectures. The paper by Fuchs and colleagues introduces a novel compiler-assisted roll-back scheme for repairing the erroneous effects of speculative instruction executions in parallel architectures. Gleeson's paper discusses the issue of why fault tolerant systems are not in as widespread use as might be expected, the cost/benefit trade-offs for fault tolerance and the market and technology challenges that lie ahead.

As CPU cycles become more freely and cheaply available, the I/O performance in a system is rapidly becoming the bottleneck constraining overall system performance. Thus the paper by Jones, describing the Stable Disk which is a high-performance RAID disk system with additional fault tolerance characteristics, covers an important issue in fault tolerant systems. Liddell's paper presents another industrial viewpoint on the problems faced by fault tolerant system designers, and overviews the design approach taken in IMP's fault tolerant computer systems. The paper by Pradhan studies schemes which can avoid the roll-back of a task's state in the face of transient failures through the use of replication. In the final paper in this section, Stiffler argues that the need for fault tolerant systems continues to grow and he surveys some of the existing commercial approaches. He presents his view on the problems that lie ahead and need to be solved in the next generation of fault tolerant systems.

The third section of papers on "Software Architectures for Fault Tolerance" has contributions from Yair Amir (Hebrew University of Jerusalem), Ken Birman (Cornell University), Elmootazbellah Elnozahy (Carnegie Mellon University), Yennun Huang (AT&T Bell Laboratories), Pete Lee (University of Newcastle upon Tyne), Jim Lipkis (Chorus Systemes), Gilles Muller (IRISA-INRIA), David Powell (LAAS-CNRS) and Santosh Shrivastava (University of Newcastle upon Tyne). Amir's paper describes the construction of a reliable distributed application build on top of the Transis environment. Birman argues that a new class of distributed application is emerging due to the manner in which organisations are using computing systems, and such applications will require advances in the techniques used to build reliable distributed software systems. It is clear that networks of workstations will be a feature of many distributed systems, and the paper by Elnozahy describes the Manetho system which provides transparent fault tolerance for parallel applications running on such systems.

A conclusion which comes out of many of the papers in the conference is that software faults remain a key problem area. The paper by Huang describes two techniques that have been successfully applied to enhance the reliability of software systems without requiring the provision of redundancy in the form of design diversity. Lee's paper is also concerned with the problems of software faults. He discusses the nature of software faults, summarises the techniques which have been proposed for tolerating such faults, and describes an overall architecture for fault tolerant software systems.

Micro-kernels are an increasingly important facet of present-day operating systems. The papers by Lipkis and by Muller address some of the issues of micro-kernel support for fault tolerance, in the Chorus and Mach systems respectively. Powell's paper presents some of the lessons learned from the Delta-4 project which was investigating fault tolerance in distributed systems. Finally in this section, Shrivastava presents some case studies in building reliable distributed applications in computing environments which consist of off-the-shelf hardware and software components with no special provisions for fault tolerance.

The section of the book entitled "Embedded and Real-Time Systems" contains papers by Rod Bark (Hewlett-Packard Laboratories), Hermann Kopetz (Technical University of Vienna), Jay Lala (Charles Stark Draper Laboratory), and Farnam Jahanian (University of Michigan). Bark's paper is concerned with the telecommunications markets, their fault tolerance requirements, and the hardware and software issues that arise. Critical, real-time systems are the focus of the paper by Kopetz, who presents some of the key design approaches for the construction of large real-time systems. Real-time systems are also addressed by Lala and Jahanian. Lala's paper discusses strategies for dealing with common-mode failures in such systems, while Jahanian argues that the traditional approaches to fault tolerance need to be re-examined for time-critical applications.

The final section of the book, on "Data and Databases", has papers by Andrea Borr (Hewlett-Packard) and Jehan-Francois Pâris (University of Houston). Borr's paper argues that special hardware provisions for fault tolerance are not a necessary part of an environment which is required to provide a high level of availability to data, and she discusses a prototype client-server system based on standard hardware and software components. Last, but by no means least, the paper by Pâris concentrates on the problems of managing replicated data. The paper provides a summary of the state-of-the-art in this area, and presents some of the unresolved issues which are likely to require attention in the years ahead.

## Conclusions

Many of the conclusions arising from this workshop are covered in the papers outlined above, since the authors have had a chance to revise their workshop presentations for this book. However, in this section we provide a selection of key fault tolerance issues that arose during the course of the 3 days.

### Hardware

- There is a strong move away from proprietary hardware solutions
- Fault tolerance measures are still needed for the hardware components in a computing system
- Hence, off-the-shelf hardware components must begin to provide support for fault tolerance mechanisms. This should be the next use of spare silicon, and the mechanisms required are well understood
- Cost is still a major issue. Customers want reliable behaviour but are not willing to pay other than a very small premium for fault tolerance. (One participant drew a parallel between selling fault tolerance and insurance!)
- Unreliable communications hardware is causing enormous software problems.

### Software

- There is a growing emphasis on software architectures as the basis for reliable distributed applications
- A set of different architectural models is emerging: group communications, atomic actions/transactions, transparent fault tolerance
- The Unix model makes life difficult for the fault tolerance implementer
- Software-fault tolerance remains a key issue
- Seemingly ad-hoc (but low-cost) techniques do seem to work in practice

December 1993

Michel Banâtre
Peter A. Lee

# Program Committee

## Chair

Michel Banâtre    IRISA/INRIA, Rennes (F)
Pete Lee          University of Newcastle upon Tyne (UK)

## Members

Ken Birman        University of Cornell (USA)
W. Kent Fuchs     University of Illinois (USA)
Farnam Jahanian   IBM, R.J Watson (USA)
David Powell      LAAS, Toulouse (F)
Jack Stiffler     Sequoia, Massachusetts (USA)

# Organizing Committee

Michel Banâtre     IRISA/INRIA, Rennes (F)
Elisabeth Lebret   IRISA/INRIA, Rennes (F)
Pete Lee           University of Newcastle upon Tyne (UK)
Christine Morin    IRISA/INRIA, Rennes (F)

A number of people contributed to the success of the workshop. We offer our sincere thanks to all of them. We are particulary grateful to Maryse Auffray, Marie-Noëlle Georgeault, Philippe Lecler, Evelyne Livache and Gilles Muller.

## Sponsors

- Bull
- CEC (Esprit)
- France telecom

# Organization

IRISA/INRIA, Rennes
University of Newcastle upon Tyne

# Table of Contents

# III Software Architectures for Fault Tolerance

# IV Embedded and Real-Time Systems

# V   Data and Databases

# I    Field Experiences with Fault Tolerant Systems

# Top Five Challenges Facing the Practice of Fault-tolerance

Ram Chillarege

IBM Thomas J. Watson Research Center, Yorktown Heights, New York 10598 **

Abstract. This paper describes key problem areas for the fault-tolerant community to address. Changes in technology, expectation of society, and needs of the market pressure the change point for fault-tolerance in their own special manner. A developer, who has only a little set of resources and limited time, responds to these pressures with a set of priorities. I believe that the top five challenges which ultimately drive the exploitation of fault-tolerant technology are: (1) Shipping a product on schedule, (2) Reducing unavailability, (3) Non-disruptive change management, (4) Human fault-tolerance, (5) All over again in the distributed world. Each of these are discussed to explore their influence on the choice for fault-tolerance. Understanding them is key to guide research-investment and structure its derivatives.

## 1. The Area of Fault-tolerance

The area of fault-tolerance is never clearly defined, however, in some quarters it is assumed that fault tolerant computing appears in a box. This is misleading given that the ideas of fault-tolerance permeate the entire industry into hardware, software, and application. Yet, it is not uncommon for industry segmentation efforts to divvy up the market and identify one of them as the fault tolerant market. This market, when quantified by adding up the revenue from fault tolerant boxes, is only in the range of two billion dollars [1]. In an industry that is estimated at more than two hundred billion dollars. However, as most engineers would agree, the perception that fault tolerant computing comes in a box, whether hardware or software, is only a very narrow view of the area.

A larger view, one I believe to be more accurate, is that the ideas and concepts of fault-tolerance permeate every segment of the industry – starting with the device, the machine and following through with systems software, the system software, application software and including the end user. However, this larger vision is confounded by the fact that there are several different forces and expectations on what is considered fault-tolerance and what is not. The single hardest problem that continues to persist in this community is the definition of the faults that need to be tolerated [2] [3]. An engineering effort to design fault-tolerance is effective only when there is a clear picture of what faults need to be tolerated. These questions need to be answered at every level of the system. There are

** This paper represents a personal view of the author and should not be interpreted as an official position of the IBM Corporation, either stated or implied.

# Top Five Challenges Facing the Practice of Fault-tolerance

Ram Chillarege

IBM Thomas J. Watson Research Center, Yorktown Heights, New York 10598 **

**Abstract.** This paper identifies key problem areas for the fault-tolerant community to address. Changes in technology, expectation of society, and needs of the market pressure the design point for fault-tolerance in their own special manner. A developer, who has only a finite set of resources and limited time, responds to these pressures with a set of priorities. I believe that the top five challenges, which ultimately drive the exploitation of fault-tolerant technology are: (1) Shipping a product on schedule, (2) Reducing unavailability, (3) Non-disruptive change management, (4) Human fault-tolerance, (5) All over again in the distributed world. Each of these are discussed to explore their influence on the choice for fault-tolerance. Understanding them is key to guide research investment and maximize its derivatives.

## 1   The Area of Fault-tolerance

The area of fault-tolerance is never clearly defined, however, in some quarters it is assumed that fault tolerant computing appears in a box. This is misleading given that the ideas of fault-tolerance permeate the entire industry into hardware software, and application. Yet, it is not uncommon for industry segmentation efforts to divvy up the market and identify one of them as the fault tolerant market. This market, when quantified by adding up the revenue from fault-tolerant boxes, is only in the range of two billion dollars [1], in an industry that is estimated at more than two hundred billion dollars. However, as most engineers would agree, the perception that fault tolerant computing comes in a box, either hardware or software, is only a very narrow view of the area.

A larger view, one I believe to be more accurate, is that the ideas and concepts of fault-tolerance permeate every segment of the industry – starting with the device, the machine and following through with systems software, sub-system software, application software and including the end user. However, this larger vision is confounded by the fact that there are several different forces and expectations on what is considered fault-tolerance and what is not. The single hardest problem that continues to persist in this community is the definition of the faults that need to be tolerated [2] [3]. An engineering effort to design fault-tolerance is effective only when there is a clear picture of what faults need to be tolerated. These questions need to be answered at every level of the system. There are

---

** This paper represents a personal view of the author and should not be interpreted as an official position of the IBM Corporation, either stated or implied.

trade-offs in cost, manufacturability, design time and capability in arriving at a design point. Utimately, like any decision, there is a substantial amount of subjective judgement used for that purpose.

Independent of the technical challenges that face the designer of fault tolerant machines, there is another dimension which is based on society and its expectations placed on computers. In the long run this has a more significant impact on what needs to be designed into machines than is ordinarily given credit. Let us for a moment go back in time and revisit the Apollo Seven disaster that took place more than two decades ago. At that time the tragedy brought about a grave sadness in our society. We let it pass, hoped it would not happen again, and continued the pursuit of scientific accomplishments for mankind. Contrasted with the Challenger disaster that took place only a few years ago, there was a very different perception in society. It was considered unacceptable that such a disaster could take place. The expectations on technology had changed in the minds of people. Technology has significantly advanced, and the average person trusted it a lot more, whether or not that trust was rightfully placed.

These changes in expectation place an enormous pressure on the designers of equipment which is used in every day life. People expect them to work and expect them to be reliable, whether or not the product has such specifications. In cases where safety is critical, there may exist an elaborate process and specification to insure safety. However, there are computers imbedded in consumer devices which may or may not have gone through the design and scrutiny to insure reliability, safety and dependability.

## 1.1  "Operating Just Below the Threshold of Pain"

The question of engineering fault-tolerance is a very critical one. Just how much fault-tolerance is needed for a system or an application is a hard question. Ideally, this question should have an engineering answer but in reality that is rare. It is one that has to be answered bearing in mind, expectation of a customer, the capability of a technology and what is considered competitive in the marketplace. I propose that a realistic answer to this question is to recognize that a system need be fault tolerant only to the extent that it *operates just below the threshold of pain.*

Fault-tolerance does not come free. Developing a system which is fault tolerant beyond customer expectation is excessive in cost and cannot be competitive. On the other hand, if the system fails too often causing customer dissatisfaction, one will lose market share. The trick is to understand what that threshold of pain is and insure that the system operates just below that threshold. This would then be the perfect engineering solution.

Understanding the threshold of pain, knowing the limits of the technology and the capability of alternate offerings is critical. One approach is to dollarize lost business opportunity to provide a quantitative mechanism to arrive at a reasonable specification. However, when the impact is customer satisfaction and lost market share, it is more complicated. When the impact is perception, it is truly difficult. When safety is in question, all bets are off. Nevertheless, the bottom line is that one has to maintain a careful balance in designing fault-tolerance capability.

## 2 Forces Driving the Prioritization

The design of fault-tolerant computing is influenced by several changes in the current industrial environment. These changes come from different directions and pressure the fault tolerant community in their own special manner. For the purposes of this paper we will discuss a few of the pressures that influence the current environment.

Component reliability and speed both have made dramatic improvements. The improvement in hard failure rate for IBM mainframes, (measured in failures per year per MIPS) decreased almost two orders of magnitude in 10 years [4]. The dramatic improvement in reliability decreases the sense of criticality on fault-tolerance, although it does not completely go away. However, this trend coupled with other effects does tend to change the focus. One of the other significant effects is standardization and commoditization, yielding a very competitive market. Standardization increases competition, reduces profit margins and on puts a very strong focus on cost. This competitiveness is experienced in almost every segment, more so in the lower price segments than the higher price segments. The net result is a tremendous focus on cost.

The belief that fault-tolerance increases cost is quite pervasive, although it is not clear that it does so from a life-cycle-cost perspective. Fundamentally, fault-tolerance in hardware is achieved through the use of redundant resources. Redundant resources cost money (or performance) and no matter how small come under perpetual debate.

The drive towards standardization has decreased product differentiation. As a result, in a market with standardized offerings every vendor is looking for product differentiators. Fault-tolerance, is certainly a key differentiator amongst equivalent function and this should help drive the need for greater fault-tolerance.

The customer's perspective on these problems is driven from a different set of forces. There is a much greater dependency on information technology as time progresses, and this dependency is not as well recognized until things go wrong. This subliminal nature of computing in the work place has resulted in much higher expectations on delivery of the service. Customers do not write down specifications on dependability, reliability, availability or serviceability. They have expectations which have grown to the point that dependability is expected as a given. As a result, the focus of the customer is on the solution and not so much on how we got to the solution. Unless a vendor recognizes these expectations and designs appropriately, the resulting solution may be far from the expectations.

Given the downturn in the economy in the last few years there has been a trend to reduce expenditure on information systems. One of the tendencies is to move off equipment which is considered higher priced and on to those considered lower priced alternatives. These moves are usually not matched with a corresponding shift in expectation as far as reliability and availability. This is particularly true where applications on centralized mainframe computers are moved to networks of distributed personal computers. While the mainframe systems had experienced staff who understood systems management, dependencies, and recovery strategies the equivalent function or skill may not exist for the distributed setup. However, with computing in the hands of the non-experts, the expectations continue to carry through while the underlying enablers may not exist, and the risks not adequately comprehended.

Given these various forces one can see that the design point for fault tolerant equipment is indeed a very nebulous issue. Although it is good to, "ask the customer," on a realistic front questions on expectation of reliability, availability, with the corresponding cost and risk are extremely hard to quantify.

## 3  The Top 5 Challenges

There is only a finite amount of time and resource that can be juggled to produce product and profit. Fault-tolerance, as a technology or a methodology to enhance a product, plays a key role in it. Without the techniques of fault-tolerance it is unlikely that any of the products would function at levels of acceptability. Yet, since the use of fault-tolerance takes a finite amount of resource (parts and development) its application is always debated. Thus, there are times when its use, though arguably wise and appropriate has to be traded due to its impact on the practicality of producing product.

There is no magic answer to the tradeoffs that are debated. Some times, there are costing procedures and data to understand the tradeoffs. Most times, these decisions have to be made with less than perfect information. Thus judgment, experience, and vision drive much of the decision making. What results are a set of priorities. The priorities change with time and are likely to be different for the different product lines. However, stepping back and observing the trends there are some generalizations that become apparent. The following sections list five items, in order, that I believe drive most of the priorities. There are numerous data sources and facts from technical, trade and news articles that provide bits and pieces of information. Although some are cited, the arguments are developed over a much larger body of information. The compilation is purely subjective and the prioritization is a further refinement of it.

### 3.1  Shipping a Product on Schedule

This is by far the single largest force that drives what gets built or not, and for the most part, rightly so. What has that to do with fault-tolerance? It worthwhile noting that producing product is always king - the source of revenue and sustenance. The current development process is under extreme pressure to reduce cycle time. Getting to market first provides advantage and the price of not being first is significant. This is driven by the need in a competitive market to introduce products faster, and a technological environment where product life times are shrinking. The reduction in cycle time impacts market opportunity realised and life-cycle costs.

The development cycle time is proportional to the amount of function being designed. The shrinking of development cycle time brings under scrutiny any function that could be considered additional. Unfortunately, this pressure does not spare function used to provide fault-tolerance. Fault-tolerance requires additional resource not only in hardware but also in design and verification, which add to development cycle time. Any extra function that doesn't directly correspond to a marketable feature comes under scrutiny. Thus, the pressure of reducing of cycle time can indirectly work against functionality such as fault-tolerance which is usually a support type of function in the background. Until fault-tolerance becomes a feature which is directly translates to customer gain, the cycle time pressures do not work in its favor.

Systems have become very complex. The complexity exists at almost every level of the system – the hardware, the software, the applications and user interface levels. Designing complex systems increases development cycle time, and also creates correspondingly complex failure mechanisms. Although automation and computer aided design techniques have helped reduce the burden, especially in hardware, they cause a new kind of problem. Errors that are inserted and the ones that dominate the development process are the higher level specification and design errors. These design errors have a large impact on the overall development cycle time, significantly impacting cost. There are no easy solutions to these problems and an understanding of the fault models is only emerging.

The classical positioning of dependable computing and fault-tolerance has been not to address the faults that escape the development process but to address the random errors attributed to nature. Unfortunately, this is probably a fairly major oversight in this industry. One of the critical paths in a business is the development cycle time. The compressed schedules can result in a greater number of errors that actually escape into the field. Unfortunately, this has never been the focus and is not easy to make the focus. It would make a difference if these error escapes were also the focus of the fault-tolerant computing research community.

## 3.2 Reducing Unavailability

From the perspective of a commercial customer, it is the loss of availability that causes a large impact. The causes of outage need to be carefully understood before one can develop a strategy for where fault tolerance needs to be applied. There have been quite a few studies that identify the various causes of outage and their impact. A widely recognized conclusion is that the Pareto is dominated by software and procedural issues, such as operator errors or user errors. Next to these errors are hardware and environmental problems. Studies show that a decade ago, hardware outage dominated the Pareto but improvements in technology and manufacturing have decreased that contribution. However, there have not been similar improvements in software which is why it now dominates the cause of outage [5]. It is common place in the industry to separate outage causes into scheduled and unscheduled outage. Given the Pareto this split is more relevant in software than in hardware.

An unscheduled outage is an act of technology or nature and is the kind of fault that is commonly the target of fault-tolerant design. Typically, these faults are due to manufacturing defects or marginal performance which result in transient or intermittent errors. Unscheduled outage can also occur due to software bugs or defects. Although there is considerable effort expended on debugging software prior to release, there is no such thing as the last bug. Bugs that cause failures but do not always result in a complete outage [6]. Infact, the severity 1 (on a scale of 1-4) implying a complete loss of function are less than 10% and severity 2, which requires some circumvention to restore operation is typically between 20%-40%. The severity 3's and 4's correspond to an annoyance and are usually the bulk of the problems. Not every software defect hits every customer. However, it is common practice to upgrade a release of software with a maintenance release. A maintenance release includes recent bug-fixes and the time required for periodic maintenance is usually accounted under scheduled outage.

The largest part of outage due to software is what may be called planned or scheduled outage. Primarily, these are for maintenance, reconfiguration, upgrade etc. Over the past few years we have seen that the proportion of scheduled outage, especially in software, has greatly increased. The mean scheduled outage in the commercial data processing center is at least twice that of an unscheduled outage. It is also the case that the total amount of outage caused, due to scheduled down time, far exceeds unscheduled outage, particularly for software. Typically commercial systems have scheduled down time to reorganize data bases, accommodate new configurations or tune for performance. This is an aspect of outage that has not been adequately studied in the academic community. Although, it may sound like a topic for systems management it impacts availability most directly.

As the industry places greater emphasis on reducing software defects and their impact, the proportion of the scheduled outage will rise. Reducing the scheduled outage down to zero is becoming a requirement in some commercial applications that call for 24x7 operation, i.e., 24 hours a day, 7 days a week [7]. To reach this design point one has to reduce outage from all sources. The difficulty is in reducing scheduled outage since, most old designs assume the availability of a window for repair and maintenance. To reach the goal of 24x7 operation one has to broaden the vision and scope of fault-tolerance to include all sources of outage. This calls for rethinking the design point. The task is much simpler for hardware, where each machine design starts with almost a clean slate. Whereas, designing software is a much more constrained, building on a base of code, whose design might not all be understood or documented.

## 3.3 Non-Disruptive Change Management

The earlier discussion on scheduled outage brings to focus a very important aspect about software maintenance. Software will always need to be maintained:

either the installation of patches, upgrade to a newer release, establishing of new interfaces, etc. All these cause disruption and more often than not demand an outage. Unless software has been designed to be maintained non-disruptively, it is unlikely this capability can be retrofit. The increasing network applications create situations where products communicate with different releases and functionality, requiring *N to N+1* compatibility. This requirement has serious implications on how software is designed, control structures maintained, and data shared. Architecting this from the very beginning makes the task of designing upgradability much easier. Trying to do this in a legacy system is invariably a hard exercise and sometimes infeasible.

There are some techniques that can be adopted towards non-disruptive change management. Broadly, they fall into a couple of major categories: one being a hot standby and the other the mythical modular construction that can be maintained on-line. With legacy system the choices are more limited given a base architecture which is inherited, and a hot standby approach is easier to conceive [8] [9]. In a hot standby, a second version of the application is brought up and users migrated from one application to the other while the first version is taken down for rework. To do this one has to maintain communication between the applications, consistency of data, and a failover capability. Alternatively, applications can be built so they are more modular and the shared resources managed to permit online maintenance.

A related problem that impacts non-disruptive change management is the very first step namely, problem isolation and diagnosis. Unlike hardware, software failures do not always result in adequate information to identify the fault or the cause of failure. In IBM parlance, this is commonly called *first failure data capture*. Studies have shown, that the first failure data capture is usually quite poor. Barring, some of the mainframe software which has traditionally had a lot of instrumentation [10]. Most software does not trap, trace or log adequate information to help diagnose the failure the first time it occurs. Furthermore, error propagation and latency make it hard to identify the root cause. The problem then requires to be *re-created* which, at the customer site, causes further disruption and outage.

In a network environment, an application can be spread across the network in a client-server relationship with data from distributed databases. Providing a non-disruptive solution for change management becomes more complicated. To reduce outage, change management has to be carefully architected. Current trends in this area are mostly adhoc and a unifying theme and architecture is certainly an opportune area for research. It would also provide for better interoperability across multi-vendor networks.

## 3.4   Human Fault-Tolerance

With the current focus on the defect problem and unscheduled outage their impact will eventually be decreased. The scheduled down time will also decrease with improved systems management. However, a new problem will then start to dominate. This problem has to do with the human comprehension of tasks being performed. In IBM parlance, we call this the *non-defect oriented problems*. As the name suggests, a non-defect is one that does not require a code change to fix the problem. The non-defect problems also includes tasks such as installation and migration, provided they are problems related to comprehensibility of instructions and tasks, as opposed to defects in the code.

A non-defect can cause work to be stopped by the human, resulting in an eventual loss of availability. This disruption in the work, can also result in calls to the vendor increasing service costs. More importantly, these problems can eventually impact the perception of the product. Increasingly, information on a product is integrated with the application making documentation more accessible and available. New graphical user interfaces have paradigms that make the execution of a task far more intuitive. Additionally, there can evolve a culture of *user is always right*. In this environment, the concept of availability needs to be re-thought and correspondingly the concepts of fault-tolerance. The classical *user error* will quickly become passe. Nevertheless, designing systems to tolerate human error is only part of the story. Designing systems to ensure a certain degree of useability perceived by a user, is certainly a new challenge for the fault-tolerant community.

## 3.5 All Over Again in the Distributed World

One of the philosophies in fault-tolerance, goes back to John von Neumann, – "the synthesis of reliable organisms from unreliable components". Stretching this to the present day, we often think of designing distributed systems using parts from the single system era. If it were single system with no fault-tolerance being used to build distributed systems, we might be luckier. However, single high end commercial systems, are amazingly fault-tolerant. When we lash a few of them together, one has to be careful in understanding the failure and recovery semantics, before designing a higher level protocol. For, we are no longer, synthesizing a reliable system with unreliable components.

The problems emanate because there are several layers of recovery management, each one optimized locally, which may not prove to be a good global optimal. For example, assume there are two paths to a disk via two different fault-tolerant controllers. If an error condition presented on a request, is re-tried repeatedly by the controller, it would be a poor choice given the configuration. Failing the request reported with an error, and re-issuing it on a different path would be preferred. However, this implies understanding the recovery semantics and disabling them to develop yet another higher level policy. The above situation only illustrates the tip of the iceberg. There are several nuances that need to be dealt with.

In essence, one has to think of the design point and the strategy *all over again in the distributed world*. There are several benefits, one of them being the availability of a substantial number of spares. With plenty of spares, *shoot and restart*, might be a better policy than trying to go through an elaborate recovery process. Assuming that error detection is available, sparing provides a nice repair policy. Contrast with a high-end commercial processor such as the IBM ES/9000 Model 900 [11], which has extensive checking but limited spares. Whereas a network of workstations, in todays technology with minimal checking can provide a lot of spares. On the other hand, the ES/9000 provides some of the highest integrity in computing. Solutions to the integrity problem in a network of workstations, when designed on the granularity of a machine, has questionable performance. This leaves open the very important question of integrity. The design for fault-tolerance in the distributed world, needs to look carefully at integrity, detection, recovery and reconfiguration at an appropriate level of granularity.

## 4 Summary

The goal of this paper is to bring to the fault-tolerant community a perspective of, what I believe are, the top five priorities for a developer in today's environment. The issues identify the factors that help or hinder the exploitation of fault-tolerant technology. Understanding the issues and placing a focus on them could eventually lead to innovation and research that will benefit the industry.

1. **Shipping a product on schedule** dominates the list and is further accentuated due to the compressed development cycle times. In an intensely competitive market with very short product life times, any extra function that might stretch the cycle time, can be argued as non critical and end up on the chopping block. Fault-tolerance function is no exception to it unless the resulting reliability is essential to the survival of the product line, or is a feature that is clearly added value. The dramatic improvements in component reliability probably do not help it. Whereas, a crisp articulation of the life-cycle-cost reduction due to fault-tolerance and overall improvement in customer satisfaction are driving forces, when applicable.

2. **Reducing Unavailability** is critical as more segments of the market bet their business on the data processing and information technology. Today, given the consolidations in commercial computing and globalization of the economy, the window for outage is quickly disappearing, driving towards the requirements of 24x7 operations. The outage due to software dominates the causes of unavailability, and is commonly separated into scheduled and un-scheduled outage. In the commercial area, scheduled dominates the two. Research in fault-tolerant computing does not directly address some of these issues, but is a relevant topic for investigation.

3. **Non-disruptive change management** will be a key to achieving continuous availability and dealing with the largest fraction of problems associated with software. Given that most software in the industry is legacy code there is an important question of how one retrofits such capability. It is likely that a networked environment, with several spares, could effectively employ a *shoot and restart* policy, to reduce unavailability and provide change management.

4. **Human Fault-tolerance** will eventually start dominating the list of causes for unavailability and the consequent loss of productivity. Currently there is a significant focus in the industry on the defect problem and the associated unavailability problems due to scheduled downtime. Eventually these will be reduced, in that order, leaving the non-defect oriented problems to dominate. This problem is accentuated by the fact that there is a significant component of graphical user interface in today's applications meant for the non-computer person. Useability will be synonymous to availability, creating this new dimension for fault-tolerance research to focus on.

5. **All over again in the distributed world** summarizes the problems we face in distributed computing environment. The difficulty is that the paradigms of providing fault-tolerance do not naturally map over from the single system to the distributed system. The design point, cost structure, failure modes, resources for sparing, checking and recovery are all different. So long as that is recognized, hopefully, gross errors in design will not be committed.

## References

1. J. Bozman, "Identifies the sources as intl. data corp.," *Computerworld*, pp. 75–78, Mar 30 1992.
2. J. J. Stiffler, "Panel: On establishing fault tolerance objectives," *The 21st Intl. Symposium on Fault-Tolerant Computing*, June 1991.
3. *IEEE Intl. Workshop on Fault and Error Models*. Palm Beach, FL, January 1993.
4. D. Siewiorek and R. Swarz, *Reliable Computer Systems*. Digital Press, 1992.
5. J. Gray, "A census of tandem system availability between 1985 and 1990," *IEEE Transactions on Reliability*, vol. 39, October 1990.
6. M. Sullivan and R. Chillarege, "Software defects and their impact on system availability - a study of field failures in operating systems," *The 21st Intl. Symposium on Fault-tolerant Computing*, pp. 2–9, June 1991.
7. J. F. Isenberg, "Panel: Evolving systems for continuous availaibility," *The 21st Intl. Symposium on Fault-Tolerant Computing*, June 1991.
8. *IMS/VS Extended Recovery Facility: Technical Reference*. IBM GC24-3153, 1987.
9. D. Gupta and P. Jalote, "Increasing system availaibility through on-line software version change," *The 23rd Intl. Symposium on Fault-Tolerant Computing*, June 1993.
10. R. Chillarege, B. K. Ray, A. W. Garrigan, and D. Ruth, "Estimating the recreate problemm in software failures," *The 4th Intl. Symposium on Software Reliability Engineering*, November 1993.
11. L. Spainhover, J. Isenberg, R. Chillarege, and J. Berding, "Design for fault-tolerance in system es/9000 model 900," *The 22nd Intl. Symposium on Fault-Tolerant Computing*, pp. 38–47, July 1992.

# Fault Tolerance Cost Effectiveness

Y. Levendel
263 Shuman Boulevard
Room 1Z108
Naperville, Illinois 60566-7050
USA
Phone: 1-708-979-1310
E-mail: levendel@att.com

## ABSTRACT

In switching applications, the implementation of fault tolerance has traditionally resulted in high hardware costs, by exclusively relying on proprietary hardware and by using monolithic recovery techniques external to the applications to achieve high quality service. The main advantages of this strategy were no unscheduled downtime, deferred maintenance, easy restart when needed, and easy growth and degrowth. While these objectives are still attractive, they can be achieved in a more cost-effective way by increased reliance on standard fault recovery components distributed closer to and inside the applications, and by using hardware recovery at the system level. A recent trend toward service customization and system distribution allows limiting the use of traditional recovery techniques where absolutely necessary to satisfy performance requirements.

## 1. PERFORMANCE REQUIREMENTS OF TELECOMMUNICATION SYSTEMS

Electronic telephone switching systems are expected by telephone customers to satisfy high reliability requirements in order to assure high quality service. Ideally, the system is expected to perform continuous, uninterrupted operation, and in principle, switching systems are designed for long range continuous operation. In practice, however, target thresholds are set in the form of maximum allowable failure rate, and different sets of requirements are applied for different types of situations. Under these conditions, the products are subjected to the following requirements.

1.  **Operation without Catastrophic Failures**
    In the USA, the system downtime is expected to be less than 1 hour for 20 years of continuous operation.

2.  **Operation without Non-catastrophic Failures**
    The system is expected to provide call processing from beginning to end, but is allowed to interrupt at most 1 call in 10,000. Dial tone must be provided with a delay not to exceed 1 sec.

3.  **Non-intrusive Office Administration and Maintenance**
    The data base, the software, and the system configuration can be changed under specific sets of circumstances without affecting call processing operation. These include: customer data modification, minor software updates, hardware growth, and hardware preventive maintenance and repairs.

4.  **Intrusive Office Provisioning**
    During intrusive Office Provisioning, such as major software or hardware upgrades, it is acceptable for a customer not to be able to initiate new calls after the beginning of the provisioning operation. However, a strict requirement applies to calls in progress: they must be maintained as long as the customers desire during the entire provisioning operation.

A large number of additional requirements further specifies internal operating conditions, such as overload conditions, performance under limited hardware availability, fault propagation restrictions, etc.

## 2. FAILURE ATTRIBUTION

Large systems, such as electronic telephone systems, are composed of a collection of hardware and software elements, each one with a certain degree of imperfection. A continuous analysis of field failure is essential to guide the effort of improving system performance. For the 5ESS® switch, the partition of field failures is given in Table 1 [CLE86, LEV90]. The proportions may vary from product to product, and depending on product maturity.

| Failure | Percentage |
|---------|-----------|
| Hardware | 30%-60% |
| Software | 20%-25% |
| Procedure | 30% |

**TABLE 1.** System Failure Attribution

Procedural errors may be due to personnel inexperience or inadequate operations manuals. Hardware failures dominate the other failure types. However, this does not reflect the current industry experience in commercial hardware where the hardware failure rate is much lower [HAR93]. This is mainly due to the fact that large segments of telephone switching hardware is highly proprietary and its reliability improvement process is slower than commercial hardware which is produced in larger quantities. Commercial hardware may reach higher dependability earlier than proprietary hardware.

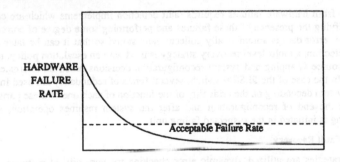

HARDWARE LIFE CYCLE

**Figure 1.** Hardware Failure Rate Improvements

Over the years, however, 5ESS® hardware failure rates have significantly dropped because of design improvements (Figure 1), and software quality improves even more rapidly (Figure 2). Actual field data can be found in a separate publication [LEV90]. New releases of hardware or software may cause a resurgence of failures.

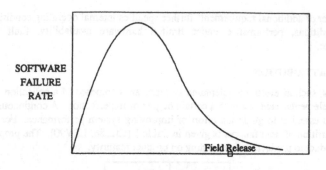

SOFTWARE
FAILURE
RATE

Field Release

RELEASE LIFE CYCLE

**Figure 2.** Software Failure Rate Improvements

## 3. RECOVERY AND RECOVERY SOFTWARE

The existence of recovery software is predicated on the assumption that it is impossible to deliver high quality hardware and software. It is the need for a system to operate correctly in the presence of these hardware or software faults that led to the development of large recovery software. In the 5ESS® switch, software development costs are an order of magnitude larger than hardware development costs, and 38% of this software deals with recovery. This represents a significant overhead cost directly related to the imperfections of hardware and software.

5ESS® recovery software has traditionally been partitioned into *Hardware Failure Recovery Software*, or in short *Fault Recovery Software*, and *Software Fault Recovery Software*, or *Software Integrity*. Of course, the boundary between the two is not totally unambiguous because some hardware failure may cause software corruptions without being clearly identifiable as hardware failures. The two segments of recovery software are regulated by recovery strategies and escalation levels [CLE86].

### 3.1 Hardware Fault Recovery

The recovery from hardware failures requires fault detection implements which are capable of rapidly identifying the presence of these failures and performing some degree of correction. At detection time, error data is automatically collected and stored so that it can be later analyzed. After error detection, a multi-level recovery strategy is used with an escalation policy, ultimately leading to resource swapping and system reconfiguration decisions based on alternate resource availability. In the case of the 5ESS® switch, several forms of redundancy are used in different parts of the system depending on the criticality of the function of each one of these parts (duplex, $m+k$,...). At the end of reconfiguration and after the system resumes operation, automatic troubleshooting is initiated in the suspected failing unit.

### 3.2 Software Fault Recovery

Two basic strategies are utilized, dynamic error checking for very critical software, and data check for the remainder of the software. The data checks assume that a software error will ultimately manifest itself as a data error or inconsistency. Here too, an escalation strategy has been commonly used.

### 3.3 External Recovery Software Strategy and Embedded Hardware Recovery Strategy

Traditionally, hardware fault recovery has partially been embedded in the hardware while its software component was external to the application. The software fault recovery has essentially been external. Embedding recovery in the hardware has resulted in extremely high cost of hardware design and manufacturing goods. This is aggravated by the high proprietary nature of the hardware preventing an economy of numbers. This also affects software portability. The external nature of the recovery software makes it difficult to tune to specific applications and makes it vulnerable to inadequacies.

## 4. SOFTWARE ERRORS

As reported earlier [CLE86], several observations about software development are essential. Two software classes can be identified:

1. *High usage software*
   This is software which deals with delivering to the customer essential system functions which will be triggered by end customer requests. These include call processing, billing, system provisioning, customer data and office administration, basic call processing, etc.

2. *Low usage software*
   This category includes software which is run infrequently and software triggered by unexpected events. Recovery software belongs to that category. Some parts of call processing may belong to low usage software depending on the selling patterns and service cost policies of the service providers.

High usage software is easier to test and will ultimately receive the highest exposure. Therefore, its quality improvement curve will be the steepest. Conversely, recovery software will the most difficult to "train." Testing it thoroughly in laboratory is impossible, and its field exposure will be the lowest, making its reliability improvement curve the flattest.

Recovery software can be triggered by errors originating from hardware or software or can be run on a routine basis. For instance, defensive diagnostic software can be routinely run in sensitive hardware areas on a low priority basis when processing cycles are available. The same can be done for routine audits which examine the consistency of software and data.

Software failures may be primary or secondary.

**Definition 1:** A software *primary* failure is a failure that originated from a single error in a segment of code.

**Definition 2:** A software *secondary* failure is a failure that originated from an erroneous reaction of a segment of software to another imperfection in software or in hardware.

**Example 1:** A software bug in call processing causes a call to be interrupted. The system routines that are in charge of cleaning up the data structures associated with interrupted calls does its job correctly. The software bug is primary.

**Example 2** As a result of a hardware failure, a segment of recovery software takes the wrong hardware unit out of service. This software error is a secondary failure to the original hardware failure.

**Example 3:** Recovery software exhibits a secondary failure as a result of a primary call routing error.

**Example 4:** As a result of a routine audit of system data, recovery software erroneously tears down all call processing in a community of 256 customers. This failure is primary in recovery software. Although such cases are possible, most of the field failures in recovery software are secondary failures.

As the product improves in the field, primary failures in hardware or in software outside the recovery software will become rarer and rarer, thus decreasing the exposure of the recovery software and slowing down its debugging. In conclusion, the recovery software is likely to remain with the highest fault density, because its improvement depends on field exposure, as for any other software.

## 5. SOFTWARE WHICH DOES NOT FAIL DOES NOT EXIST

Table 2 summarizes the field fault densities ($x$) and the fault densities during development ($y$) for a given product release. This release was composed of a significant hardware configuration change and a large increment of software (850,000 lines of code). The results were measured over 4 years.

| Software Increment Size | Development Fault Density ($y$) | Field Fault Density ($x$) | Training Ratio $x/y$ | Software Type |
|---|---|---|---|---|
| 42069 | 0.0285 | 0.0072 | 0.2543 | Preventive Maintenance |
| 5422 | 0.0673 | 0.0210 | 0.3123 | Billing |
| 9313 | 0.0793 | 0.0277 | 0.3491 | Field Update Software |
| 14467 | 0.0265 | 0.0072 | 0.2741 | System Growth |
| 165042 | 0.1016 | 0.0053 | 0.0534 | Hardware Fault Recovery |
| 16504 | 0.0841 | 0.0020 | 0.0237 | Software Fault Recovery |
| 38737 | 0.1494 | 0.0058 | 0.0393 | Hardware and Software System Integrity |

**TABLE 2.** Development and Field Fault Density Comparison

The development and field fault density [LIP82] are obtained by dividing the the number of development and field errors by the size of the code. $x/y$ is the *training ratio*.

The data in Table 2 demonstrates the high "training" experienced by the high usage software (upper segment of Table 2). It is therefore likely that the high usage software has significantly improved as a result of this "training." Conversely, the low usage software (lower segment of Table 2) receives poor field training and displays a significantly lower training ratio.

### 5.1 Software Exposure and Software Improvement

The improvements of hardware and software (Figures 1 and 2) due to field exposure cause a rapid irrelevance of large amounts of recovery software. After a short interval in the field, the improvement of recovery software becomes very slow, postponing its maturation.

Most of the impact of fault recovery software occurs during system development, and helps maintain reasonable system cycling when the system has not yet reached field grade. In a laboratory experiment, system integrity software was turned off at various points during the development cycle to measure a global software quality metric. At the worse point in development (highest software failure rate in Figure 2), the system could not stay up beyond ten minutes without system integrity software. A few days before release the system remained up for one week before the experiment was stopped. In a sense, this indicates that a large part of the role of recovery software is aimed at maintaining a satisfactory design environment by allowing the system to run in the lab in spite of a relatively high number of hardware failures and software errors. It also allows to deliver to the field a product that is still imperfect. But, over a short period of time, the hardware and software reliability improvements make the recovery software somewhat irrelevant. However, when invoked recovery software may exhibit secondary failures. Therefore, excessive reliance in the field on imperfect recovery software may prove to be more detrimental than it is beneficial since it is based on partially immature software, as exhibited in recent noted field incidents.

Given the decreasing number of field failure triggers, the time to significantly improve this software may go beyond the product useful life. Certainly, because of its sheer size (38% of the total software), large recovery software represents a costly strategy for achieving system dependability. On the other hand, since the cost of injecting failures in the laboratory prior to field release proves equally prohibitive, one cannot realistically avoid relying on field training of recovery software.

There also is a hidden cost of using "untrained" recovery software. Unattended errors will tend to absorb excessive hardware resources further increasing the cost to performance ratio of the hardware.

In conclusion, recovery software may end up serving as a placebo, in the best case, and being detrimental, in the worst case.

## 6. A STRATEGY FOR DEPENDABLE SYSTEMS

Some of the proposals below are consistent with Bernstein and Yuhas [BER93].

### 6.1 Better Upfront Hardware Dependability

An essential step of a better strategy for system dependability is to increase up front dependability of its components. Several techniques are available.

1. **Increased Reliance on Off-the-shelf Components**

   Excessive utilization of specialized designs causes excessive failure rates and excessive reliance on recovery software. Conversely, using commercial components will allow the system designers to "ride" on commercial quality and performance curves, achieving earlier hardware maturation. This in turn will allow lowering the investment in recovery software.

   The use of commercial hardware components brings with it the potential of increasing the usage of commercial processors and their software, furthering the dependability of the system components.

2. **Decrease Reliance on Duplex Configurations**

   With an increase in commercial computers dependability, it may be feasible to rely less on duplex recovery mode in favor of $m + k$ techniques which may be more economical.

3. **System and Functionality Distribution**

   Distribution of functionality allows to reduce system complexity and therefore decreases the cost of achieving reliability targets. This technique enhances the usability of off-the-shelf system components.

   This technique also allows to better choose hardware quality (and cost) in a range of possibilities and limit the use of proprietary hardware where absolutely necessary:

   a. Fault tolerant hardware for high performance application segments.

   b. High availability commercial hardware for mid-range applications.

   c. Regular commercial hardware for the remainder.

   Interestingly enough, this trend may already be emerging in telecommunication and will affect its economy in the same way computer distribution to the end-user's desk has affected computing.

4. **Use of Client-server Model**
   This models strengthen our ability to implement a choice of hardware attributes and makes it a better fit for a simplified recovery software [BOR93].

## 6.2 Better Upfront Software Dependability

While recovery software principles have remained practically constant over the years, improvements in software technologies have continued to happen. Fundamentally, software engineers can now write software with a large "expansion factor" by using better languages and technologies. These techniques can improve the initial quality of software deliveries making the reliance on recovery software less necessary. Continued emphasis on initial software quality may prove to be a more economical route.

## 6.3 More Reliance on Recovery Software Methodologies

The aforementioned strategy step allows to rethink and modernize the strategy for recovery from hardware failures and software errors. Using more dependable components will release the fault tolerance designer from the need to worry about the internal behavior of the components as a result of faults, and focus instead on the system as a whole. In addition to the standard reliability techniques used in commercial products, it may be feasible to implement "boundary" hardware reliability techniques to aid system recovery.

In rethinking the recovery strategy, it is important to distribute it when appropriate and move it from hardware to software as much as possible. Coupled with an appropriate choice of "fault-tolerance quality," this allows the appropriate hardware cost and performance overhead choices.

Huang and Kintala [YUA93] recognize 4 levels of recovery:

— **Level 1**: detection and restart; data may still be inconsistent.

— **Level 2**: periodic check of dynamic data and of internal states.

— **Level 3**: check of static data

— **Level 4**: continuous operation by duplication (hot spares, etc.).

They experimented with fault tolerant software that can address levels 1,2 and 3, and recover from faults undetected by hardware. The method incurred a performance overhead of 0.1% to 14%. The strategy is composed of the following three components:

1. *A watchdog daemon process (watchd)*:
   It watches the cycle of local application process, recovers to the last checkpoint or to a standard state, can watch other watchdogs and reconfigure the network, and can watch itself to a certain extent.

2. *A library of C-functions for fault tolerance (libft)*:
   They can be used in application programming to specify checkpoints and establish the recovery strategy. They allow tuning of the performance/resilience ratio of the recovery.

3. *A multi-dimensional file system (nDFS)*:
   It allows the replication of critical data and is built on top of UNIX, which lowers design costs.

As opposed to hardware recovery, these techniques allow transferring the design effort from designing a complex mechanism to that of designing a strategy that is easily implementable by "off-the-shelf" software components (libraries). Since these techniques lend themselves to some degree of "mechanization" in implementing recovery software, they can help tune the strategy with respect to the frequency and amount of dynamic data (as well as static data) to be recovered. This can also facilitate software portability, making hardware upgrades easier.

## 7. APPLICATION TO INTELLIGENT NETWORK COMPONENTS

In addition to using the aforementioned software recovery techniques, variable service dependability can be achieved by replicating on multiple platforms services and/or service resources, depending on their criticality [BAR93] and the economic value of the desired level of service dependability. Evidently, a successful application of service component replication depends on more rigorous application programming technologies.

## 8. ACKNOWLEDGEMENTS

This paper is based on the work of many engineers who, over the years, have made the 5ESS® switch a success. They have met the challenges of producing a very large system which has exceeded customers quality and availability expectations. The experience gained and the dependability improvements achieved over the years can now be embodied in a "leaner" recovery strategy more in line with the economic trends of the nineties.

I am deeply indebted to L.Bernstein whose challenging questions and insights have contributed to shape the viewpoints expressed here. My thanks also go to the team of Steel Huang which has produced some of the data used here.

## REFERENCES

[BAR93]  Bark, Rod, "Fault-Tolerant Platforms for Emerging Telecommunications Markets," *Proceedings of the Workshop on Hardware and Software Architectures For Fault Tolerance: Perspectives and Towards a Synthesis*, Le Mont Saint Michel, France, June 14-16, 1993.

[BER93]  Bernstein, L. and C.M.Yuhas, "To Err is Human; to Forgive, Fault Tolerance," to be published.

[BOR93]  Borr, Andrea, and Carol Wilhelmy, "Highly-Available Data Services for UNIX Client-Server Networks: Why Fault-Tolerant Hardware isn't the Answer," *Proceedings of the Workshop on Hardware and Software Architectures For Fault Tolerance: Perspectives and Towards a Synthesis*, Le Mont Saint Michel, France, June 14-16, 1993.

[CLE86]  Clement, George F., "Evolution of Fault Tolerant Computing at AT&T," *Proceedings of the One-day Symposium on the Evolution of Fault Tolerant Computing*, Baden, Austria, pp. 27-37, 1986.

[HAR93]  *Hardware and Software Architectures For Fault Tolerance: Perspectives and Towards a Synthesis*, Le Mont Saint Michel, France, June 14-16, 1993.

[HUA93]  Huang, Y. and C.M.R. Kintala. "Software Implemented Fault Tolerance: Technologies and Experience" *Proceedings of the 23rd International Symposium on Fault Tolerant Computing (FTCS-23)*, Toulouse, France, June 22-23, 1993.

[LEV90]  Levendel, Y., "Reliability Analysis of Large Software Systems: Defect Data Modeling," *IEEE Transactions on Software Engineering*, February 1990.

[LIP82]  Lipow, M., "Number of Faults per Line of Code," *IEEE Transactions on Software Engineering*, Vol. SE-8, No. 5, pp. 437-439, July 1982.

# Fault Tolerant Applications Systems; A Requirements Perspective

## C. Douglass Locke

IBM Federal Systems Company, Bethesda, MD 20817, USA

**Abstract.** From the applications perspective, the requirements for fault tolerance are not intrinsic to the problem being solved. Fault tolerance requirements are at least two levels removed from the top level requirements; fault tolerance requirements are derived from the confluence of response time and availability requirements. Response time and availability requirements, in turn, are derived from several top-level requirements, most notably accuracy and performance requirements. This second-order requirements derivation results in a wide variety of responses in system architectures constructed to meet them.

## Introduction

We have become accustomed to discussing fault tolerant applications as if they were a separate class of applications distinct from non fault tolerant applications. In practice, the distinction is quite fuzzy, and is dependent on the relationships between multiple requirements. This paper will briefly discuss the origins of the requirements for fault tolerance, and the implications of these origins on the application fault tolerance structures that result. In this paper, fault tolerant systems which must continue to meet their functional and performance requirements in the presence of failures are distinguished from highly available systems for which a probability of being ready for service at any moment must meet or exceed some specified value. Fault tolerance and high availability are not independent; as discussed in this paper, fault tolerant designs are one of several responses to requirements for high availability.

All functional and performance characteristics of well-designed applications are intended to be responsive to the top-level requirements for the application. These top-level requirements are defined by the persons or organizations procuring the system. Requirements are properly viewed as a hierarchical collection of assertions about one or more of these characteristics. At the top level of the hierarchy can be found the fundamental operational characteristics, including statements such as "The Automatic Teller Machine (ATM) shall contain currency of multiple denominations which can be securely held and distributed in immediate response to customer requests under control of a remote account management computer."

These top level requirements are supported by lower level requirements which provide detailed capabilities that, taken together, result in the ability to meet the top-level requirements. These requirements include definitions for concepts described in the top-level requrements, such as the terms "immediate", "securely", "multiple", "account" used in this example.

As lower level requirements are defined, additional requirements are created which are derived from the higher level requirements. Thus, for example, the ATM machine may be required to have a keypad with which the customer can make the required requests.

The total set of requirements for many of today's complex systems are composed almost exclusively of natural language expressions in such a hierarchy of requirements, and result in the production of very large requirements documents.

## Application Requirements for Fault Tolerance

At the outset, we note that the presence of a potential for faults does not directly imply a requirement for fault tolerance. Fault tolerance represents one of several responses to requirements for continued operation in the presence of faults. Selection of fault tolerance as a response to such requirements is the result of a confluence of multiple actual requirements.

Thus, it is important to recognize that the requirements for fault tolerance, in the same way as for requirements for bounded response time (i.e., real-time), are *derived* requirements rather than primary requirements. In fact, requirements for fault tolerance are second-order derived requirements in that they are derived from multiple other derived requirements. This is the basic reason for the wide diversity of responses in actual system architectures to their fault tolerance requirements.

For example, it is well known that NASA's Space Shuttle requires a high degree of fault tolerance. However, the primary requirement for the Space Shuttle is to provide the capability to repeatedly place a given mass into low earth orbit within given time bounds. From this requirement can be inferred a requirement for processor response time based on vehicle dynamics in various flight domains, as well as a requirement for a high level of processor availability, to ensure that the shuttle will be able to place the payload into the proper orbit at the proper time.

Similarly, air traffic control systems are well known to require fault tolerance, but their primary requirement is to track and control some number of aircraft, maintaining a given level of aircraft separation, within a given amount of airspace as aircraft move from one airport to another. The requirement to track moving aircraft implies a requirement to respond to sensors (e.g., radars) and operators within bounded response times. The requirement to track aircraft and maintain separation continuously implies that the system be highly available over an extended period of time.

In both of these examples, it is the combination of the twin requirements for bounded response time and the requirement for high availability that produces the requirement for fault tolerance. If either of these requirements were removed or significantly reduced, fault tolerance would become unimportant. For example, if response time bounds were removed, processor failure could be handled using pyhsical repair or replacement, examples of fault detection/correction, rather than fault tolerance. If high availability is not required, the system can simply be taken off-line, again using fault detection/correction rather than fault tolerance.

From this we can see the basic reason for the relative scarcity of truly fault tolerant systems. The importance of fault tolerant systems is not because they are, or perhaps will ever be, widely prevalent, but rather because of the critical importance of the systems which require fault tolerance to safety or mission completion.

Further, the need for fault tolerant systems will be likely to increase because of the rapid growth in systems with short response time and high availability requirements. Recent examples include global positioning satellite systems, air traffic control, space stations, and manufacturing control systems.

There are examples of application systems with real-time response requirements that have not typically been designed for fault tolerance, such as Automatic Teller Machines. ATM's have requirements for real-time response, but not for high availability; thus, they are usually designed to respond to faults using detection/correction techniques. In addition, an example of an application system with a high requirement for availability but without a real-time response requirement is a payroll system, which is also likely to be designed to respond to faults using detection/correction techniques.

## Design Responses to Fault Tolerance Requirements

In actual systems with fault tolerance requirements in use today, there are a number of design responses to the derived requirements for fault tolerance. The Space Shuttle, for example, is designed using hardware-assisted fault tolerance using redundant processors communicating on a bus. During critical flight domains, such as ascent and reentry, all processors receive all inputs and generate all outputs, using software voting and hardware consensus techniques to prevent propagation of faults. This approach reflects the solutions available to its designers in the mid-1970's, when the largest and fastest available space-qualified processors were approximately 1 MIP and had approximately 400KB of memory. It was determined that most of the computational power of the processor would be needed to perform the vehicle control tasks, and that the required redundancy should therefore be provided principally in the hardware.

The US air traffic control application has been designed to emphasize the use of commercial processors, communications devices, and operating systems. Thus, its need for fault tolerance is being supported using a combination of software redundancy and hardware redundancy. Each critical application function consists of a set of software modules in a primary/backup configuration, with a software availability manager determining the current health of each module. If the availability manager determines the necessity to recover from a fault, either due to hardware or software failure, it initiates a switchover between primary/backup modes, and carries out the recovery. The backup will have maintained a capability to complete the recovery within the required response time; in some cases this will require that it maintain a complete duplicate of the primary state, while in others it will require only an ability to capture a recent checkpoint, depending on the functional and performance requirements associated with the operation.

## What Faults Must be Tolerated?

Existing systems requiring fault-tolerance are designed to be tolerant to only certain faults, in certain combinations. The faults and combinations are determined by a tradeoff between the likelihood of certain types and combinations of faults, the cost of maintaining tolerance to them, and the importance to the end user of doing so. Thus, the Data Management System of the Space Station is not designed to be tolerant to faults in workstations, because life/mission critical functions do not depend on their continuous availability. On the other hand, functions (such as atmosphere maintenance actions) that are life/mission critical are designed to withstand individual processor faults as well as network faults (i.e., network partitioning). Thus, the cost of maintaining continuous operation in the presence of faults is limited to small clusters of processors with simple local interconnections.

On the opposite extreme, an air traffic control system must maintain continuous availability for extended periods of time. This does not mean, however, that the loss of a single controller console is catastrophic, but that such a loss does not result in the loss of any other related function, and that the controller has the ability to immediately resume operations on a different physical console. Thus, the use of multiple hot-spare processes, rather than hot-spare processors allows any lost function due to the loss of a processor to be immediately restored on a neighboring console processor. On the other hand, in such a system, a network partition would be much more serious, since some part of the system would become instantly non-functional. The design response to the requirement for continuous connectivity is to use not only multiple redundant communications cabling, bridges, and cards throughout, but even to use multiple communications technologies to prevent a possible common-mode failure.

In military systems, individual systems are seldom fault-tolerant, but multiple copies of identical systems, as well as multiple subsystems with overlapping requirements are used to provide sufficient fault tolerance. For example, long-range transport aircraft use not only multiple inertial navigation systems (INS) to ensure continuous navigation capability, but also provide doppler navigation, satellite navigation, LORAN, and air-mass dead reckoning to ensure that some navigation solution will be continuously available.

# Conclusions

The Fault-Tolerance literature contains many potential techniques for maintaining fault tolerance, particularly for fault tolerant processing and communications, but their actual use can be seen to be dictated by multiple, diverse requirements which are reflected in a variety of designs.

Since most of the actual requirements from which fault tolerance requirements are derived are met by software-intensive solutions in recent systems, it follows that the most critical fault tolerance techniques are more closely related to software designs than hardware designs. Clearly, the use of, for example, highly available processors will result in longer MTBF's, but the identification of alternative processor and communications configurations in response to the actual faults must occur in software.

Increasingly, it is critical to note that software faults dominate hardware faults as the source of potential system failure; tolerance to software faults still represent an important research area. This problem is made significantly more intractable when we reflect on the fact that fault tolerance requirements derive from the combination of response time requirements and high availability requirements, both of which are likely casualties of software faults. The known general fault tolerance solutions become much more expensive in the context of software faults.

II. Hardware Architectures for Fault Tolerance

# II  Hardware Architectures for Fault Tolerance

# Scalable Shared Memory Multiprocessors: Some Ideas to Make Them Reliable

Michel Banâtre, Alain Gefflaut, Christine Morin

IRISA-INRIA
Campus universitaire de Beaulieu
F-35042 Rennes Cedex
France
email : {banatre,gefflaut,morin}@irisa.fr

Abstract. Scalable shared memory multiprocessors are promising architectures to achieve teraflops computational power. As they contain a large number of processor and memory elements, such machines have a high probability of failure. In this paper, we investigate an approach based on backward error recovery to provide a highly available scalable shared memory architecture tolerating transient and permanent processor and memory failures.

## 1. Introduction

Grand challenges applications defined by the HPCC program, such as climate modeling or human genome, will require processing power that is not currently available. Solving these new problems requires the use of new and better suited architectures. The size and complexity of these applications are so important that the underlying machines must include a large number of processors working in parallel. Scalable Shared Memory Multiprocessors (SSMM) have been developed to provide this computing power as well as a simple programming model based on shared memory. The architecture scalability results from the scalability of the interconnection network which allows the interconnection of a large number of processor and memory elements.

In general, the reliability of a computing system decreases as the number of its components increases. However, in a shared memory multiprocessor architecture, the failure of a processor or memory element leads to the unavailability of the whole machine. Furthermore, the meantime between failures (MTBF) of a scalable architecture might be very low. Consider

# Scalable Shared Memory Multiprocessors: Some Ideas to Make Them Reliable

Michel Banâtre, Alain Gefflaut, Christine Morin

IRISA-INRIA
Campus universitaire de Beaulieu
F-35042 Rennes Cedex
France
*email : {banatre,gefflaut,morin}@irisa.fr*

**Abstract.** Scalable shared memory multiprocessors are promising architectures to achieve teraflops computational power. As they contain a large number of processor and memory elements, such machines have a high probability of failure. In this paper, we investigate an approach based on backward error recovery to provide a highly available scalable shared memory architecture tolerating transient and permanent processor and memory failures.

## 1 Introduction

Grand challenges applications defined by the HPCC program, such as climate modeling or human genome, will require processing power that is not currently available. Solving these new problems requires the use of new and better suited architectures. The size and complexity of these applications are so important that the underlying machines must include a large number of processors working in parallel. Scalable Shared Memory Multiprocessors (SSMM) have been developed to provide this computing power as well as a simple programming model based on shared memory. The architecture scalability results from the scalability of the interconnection network which allows the interconnection of a large number of processor and memory elements.

In general, the reliability of a computing system decreases as the number of its components increases. However, in a shared memory multiprocessor architecture the failure of a processor or memory element leads to the unavailability of the whole machine. Furthermore, the meantime between failures (MTBF) of a scalable architecture might be very low. Consider for instance a system made of a thousand basic elements with a MTBF of 10 000 hours. The average working time of the resulting architecture is then about 10 hours. Hence, availability is a key point in the design of a scalable shared memory multiprocessor architecture. It is necessary to provide fault tolerance mechanisms in order to mask failures of the architecture components to ensure high availability of the global machine. In this paper, we investigate an approach based on backward error recovery to provide transparent recovery from transient and permanent failures of processors as well as memory elements. This is quite different from other studies on backward error recovery in which storage is often assumed reliable.

A backward error recovery scheme is considered because we believe that it is well suited to the target architecture. Solutions ranging from double redundancy to quadruple redundancy (e.g. Tandem [6], Stratus [13]) drastically increase system complexity and cost. Moreover, consecutive failures of the same element are not treated by these approaches. Process replication (Targon [8], Tandem Non-stop [6]) for parallel programming could also be used but it reduces the communication bandwidth, and increases the message subsystem latencies in an unacceptable way.

The purpose of this paper is not to describe a definite solution to availability in SSMM but rather to give insight into alternative approaches and to discuss their potential advantages and drawbacks. The remainder of this paper is organized as follows. In Section 2, we present scalable shared memory multiprocessor architectures and introduce the one chosen for our study. Backward error recovery in SSMM is investigated in Section 3 emphasizing the issues of recoverable memory implementation. Section 4 is devoted to the data sharing problem in backward error recovery schemes. Concluding remarks are given in Section 5.

# 2 Scalable Shared Memory Multiprocessors

Shared memory multiprocessors provide a simple and efficient programming model since the shared memory programming actually represents a direct extension of the sequential programming style. A single address space eases parallel machine programming by reducing the problem of data partitioning and dynamic load balancing. Moreover, shared memory simplifies automatic parallelization and supports standard operating systems and multiprogramming.

## 2.1 Main Features

Traditional small-scale shared memory multiprocessors use a common bus for memory access. However, the limited bandwidth of the common bus prevents them from supporting more than a few number of processors (less than 20 with recent microprocessors). To provide more computing power through a larger number of processors, scalable shared Memory multiprocessors have been developed. These machines still provide the single address space ease of programming while supporting scalability of distributed memory machines. Basically, a SSMM is composed of a distributed shared memory, and a scalable interconnection network (see Fig. 1). Scalability of the architecture is made possible by the interconnection network, which provides a high bandwidth, and the use of multiple memory modules.

The majority of these shared address space distributed memory multiprocessors can be classified as Non Uniform Memory Access (NUMA) machines. In NUMA machines, a node contains a processor, associated caches, a static portion of the shared memory and an interface to the

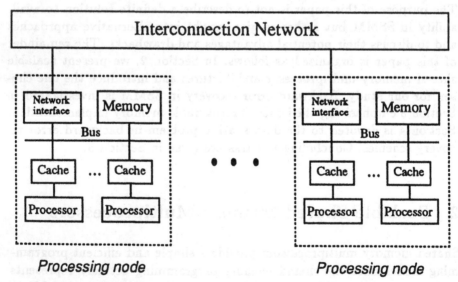

Fig. 1. Architecture of a scalable shared memory multiprocessor

interconnection network. These systems are called NUMA as the memory access time is non-uniform and depends upon whether the location addressed is either in the cache, in local memory or in a remote memory. When such an architecture uses coherent caches, it is called a Cache Coherent Non Uniform Memory Access (CC_NUMA) architecture. Examples of CC_NUMA architectures include the Stanford DASH [16] or the MIT Alewife multiprocessors [2]. In a CC_NUMA architecture, cache coherence is maintained by a directory based protocol. For each memory line, a directory entry stores the line state and the identities of remote nodes sharing the line. Directory based protocols [1] allow the sending of point to point messages to maintain coherence and thus limit network contention compared to snooping schemes [4] which require information broadcast. Handling a miss in a CC_NUMA requires knowledge about the home node for the corresponding memory block. The home node is the processing node where the data is physically allocated (it is usually determined by the highest order bits of the address). This home node is in charge of managing coherence of the corresponding memory block by maintaining the directory entry of the block. Upon a miss, a node first sends its request to the home node of the required memory block. If the block is not modified, the home node provides the block directly from its local memory. Otherwise, the request is forwarded to the node that has the dirty copy of the block.

Recently, a second class of scalable shared memory architecture has emerged. Like a CC_NUMA, a Cache Only Memory Architecture (COMA) machine consists of nodes connected by an interconnection network. Each processing node has a processor, a cache and a portion of the global memory. The difference is that the memory associated with each node acts as a large cache of the global address space. As a consequence location of a data item is completely decoupled from its physical address. In a COMA machine, data items are automatically migrated or replicated in main memory depending on the memory reference pattern. Coherence between blocks replicated in different memories of the architecture is maintained by a directory based protocol. Unlike a CC_NUMA, there is no notion of memory block home node. Localizing a remote memory block is then much more complicated than in a CC_NUMA. To avoid broadcasting on a miss, COMA machines usually use a *hierarchical directory scheme* and a corresponding hierarchical interconnection network. Each directory maintains state information about all blocks stored in the descendent subsystems. This hierarchical organization simplifies the block-search algorithm used upon a miss in the local memory. The request propagates up the hierarchy until a directory indicates it has a copy of the block and then propagates down to a node that has the copy. The node returns the block along the same path as the request. Example of COMA architectures are the DDM (Data Diffusion Machine) [12] that uses a hierarchy of busses, and the KSR1 [10] which uses a hierarchy of rings.

## 2.2 Considered Organization

The goal of this study is to cope with permanent failures in a SSMM. We focus here on CC_NUMA architectures. We do not consider further COMA architectures because of their hierarchical organization. We think that hierarchical organizations are not suited to tolerating failures since the failure of the root of a subsystem implies the loss of the whole subsystem.

The target architecture consists of a set of nodes connected to a scalable interconnection network. We assume a reliable network and hence no architecture partitioning (the network topology provides several paths between two distinct nodes). Each processing node is made of a processor, its cache, a memory and a network interface in charge of managing the directory information to maintain coherence. To prevent faulty processing nodes from sending corrupted information on the network, we assume fail-silent nodes. Finally, we suppose that the failure of any component of a node leads to the whole node failure. Fault detection is achieved by nodes associating watchdogs with requests.

Recovery of processor failures has been largely investigated by researchers [15]. However, most of the existing studies assume a reliable storage for saving checkpoints. In this paper we do not consider any reliable storage. We present solutions where checkpoints are maintained in the architecture global memory, which is not assumed to be reliable. Consequently, new mechanisms must be provided to also tolerate loss of memory elements.

## 3 Backward Error Recovery in a SSMM

Backward error recovery [9] can be defined as the capability of a system to return to a consistent state that existed before it failed. A checkpoint is then defined as a consistent state from which the execution can be restarted. Backward error recovery is implemented by saving checkpoints for each processor of the architecture and by using these checkpoints to restart execution after a component failure.

As presented in [9], the system memory hierarchy can be used to implement checkpoints. The upper levels of the memory hierarchy hold the modified data while the changes are not yet reflected in the lower levels. For example, caches can be used to hold modified data until a cache line, which must be written back, forces a new checkpoint to be taken. This approach is used in the Sequoia architecture [7] and in the CARER proposal [3, 19]. However, this *level* scheme implies a large number of checkpoint establishments, which can degrade the architecture performance [5].

We plan to use a *dual* scheme where active and checkpoint data live together in the same level of the memory hierarchy. To minimize the checkpoint establishment duration, the architecture global memory is used to save checkpoints. The interest of such a solution is that checkpoint rate does not depend on the cache features (size, associativity) and hence can remain low. The presence of a fast interconnection network provides a simple and efficient way to transfer memory blocks between different memories in order to take checkpoints. As a consequence, a part of the memory is inaccessible to processors since it contains checkpoint data.

## 3.1  Stability

Any backward error recovery technique must ensure the memory stability. We define memory stability as the property that the memory system delivers either the current data or at least the checkpoint data of a memory block despite the architecture failures. To ensure this property with our dual scheme, we use the fact that the memory system consists of multiple independent memory elements. We then just have to place a current data and its checkpoint counterpart on distinct memory elements.

To implement stable storage, we use a dynamic replication mechanism where each memory block belongs to a primary segment and a secondary segment located on distinct nodes. We define a segment as a page or a group of pages. A primary segment is directly accessed by processors during execution and contains active data. A secondary segment is part of the checkpoint and is used at commit and recovery time. A node may contain both types of segments. For reconfiguration purposes, primary and secondary segments must not be attached to any particular memory element. They must rather be able to move from one memory node to another according to reconfigurations. This requires a localization mechanism in order to maintain the association between primary and secondary segments. Replication tables are used on each node to maintain this information. For each segment (primary or secondary) on a particular node, an entry of the replication table contains the segment type as well as the address of its associated segment. As a consequence, a primary segment knows where its secondary segment is located, and symmetrically, a secondary segment knows where its primary segment is stored. This double knowledge allows the identification of lost segments when a memory failure occurs. Figure 2 gives an example of the memory organization.

35

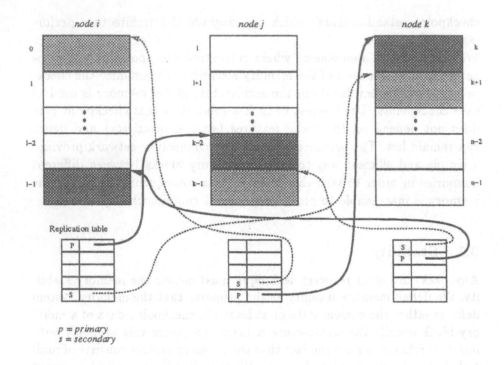

p = primary
s = secondary

**Fig. 2.** Ensuring memory stability

The size of the replication tables depends on the replication granularity. Replication at block level would require large tables and so a large amount of memory. A replication at page or even at page group granularity seems more appropriate to limit the memory overhead.

## 3.2 Memory Reconfiguration after Failure

One of the major interests of our study is that memory failures are handled through memory reconfiguration in order to ensure the memory stability property. After a processing node failure, a part of the memory is lost and some segments are no longer accessible. The reconfiguration phase aims at restoring these lost segments. It is divided into two steps. The first step consists in identifying lost memory segments. During this step all the nodes have to scan their replication table to find the address of lost segments. Once lost segments have been discovered, the second step consists in allocating again these segments on safe processing nodes. Two types of segments may be lost. Recovering secondary segments is done by allocating a new memory segment followed by a commit to update this new secondary segment. Loss of primary segments is more complex to deal with. The problem is that CC_NUMA architectures statically distribute physical addresses on the different nodes. Consequently, when a node stops subsequently to a failure, the primary segments it owns are no longer accessible. The reconfiguration creates a new primary segment on another safe node. However, physical addresses of this segment are different from the previous ones. To address these segments, processors have to take into account the address modification.

A direct solution to this problem would be to use the virtual to physical address translation mechanism by modifying the translation tables of all processes using the segment. However, this solution does not seem realistic as the operating system may directly access some part of the physical address space, bypassing the translation mechanism (root pointer of a translation table for example) and thus disabling address changes.

A better solution to the reconfiguration problem is to use an additional level in the address translation mechanism. By introducing an *absolute* address space between virtual and the physical addresses, the modification of primary segment addresses can be kept transparent to the processors. The *absolute* address space is a linear address space which represents the global address space shared by all processors of the architecture. Each time a request has to access a remote node, an absolute to physical address translation is performed. A processor manipulates only absolute addresses and does not care about physical addresses. Upon failure and reconfiguration, the modification of a physical address is realized by modifying the absolute to physical address translation. Processors still access the segment with the same *absolute* address. Implementation of this solution requires the use of an absolute to physical translation mechanism located on each node and updated on each memeory reconfiguration. The size of the information needed for the translation depends on the fragmentation of the absolute address space.

## 3.3   Checkpointing a Single Processor

Taking a new checkpoint implies updating the previous one as only one checkpoint is maintained. To limit the checkpoint duration, *incremental* checkpointing [9] is used. Memory blocks modified by the processor since the last checkpoint must be written to their corresponding checkpoint block. Moreover, the processor's internal registers have also to be checkpointed. In order to identify memory blocks that have to be copied onto their checkpoint counterparts to establish a new checkpoint, a field is added to each directory entry to record the identity of the *active writer* of a memory block. A processor $p$ is said to be the *active writer* of a memory block $b$ if $p$ has written to $b$ since its last checkpoint and $b$ has not been written to subsequently by another processor. The *active writer* field is maintained by the directory controller of the block because all modifications of the block have to go through it.

Another problem is the atomicity of checkpoint establishment needed to ensure the presence of a consistent state even if a failure occurs during this operation. If a memory element, containing active data, fails after modification of part of the checkpoint data, then the checkpoint data are partially updated and cannot be used to restart execution. To ensure checkpoint establishment atomicity, one solution is to use two secondary segments instead of only one and a two-phase commit protocol to update both segments. This new secondary segment is managed by the replication tables which now have an additional pointer to the second associated segment.

The checkpoint algorithm can be divided in four phases. In the first phase, the processor has to flush its cache and internal registers. All modified blocks located in the processor cache are then copied back to their primary locations. Internal registers are saved as standard memory blocks by being first written into the cache. In order to perform the second phase, the node has to record the identity of all nodes where it has written back a modified memory block either during normal processing when a memory block is written back due to cache conflict or during the flush.

In the second phase, the node sends a message to each node where it wrote back a memory block (during flush or normal computation), asking them to update the first secondary location of blocks whose active writer is the requesting node. Each of these node controllers checks its directory entries to identify which memory blocks have to be sent to their first checkpointing data. This information is delivered by the active writer field of the directory entries. To identify the target node where the corresponding replicated block is stored, the controller uses its replication tables. When all checkpointing data have been updated, the node sends an acknowledgement message to the requesting processor.

The third phase begins as soon as all the acknowledgments from remote nodes have been received. Again the processor sends a message to each node where it wrote back a memory block. These nodes update the second checkpoint data and respond with an acknowledgement signal when this operation is performed.

Finally after having received all the acknowledgment signals, the execution of the processor can resume[1].

## 3.4 Recovering a Node Failure

Recovery of a processor means in fact updating all active data for which the faulty processor is the active writer, with the corresponding checkpoint data. In the event of a node failure, not only the faulty node processor but also all processors which were active writers of (active) memory blocks located on the faulty node, have to roll back. The reason is that a part of their current state has been lost. To identify these processors, we must duplicate the active writer information. This can be done in the directory entries of nodes containing the corresponding checkpoint data. When a node failure is detected, each remaining node has then to scan its directory to find which processor has to rollback. This is done by searching for checkpoint memory blocks whose active data was located on the faulty node. The active writer field of such blocks indicates the identity of the processor which has to roll back. Once these processors have been identified, they have to stop their execution and to invalidate their caches. After memory reconfiguration, all nodes of the architecture have to scan their directories in order to identify which memory blocks have to be updated. Those blocks are current memory blocks whose active writer is one the roll backing processors. When the recovery of updated data is performed, the stopped processors can restart their computation.

# 4 The data Sharing Problem and its Solutions

Recording a checkpoint in a single processor environment is quite simple. Using multiple processors that communicate through shared variables complicates the problem. In a multiprocessor environment, the goal of the recovery protocol is to ensure that there always exists a consistent recovery state from which the execution can be restarted. This consistent recovery state formed by the different processor checkpoints is called a recovery line [15]. Because we keep only one checkpoint per processor (pessimistic approach), we must ensure that the set of checkpoints always forms a recovery line.

---

[1] Note that the above protocol does not guarantee the atomicity of checkpoint establishment if a memory element contains both types of segment (primary and secondary). The loss during the second phase of a segment containing the primary copy of a block and one of the secondary copies of another block cannot be recovered. None of the current and recovery states can be restored as one of the two secondary copies of each block is partially updated while a block has lost its current copy and the second one has lost its second (unmodified) secondary copy. This problem may be solved by temporary having an additional copy of blocks which have to be copied.

## 4.1 Processor Dependencies

We show in Fig. 3 the two types of interactions that two processors can have in a shared memory environment. The first interaction is referred to as the *Write-Read* interaction. In this case, maintaining a consistent global state after $Q$ has read the shared data in the event of failure and rollback of $P$ requires a rollback of $Q$ to its previous checkpoint $Cq$. Otherwise, $Q$ would be in an *inconsistent state* where it has read a data not yet written. This is quite similar to the notion of consistent state, in a message passing environment, defined by Lamport in [14]. Moreover, our pessimistic approach implies to ensure that the set of checkpoints always forms a consistent global state. Hence, if processor $Q$ commits after reading the shared data, the global state formed by $Cp$ and $Cq'$ checkpoints is not consistent since it represents a state where processor $Q$ has read a not yet written data. To maintain a consistent global recovery state, $P$ has to commit when $Q$ takes checkpoint $Cq'$.

The second interaction is referred to as the *Write-Write* interaction. The effect of this interaction is not due to the need to keep consistent states but is a consequence of the physical implementation of the architecture. A shared memory multiprocessor implements a hardware coherence protocol which usually allows only one version for each shared data. Let us consider the second example, where processor $Q$ writes a shared variable which has been previously modified by $P$. When $Q$ performs its write, the value previously written by P is updated and any other read by $P$

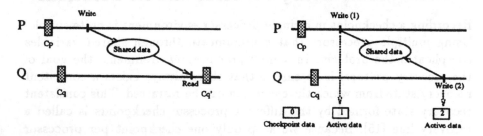

**Fig. 3.** Interactions between two processors

will return the value written by $Q$. Consider now that $Q$ must rollback. The recovery protocol can only restore the last checkpointed data of the shared data (0 in the example) which is not the last write performed by $P$ (1 in the example). Consequently, any read by processor $P$ will not return a correct value since the returned value should correspond at least, because of causality relation, to the last write performed by $P$ (1, here, if we assume a sequential consistency model [14]). Potentially, $P$ is in an inconsistent state since it could violate sequential consistency. To solve this problem, processor $P$ has to rollback if processor $Q$ rolls back. If now, $P$ decides to take a new checkpoint after $Q$ has performed its write, then $Q$ is forced to take a new checkpoint too. The reason is that the new checkpoint of $P$ prevents $Q$ from rolling back to a state prior to its write in the event of failure.

## 4.2 Proposals

Different solutions exist to solve the problem of data sharing in a backward error recovery environment. The first solution is certainly the simplest. The strategy is to identify a recovery line by ensuring that all the architecture processors establish a checkpoint simultaneously. We call this first solution *global checkpoint*. To ensure a global consistent state after failure of a processor, all the processors have to roll back to their previous checkpoint.

Another method is to avoid the need to identify a recovery line by ensuring that there is no inter-processor dependency due to data sharing. This can be achieved by synchronizing checkpoint establishments and communications. A processor has then to establish a new checkpoint before a communication occurs. This is sufficient to ensure that there is always a recovery line. Moreover, as no processor is able to communicate without checkpointing its state beforehand, roll back concerns only one faulty processor. Such a solution has been proposed in [19] and [3]. It applies to bus based shared memory multiprocessors as well as to distributed shared virtual memory. In this approach, a processor $p$ is required to take a new checkpoint whenever one of the data modified by $p$ since its last checkpoint is to be read by another processor $q$. Another implementation of this strategy has been used in the Sequoia [7] architecture. Sequoia avoids dependencies between processors by forcing a processor to checkpoint each time it accesses shared data. To realize this, shared data have to be accessed within explicit critical sections protected by test-and-set locks. At the end of each critical section, a new checkpoint is established preventing any processor dependency. An advantage of this strategy is that it avoids the computation of a recovery line when a processor rolls back. Only the faulty processor is required to roll back. Moreover, checkpointing involves only one processor.

A third solution to the data sharing problem consists in managing dependencies between communicating processors in order to compute the dependency group which is the set of processors that have to roll back or establish a checkpoint when a processor fails or when a processor takes a checkpoint. Two categories of dependencies are distinguished, dependencies forcing a roll back and dependencies forcing the establishment of a checkpoint. When a processor is to establish a checkpoint, its dependency group is computed. Processors belonging to this dependency group are forced to take a new checkpoint to ensure that the set of all checkpoints always forms a recovery line. Symmetrically, to ensure that the current state formed by all processor states is consistent, roll back of a particular processor forces the roll back of a set of dependent processors. This solution has been evaluated for a bus based architecture. Dependencies between processors are recorded by a recoverable shared memory that also stores processor checkpoints [5]. Dependency tracking is realized through snooping of the cache coherence protocol transactions.

## 4.3 Implementation in a SSMM

In the context of a SSMM, the way data sharing is dealt with will certainly influence performance of the architecture. Our goal is to keep the performance degradation as low as possible. Performance degradation is directly related to the number of checkpoint establishments that are realized in the system. Any of the three solutions proposed above could be applied. As we have not yet evaluated them for an SSMM architecture, we try here to analyze their respective advantages and drawbacks. Our comparison criterion is essentially based on performance degradation that the solution should report. We are also concerned with the implementation complexity of each solution.

*Global checkpointing* is certainly the most simple solution. It requires no overhead to manage interactions between processors and moreover, it imposes no particular assumption on the checkpoint rate. This last remark is very important since the number of checkpoint establishments will directly fix the performance degradation. The main drawback of this solution is that it potentially forces a large number of processors to commit together though a number of them would not need to.

Synchronization of communications and checkpoint establishments could be used also without great modifications of the existing hardware architecture. The main problem here is to identify when a processor accesses a memory block previously modified by another one. The directory based coherence protocol gives this information. Each time a processor has a miss, it sends a request to the home node of the memory block. As presented in the description of the memory, the home node always maintains the *active writer* of a memory block. It can hence send a checkpoint establishment message to the *active writer* processor and wait for the end of the checkpoint establishment before delivering the memory block.

From the point of view of checkpoint rate and the number of processors included in a checkpoint establishment operation, managing dependencies between communicating processors is the best solution. As studied in [5] where it is implemented in a bus based shared memory multiprocessor, it leaves the checkpoint rate independent of the communication patterns of the application programs. Moreover, the dependency management mechanism implemented in shared memory minimizes the number of processors that are affected by the commit. An implementation in a SSMM could be possible since like the previous solution, we just need to identify communications between processors. Again, the information delivered by the directory coherence protocol is sufficient for this purpose. Only few messages should be added to the protocol in order to record, for each node, the dependencies it has with other nodes. If this solution is quite simple to implement in a bus based shared memory multiprocessor, it is much more complicated in a SSMM. In the bus based approach, snooping coherence protocols allow a centralized management of dependencies. Thus, the checkpoint establishment time is not disturbed by the group computation which is not time consuming. By contrast, dependency management is distributed in a SSMM. The main problem is that the group computation has to be implemented by a distributed protocol which must ensure some atomicity property. In particular a group computation must guarantee completeness of a dependency group. The complexity of this algorithm is likely to outweigh the advantage of managing dependencies because a large number of messages could be exchanged. Clearly this strategy could be valid if the group computation time remains reasonable.

## 5  Conclusion

Availibility is a key point in the design of scaclable shared memory multiprocessors as the MTBF of such architectures may be very low. In this paper, we have presented a solution to the availability problem of NUMA scalable shared memory multiprocessors. Our approach is based on backward error recovery and uses the presence of multiple memory elements in the architecture to provide a recoverable shared memory. To tolerate the loss of memory elements, a mechanism permitting memory reconfiguration has been proposed. This reconfiguration mechanism leads to an organization of the machine which can still tolerate a single failure of any safe node.

The data sharing problem has been addressed but we have no final solution for the time being. We think that dependency management between nodes may be too fine-grained in a SSMM. Clustering techniques used for operating system [18] could be applied to divide the architecture into static dependent groups of processors which always establishes a checkpoint or roll back together. Dependencies would then be used between communicating groups of processors. These solutions have to be further investigated.

We are currently developing a simulator for SSMM. This tool uses address traces of parallel applications [11] and will permit the performance evaluation of the different approaches. Clearly, the key point to obtain a low performance degradation is to limit the overhead of checkpoint establishments, which could be quite high since memory blocks have to move from node to node. Consequently, we also plan to study some solutions to speed up checkpoint establishment. In particular, saving checkpoints concurrently with execution is certainly a promising solution.

Another field of interest is to investigate solutions to provide highly available flat COMA (COMA-F) architectures [17] which are non hierarchical architectures combining the advantages of both CC_NUMA and COMA.

# References

1. A. Agarwal, D. Chaiken, C. Fields, and K. Kurihara. Directory-based cache coherence in large-scale multiprocessors. *IEEE Computer*, 49–58, June 1990.
2. A. Agarwal, D. Chaiken, K. Johnson, D. Kranz, J. Kubiatowi cz, K. Kurihara, B. Lim, G. Ma, and D. Nussbaum. *The MIT Alewife Machine : A Large-Scale Distributed Memory Multiprocess or*. Research report MIT/LCS/TM-454, MIT Laboratory for Computer Science, June 1991.
3. R.E. Ahmed, R.C. Frazier, and P.N. Marinos. Cache-aided rollback error recovery (carer) algorithms for shared-memory multiprocessor systems. In *Proc. of 20th International Symposium on Fault-Tolerant Computing Systems*, pages 82–88, Newcastle, June 1990.
4. J. Archibald. *The Cache Coherence Problem in Shared-Memory Multiprocessors*. PhD thesis, University of Washington, December 1987.
5. M. Banâtre, A. Gefflaut, P. Joubert, P.A. Lee, and C. Morin. *An Architecture For Tolerating Processor Failures In Shared-Memory Multiprocessors*. Research report 1965, INRIA, March 1993.
6. J. Bartlett, J. Gray, and B. Horst. Fault tolerance in tandem computer systems. In A. Avizienis, H. Kopetz, and J.C. Laprie, editors, *The Evolution of Fault-Tolerant Computing*, pages 55–76, Springer Verlag, 1987.

7. Ph. A. Bernstein. Sequoia: a fault-tolerant tightly coupled multi-processor for transaction processing. *IEEE Computer*, 21(2):37–45, February 1988.

8. A. Borg, W. Blau, W. Graetsch, F. Herrmann, and W. Oberle. Fault tolerance under unix. *ACM Transactions on Computer Systems*, 7(1):1–24, 1989.

9. N. S. Bowen and D. K. Pradhan. Processor- and memory- based checkpoint and rollback recovery. *IEEE Computer*, 22–31, February 1993.

10. S. Frank, H. Burkhardt III, and J. Rothnie. The ksr1: bridging the gap between shared memory and mpps. In *COMPCON93, 38th IEEE Computer Society International Conference*, pages 285–294, San Francisco, February 1993.

11. A. Gèfflaut and P. Joubert. *SPAM : A Multiprocessor Execution Driven Simulation Kernel*. Research report 1966, INRIA, March 1993.

12. E. Hagersten, A. Landin, and S. Haridi. Ddm - a cache-only memory architecture. *IEEE Computer*, 25(9):44–54, September 1992.

13. E. S. Harrison and E. Schmitt. The structure of system/88, a fault-tolerant computer. *IBM Systems Journal*, 26(3):293–318, 1987.

14. L. Lamport. How to make a multiprocessor computer that correctly executes multiprocess programs. *IEEE Transactions on Computers*, 28(9):690–691, September 1979.

15. P. Lee and T. Anderson. *Fault Tolerance: Principles and Practice*. Volume 3 of *Dependable Computing and Fault-Tolerant Systems*, Springer Verlag, second revised edition, 1990.

16. D. Lenoski, J. Laudon, K. Gharachorloo, W. Weber, A. Gupta, J. Hennessy, M. Horowitz, and M. Lam. The stanford dash multiprocessor. *IEEE Computer*, 25(3):63–79, March 1992.

17. P. Stenstrom, T. Joe, and A. Gupta. Comparative performance evaluation of cache-coherent numa and coma arch itectures. In *Proc. of 19th Annual International Symposium on Computer Architecture*, pages 80–91, May 1992.

18. M. Stumm, R. Unrau, and O. Krieger. Designing a scalable operating system for shared memory multiprocessors. In *Usenix workshop, Micro-kernels and Other Kernel Architectures*, pages 285–303, Seattle, Washington, April 1992.

19. K. L. Wu, W. K. Fuchs, and J. H. Patel. Cache-based error recovery for shared memory multiprocessor systems. In *Proc. of 1989 International Conference on Parallel Processing*, pages 159–166, University Park, Pennsylvania, 1989.

# Application of Compiler-Assisted Rollback Recovery to Speculative Execution Repair*

Neal J. Alewine[1], W. Kent Fuchs[2], and Wen-mei Hwu[2]

[1] International Business Machines Corporation, Boca Raton, Fl.
[2] Coordinated Science Laboratory, University of Illinois, Urbana, IL

**Abstract.** Speculative execution is a method to increase instruction level parallelism which can be exploited by both super-scalar and VLIW architectures. The key to a successful general speculation strategy is a repair mechanism to handle mispredicted branches and accurate reporting of exceptions for speculated instructions. Multiple instruction rollback is a technique developed for recovery from transient processor failures. This paper investigates the applicability of a recently developed compiler-assisted multiple instruction rollback scheme to aid in speculative execution repair. Extensions to the compiler-assisted scheme to support branch and exception repair are presented along with performance measurements across ten application programs. Our results indicate that techniques used in compiler-assisted rollback recovery are effective for handling branch and exception repair in support of speculative execution.

## 1 Introduction

Super-scalar and VLIW architectures have been shown effective in exploiting instruction level parallelism (ILP) present in a given application [1, 2, 3]. Creating additional ILP in applications has been the subject of study in recent years [4, 5, 6]. Code motion within a basic block is insufficient to unlock the full potential of super-scalar and VLIW processors with issue rates greater than two [3]. Given a trace of the most frequently executed basic blocks, limited code movement across block boundaries can create additional ILP at the expense of requiring complex compensation code to ensure program correctness [7]. Combining multiple basic blocks into *superblocks* permits code movement within the superblock without the compensation code required in standard trace scheduling [3].

General upward and downward code movement across trace entry points (joins) and general downward code motion across trace exit points (branches, or

---

* This research was supported in part by the National Aeronautics and Space Administration (NASA) under grant NASA NAG 1-613, in cooperation with the Illinois Computer Laboratory for Aerospace Systems and Software (ICLASS), and in part by the Department of the Navy and managed by the Office of the Chief of Naval Research under Contract N00014-91-J-1283.

forks) is permitted without the need for special hardware support [7]. Sophisticated hardware support is required, however, for upward code motion across a branch boundary. Such code motion is referred to as *speculative execution* and has been shown to substantially enhance performance over nonspeculated architectures [8, 9, 10]. This paper focuses on the support hardware for speculative execution, which is responsible to ensure correct operation in the presence of excepting speculated instructions (referred to as exception repair) and of mispredicted branches (referred to as branch repair). It is shown that data hazards which result from exception and branch repair are very similar to data hazards that result from multiple instruction rollback, and that techniques used to resolve rollback data hazards are applicable to exception and branch repair.

The remainder of the paper is organized as follows. Section 2 gives a brief overview of a compiler-assisted multiple instruction rollback (MIR) scheme to be used as a base for application to speculative execution repair (SER). Section 3 describes speculative execution and the requirements for exception repair and branch repair. Section 4 introduces a *schedule reconstruction* scheme and extends the compiler-assisted rollback scheme. Section 5 describes *read buffer* flush costs and Section 6 presents performance impacts which result from read buffer flushes.

## 2   Compiler-Assisted Multiple Instruction Rollback Recovery

### 2.1   Hazard Classification

Within a general error model, data hazards resulting from instruction retry are of two types [11, 12, 13]. On-path hazards are those encountered when the instruction path after rollback is the same as the initial path and branch hazards are those encountered when the instruction path after rollback is different than the initial path. As shown in Figure 1(a), $r_x$ represents an on-path hazard where during the initial instruction sequence $r_x$ is written and after rollback is read prior to being re-written. As shown in Figure 1(b), $r_y$ represents a branch hazard where the initial instruction sequence writes $r_y$ and after rollback $r_y$ is read prior to being re-written however this time not along the original path.

### 2.2   On-path Hazard Resolution Using a Read Buffer

Hardware support consisting of a read buffer of size $2N$, as shown in Figure 2, has been shown to be effective in resolving on-path hazards [11, 12, 13]. The read buffer maintains a window of register read history. If an on-path hazard is present, then prior to writing over the old value of the hazard register, a read of that value must have taken place within the last $N$ instructions (else after rollback of $\leq N$, a read of the hazard register would not occur before a redefinition). Key to this scenario is the fact that the original path is repeated. Branch hazard resolution is left to the compiler. At rollback, the read buffer is flushed back to the general purpose register file (GPRF), restoring the register

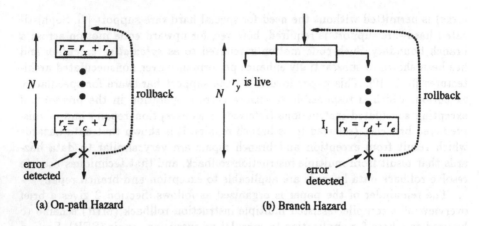

(a) On-path Hazard          (b) Branch Hazard

**Fig. 1.** Data Hazards.

file to a restartable state. The primary advantage of the read buffer is that it does not require an additional read port as with a history buffer, duplications of the GPRF as with the future file, or bypass logic as with the reorder buffer or delayed write [14, 15].

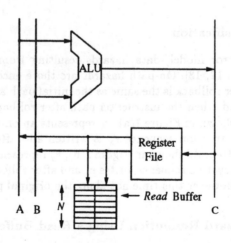

**Fig. 2.** *Read* Buffer.

### 2.3 Branch Hazard Removal Compiler Transformations

Compiler transformations have been shown to be effective in resolving branch hazards [11, 12]. Branch hazard resolution occurs at three levels; 1) pseudo code, 2) machine code, and 3) post-pass. Resolution at the pseudo code level would be accomplished by renaming the pseudo register $r_y$ of instruction $I_i$ (Figure 1) to $r_z$. Node splitting, loop expansion and loop protection transformations aid in breaking pseudo register equivalence relationships so that renaming can be performed. After the pseudo registers are mapped to physical registers, some branch hazards could re-appear. This is prevented at the machine code level by adding hazard constraints to live range constraints prior to register allocation. Branch hazards that remain after the first two levels can be resolved by either creating a "covering" on-path hazard or by inserting nop instructions ahead of the hazard instruction until the rollback is guaranteed to be under the branch. Given the branch hazard of Figure 1, a covering on-path hazard is created by inserting an MOV $r_y, r_y$ instruction immediately before the instruction in which $r_y$ is defined. This guarantees that the old value of $r_y$ is loaded into the read buffer and is available to restore the register file during rollback.

# 3 Speculative Execution

Figure 3 illustrates the two basic problems which are encountered when attempting upward code motion across a branch. First, if the speculated instruction (i.e., an instruction moved upward past one or more branches) modifies the system state, and due to the branch outcome the speculated instruction should not have been executed, program correctness could be affected. Second, if the speculated instruction causes an exception, and again due to the branch outcome, the excepting instruction should not have been executed, program performance or even program correctness could be affected.

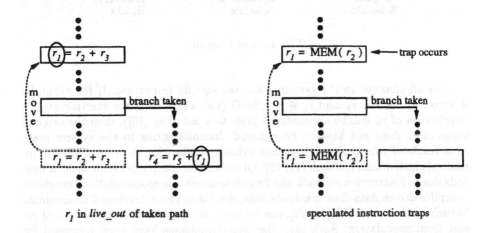

**Fig. 3.** Speculative execution.

49

## 3.1 Branch Repair

Figure 4 shows an original instruction schedule and a new schedule after speculation. Instructions $d$, $i$, and $f$ have been speculated above branches $c$ and $g$ from their respective fall-through paths.[3] Speculated instructions are marked "(s)." The motivation for such a schedule might be to hide the load delay of the speculated instructions or to allow more time for the operands of the branch instructions to become available. If $c$ commits to the taken path (i.e., it is mispredicted by the static scheduler), some changes to the system state that have resulted from the execution of $d$, $i$, and $f$, may have to be undone. No update is required for the PC; execution simply begins at $j$. If instead, $c$ commits to the fall-through path but $g$ commits to the taken path, then only $i$'s changes to the system state may have to be undone.

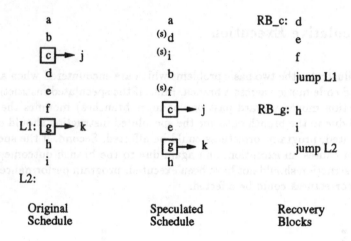

**Fig. 4.** Branch repair.

Not all changes to the system state are equally important. If for example, $d$ writes to register $r_x$ and $r_x \notin live\_in(j)$ (i.e., along the path starting at $j$, a redefinition of $r_x$ will be encountered prior to a use of $r_x$ [16]), then the original value of $r_x$ does not have to be restored. Inconsistencies to the system state as a result of mispredicted branches exhibit similarities to branch hazards in multiple instruction rollback [11, 12]. Given this similarity between branch hazards due to instruction rollback and branch hazards due to speculative execution, compiler-driven data-flow manipulations, similar to those developed to eliminate branch hazards for MIR [11, 12], can be used to resolve branch hazards that result from speculation. Such compiler transformations have been proposed for branch misprediction handling [9]. Since re-execution of speculated instructions

---

[3] For this example it is assumed that the fall-through paths are the most likely outcome of the branch decisions at $c$ and $g$.

is not required for branch misprediction, compiler resolution of branch hazards becomes a sufficient branch repair technique.

## 3.2 Exception Repair

Figure 4 also demonstrates the handling of speculated trapping instructions. If $d$ is a trapping instruction and an exception occurred during its execution, handling of the exception must be delayed until $c$ commits so that changes to the system state are minimized, and in some cases to ensure that repair is possible in the event that $c$ is mispredicted. If $c$ commits to the taken path, the exception is ignored and $d$ is handled like any other speculated instruction given a branch mispredict. If $c$ was correctly predicted, three exception repair strategies are possible. The first is to undo the effects of only those instructions speculated above $c$ (i.e., $d$, $i$, and $f$) and then branch to a recovery block $RB\_c$ [10] as shown in Figure 4. The address of the recovery block can be obtained by using the PC value of the excepting instruction as an index into a hash table. This strategy ensures precise interrupts [14, 17] relative to the nonspeculated schedule but not relative to the original schedule. Recovery blocks can cause significant code growth [10]. The second strategy undoes the effects of all instructions subsequent to $d$ (i.e., $i$, $b$, and $f$), handles the exception, and resumes execution at instruction $i$ [9]. This latter strategy provides restartable states and does not require recovery blocks. A third exception repair strategy undoes the effects of only those subsequent instructions that are speculated above $c$ (i.e., only $i$ and $f$), handles the exception, and resumes execution at instruction $i$, however, this time only executing speculated instructions until $c$ is reached. The improved efficiency of strategy 3 over that of strategy 2 comes at the cost of slightly more complex exception repair hardware.

When a branch commits and is mispredicted, the exception repair hardware must perform three functions: 1) determine whether an exception has occurred during the execution of a speculated instruction, 2) if an exception has occurred, determine the PC value of the excepting instruction, and 3) determine which changes to the system state must be undone. Functions 1 and 2 are similar to error detection and location in multiple instruction rollback. Function 3 is similar to on-path hazard resolution in multiple instruction rollback [18, 11, 12]. On-path hazards assume that after rollback the initial instruction sequence from the faulty instruction to the instruction where the error was detected is repeated.

Figure 5 illustrates the speculation of a group of instructions and re-execution strategy 3. The load instruction traps, but the exception is not handled until the branch instruction commits to the fall-through path. Control is then returned to the trapping instruction. This scenario is identical to multiple instruction rollback where an error occurs during the load instruction and is detected during the branch instruction. For this example, only $r_1$ must be restored during rollback since $r_4$ and $r_5$ will be rewritten prior to use during re-execution. Figure 5 shows that exception repair hazards in speculative execution are the same as on-path hazards in multiple instruction rollback, and a read buffer as described in Section 2 can be used to resolve these hazards. The depth of the read buffer is the maximum distance from $I_b$ to $I_n$ along any backwards walk[4], where $I_n$ is a trapping instruction that was speculated above branch instruction $I_b$.

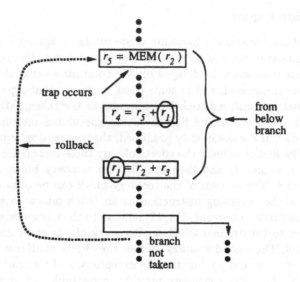

**Fig. 5.** Exception repair.

## 3.3 Schedule Reconstruction

Assumed in Figures 4 and 5 are mechanisms to identify speculative instructions, determine the PC value of excepting speculated instructions, and determine how many branches a given instruction has been speculated above. An example of the latter case is shown in Figure 4 where instructions $d$, $i$, and $f$, are undone if $c$ is mispredicted; however, only $i$ must be undone if $g$ is mispredicted.

If the hardware had access to the original code schedule, the design of these mechanisms would be straightforward. Unfortunately, static scheduling reorders instructions at compile-time and information as to the original code schedule is lost. To enable recovery from mispredicted branches and proper handling of speculated exceptions, some information relative to the original instruction order must be present in the compiler-emitted instructions. This will be referred to as *schedule reconstruction*.

By limiting the flexibility of the scheduler, less information about the original schedule is required. For example, if speculation is limited to one level only (i.e., above a single branch), a single bit in the opcode field is sufficient to indicate that the instruction has been moved above the next branch [8]. The hardware

---

[4] A *walk* is a sequence of edge traversals in a graph where the edges visited can be repeated [19].

would then know exactly which instruction effects to undo (i.e., the ones with this bit set). Also, removing branch hazards directly with the compiler permits general speculation with no schedule reconstruction for branch repair [9].

# 4 Implicit Index Schedule Reconstruction

*Implicit index* scheduling supports general speculation of regular and trapping instructions. The scheme was inspired by the handling of stores in the sentinel scheduling scheme [9] and was designed to exploit the unique properties of the read buffer hardware design described in Section 2. Schedule reconstruction is accomplished by marking each instruction *speculated* or *nonspeculated* by including a bit in the opcode field, and using this encoding to maintain an operand history of speculated instructions in a FIFO queue called a speculation read buffer (SRB). The SRB operates similar to a read buffer with additional provisions for exception handling.

## 4.1 Exception Repair Using a Speculation Read Buffer

Figure 6 shows an original code schedule and two speculative schedules, along with the contents of the SRB at the time branches $I_c$ and $I_g$ commit. Instructions $I_d$ and $I_f$ have been speculated above branch instruction $I_c$, and $I_i$ has been speculated above both $I_g$ and $I_c$. The encoding of speculated instructions informs the hardware that the source operands are to be saved in the SRB, along with the source operand values, corresponding register addresses, and the PC of the speculated instruction.

Speculated instructions execute normally unless they trap. If a speculated instruction traps, the exception bit in the SRB which corresponds to the trapping instruction is set and program execution continues. Subsequent instructions that use the result of the trapping instruction are allowed to execute normally.

A *chk_except(k)* instruction is placed in the home block of each speculated instruction. Only one *chk_except(k)* instruction is required for a home block. As the name implies, *chk_except(k)* checks for pending exceptions. The command can simultaneously interrogate each location in the SRB by utilizing the bit field $k$. As shown in schedule 1 of Figure 6, *chk_except(001111)* in $I'_c$ checks exceptions for instructions $I_d$ and $I_d$. If a checked exception bit is set, the SRB is flushed in reverse order, restoring the appropriate register and PC values. Execution can then begin with the excepting instruction.

Figure 6 illustrates several on-path hazards which are resolved by the SRB. In schedule 1, if $I_i$ traps and the branch $I_c$ commits to the taken path, $I_i$ has corrupted $r_2$ and $I_f$ has corrupted $r_7$. Flushing the SRB up through $I_i$ restores both registers to their values prior to the initial execution of $I_i$. Note that register $r_6$ is also corrupted but not restored by the SRB, since after rollback $r_6$ will be rewritten with a correct value before the corrupted value is used.

As an alternative to checking for exceptions in each home block, the exception could be handled when the exception bit reaches the bottom of the SRB. This is

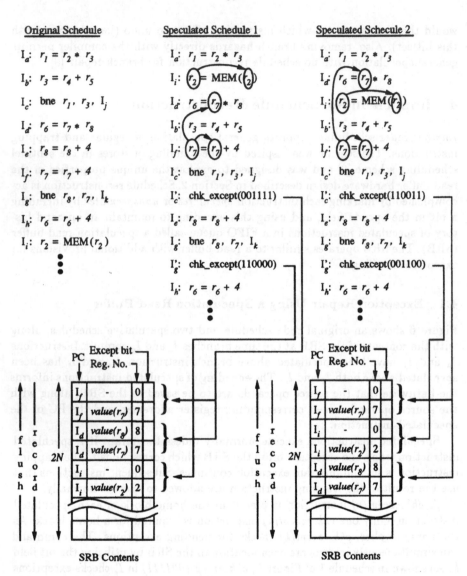

**Fig. 6.** Exception repair using a speculation read buffer (SRB).

similar to the reorder buffer used in dynamic scheduling [14] and eliminates the cost of the *chk_except(k)* command, however, increases the exception handling latency which can impact performance depending on the frequency of exceptions.

Implicit index scheduling derives its name from the ability of the compiler to locate a particular register value within the SRB. This is possible only if the dynamically occurring history of speculated instructions is deterministic at branch boundaries. Superblocks guarantee this by ensuring that the sole entry into the superblock is at the header and by limiting speculation to within the superblock. For standard blocks, bookkeeping code [7] can be used to ensure this deterministic behavior.

## 4.2 Branch Repair Using a Speculation Read Buffer

As described in Section 2, branch repair can be handled by resolving branch hazards with the compiler. Branch hazard resolution in multiple instruction rollback can be assisted by the read buffer when "covering" on-path hazards are present, reducing the performance cost of variable renaming [11, 12]. In a similar fashion, the SRB can assist in branch repair. Figure 7 shows the original code schedule and the two speculative schedules of Figure 6. For this example, it is assumed that $r_2$, $r_3$, $r_6$, and $r_7$ are elements in both $live\_in(I_j)$ and $live\_in(I_k)$.

As shown in schedule 1, if branch instruction $I_c$ commits to the taken path, $r_2$, $r_6$, and $r_7$, which were modified in $I_i$, $I_d$, and $I_f$, respectively, must be restored. If instead, $I_c$ commits to the fall-through path and $I_g$ commits to the taken path, only $r_2$ must be restored. Registers $r_2$ and $r_7$ are rollback hazards that result from exception repair; therefore, the SRB contains their unmodified values. By including a *flush(k)* command at the target of $I_c$ and $I_g$, the SRB can be used to restore $r_2$ and/or $r_7$ given a misprediction of $I_c$ or $I_g$.

The *flush(k)* command selectively flushes the appropriate register values given a branch misprediction. For example, in schedule 2 of Figure 7, if $I_c$ is predicted correctly and $I_g$ is mispredicted, the SRB is flushed in reverse order up through $I_i$, restoring $value(r_2)$ from $I_i$ but not restoring $value(r_7)$ from $I_f$. Since speculation is always from the most probable branch path, the *flush(k)* command is always placed on the most improbable branch path, minimizing the performance penalty. Not all branch hazards are resolved by the presence of on-path hazards. These remaining hazards can be resolved with compiler transformations.

## 5    SRB Flush Penalty

The examples of Section 4 demonstrate that compiler-assisted multiple instruction rollback can be applied to both branch repair and exception repair in a speculative execution architecture. The flush penalty of the read buffer is not a key concern in multiple instruction rollback applications since instruction faults are typically very rare. In application to exception repair in speculative execution, the SRB flush penalty is also not a major concern due to the infrequency of

55

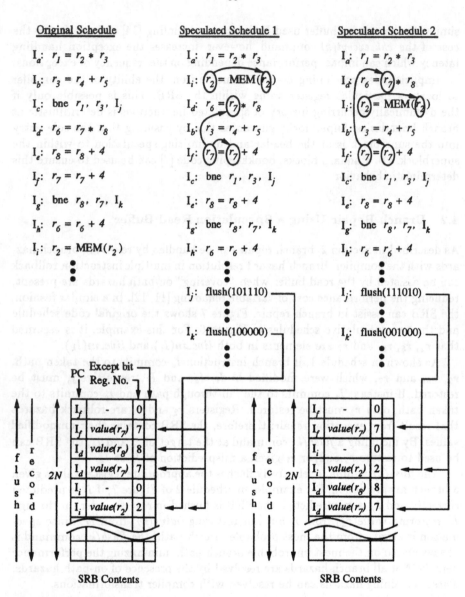

**Fig. 7.** Branch repair using a speculation read buffer (SRB).

exceptions involving speculated instructions. However, in application to branch repair, the SRB flush penalty could produce significant performance impacts. Studies of branch behavior show a conditional branch frequency of 11% to 17% [20]. Static branch prediction methods result in branch mispredictions in the range of 5% to 15%. This results in a branch repair frequency as high as 2.5%. Assuming a CPI (clock cycles per instruction) rate of one and an average SRB flush penalty of ten cycles, the performance overhead of the flush mechanism would reach 22.5%. This indicates the importance of minimizing the amount of redundant data stored in the SRB so that the flush penalty is reduced.

Recently, a technique was proposed to reduce the amount of redundant data in a read buffer so that the read buffer size could be reduced [12, 13]. A similar technique can be used to assure that only the data required for branch and exception repair is stored in the SRB. In the implicit index scheme of Section 4, a bit indicating whether an instruction is speculated is added to the opcode field. By expanded this field to two bits, operand storage requirements can be specified. Figure 8 shows the reduced contents of the SRB given schedule 1 of Figure 7. In the modified scheme, only the first read of $r_7$ must be maintained. Register $r_8$ is not required since it was not modified. The improved scheme also eliminates blank spaces in the SRB. For this example, the misprediction of $I_c$ in schedule 1 of Figure 7 results in four less variables to flush.

The coding of the two speculation bits would be as follows: 00) no save required, 01) save operand 1, 10) save operand 2, and 11) save both operands. If neither operand of a speculated instruction has be saved in the SRB, the instruction is not marked as speculated. This is not a problem for branch repair: however, if such an instruction traps, the hardware would have no way of knowing not to handle the exception immediately. There would also be no entry in

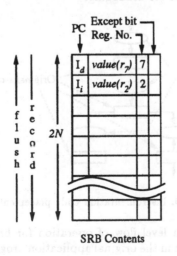

**Fig. 8.** SRB with reduced content.

the SRB for the exception bit or for the corresponding PC value. One solution to the problem would be to add another bit to the opcode field which marks speculated trapping instructions. A better solution is to code all speculated trapping instructions which have no operands to save as 01. This will indicate that exception handling is to be delayed and cause a reservation of an entry in the SRB, and also will slightly increase the flush penalty during branch repairs.

# 6 Performance Evaluation

## 6.1 Evaluation Methodology

In this section, results of a read buffer flush penalty evaluation are presented. The instrumentation code segments of Figure 9 call a branch error procedure which performs the following functions:

1. Update the read buffer model.
2. Force actual branch errors during program execution, allowing execution to proceed along an incorrect path for a controlled number of instructions.
3. Terminate execution along the incorrect path and restore the required system state from the simulated read buffer.
4. Measure the resulting flush cycles during the branch repair.
5. Begin execution along the correct path until the next branch is encountered.

An example instrumentation code segment is shown in Figure 10. Parameters, such as operand saving information, current PC, branch fall-though PC, and branch target PC values, are passed by the instrumentation code to the branch error procedure. An additional miscellaneous parameter contains instruction type and information used for debugging.

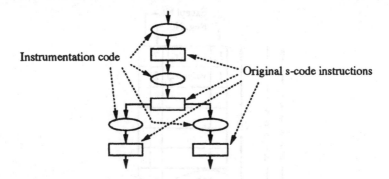

**Fig. 9.** Instrumentation code placement.

Figure 11 gives a high level flow of operation for branch error procedure. When a branch instruction in the original application program is encountered, an *arm_branch* flag is set. Prior to the execution of the next application instruction, the *arm_branch* flag is checked, and if set, the branch decision made by the

```
$_simlb_2_24_0:
# instruction 24
#   Begin brsim_sim hook: s1 = 16, s2 = 0: normal
        subu    $sp,    44
        la      $at,        $_simlb_2_24_0  ◄─── hook address
        sw      $at,    20($sp)
        la      $at,        $_simlb_2_24_1  ◄─── instruction adress
        sw      $at,    24($sp)
        la      $at,        $_simlb_2_25_0  ◄─── next hook address
        sw      $at,    28($sp)
        li      $at,        8216  ◄────────── miscellaneous
        sw      $at,    32($sp)
        li      $at,        16  ◄──────────────── directs read buffer to save
        sw      $at,    40($sp)                   register 16
        move    $at,    $sp
        j               brsim_save
#   End brsim_sim hook.
$_simlb_2_24_1:
```

| addu | $16, | $16, | 4 | ◄─── original instruction |

```
$_simlb_2_25_0:
# instruction 25
#   Begin brsim_sim hook: s1 = 16, s2 = 9: branch
        subu    $sp,    44
        la      $at,        $_simlb_2_25_0  ◄─── hook address
        sw      $at,    20($sp)
        la      $at,        $_simlb_2_25_1  ◄─── instruction adress
        sw      $at,    24($sp)
        la      $at,        $_main_6  ◄────────── next hook address
        sw      $at,    28($sp)
        li      $at,        532505  ◄──────────── miscellaneous
        sw      $at,    32($sp)
        la      $at,        $_main_5  ◄────────── target address
        sw      $at,    36($sp)
        li      $at,        304  ◄─────────────── directs read buffer to save
        sw      $at,    40($sp)                   registers 16 and 9
        move    $at,    $sp
        j               brsim_save
#   End brsim_sim hook.
$_simlb_2_25_1:
```

| bne | $16, | $9, | $_main_5 | ◄─── original instruction |

```
$_main_6:
```

**Fig. 10.** Instrumentation code sequences.

application program is set aside. The branch is then predicted by the branch prediction model. Four models are used in the evaluation: 1) predict taken, 2) predict not taken, 3) dynamic prediction, and 4) static prediction from profiling information. The dynamic prediction model is derived from a two bit counter branch target buffer (BTB) design [21] and is the only model that requires updating with each prediction outcome.

After the branch is predicted, the prediction is checked against the actual branch path taken by the application program. If the prediction was correct,

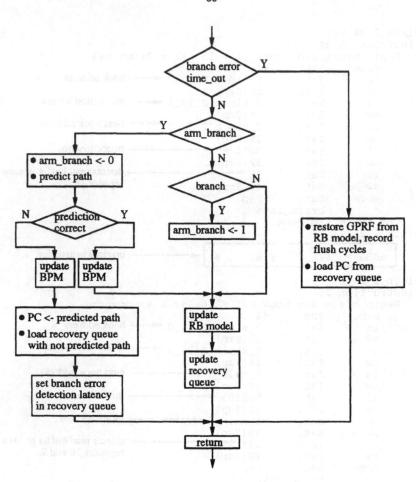

PC    - program counter

GPRF  - general purpose register file

RB    - read buffer

BPM   - branch prediction model

**Fig. 11.** Branch error procedure operation.

execution proceeds normally. If the prediction was incorrect, the correct branch path is loaded into the recovery queue along with a branch error detection (BED) latency, and the predicted path is loaded into the PC. The BED latency indicates how long the execution of instructions is to continue along the incorrect path. The *branch error time_out* flag is set when the BED latency is reached. When a branch error is detected, the register file state is repaired using the read buffer contents. The PC value of the correct branch path is obtained from the recovery queue. During branch error rollback recovery, the number of cycles required to flush the read buffer during branch repair is recorded.

It is assumed for this evaluation that two read buffer entries can be flushed in a single cycle. This corresponds to a split-cycle-save assumption of the general purpose register file [12]. Performance overhead due to read buffer flushes (% increase) is computed as

$$Flush\_OH = 100 * \frac{flush\_cycles}{total\_cycles}$$

All instructions are assumed to require one cycle for execution. This assumption is conservative since the MIPS processor used for the evaluation requires two cycles for a load. The additional cycles would increase the *total_cycles* and thereby reduce the observed performance overhead. In addition to accurately measuring flush costs, the evaluation verifies the operation of the read buffer and its ability to restore the appropriate system state over a wide range of applications.

The instrumentation insertion transformation operates on the s-code emitted by the MIPS code generator of the IMPACT C compiler [3]. The transformation determines which operands require saving in the read buffer and inserts calls to the *initialization*, *branch error*, and *summary* procedures. The resulting s-code modules are then compiled and run on a DECstation 3100. For the evaluation, BED latencies from 1 to 10 were used. Table 1 lists the ten application programs evaluated. *Static Size* is the number of assembly instructions emitted by the code generator, not including the library routines and other fixed overhead.

## 6.2 Evaluation Results

Experimental measurements of read buffer flush overhead (*Flush OH*) for various BED latencies are shown in Figures 12 through 16 (pp. 18 through 20). The four branch prediction strategies used for the evaluation are: 1) predict taken

**Table 1.** Application programs.

| Program | Static Size | Description |
|---------|-------------|-------------|
| QUEEN | 148 | eight-queen program |
| WC | 181 | UNIX utility |
| QSORT | 252 | quick sort algorithm |
| CMP | 262 | UNIX utility |
| GREP | 907 | UNIX utility |
| PUZZLE | 932 | simple game |
| COMPRESS | 1826 | UNIX utility |
| LEX | 6856 | lexical analyzer |
| YACC | 8099 | parser-generator |
| CCCP | 8775 | preprocessor for gnu C compiler |

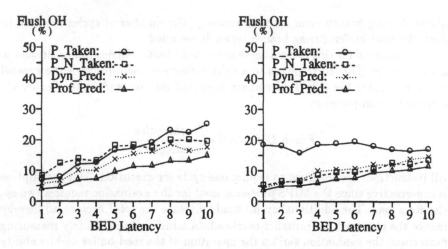

**Fig. 12.** Flush penalty: QUEEN, WC.

(*P_Taken*), 2) predict not taken (*P_N_Taken*), 3) dynamic prediction based on a branch target buffer (*Dyn_Pred*), and 4) static branch prediction using profiling data (*Prof_Pred*).

Flush costs were closely related to branch prediction accuracies, i.e., the more often a branch was mispredicted, the more often flush costs were incurred. In a speculative execution architecture, branch prediction inaccuracies result in performance impacts in addition to the impacts from the branch repair scheme. Branch misprediction increases the base run time of an application by permitting speculative execution of unproductive instructions. Increased levels of speculation increase the performance impacts associated with branch prediction inaccuracies. Only the performance impacts associated read buffer flushes are shown in Figures 12 through 16.

For nine of the ten applications, *P_N_Taken* was significantly more accurate or marginally more accurate in predicting branch outcomes than *P_Taken*. For QSORT, *P_Taken* was significantly more accurate than *P_N_Taken*. This result demonstrates that in a speculative execution architecture, it is difficult to guarantee optimal performance across a range of applications given a choice between predict-taken and predict-not-taken branch prediction strategies.

For all but one application, *Prof_Pred* was more accurate than either *P_Taken* or *P_N_Taken*. For CMP, *Prof_Pred*, *P_N_Taken*, and *Dyn_Pred* were nearly perfect in their prediction of branch outcomes. *Prof_Pred* marginally outperformed *Dyn_Pred* in all applications except LEX.

The purpose of measuring read buffer flush costs given the recovery from injected branch errors is to establish the viability of using a read buffer design for branch repair for speculative execution. Although in such a speculative schedule only static prediction strategies would be applicable, the *Dyn_Pred* model was included to better assess how varying branch prediction strategies impact flush costs. Overall, the accuracy of *Dyn_Pred* fell between *P_Taken*/*P_N_Taken* and *Prof_Pred*.

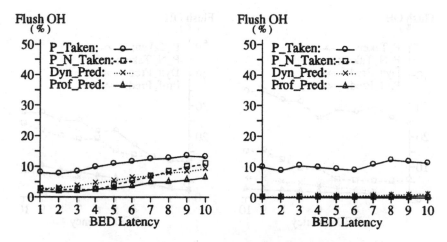

**Fig. 13.** Flush penalty: COMPRESS, CMP.

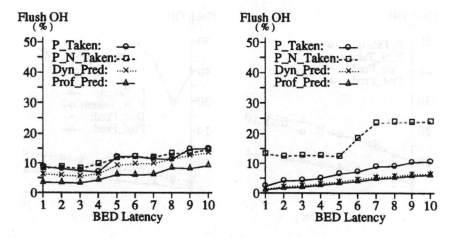

**Fig. 14.** Flush penalty: PUZZLE, QSORT.

Over the ten applications studied, read buffer flush overhead ranged from 49.91% for the P_Taken strategy in CCCP to .01% for the *P_N_Taken* strategy for CMP given a BED of ten. It can be seen from Figures 12 through 16 that a good branch prediction strategy is key to a low read buffer flush cost. The results show that given a static branch prediction strategy using profiling data, an average BED of ten produces flush costs no greater than 14.8% and an average flush cost of 8.1% across the ten applications studied. This performance overhead is comparable to the overhead expected from a delayed write buffer scheme with a maximum allowable BED of ten [15]. Given a maximum BED of ten and an average BED of less than ten, the flush costs of the read buffer would be less than that of a delayed write buffer, since a delayed write buffer is designed for a worst-case BED and the flush penalty of a read buffer is based on the average BED. The

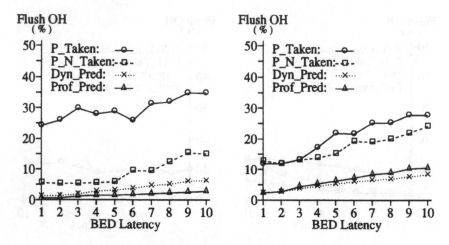

**Fig. 15.** Flush penalty: GREP, LEX.

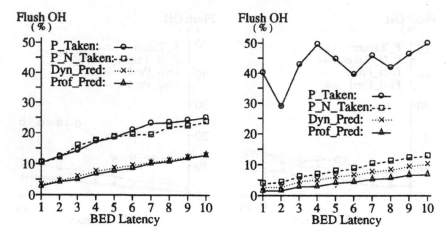

**Fig. 16.** Flush penalty: YACC, CCCP.

observed flush costs are small in comparison to the substantial performance gain of speculated architectures over that of nonspeculated architectures [8, 9, 10].

The BED for a given branch in this evaluation corresponds to the number of instructions moved above a branch in a speculative schedule. The results of the evaluation indicate that if the average number of instructions speculated above a given branch is $\leq$ 10, then the read buffer becomes a viable approach to handling branch repair.

# 7 Summary

Speculative execution has been shown to be an effective method to create additional instruction level parallelism in general applications. Speculating instructions above branches requires schemes to handle mispredicted branches and speculated instructions that trap.

This paper showed that branch hazards resulting from branch mispredictions in speculative execution are similar to branch hazards in multiple instruction rollback developed for processor error recovery. It was shown that compiler techniques previously developed for error recovery can be used as an effective branch repair scheme in a speculative execution architecture. It was also shown that data hazards that result in rollback due to exception repair are similar to on-path hazards suggesting a read buffer approach to exception repair.

Implicit index scheduling was introduced to exploit the unique characteristics of rollback recovery using a read buffer approach. The read buffer design was extended to include PC values to aid in rollback from excepting speculated instructions.

Read buffer flush penalties were measured by injecting branch errors into ten target applications and measuring the flush cycles required to recover from the branch errors using a simulated read buffer. It was shown that with a static branch prediction strategy using profiling data, flush costs under 15% are achievable. The results of these evaluations indicate that compiler-assisted multiple instruction rollback is viable for branch and exception repair in a speculative execution architecture.

# References

1. R. P. Colwell, R. P. Nix, J. O'Donnell, D. B. Papworth, and P. K. Rodman, "A VLIW Architecture for a Trace Scheduling Compiler," in *Proc. 2nd Int. Conf. Architecture Support Programming Languages and Operating Syst.*, pp. 105–111, Oct. 1987.

2. J. C. Dehnert, P. Y. Hsu, and J. P. Bratt, "Overlapped Loop Support in the Cydra 5," in *Proc. 3rd Int. Conf. Architecture Support Programming Languages and Operating Syst.*, pp. 26–38, April 1989.

3. P. Chang, W. Chen, N. Warter, and W.-M. W. Hwu, "IMPACT: An Architecture Framework for Multiple-Instruction-Issue Processors," in *Proc. 18th Annu. Symp. Comput. Architecture*, pp. 266–275, May 1991.

4. B. R. Rau and C. D. Glaeser, "Some Scheduling Techniques and an Easily Schedulable Horizontal Architecture for High Performance Scientific Computing," in *Proc. 20th Annu. Workshop Microprogramming Microarchitecture*, pp. 183–198, Oct. 1981.

5. M. S. Lam, "Software Pipelining: An Effective Scheduling Technique for VLIW Machines," in *Proc. ACM SIGPLAN 1988 Conf. Programming Language Design Implementation*, pp. 318–328, June 1988.

6. A. Aiken and A. Nicolau, "Optimal Loop Parallelization," in *Proc. ACM SIGPLAN 1988 Conf. Programming Language Design Implementation*, pp. 308–317, June 1988.

7. J. A. Fisher, "Trace Scheduling: A Technique for Global Microcode Compaction," *IEEE Trans. Comput.*, vol. c-30, no. 7, pp. 478-490, July 1981.

8. M. D. Smith, M. S. Lam, and M. Horowitz, "Boosting Beyond Scalar Scheduling in a Superscalar Processor," in *Proc. 17th Annu. Symp. Comput. Architecture*, pp. 344-354, May 1990.

9. S. A. Mahlke, W. Y. Chen, W.-M. W. Hwu, B. R. Rao, and M. S. Schlansker, "Sentinel Scheduling for VLIW and Superscalar Processors," in *Proc. 5th Int. Conf. Architecture Support Programming Languages and Operating Syst.*, pp. 238-247, Oct. 1992.

10. M. D. Smith, M. A. Horowitz, and M. S. Lam, "Efficient Superscalar Performance Through Boosting," in *Proc. 5th Int. Conf. Architecture Support Programming Languages and Operating Syst.*, pp. 248-259, Oct. 1992.

11. N. J. Alewine, S.-K. Chen, C.-C. J. Li, W. K. Fuchs, and W.-M. W. Hwu, "Branch Recovery with Compiler-Assisted Multiple Instruction Retry," in *Proc. 22th Int. Symp. Fault-Tolerant Comput.*, pp. 66-73, July 1992.

12. N. J. Alewine, *Compiler-assisted Multiple Instruction Rollback Recovery using a Read Buffer*. PhD thesis, Tech. Rep. CRHC-93-06, University of Illinois at Urbana-Champaign, 1993.

13. N. J. Alewine, S.-K. Chen, W. K. Fuchs, and W.-M. W. Hwu, "Compiler-assisted Multiple Instruction Rollback Recovery using a Read Buffer," Tech. Rep. CRHC-93-11, Coordinated Science Laboratory, University of Illinois, May 1993.

14. J. E. Smith and A. R. Pleszkun, "Implementing Precise Interrupts in Pipelined Processors," *IEEE Trans. Comput.*, vol. 37, pp. 562-573, May 1988.

15. Y. Tamir and M. Tremblay, "High-Performance Fault-Tolerant VLSI Systems Using Micro Rollback," *IEEE Trans. Comput.*, vol. 39, pp. 548-554, Apr. 1990.

16. A. V. Aho, R. Sethi, and J. D. Ullman, *Compilers: Principles, Techniques, and Tools.* Reading, MA: Addison-Wesley, 1986.

17. M. Johnson, *Superscalar Microprocessor Design.* Englewood Cliffs, NJ: Prentice-Hall, Inc., 1991.

18. C.-C. J. Li, S.-K. Chen, W. K. Fuchs, and W.-M. W. Hwu, "Compiler-Assisted Multiple Instruction Retry." Manuscript, May 1991.

19. J. A. Bondy and U. Murty, *Graph Theory with Applications.* London, England: Macmillan Press Ltd., 1979.

20. J. L. Hennessy and D. A. Patterson, *Computer Architecture: A Quantitative Approach.* San Mateo, CA: Morgan Kaufmann Publishers, Inc., 1990.

21. J. K. Lee and A. J. Smith, "Branch Prediction Strategies and Branch Target Buffer Design," *Computer*, vol. 17, no. 1, pp. 6-22, Jan. 1984.

# Fault Tolerance: Why Should I Pay For It?

*Barry J. Gleeson*
Unisys Corporation
2700 North First St.
San Jose, CA 95134
barry@sj.unisys.com

*Abstract.* Fault tolerant systems are not as widely used today as one might expect from an analysis of the costs of failures. System developers must consider other factors as well: where should development dollars be spent for maximum leverage? Will development in one area (e.g. fault tolerance) impede development in others? Development of fault tolerance techniques that are *orthogonal* to other development efforts must be a high priority. Market forces are driving a number of new technologies into products; our analysis suggests that these new technologies will change the trade-offs in both the performance cost and development cost areas.

## 1. Introduction

If fault tolerant architectures are to make any significant impact on the world of commercial computing, a real change of perspective is required. Unless we become far more focussed on issues of cost in all its dimensions, fault tolerant architectures will remain on the sidelines.

## 2. The Customer's Perspective

Why is it that fault tolerant architectures have not bloomed in the market place? It is clear that failures cost companies time and money - often significant amounts of money. Why is this not sufficient motivation to invest in fault tolerant machines?

The 1980s were dominated by the explosive growth of commercial, off-the-shelf microprocessor technology. PCs and workstations proliferated and captured the imagination; fault tolerance was simply irrelevant. Ethernet and token ring moved these systems from being isolated islands of inconsistent information to networked nightmares. Network management became a much more valuable (read: profitable) venture than fault tolerance.

Thus, the answer is simple: the money has been better spent on other things. For most commercial system users, failures have been far from their most significant problem. Fault tolerance techniques have been aimed at system or box level availability, while our customers have come to focus on the much more important problem of *information availability*.

Today, most companies have much valuable data locked up inaccessibly in their mainframes. PCs and workstations abound, but they do not talk to each other well, let alone give access to the mainframe's data in any convenient fashion. The result: inconsistent data, usually trapped in spreadsheets scattered around an organization.

This problem has been compounded by the recent boom in laptop systems. When PCs were close relatives of boat anchors, most users had just one copy of any particular piece of information. Today, they have at least two: one in their desktop machine, and one in their laptop. Opportunities for inconsistency have suddenly multiplied.

Of course, many vendors have been working on solving these problems for some time now. The major PC software houses are vying to establish the standards by which objects can be shared across a network; similar standards are also being developed in a more general forum [OMG91]. Besides improving the interoperability of applications, these distributed application development frameworks will begin to ease the problems of multiple, inconsistent copies of data.

The fundamental problem is that trying to provide fault tolerance gets in the way of solving these other more pressing problems. The individual boxes that make up a system today already have excellent availability. Adding cost and complexity is simply unwarranted.

Of course, there is another perspective. It is much easier to sell functionality than availability. There is usually an implicit assumption of some reasonable level of availability by all parties. When the customer's (often unstated) expectations about availability are not met, it's the vendor's problem.

There are changes on the horizon, however. The emergence of distributed object linkage and invocation facilities will have a significant impact on this picture. While linking to information rather than copying it removes the inconsistency problem, it introduces availability dependencies. Every system to which one has links must be up simultaneously. The availability of a whole interconnected web of machines will quickly and surely become crucial.

## 3. Costs and Benefits

One way to analyze the situation in more detail is to look at the costs and benefits of various fault tolerant schemes. For which customers and situations do the benefits outweigh the costs? Can we reduce the costs, or increase the benefits to the point where fault tolerant systems will be more widely employed?

There are at least three dimensions to the cost/benefit problem:

* *Performance Costs.* How efficient is the fault tolerant scheme? What is the incremental cost to the customer who needs x cycles of work done per day?

* *Development Costs.* How much does the fault tolerant architecture increase time to market? How much does it complicate (and therefore delay) the development of new functionality?

* *Faults Tolerated.* What fraction of real system failures does the fault
tolerant architecture deal with successfully? Is the benefit really worth
the cost?

Current fault tolerant architectures are far too expensive in either the performance
cost or development cost dimensions. For example, systems with high levels of
hardware redundancy, such as Stratus' systems [Freiburghouse82], or the more
recent Tandem Integrity systems, have very high performance costs. On the other
hand, their hardware development costs are not high, and their software development
costs are minimal.

System such as the Tandem Guardian systems [Katzman77, Bartlett78] have lower
performance costs, but much higher software development costs. The rate at which
operating system and application software is evolving makes this cost prohibitive for
many potential customers.

In addition, these architectures have significant differences in terms of the kinds of
failures they tolerate. The Stratus and Integrity systems cannot tolerate operating
system failures of any kind. Experience with Guardian systems shows that they
tolerate most real operating system failures. Of course, Stratus and Tandem have
spent much time and money to ensure that their operating systems are not the
primary cause of system failure. This can itself be a problem in the market: so much
time and effort must be devoted to testing and bullet-proofing the operating system
that little bandwidth remains for the addition of new functionality.

The Auragen - later Targon/32 - system [Borg83, Borg89], although not commercially successful, was an innovative attempt to address both performance and
development costs simultaneously. There is a significant drawback to this scheme,
however: it is unable to deal with nondeterministic process behaviour. In particular,
it could not deal with processes sharing memory.

Much thought has since been given to fault tolerance schemes that employ checkpoints alone, or in combination with logging of some sort [Strom85, Chandry85,
Koo87, Johnson87, Johnson88]. Such schemes have the attractive property of
pushing performance costs into the failure case: they keep the cost of normal
operation low, at the expense of recovery time. For applications without strong real-
time response constraints, this trade-off is worthwhile. Fortunately, most commercial applications fall into this category.

The problems associated with nondeterministic execution are significant - especially
for computations that interact frequently with the external world. Before dispensing
cash from an automated teller machine, printing a paycheck, or issuing an airline
ticket, we must be sure that failure recovery will lead to the same external action,
despite any nondeterminism inherent in the system. Some actions are hard to retract.

Most commercial applications interact with the external world frequently. This
suggests that we should study nondeterminism and its sources carefully. In fact,
there are very few intrinsic sources of nondeterminism in most systems - especially
in systems where CPUs do not share memory. Multi-threading, interrupts, and
registers or 'memory' that can be modified by external hardware (e.g. I/O devices)
are usually the only sources of nondeterministic system behaviour.

A small amount of hardware or compilation system support can be used to measure (and therefore eliminate) the first two of these sources of nondeterminism. It is conceivable that future off-the-shelf microprocessors will include the required support. Removing nondeterminism in this way not only enables the use of a wide range of logging techniques, but also provides a major benefit to the software developer: more time is spent trying to reproduce timing related problems than in any other software debugging endeavour.

Memory mapped I/O devices can also be dealt with using a variety of techniques.

Given the rate at which operating systems are evolving, operating system development costs are a significant issue. This suggests that we should attempt to apply general purpose logging schemes to the operating system as well as to applications.

The analysis above really looks at fault tolerant architectures in isolation from the rest of the market. In fact, there are several trends in the general market today that will significantly affect both development cost and performance cost for fault tolerant systems.

## 4. Nomadic Systems

Portability is clearly highly valued today. Witness the speed with which so-called luggable systems became portables, and portables became laptops. Palmtops and pen based computers have captured the imaginations and wallets of users and venture capitalists alike. How is this connected to the fault tolerance market?

Portable machines, by their very nature, spend most of their life disconnected from the network umbilical cord. While significant amounts of money are currently being spent to extend networks across the airwaves, it seems likely that 'disconnected operation' will be the norm for quite some time, and will probably never go away completely.

Some interesting work on file systems for portable machines has been done at Carnegie Mellon University [Satyanarayanan90]. In the PC world, tools to get data in laptop and desktop machines synchronized before and after each trip have come to market in the last few months.

Clearly, the large demand for portable machines will ensure that good solutions to these problems are found. Tools for dealing with replication of files, network partitions, and restoring consistency of replicas when partitions are healed will be developed post haste - even if this requires that all applications be extended with replica reconciliation functions.

The challenge will be to adapt the tools and mechanisms created for portable systems to the operating systems and applications that run on servers and larger systems.

# 5. Parallel Architectures Emerge

Much attention is being paid today to parallel processing systems. There appears to be a consensus building that widespread commercial application of such systems will soon be feasible. Cost and scalability considerations are driving this trend: the intention, of course, is to apply commodity microprocessors and related hardware components to larger problems.

While cost and scalability are driving this trend, there are several significant side effects. From a hardware fault tolerance viewpoint, the obvious side effect is that parallel machines of the non-shared memory variety can be thought of as many identical, interchangeable failure domains.

There is a more subtle side effect as well. Clearly, the key issue for such architectures is the development of parallel applications, and the operating systems to support them. Today, the development costs for such applications are huge. On the other hand, the potential performance cost benefits of these architectures are so large that there is a significant incentive to solve the development cost problem.

In the general case, this is a very difficult problem. How does one take an arbitrary program and parallelize it? Fortunately, we do not need a solution to the general problem to realize significant benefits. Solutions for several large problem classes may be sufficient. In fact, solutions for some commercially important problems are already emerging.

Databases are at the heart of many commercial applications. This is good news: the problems of parallelizing databases are fairly well understood [Ceri84, Graefe90, DeWitt92]. It is reasonable to expect that the commercial database suppliers will over the next few years compete to provide parallel database solutions [Tandem87, Rudin90].

Another class of applications for which a solution is emerging of its own accord is applications that do not need to be internally parallelized. There is a large set of existing applications that already consist of many processes with little interaction. For example, most Unix tools consist of one or more processes per user, where each process does not need more compute power than that provided by a single node. Similarly, running *make* to create a large piece of software is already essentially parallelized.

These applications are difficult to move to today's parallel machines, basically because the operating systems provided are often very simple, and almost always proprietary. The emergence of so-called 'Single System Image' Unix-like operating systems for this class of platform [Popek85, Batlivala92, Zajcew93] will remove this barrier.

These two application classes between them cover a very large fraction of today's commercial systems.

More general use of parallel machines will have two important effects on the fault tolerant market: first, it will clearly increase the demand; second, it will lower the hurdle end users face in moving to fault tolerant architectures. No longer will the vendor need to develop a parallel database, as Tandem and Auragen had to do. The incremental development cost for end users to move their applications would be substantially reduced. No longer would the end user have to adapt to the single database system provided by the system vendor; they could continue to use their existing DBMS.

Further, it should be possible to apply a general purpose logging scheme to all the applications that run on these machines. No longer would the end user be stuck if the fault tolerant vendor's applications did not have the required functionality.

## 6. Hardware Implications

Clearly, one component of any cost effective fault tolerance architecture is failure detecting hardware. How can we lower the performance cost and development cost for such hardware?

From one perspective, this problem is well understood [Sellers68, Siewiorek82]. Extensive failure detection has been a feature of mainframe systems for many years, and is usually an integral part of the system maintenance mechanisms [Ciacelli81, Bossen82, Tendolkar82]. A failure detector points to a field replaceable unit; this ensures that intermittent hardware failures are removed from the system quickly and cost effectively.

This technology has not found its way into smaller machines such as PCs, workstations and low end servers. They have very few field replaceable units, and the software is simple enough that distinguishing hardware failures from software failures is usually not difficult. The failure detection hardware development costs are too high and the benefits too small, relative to the cost of failure to the end user.

It could be argued that for single user systems such as PCs and workstations, this situation will not change in the foreseeable future. On the other hand, there are significant cost advantages to using PC and workstation components in larger, shared systems.

Hence, the challenge must be to find a way to reduce the development cost of failure detecting hardware to the point where it is incorporated in commodity hardware components as a matter of course. It must come almost free from the chip and board designer's perspective.

One obvious way to attack this is through the CAD systems that are used to design chips and boards. Much progress has been made in the last ten years in automating the development of chunks of logic based on high level descriptions of required functionality. Logic synthesis tools are now capable of generating high quality designs for significant parts of a system. Today, there is a conflict between the use of logic synthesis and the need for fault detection. Current synthesis tools attempt to generate space or time efficient designs. Any redundancy - fault detection included - is removed.

There has been some interest commercially in logic synthesis tools that automatically generate testable designs; it seems a small conceptual step to fault detecting designs.

Another challenge in the hardware area will be to ensure that chips developed by different vendors work together in a fault detecting sense as well as a functional sense. This will require that consensus be built in the industry about which fault detection methods are appropriate in different areas of a system.

## 7. Software Implications

Software is changing at an amazing rate. Even in the operating system area - which arguably should have the lowest rate of change - things are evolving at breakneck speed. One has only to monitor groups such as Unix International to see that today's operating systems are far from being considered adequate [UI92].

In the applications development area, the flow of new software is best described as a deluge.

The challenge is to make fault tolerance an orthogonal issue - one that the application and operating system developers do not need to think much about. In the operating system arena, microkernels would appear to be of some assistance in this regard. They are being adopted today for two pragmatic reasons: first, the division of an operating system into servers with well defined interfaces makes complex systems easier to build and manage; second, location and migration transparent communication between servers provides a good foundation for building operating systems for parallel non-shared memory machines. [Rozier88, Armand89, Guillemont91, Zajcew93].

How can microkernels assist the development of fault tolerant systems? They provide a natural environment for checkpoint and log based recovery mechanisms, because interactions between components are exposed to the microkernel. They provide an obvious place to monitor and record interactions among the set of user processes and servers.

More subtly, microkernels enable one to separate an operating system into deterministic and nondeterministic parts. Nondeterminism can with care be confined to the microkernel itself, plus the servers that contain device drivers. In some implementations, drivers are isolated into special driver servers [Armand91]. Thus, a checkpoint and logging scheme could be used both for applications *and* for much of the operating system.

It is clear that the microkernel in such a system should not dictate the fault tolerance mechanisms employed by operating system servers and user processes. Some servers are intrinsically nondeterministic; failure recovery for those servers may be done using different mechanisms than those employed by the deterministic servers. Servers or user processes may be able to optimize based on their knowledge of messages semantics; checkpoint size can be reduced for servers that use software caching by taking advantage of the cache's characteristics.

Thus, the microkernel should provide a set of mechanisms that can be used to support a wide variety of fault tolerance mechanisms. Policy should be left to the servers and user processes.

Much work remains to determine what mechanisms should be provided. We do not yet have a clear idea of the range of possible choices. We must strive to make the failure semantics presented by the microkernel to servers as clean and simple as possible.

One area where failure semantics are particularly gruesome today is communications. The traditional communications tools typically only provide enough information for the user to gracefully report the apparent failure of a server. Failures are usually detected independently by each service user; there is no guarantee that users will have a consistent view of the state of the server - or indeed that the apparent failure was any more than a temporary overload of a particular route through the network.

Much theoretical work has been done in the last few years to show what can and cannot be done to provide simple failure semantics in distributed systems. It has become clear that there is a fundamental distinction between synchronous and asynchronous systems [Fischer85], and that the ability to detect failures is at the heart of this difference [Chandra92].

Market reality intrudes here: commercial systems can be neither completely asynchronous nor completely synchronous. To be completely synchronous, there must be an absolute upper bound on the total system load. The system works when the load is below this bound, and fails when it is exceeded. This is not acceptable behaviour for most commercial systems: rather, system response time should degrade gracefully as system load is increased. Asynchronous algorithms are also attractive because they usually have better 'average' performance than their synchronous equivalents.

On the other hand, end users detect system failure synchronously: they will not wait forever for a response.

Real systems, then, will consist of both synchronous and asynchronous parts. For example, in the ISIS system [Birman87, Birman89, Birman91, Ricciardi91], low level message transport is timed, so that failures can be detected quickly. The upper layers - including the applications using ISIS - are asynchronous.

There are difficult choices to be made with respect to the way that failures and potential partitions are presented to the users of a set of communication facilities. It seems that integrated failure reporting and message delivery, as provided in ISIS, is a useful simplification from the user's perspective. Providing such services at the microkernel level will simplify the problems confronting operating system developers considerably.

The long term goal must be to provide software developers with simple tools for building fault tolerant applications.

# 8. Conclusion

Some fairly fundamental changes are occurring in the computer industry today. Parallel machines are slowly moving towards the mainstream; operating system architectures are being revisited; networks of machines are the norm; the object invocation paradigm is being extended to cross networks transparently - and applications that use this extended paradigm are beginning to appear.

In broadest terms, the challenge is to repeat the success of the telephone system: to make computing services ubiquitous, dependable, and natural to use: "... the test of a well made tool ... is the speed with which it vanishes from the consciousness of its user." [Hapgood93]. Initially, the telephone system was limited in extent, and unreliable. As the network became more universal, and as use became more common, service availability demands skyrocketed. Fortunately, the telephone network has a very limited, focused and *stable* function - the rate of change in what it is expected to do has been extremely low. Thus, essentially ad hoc availability techniques were appropriate. Now we must learn to provide the same level of availability for networks with arbitrary, rapidly evolving functionality.

## 9. Acknowledgments

The author would like to thank Rajiv Sinha and Jim Hamrick for their careful reading of and thoughtful suggestions for this paper.

## 10. References

[Armand89] Armand, F., Gien, M., Herrmann, F., Rozier, M. Revolution 89, or Distributing UNIX Brings it Back to its Original Virtues. In *Proceedings of Workshop on Experiences with Building Distributed (and Multiprocessor) Systems,* October 1989.

[Armand91] Armand, F. Give a Process to your Drivers! In *Proceedings of the EurOpen Autumn 1991 Conference,* Budapest, Hungary, September, 1991.

[Bartlett78] Bartlett, J. A 'Non-Stop' Operating System. In *Proceedings of the Hawaii International Conference of System Sciences,* 1978.

[Batlivala92] Batlivala, N., Gleeson, B., Hamrick, J., Lurndal, S., Price, D., Soddy, J., Abrossimov, V. Experience with SVR4 over Chorus. In *Proceedings of the USENIX Workshop on Micro-Kernels and Other Architectures,* April 1992.

[Birman87] Birman, K., Joseph, T. Exploiting Virtual Synchrony in Distributed Systems. In *Proceedings of the Eleventh ACM Symposium on Operating System Principles,* Austin, Texas, November 1987.

[Birman89] Birman, K., Joseph, T. Exploiting Replication in distributed systems. In Sape Mullender, editor, *Distributed Systems,* ACM Press, Addison Wesley, 1989.

[Birman91] Birman, K., Schiper, A., Stephenson, P. Lightweight causal and atomic group multicast. In *ACM Transactions on Computer Systems,* Vol. 9, No. 3, August, 1991.

[Borg83] Borg, A., Baumbach, J., Glazer, S. A Message System Supporting Fault Tolerance. In *Proceedings of the 9th Symposium on Operating System Principles,* October, 1983.

[Borg89] Borg, A., Blau, W., Graetsch, W., Herrmann, F., Oberle, W. Fault Tolerance under UNIX. In *ACM Transactions on Computer Systems,* Vol. 7, No. 1, February 1989.

[Bossen82] Bossen, D., Hsiao, M. Model for Transient and Permanent Error-Detection and Fault-Isolation Coverage. In *IBM Journal of Research and Development,* Vol. 26, No. 1, January 1982.

[Ceri84] Ceri, S., Pelagatti, G. *Distributed Databases: Principles and Systems.* McGraw Hill, New York, 1984.

[Chandra92] Chandra, T., Hadzilacos, V., Toueg, S. The Weakest Failure Detector for Solving Consensus. In *Proceedings of the Eleventh Annual ACM Symposium on Principles of Distributed Computing,* August 1992.

[Chandry85] Chandry, K., Lamport, L. Distributed Snapshots: Determining global states of distributed systems. In *ACM Transactions on Computer Systems,* Vol. 3, No. 1, February 1985.

[Ciacelli81] Ciacelli, M. Fault Handling on the IBM 4341 Processor. In *Proceedings of the 11th Annual International Symposium on Fault Tolerant Computing,* 1981.

[DeWitt92] DeWitt, D., Gray, J. Parallel Database Systems: The Future of High Performance Database Systems. In *Communications of the ACM,* Vol. 35. No. 6, June 1992.

[Fischer85] Fischer, M., Lynch, N., Paterson, M. Impossibility of Distributed Consensus with One Faulty Process. In *Journal of the ACM,* Vol 32, No. 2, April 1985.

[Freiburghouse82] Freiburghouse, R. Making processing fail-safe. In *Mini-Micro Systems,* Vol. XV, No. 5, May 1982.

[Graefe90] Graefe, G. Encapsulation of Parallelism in the Volcano Query Processing System. In *Proceedings of the 1990 ACM-SIGMOD International Conference on Management of Data,* May 1990.

[Guillemont91] Guillemont, M., Lipkis, J., Orr, D., Rozier, M. A Second-Generation Microkernel Based UNIX; Lessons in Performance and Compatibility. In *Proceedings of the Winter 1991 USENIX Conference.*

[Hapgood93]  Hapgood, F.  *Up the Infinite Corridor: MIT and the Technical Imagination.* Addison Wesley, 1993.

[Johnson87] Johnson, D., Zwaenopoel, W.  Sender-based message logging.  In *The Seventeenth International Symposium on Fault-Tolerant Computing,* IEEE Computer Society, 1987.

[Johnson88] Johnson, D., Zwaenopoel, W.  Recovery in distributed systems using optimistic message logging and checkpointing.  In *Proceedings of the Seventh Annual ACM Symposium on Principles of Distributed Computing,* ACM, August 1988.

[Katzman77] Katzman, J. *A Fault-Tolerant Computing System.* Tandem Computers, Inc., Cupertino CA, 1977.

[Koo87] Koo, R., Toueg, S.  Checkpointing and rollback recovery for distributed systems.  In *IEEE Transactions on Software Engineering,* Vol. 13, No. 1, January 1987.

[OMG91] *Object Management Group Architecture Guide,* Issue 1.0, November 1, 1990.

[Popek85] Popek, G., Walker, B.  *The LOCUS Distributed System Architecture,* MIT Press, 1985.

[Ricciardi91] Ricciardi, A., Birman, K. Using process groups to implement failure detection in asynchronous environments.  In *Proceedings of the Eleventh ACM Symposium on Principles of Distributed Computing,* Montreal, Quebec, August 1991.

[Rozier88] Rozier, M., Abrossimov, V., Armand, F., Boule, I., Gien, M., Guillemont, M., Herrmann, F., Kaiser, C., Langlois, S., Leonard, P., Neuhauser, W. CHORUS Distributed Operating Systems.  In *Computing Systems Journal,* Vol. 1,  No. 4, The USENIX Association, December 1988.

[Rudin90] Rudin, K. *Oracle for Massively Parallel Systems: Technology Overview.* Oracle Corporation, 1990.

[Satyanarayanan90]  Satyanarayanan, M. Scalable, Secure, and Highly Available Distributed File Access. In *IEEE Computer,* May 1990.

[Sellers68] Sellers, F., Hsiao, M., Bearnson, L. *Error Detecting Logic for Digital Computers.* McGraw Hill, New York, 1968.

[Siewiorek82] Siewiorek, D., Swarz, R. *The Theory and Practice of Reliable System Design.* Digital Press, Bedford, Mass., 1982.

[Strom85] Strom, R., Yemeni, S.  Optimistic recovery in distributed systems.  In *ACM Transactions on Computer Systems,* Vol. 3, No. 3, August, 1985.

[Tandem87] Tandem Database Group. NonStop SQL, a Distributed, High-Performance, High Reliability Implementation of SQL. *Workshop on High Performance Transaction Systems*, Asilomar, CA, Sept. 1987.

[Tendolkar82] Tendolkar, N., Swan, R. Automated Diagnostic Methodology for the IBM 3081 Processor Complex. In *IBM Journal of Research and Development*, Vol. 26, No. 1, January 1982.

[UI92] UNIX International. *1992 System V Roadmap*, January 1992.

[Zajcew93] Zajcew, R., Roy, P., Black, D. Peak, C., Guedes, P., Kemp, B., LoVerso. J., Liebensperger, M., Barnett, M., Rabii, F., Netterwala, D. An OSF/1 UNIX for Massively Parallel Multicomputers. In *Proceedings of the Winter 1993 USENIX Conference.*

# Stable Disk - A Fault-Tolerant Cached RAID Subsystem

Jeremy Jones & Brian Coghlan

Department of Computer Science,
Trinity College, Dublin 2,
Ireland

jones@cs.tcd.ie
coghlan@cs.tcd.ie

Abstract: Lack of I/O performance is becoming a limiting factor in many computing systems. The Stable Disk is a high performance fault-tolerant cached RAID subsystem which exploits write-cacheing. A memory-mapped stable memory is used as a fault-tolerant cache, the design of which incorporates VRAMs to support switch-mode checkpointing and to provide a fast, direct path to disk.

## 1. Introduction

Single chip microprocessors are continuing to double in speed every 18 months and symmetric shared memory multiprocessor systems constructed from such devices are fast becoming the norm. Given the continuing race to provide more MIPS, it is unfortunate that there has not been a corresponding effort to improve disk I/O performance (in particular). It is evident that exploring solutions to the disk I/O bottleneck is an important research topic - paraphrasing Amdahl's law, a system is only as fast as its slowest component.

The RAID [PATT-88][PATT-89] approach to the disk I/O bottleneck is to use many small inexpensive disks instead of a single large expensive one. The concurrency and data transfer rate from many small inexpensive disks are potentially far greater than that of a single large expensive disk. Concurrent accesses to the different disks in a RAID, allow applications such as file servers and transaction processing systems to access "unrelated" items in parallel. Striped operation where all disks in a RAID stripe perform identical operations in unison can improve the data transfer rate for data hungry applications such as multi media. As a bonus, RAID solves the problem of disk reliability in a cost-effective manner by using "parity disks" rather than disk mirroring.

A RAID, like any single expensive disk, has a limit on the number of disk operations that can be performed per second. A general strategy to increase throughput is to minimise seek times, reduce disk latency and to maximise the amount of data transferred per I/O request. This is exactly the approach adopted by a log structured file system [OUST-88]. The disk is written progressively from the first to the last track to minimise seeking. Modified blocks are collected together and written in a single operation to improve the overall transfer rate. If there is a large enough read cache, there need only be occasional seeks for reads.

Further improvements in I/O performance can be made by exploiting RAM based write caches [STON-87][OUST-88][COPE-89]. Read caches are widely used, but write caches suffer the risk of losing data on a system failure. Write cacheing can be exploited provided the implementation is fault-tolerant. Write cacheing allows synchronous writes to be turned into asynchronous ones. This can be particularly effective, for example, when writing the log file of a transaction manager (eg. Tuxedo) by taking the time consuming synchronous disk write, which is needed for fault-tolerance, out of the critical path. File I/O can be speeded up by taking advantage of the short lifetime of many files - they can safely be created, updated and deleted entirely within the write-cache without ever being written to disk.

The remainder of this paper shows how a fault-tolerant write cache can be integrated into a RAID controller to make a high performance disk subsystem which will go some way towards meeting the I/O requirements of the next generation of multiprocessors.

## 2. Background

The critical issues in the design of a high performance RAID subsystem are (i) to provide a high speed, direct data path between memory and the disks (ii) to provide fault tolerant cacheing and (iii) to work in a multiprocessor environment.

A RAID can contain many disks. The objective is to keep the disks as busy as possible transferring data to/from memory. Disk bit recording densities and disk revolution speeds are slowly improving and the data rate from the head (of an inexpensive disk) is approaching 2MB/s. If a RAID contains 50 disks, which can occupy a surprisingly small volume given the advent of 2.5" and 1.8" disks, then a bandwidth of 100MB/s is required between memory and the disks. Many RAID controllers are driven through a single SCSI interface which has a bandwidth of only 20MB/s (16 bit wide & fast) or 40MB/s (32 bit wide & fast) - clearly a bottleneck. Furthermore, the effect of the disk traffic on the system bus creates another bottleneck. Dual ported write caches can solve both of these problems since one port can be connected to the host processor and the other can be used to supply data to/from the disks at rates in excess of 100MB/s with negligible interaction with the host processor port. Below we show that video RAMs (VRAMs) have an architecture that ideally suit such a write cache.

Write-caches are generally internal to a disk controller and are accessed in the same manner as the disk - through an I/O port by following a complex sequence of operations. If battery-backed, it can give the same illusion of atomicity that a disk provides. This I/O port is a potential bottleneck, especially if it has a SCSI interface like a disk. Given a VRAM memory mapped disk I/O cache, it is interesting to consider adding functionality to make it atomic. A simple battery-backed VRAM cache is <u>not</u> sufficient because on a failure (i) its contents may be damaged (by an errant CPU) and (ii) the "state" accessible in VRAM may not be consistent or complete. An alternative approach, adopted within the Stable Disk, is to convert the memory mapped I/O cache into a stable memory [LAMP-81][BANA-86].

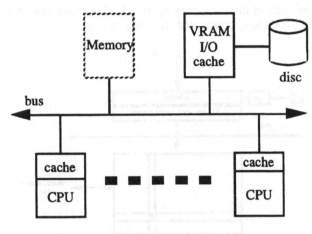

General Architecture

The normal view of a stable memory is two battery-backed banks of memory A & B. Data in bank A is updated by normal host accesses and checkpoints are taken by copying data atomically from bank A to bank B. The checkpointed data could be a data structure, the data modified by a process between context switches or, perhaps, the data modified by a processor since the last checkpoint. Enough data must be saved in memory so that "execution" can be resumed from the checkpoint. This may require the flushing of internal CPU registers and any dirty cache lines to memory before the checkpoint is taken. If a hardware or software failure occurs, it is possible to roll back to a previous checkpoint state held in stable memory. Mapping data structures directly into stable memory can reduce overheads - for example the Tuxedo bulletin board can be stored and checkpointed in situ rather than converting it into a disk record especially for writing to a log.

The operation of a VRAM I/O cache within a multiprocessor environment has to be considered in the light of its use as (i) an I/O buffer and (ii) a stable memory. Transferring data directly into the VRAMs from disk can lead to problems with maintaining cache coherency. Data can be transferred from disk into VRAM without the local CPU caches being aware of the transaction. One solution is simply to declare the VRAM cache as being non cacheable, but this does not help performance. If a write-through protocol is used, coherency can be achieved by invalidating cached copies when the new "disk page" is first accessed after an I/O read - the VRAM cache could be accessed by a new "alias" addresses whenever it is updated by the disk, potentially avoiding the invalidation of the local CPU caches all together. Write-back caches are more problematical as they require modified data to be flushed back to memory before it is to written to disk or a checkpoint taken. A multiprocessor system which allows different cacheing policies to operate in parallel and provides primitives to invalidate and flush cache lines at the page granularity would clearly be a bonus in this situation.

## 3. VRAM Organisation & Operation

The organisation & operation of a VRAM is now described in order to show that transferring data to/from disk and copying for checkpointing can be handled very effectively if the I/O cache is constructed from such devices.

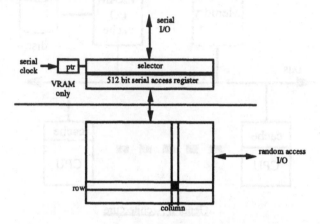

**VRAM Block Diagram**

A VRAM is a DRAM with the addition of a 512-bit (usually) serial access register and a serial port. In addition to the standard DRAM read, write & refresh cycles, transfer and shift operations can be performed on the serial access register and the serial port. A transfer operation transfers a complete memory row (512 bits) between the memory array and the serial access register or vice-versa. A shift operation selects the next data bit in the serial access register to be output on the serial I/O port or vice versa.

An I/O cache of reasonable size would comprise a number of VRAM banks. For simplicity the following diagram shows an I/O cache comprising two VRAM banks.

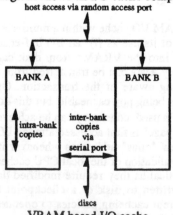

**VRAM based I/O cache**

The additional VRAM cycles can be used to (i) copy rows of data within the same VRAM bank [intra-bank] and (ii) transfer data between the serial port & the disks or copy data between different VRAM banks [inter-bank].

An intra-bank transfer requires a read transfer cycle followed by a write transfer cycle. If each bank of the VRAM is 64 bits wide, then the 64 serial access registers hold 4KB (64x 512/8) of data which can be transferred in two memory cycles (≈400ns or 10GB/s).

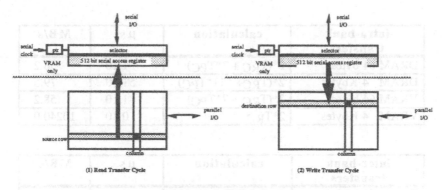

**An Intra-bank Transfer**

An inter-bank transfer requires three steps (i) read transfer of source VRAM (ii) serial transfer between serial access registers using 512 serial clocks and (iii) write transfer of destination VRAM. A complete row is transferred with 2 memory cycles and 512 serial clocks. If the serial clock operates at 25MHz and the memory is 64bits wide, 4KB of data is transferred in 15.76µs. The VRAM random access port is only occupied for the two transfer cycles (≈400ns) resulting in negligible reduction (≈3%) in host bus bandwidth. Note that instead of transferring data between two VRAM banks, inter-bank transfers can also be used to transfer data between a VRAM bank and the disks.

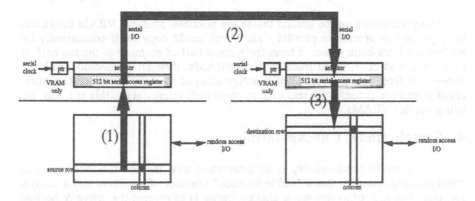

**An Inter-bank Transfer**

A comparison is now made between the copying performance of DRAM and VRAM based I/O caches. The calculations assume a 64bit data path. Comparisons are made for intra-bank and inter-bank copies of 64 bytes of data which corresponds to a typical cache line size (eg. Futurebus+) and 4 Kbytes of data which corresponds to a typical virtual memory page. For DRAM copying, page mode accesses and the existence of an external FIFO for storing data during intra-bank transfers are assumed. Typical values of $T_{ReadCycle}$=200ns, $T_{PageCycle}$=50ns & $T_{ShiftCcycle}$=40ns are used in the calculations, but remember that these figures are continually improving.

| intra-bank transfers | calculation | $\mu s$ | MB/s |
|---|---|---|---|
| DRAM 64 bytes | $2*(T_{RC} + 7*T_{PC})$ | 1.10 | 58.2 |
| DRAM 4 Kbytes | $2*(T_{RC}+ 511*T_{PC})$ | 51.50 | 79.5 |
| VRAM 64 bytes | $2*(T_{RC} + 7*T_{PC})$ | 1.10 | 58.2 |
| VRAM 4 Kbytes | $2*T_{RC}$ | 0.40 | 10240.0 |

| inter-bank transfers | calculation | $\mu s$ | MB/s |
|---|---|---|---|
| DRAM 64 bytes | $T_{RC} + 7*T_{PC}$ | 0.50 | 116.4 |
| DRAM 4 Kbytes | $T_{RC} + 511*T_{PC}$ | 25.75 | 159.1 |
| VRAM 64 bytes | $3*T_{RC} + 8*T_{SC}$ | 0.84 | 76.2 |
| VRAM 4 Kbytes | $2*T_{RC} + 512*T_{SC}$ | 15.76 | 260.0 |

It is clear that VRAMs offer superior performance especially for page sized copying operations. Unfortunately, an extra price has to be paid for this additional performance. VRAMs currently lag their equivalent DRAMs by a generation and are ≈1.5 the cost, although there is no strong technical reason why this should be so (apart from a larger package) if they were to be manufactured in the same quantities.

Many variations on the general theme are possible. Multiple VRAM banks can be organised to operate in parallel - each bank could copy itself concurrently by performing intra-bank transfers from the bottom half of memory to the top half. If each bank was constructed from 256Kx4 VRAMs, then all of memory could be copied in a fixed time (≈100μs) that is independent of memory size. A deterministic checkpoint time is useful for real time systems and, interestingly, this is a case for using smaller VRAMs.

## 4. Switch-mode Checkpointing

Switch-mode checkpointing is an interesting new method for achieving fast checkpointing. Assume that a "stable location" consists of an active and a backup location. The idea of switch-mode checkpointing is to reverse the active & backup roles by writing to a control register which essentially gives instantaneous checkpointing.

Each active/backup location has two status bits associated with it. The M(odified) bit indicates whether the location has been modified since the last checkpoint. Immediately after a checkpoint, the active & backup locations are in the same bank until modified. The AB bit indicates which is the active bank (ie. most up to date). The mechanism assumes that the M bits are stored in a memory which can be reset in a single operation - resetable static RAMs that can be cleared in under 50ns are widely available. Circuit operation is explained by the following state transition diagram and truth table for a single active/backup pair.

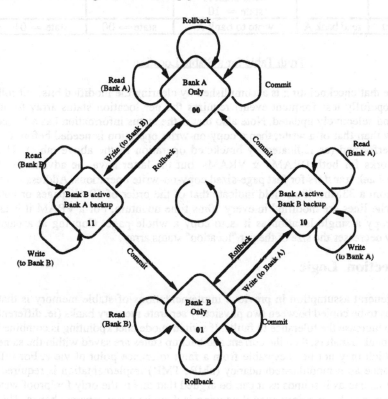

### State Transition Diagram for a Stable Location

If M = 0 (unmodified) and AB = 0 (state 00) then reads are from bank A (assume this is the initial state of all locations) until a write occurs which is directed to bank B, while the state is simultaneously set to 11. Subsequent reads are now from bank B and the M bit has been set to indicate that the location has been modified. If a failure occurs at this point, roll back is achieved by simply reverting back to state 00. On a checkpoint the M bit is cleared to move into state 01. Checkpointing in states 01 (& 00) leaves the state unchanged as the backup & active locations are in the same bank.

| state | | | | | |
|---|---|---|---|---|---|
| M | A B | read | write | checkpoint | rollback |
| 0 | 0 | read bank A | (bank A ⇒ bank B) write to bank B state ⇒ 11 | state ⇒ 00 | state ⇒ 00 |
| 1 | 1 | read bank B | write to bank B | state ⇒ 01 | state ⇒ 00 |
| 0 | 1 | read bank B | (bank B⇒ bank A) write bank A state ⇒ 10 | state ⇒ 01 | state ⇒ 01 |
| 1 | 0 | read bank A | write to bank A | state ⇒ 00 | state ⇒ 01 |

### Truth Table for a Stable Location

Notice that checkpointing is accomplished by clearing the modified bits, but roll back (a hopefully less frequent event) requires the per location status array to be scanned and selectively updated. Note also that if the status information has a larger granularity than that of a write, then a copy-on-write operation is needed before the write is performed (as indicated by bracketed operation in the above table). The scheme works for both DRAMs & VRAMs, but the latter have the advantage of using intra-bank transfers for fast page-sized copy-on-write operations. Address trace analysis from a 33Mhz 486 would indicate that of the order of 50 4K pages or 600 16byte cache lines are modified in every 10ms time quantum. For a VRAM it is as quick to copy a single location as it is to copy a whole page. Copying at a page granularity decreases the size of the per "location" status array.

## 5. Protection Logic

The general assumption in previous implementations of stable memory is that the data has to be copied between two physically separate memory banks (ie. different devices) to increase the tolerance to faults. If switch-mode checkpointing is combined with intra-bank transfers, then the current and backup states are saved within the same VRAM which may not be acceptable from a fault tolerance point of view. For full fault-tolerance an n-modular-redundancy (nMR, TMR) implementation is required. This is not as bad as it sounds as it can be argued that this is the only foolproof way to implement a stable memory even if copying is done between separate banks. This results in a 6 fold increase in memory useage for a TMR implementation.

Since the active and backup locations are in the same bank, protection logic is necessary to prevent access to the backup copy. In the Stable Disk, the protection logic also attemps to detect CPU failures (by catching illegal accesses) in the case that the CPUs are not fail-stop. The logic checks, on each access, that a given CPU is allowed access to the requested location - this checking is additional to that provided by the memory management units.

It is possible to consider an experimental system where all of memory is comprised of VRAM I/O cache. In such a system, there is a need to provide non-stable memory as it makes no sense to use stable memory for text regions or to roll-back some external I/O event which has updated memory. It is more convenient to be able to allocate memory as either stable or non-stable - for "normal" pages a single page is allocated whilst for a "stable" page two are allocated, but with only the active page accessible. The protection logic is used to implement this feature.

## 6. Stable Disk Hardware Overview

A prototype Stable Disk that incorporate the ideas presented above, has been constructed for an EISA i486 PC and a Corollary multiprocessor (a multiprocessor PC). These are attractive targets on account of their widespread use, cost effective hardware and extensive software support, especially OSF/1.

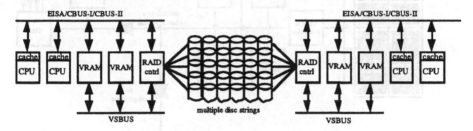

### Stable Disk Organisation for a Dual Corallary System

The Stable Disk is made up of VRAM and RAID controller boards both of which are described briefly below. The boards are attached to the CPUs via the host bus and are interconnected by a high speed private VSBUS modeled on DT-Connect II. Each RAID controller can drive five 32bit SCSI-II disk strings. Above is a sample configuration based on a dual Corollary multiprocessor system - note how the disks straddle the two machines.

## 7. VRAM Board

The VRAM board has 8MB (or 32MB) of ECC protected memory organised as 8 banks of 10 VRAMs each. The host CPUs access the VRAMs as normal memory from the host bus using the VRAM random access port. The VRAM serial ports are interconnected via a local bus which is in turn connected via buffers to the VSBUS.

Memory can be dynamically partitioned into stable and non-stable 4KB pages. Two pages are allocated for a stable page - one active and the other as a backup. After a system failure, data stored in a stable page is recoverable from the backup copy. A number of checkpointing methods are supported. Switch-mode checkpointing reverses the active and backup roles by simply writing to a control register while the other checkpointing methods are based on physically copying between the active and backup pages, the speed of which is greatly enhanced by the use of VRAMs.

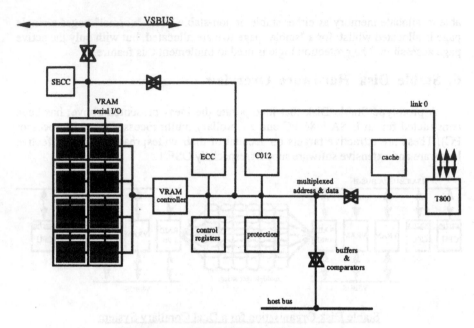

VSBUS

SECC

VRAM
serial I/O

link 0

ECC

C012

cache

VRAM
controller

multiplexed
address & data

T800

control
registers

protection

buffers
&
comparators

host bus

### VRAM based Stable Memory Block Diagram

Operation is controlled by a set of memory mapped control registers located at the top of the VRAM address space. There is an embedded transputer (t800) controller. All control registers are accessible from the host bus and the t800 so that board operation can be controlled by either. It is also possible for t800 "firmware" in VRAM to execute "high level" commands on behalf of the host CPUs. To reduce contention for VRAM access, a 32KB write-through cache has been provided for the transputer. The t800 transputer links may be used for remote recovery of VRAM data. An ISA addressable c012 link adapter is also provided for compatibility with the transputer development system (TDS).

Fault-tolerance is further enhanced by on-board protection against erroneous accesses. The protection logic checks if a CPU has the necessary rights to access a particular memory page. It also updates per page status information. Protected window slots are provided in the address space for access to companion I/O boards. When a companion I/O board is accessed using the host bus the protection is provided by the VRAM board. It is also possible to access the I/O boards in the same protected manner via the VSBUS. This path is needed, for example, if the host bus fails - in this case the t800 can control the I/O boards directly.

A single VRAM board is clearly a single point of failure, although it may well be reliable enough for certain applications. For fault-tolerant operation a number of boards can operate together in a nMR fault-tolerant arrangement. For example, 3 boards may work in a triple modular redundancy (TMR) arrangement. The host CPUs broadcast data and commands to all replicas. The host CPUs would read data from all replicas. If a board detects a difference between the data on the host bus and the data at the input to its output buffers, it traps to an error handler. The faulty board isolates itself from the bus and indicates that it needs repair. A tri-state host bus such as EISA is not entirely suited to this arrangement (a wire-OR host bus such as the open-collector Futurebus+ would suit better), so the board has a generic host bus interface allowing a single active master with multiple passive slaves, with role reversal if needed. If the bus itself turns out to be the point of failure, then the transputer links can be used to transfer the data held in the VRAMs to an alternate system.

# 8. RAID Controller

The RAID controller contains up to five SCSI-2 disk interfaces and up to four RAID array data path devices. It allows high-performance fault-tolerant disk subsystems to be constructed that have up to five 32bit RAID strings, each with up to seven ranks (fifteen with 16bit SCSI disks), and with multiplex controllers. The hardware comprises a host bus interface for programmed I/O, an external VSBUS interface for independent DMA I/O, an array data path that provides hardware support for RAID operations, and a set of disk controllers for interfacing to disks. The VSBUS is used to interconnect RAID & VRAM boards. Data is transferred between a master and a number of slaves - no hardware arbitration is required. Transfers along the VSBUS take place at 100MB/s with negligible reduction in host bandwidth (~3%).

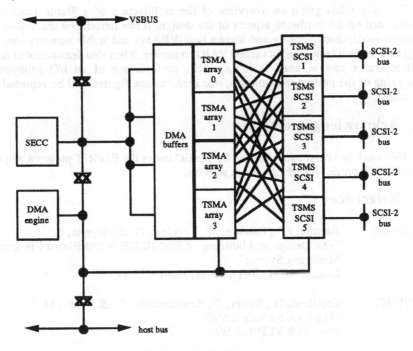

### RAID Controller Block Diagram

Control of the array data path and disk interfaces is separated. An array module (NCR 53C920 RAID data path) implements an 8bit slice of the array data path. A

SCSI module (NCR 53C916 + optional 53C932 extender for 32bit SCSI) implements a single SCSI interface. The minimal configuration would comprise a single SCSI module which supports 8, 16 or 32bit SCSI-2 disks and can be configured for asynchronous, synchronous, fast or wide SCSI bus protocols. A maximum of 5 SCSI modules can be accommodated.

To construct a minimal array configuration with hardware support, at least one array module must be installed. The array module transfers data between the 32bit EISA/VSBUS interfaces and upto five 8bit SCSI modules. This allows an array with 8bit SCSI interfaces. For 16bit interfaces, two array data path modules must be installed, whilst for 32bit interfaces all four array modules must be installed. These modules provide hardware support for RAID levels 0, 1, 3 and 5 and for up to seven ranks. The RAID board includes a 128KB DMA buffer for read data, and another of the same size for write data. The DMA buffers can also be used for host bus burst transfers to or from the array data paths. The array data path modules are not necessary for an array subsystem, but if configured in this way it will not be able to take advantage of the hardware support for array operations provided by the array data path module.

# 9  Conclusions

This paper has given an overview of the architecture of a Stable Disk and concentrated on the hardware aspects of the design. It has introduced the notion of switched-mode checkpointing and shown how VRAMs and stable memory can be integrated inside a fault-tolerant cached RAID controller. It has also demonstrated how fault tolerance can be used to increase the performance of an I/O subsytem. Debugging of the prototype continues, real performance figures will be reported in due course.

# 10.  Acknowledgements

This work has been partly funded by the EC under the ESPRIT program as part of the FASST project for which we are grateful.

# 11.  References

[BANA-86]     Banatre, J.P., Banatre, M., Lapalme, G. & Ployette, F.
              "The Design and building of ENCHERE, a distributed Electronic
              Marketing System"
              Comm. ACM, 29(1); 19-29, January 1986.

[COPE-89]     Copeland, G., Keller, T., Krisnamurthy, R. & Smith, M.
              "The Case for Safe RAM"
              Proc. 15th VLDB, 1989

[LAMP-81]     Lampson, B., ed.
              "Distributed Systems Architecture and Implementation : an
              Advanced Course"
              LNCS 105, 1981.

[OUST-88]    Ousterhout, J. & Douglis, F.
             "Beating the I/O Bottleneck: A Case for Log-Structured
             FileSystems"
             Report No. UCB/CSD 88/467, University of California.

[PATT-88]    Patterson, D.A., Gibson G., Katz, R.H.,
             "A Case for Redundant Arrays of Inexpensive disks (RAID)"
             ACM SIGMOD 88, pp. 109-116 (June 1988).

[PATT-89]    Patterson, D.A., Gibson G., Katz, R.H.,
             "Introduction to Redundant Arrays of Inexpensive disks (RAID)"
             Proceedings of IEEE COMPCON, Spring 1989.

[STON-87]    Stonebraker, M.
             "The Design of the Postgres Storage System"
             13th International Conference on VLDB 1987.

# Simple Design makes Reliable Computers

David Liddell, Chief Technical Officer, IMP Ltd., Consett, UK

## Abstract

This paper puts forward the hypothesis that the way to design reliable computers is to design simple computers. It examines the trade-off between adding complexity to solve a potential reliability problem and the unreliability incurred due to the complexity added. Some examples of simple design are then given from IMP's fault tolerant computers.

## Introduction

*A system should be as simple as possible in order to achieve its required function - and no simpler*

*Perfection is not reached when there is nothing to add, but when there is nothing to take away.*

The above "sayings" sum up the design theory I am expounding. When designing reliable systems one of the major problems to address is how to estimate the reliability that has actually been achieved. Estimating the reliability of highly complex software is effectively impossible and the situation with the hardware is actually not much better. There are good methods for estimating hardware reliability but these break down when attempting to deal with the effects of failures. The normal statement for hardware based fault tolerant systems is that there are no single points of failure but how can this be proved? The more complex the system the harder this becomes, in fact the position begins to mirror the situation with software where for any reasonably complex system proving it is correct is effectively impossible. It is hard enough designing non tolerant hardware which is bug free; to add the requirement that the design must behave predictably with random failures increases the difficulty massively.

A trade-off that continuously needs to be made is between a potential failure mode and the additional complexity to mask that mode. A good example of this is latent fault checking. Given enough time any latent fault which is unchecked will eventually cause a system to fail but testing for latent faults is notoriously difficult.

Our approach is to design very simple systems which have a higher chance of being correct and also are easier to prove correct. One of the ways to help is to design the components to be as reliable as possible so that there are no failures to mask therefore no opportunity for the masking mechanisms to fail.

## Error Free Virtual machine

One of the aims of our fault tolerant architecture is to keep the systems as similar to a non FT system as possible. We wanted to simplify the FT part of the system by using as much as we could from the non-FT system. We take the processor (including multiple processors) and memory from a non-FT system and build an error free version of this using a combination of hardware and software. This forms a virtual machine on top of which a standard operating system can run. This virtual machine has the useful property that it is reliable, we call this the reliable core. We make the IO system reliable by using duplicated but unreliable hardware with a driver running in the reliable core which runs an error detecting/correcting protocol (which is different for different IO devices) to mask this unreliability. This is standard practice and will not be discussed further.

## The Reliable Core

The core is built by duplicating or triplicating the processor/memory subsystem (each of which we call a CpuSet). CpuSet fault detection works by ensuring that each CpuSet is performing exactly the same operations at exactly the same time and comparing IO cycles. All the CpuSets run from a common clock to ensure lock step operation. Why this is not a single point of failure is discussed later.

Note that in a symmetric multi-processor implementation each processor on a single CpuSet will be performing different instructions. However the corresponding processors on adjacent CpuSets will be executing exactly the same operations. Performance is increased by adding more processors to a CpuSet, reliability is increased by adding more CpuSets.

When the CpuSets reach an IO transaction they should all perform the same operation at the same time. If CpuSets request different operations or fail to make any IO transaction at all the CpuSets must have diverged from identical operation. The cause of this divergence must be some failure within the CpuSet, for example memory corruption, or microprocessor failure (such as $2 + 2 = 5$). The IO bus design incorporates mechanisms to detect this divergence.

The IO bus (called the FTIO bus) interface on a CpuSet has two modes of operation, master and checker. All of the CpuSets in a system have the checker mode enabled, but only one also has the master mode enabled. When an I/O operation is requested the master CpuSet will put the IO transaction request onto the FTIO bus, address and data for a write cycle, address only for a read cycle. In the case of a write cycle, all of the CpuSets compare the requested address and data with the address and data which they would have put onto the FTIO bus.

During a read cycle the master places the address on the FTIO bus and all CpuSets compare this with the address they would have put onto the FTIO bus. The data portion of a read request differs from a write since neither the master nor the checker CpuSets have foreknowledge of the data they wish to read and therefore cannot make a comparison with a known value. Instead, during the data-in phase of a read request, each CpuSet checks parity, this ensures data entering the CpuSets is identical. Note that this will only guarantee that all of the CpuSets read the same data and not that the data itself is correct, for example, a disk controller could have corrupted the data before passing it to the CpuSets. The integrity of the data is protected by the detecting/correcting protocol mentioned previously.

If there is no disagreement between CpuSets, which is the normal case, the IO transaction completes successfully and processing continues. If the CpuSets disagree an exception is raised and the CpuSets enter a diagnostic routine to determine which CpuSet failed. When the diagnostics complete the good CpuSet takes the failed CpuSet off-line using a maintenance bus. In a Triple Modular Redundant (TMR) system the good CpuSet takes all the other CpuSets off-line and then reintegrates the other good CpuSet. This scheme allows the configuration of Dual Modular Redundant (DMR) or TMR systems.

A TMR system guarantees to correctly diagnose the faulty CpuSet. In a DMR when a disagreement is detected the CpuSets attempt to diagnose whether they have failed. The hardware is designed to allow fast self diagnosis with a high fault coverage. They also maintain an audit trail which records unexpected events such as illegal instruction exceptions and this is used to help with diagnosis. In practice the DMR systems correctly diagnose the faulty CpuSet but if data integrity (rather than continuous availability) is paramount then a TMR system should be used.

In order to avoid the clock generator being a single point of failure each CpuSet has the ability to generate and receive the system clock. One CpuSet generates the system clock and the others receive that clock. If the clock generator fails each CpuSet reverts to working from it's own clock generator. At the next IO transaction the CpuSets detect they are out of sync and the process described above determines the survivor.

## Configuration Management System (CMS)

The CMS intelligently manages the system's response to change. Changes in configuration occur whenever modules are added, fail, or are replaced. When failures are detected messages are passed to the CMS which parses the messages into state changes. The CMS models the systems as a finite state machine. When a state transition occurs the CMS recalculates the state of the system and any state transitions which occur can trigger "responses". Responses include warning messages, "phone home" error reporting, shell scripts or UNIX commands. The CMS runs as a user process.

Failures or changes in the operation of a controller are reported by the UNIX device drivers using the kernel error logging channel. The error device passes the messages to a user level demon which writes the message to the console device, makes a permanent copy in the status log and directs a second copy to the configuration manager. To ensure extra traceability of intermittent errors, a log of the last seven days errors is held on the system. The status logs can then be consulted to establish the exact sequence of events prior to a failure.

The configuration manager interprets all incoming kernel messages for state changes which may have occurred. A knowledge base of system modules is built up as a series of "rules" which are held in the CMS rules file. Each module in the system called an object, has a unique name. Examples are disks, CpuSets, controllers, and each tty line. Objects are then grouped according to dependencies on other objects, for example ttys are grouped into driver cards (8 ttys per driver card) then driver cards into VICP controllers (1-4 drivers per controller). Thus by applying the rules, the failure of a higher level objects marks the lower objects as failed.

The CMS has two user interfaces, fixit and sysconfig. Fixit is the normal user interface with the CMS. On request it displays all of the failed modules within the system, and whether the failure has been acknowledged.

The system has three status lights: green for "Operating System Running", yellow for "Needs Service" and Red for "New Fault". When a failure occurs the CMS, in addition to it's other tasks, sets the red light. The red light will remain on until the user takes an action to fix the machine. The first step is to invoke fixit to determine which module or modules are flagged with a failure. The user then contacts his/her support organization to log the fault. After taking this action the user can acknowledges the fault using fixit as a reported fault which needs service. Alternatively the CMS can automatically "phone home" to a service center to report the failure. In either case the red light is then extinguished and the yellow light is set. If another failure occurs while the user is waiting for the first to be fixed the red light may be set again, indicating a new fault. When a new module arrives on site the user will remove the failed module, replace the new module and finally use fixit to re-integrate the module into service. If the re-integration is successful the yellow light is extinguished.

Sysconfig is a system configuration tool used to display and change the system configuration, it is intended for use by system developers and service engineers.

## Conclusion

The emphasis on avoiding complexity has allowed a small engineering team to design a fault tolerant computer which really works. At every opportunity we ask ourselves if there is a simpler way to achieve our goal.

The architecture of the core means we can use straightforward hardware design techniques without resorting to self-checking logic of which there is only one small piece on the CpuSet. The error free virtual machine allows an unmodified operating system to be used. This greatly simplifies support for the current OS and changes to a new OS.

The CMS has allowed us to remove a lot of complexity from the kernel drivers, replacing it with a finite state machine which models the system configuration and also runs as a user process.

# Roll-Forward Checkpointing Schemes

Dhiraj K. Pradhan   Debendra Das Sharma   and   Nitin H. Vaidya

Department of Computer Science
Texas A&M University
College Station, TX 77843-3112.
E-mail: [pradhan, ddsharma, vaidya]@cs.tamu.edu

**Abstract.** In modular redundant systems, tasks are replicated to achieve fault-tolerance. Checkpointing schemes that exploit replication can achieve better performance than the ones that ignore how the fault detection mechanism is implemented [24]. This Chapter presents two such schemes named *Dynamic Roll-Forward Checkpointing Scheme* and the *Static Roll-Forward Checkpointing Scheme*.

In the dynamic scheme for duplex systems, each task is assumed to be executing simultaneously on two processing modules. At each checkpoint, the state of the two modules executing the task is compared for detection of faults. If a fault is detected, instead of the usual roll-back, both the modules continue execution to the next checkpoint interval. The failed checkpoint interval is 'retried' on a spare module, which helps in identifying the failed processing module and making its state consistent. It is demonstrated that this scheme increases the likelihood of a task completing within a specified deadline in spite of transient faults. The dynamic scheme also results in a lower average execution time with a lower variance as compared to the usual duplex roll-back schemes.

The dynamic scheme avoids a roll-back in most cases if the transient faults are independent. However, for correlated faults, it may cause multiple roll-backs. The static scheme is capable of tolerating both independent and correlated faults. In the static scheme for triplex systems, each task is assumed to be executing on three processing modules. At each checkpoint, the state of the three processing modules is compared for detection of faults. Thus, it can tolerate all single faults by masking. In the event of multiple failures, none of the checkpoints match. In that case, various recovery actions are possible depending on the choice of *concurrent depth*. For initiating a roll-forward action, one of the three processing modules is rolled back to execute the interval that experienced failure, while the other two modules continue execution to the next checkpoint interval. The module that was rolled back helps in identifying the faulty modules and the recovery action continues. In this roll-forward scheme, we do not require any spare modules; thereby avoiding the need for task migration. Simulation results indicate that this scheme outperforms the dynamic scheme in meeting deadlines in the presence of correlated faults. It also results in a lower execution time with lower variance as compared to the static scheme.

* Research supported in part by ONR

# 1 Introduction

In ultra-reliable systems, whenever a fault is detected, the task is retried to obtain correct results. Performance degradation due to task retry in the presence of faults is the cost of achieving high reliability in such systems. In addition, there could be performance degradation due to the error detection mechanism. Many life-critical real-time systems such as fly-by-wire systems, nuclear reactor controllers, space borne computers etc., have the conflicting requirements of ultra high reliability and minimal task completion times. Inability to complete a task correctly within a hard deadline may result in a system failure. Checkpointing and Rollback Recovery (CRR) is a standard technique for minimizing the mean task completion time by reducing the time spent in retrying a task [3, 7, 10, 18, 20]. This Chapter presents two such schemes that can achieve a lower mean task completion time with higher predictability, as compared to the traditional CRR scheme.

In a CRR scheme, the processing modules periodically checkpoint their state onto a stable storage. Whenever a fault is detected, the state of the processing modules is restored to the last saved checkpoint. This eliminates the need to retry the task from the beginning and only the computation since the last checkpoint is lost. However, a checkpoint interval of computation is lost everytime a fault occurs. This could be a serious drawback in hard realtime systems where the amount of slack available may be small and the loss of even one checkpoint interval may not be tolerated. Roll-backs could be a source of concern even for real-time systems with some slack where multiple faults may occur during the execution of the task. Hence, schemes that avoid 'roll-back' to the previous checkpoint interval in the event of a fault are of utmost importance for realtime systems with high reliability and tight deadline requirements. In this Chapter, we present two such schemes that are capable of avoiding roll-back. Due to their capability of avoiding roll-backs in the presence of faults, these schemes are termed as 'Roll-Forward Checkpointing Schemes' (RFCS).

Task replication on multiple processing modules is used as a means of achieving fault detection in the proposed schemes. In this Chapter, we discuss duplex and triplex systems only. However, the ideas can be extended to all modular redundant systems. Fault detection is achieved by checkpointing the copies of the task periodically and comparing them. Comparing the checkpoints ensures a higher reliability than what the embedded fault detection mechanism of each individual processor may offer, since corrupt registers or buses can not be detected without extensive coding at all levels. Coding at the the register level may severely degrade the performance and require special design of the entire processing modules instead of using off-the-shelf components. In addition, replication also helps in avoiding roll-backs in the event of fault(s), as shown in this Chapter.

Two roll-forward checkpointing schemes have been proposed in this Chapter: *Dynamic Roll-Forward Checkpointing* and *Static Roll-Forward Checkpointing*. The dynamic scheme requires each task to be executed on a pair of processing modules and their checkpoints are compared periodically. If both the copies match, the checkpoint is *committed* and both the modules continue execution to the next checkpoint interval. In the event of a fault, the two checkpoints do not match and a non-dedicated spare is used to identify the faulty processing module. The basic idea is that after a fault is detected at a checkpoint, the two processing modules are allowed to continue execution of the task beyond the checkpoint, while the spare re-executes the task, starting from the previous (committed) checkpoint. At the end of one checkpoint interval, the checkpoint state of the spare is compared with the states of the two processing modules in the duplex where the fault was detected. The faulty processing module(s) can be identified after this comparison and various recovery actions can be taken depending on the fault scenario. This scheme is effective in avoiding roll-backs in the presence of independent faults.

The dynamic scheme performs well when the faults in the processing modules are independent. However, if the faults in the modules are correlated and in situations where faults occur in consecutive checkpoint intervals, the dynamic scheme requires multiple roll-backs. Recent studies have indicated that correlated transient failures have a significant impact on system reliability [9, 14, 23]. Environmental disturbances may cause a sudden increase in failure rates encountered by a system [8, 9] and cause correlated faults. For example, a space borne computer system may be vulnerable to the intermittent impulse radiation caused by solar flares [8]. This may cause multiple faults in various processing modules during the same checkpoint interval (space correlation) or faults in consecutive checkpoint intervals (time correlation). In order to avoid roll-backs even in the presence of correlated faults, we have proposed a static roll-forward checkpointing scheme. The static scheme uses three processing modules, forming a triplex. Thus, all single faults in one checkpoint interval can be identified during checkpoint comparison and can be masked by copying a correct checkpoint to the faulty processing module. In addition, it is capable of tolerating multiple faults in the same checkpoint interval as well as faults in consecutive checkpoint interval without requiring a roll-back, in many cases. Existing strategies do not provide such recovery capabilities. In the event of multiple faults in one checkpoint interval, none of the checkpoints match. Instead of loading the executable code and checkpoint onto a spare through the network and re-executing the interval, we select one of the three processing modules in the triplex to roll back to the previous checkpoint interval; the other two continue execution onto the next checkpoint interval. The processing module that rolls back helps in identifying the faulty processing modules and various recovery actions may be taken depending on the various fault scenarios. It has been shown that this scheme avoids roll-backs even in the presence of correlated faults without requiring any additional spare processing capability. Thus, such a scheme is suitable for real-time applications with tight deadlines in a hostile environment, where faults may occur in bursts.

The Chapter is organized as follows. The following Section provides a brief overview of the existing recovery strategies. The logical system architecture required by the proposed schemes is delineated in Section 3. Section 4 describes the dynamic roll-forward checkpointing scheme and compares its performance with the traditional duplex-based roll-back scheme. The static roll-forward checkpointing scheme is described in Section 5 along with its performance analysis and comparison with the dynamic scheme. The conclusion appears in Section 6.

## 2   Review of Previous Work

Some of the commercial fault-tolerant systems use CRR techniques to reduce the mean task execution time in the presence of failure. In the Sequoia system [2], each processing element (PE) consists of two processors operating in lock-step. A comparator tests for identical operation on each clock cycle. Each PE has a write-back cache. The cache is flushed to the main memory under OS control. The cache is flushed to the main memory in response to events such as cache overflow and context switch. The state saved in the main memory is considered to be stable. Whenever a fault is detected, the task is rolled back to the previous state saved in the main memory. Unlike the Sequoia system, the proposed schemes neither require tight synchronization among the processing modules nor a comparison at every access through the data/address bus. In addition, the proposed schemes try to avoid roll-back even in the presence of fault(s).

Tandem uses the *process pair* approach to achieve fault-tolerance [6]. A process pair consists of two processes, primary and backup, executing on two processors. The primary process periodically sends its state (checkpoint) to the backup. Whenever a primary process fails, the secondary becomes active and starts execution from the last checkpoint received from the primary. Hence, effectively the process rolls back in the event a failure is detected. The proposed schemes do not require a roll-back in the event of failures and do not assume the processors to be fail-stop.

The roll-forward strategies developed here has its root in our earlier work [17]. Independent work has also been done by Long *et al.*, termed as the *Look-ahead strategy* [12, 13]. The Dynamic RFCS scheme can be implemented using lesser redundancy than the look-ahead strategy. However, the look-ahead scheme may have a slight performance advantage over our Dynamic RFCS scheme due to its higher redundancy requirements. The Static RFCS scheme is expected to outperform the look-ahead scheme proposed in [13], as it can correct all single faults in one checkpoint interval (even consecutive ones) by majority voting. In many cases, it is capable of withstanding multiple faults in the same as well as consecutive checkpoint intervals. The look-ahead scheme proposed in [13, 12] is not capable of withstanding multiple faults in the same checkpoint interval and may require multiple roll-backs due to multiple faults in consecutive checkpoint intervals in many cases. In addition, the number of spare processors required increases with the validation depth; validation depth being the number of intervals one can go ahead without committing a checkpoint. For example, a validation depth of 1 will require three spare processors, whereas a validation depth of 2 will require upto nine spare processors. While a higher validation depth may be essential for a hard real-time application with little or no slack, the increase in the number of spare processors per retry may exhaust all the available spare processors in the system. This may cause a much higher failure probability especially in a hostile environment due to the large number of processors involved. In addition, task migrations over the network to spare processors may slow down the task execution. The proposed Static RFCS scheme requires three dedicated processing modules and can implement any validation depth without any additional processors and without involving any task migration.

## 3  System Architecture

The multiprocessor environment to be considered relies on task replication to achieve fault-tolerance. Figure 1 illustrates a multiprocessor system organization that can implement the proposed roll-forward checkpointing scheme. Each processing module (PM) is assumed to consist of a processor and a private volatile storage (VS). All the processing modules are assumed identical. It is further assumed that each PM can access a stable storage (SS). The stable storage associated with each PM is accessible by the other modules in the presence of PM failure. A *Checkpoint Processor* (CP) is assumed accessible from all the processing modules in the system. The CP can be centralized or distributed and orchestrates the fault detection and recovery functions. The CP detects module failures by comparing the state of each pair of processing modules (PMs) which perform the same task. The state of a process is an image of all the variable memory and registers associated with the process [15]. One can either compare the complete checkpoints or just signatures of the checkpoints for efficiency.

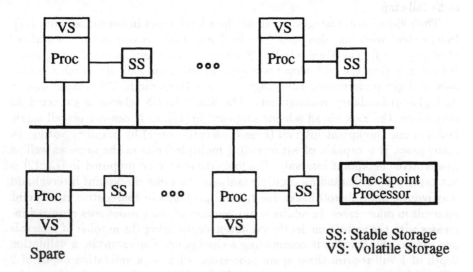

**Fig. 1.** Logical system architecture

In the Dynamic RFCS scheme it is assumed that a small number of modules are available as spares in addition to the processing modules executing duplicated tasks. These modules may be non-dedicated spares to be used temporarily for fault recovery. If spares are not available, it is assumed that active modules with spare capacity can be interrupted and used temporarily as spares. The Static RFCS scheme requires three dedicated processors and can operate with just three isolated PMs having an access to a stable storage without requiring any spare for fault recovery.

The architecture of Figure 1 is used as an example to guide the discussion in the paper. Figure 1 illustrates only the connectivity between the modules, the stable storage and the Checkpoint Processor (CP) as required by the proposed schemes. Actual implementation may be quite different. Each PM, for example, may not have independent stable storage and the PMs may share a stable storage. The physical interconnection structure can be different from that shown in Figure 1.

The procedure for state or checkpoint comparison is as follows. Whenever a task checkpoints its state into the stable storage, the state is sent to the CP. When the CP receives the states from all the modules executing a task, it compares the states. If two of the states match, they are considered correct and the previous checkpoint is replaced by the new one. If a mismatch occurs, then the previous checkpoint is not discarded and the recovery mechanism discussed in this paper is initiated.

When a write-back cache memory represents the volatile state and the main memory is stable (e.g., the Sequoia architecture [2]), the volatile storage (VS) block in a processing module in Figure 1 represents the write-back cache and the stable storage (SS) block represents the stable main memory. In this case, apart from periodic checkpointing, checkpoints need to be taken whenever the cache overflows. The contents of the stable memory locations are not overwritten at a checkpoint until the comparison of the caches in the two modules in a duplex is completed by the CP. The cache contents may need to be buffered in a separate area in the SS modules (in this case, the stable main memory) until the comparison is complete.

The following discussion and performance analysis implicitly assumes that two faulty modules will always produce different checkpoints. The likelihood that a correlated failure will produce exactly identical checkpoints in both processors can be seen to be insignificant. For further discussion of this issue the reader is referred to [24].

# 4   Dynamic Roll-Forward Checkpointing Scheme

As mentioned earlier, this scheme requires the task to be executed on two processing modules. At the end of every checkpoint interval, the two checkpoints are compared. If both the checkpoints match, the checkpoint is committed and both the processing modules continue execution to the next checkpoint interval (Fig. 2). If the two checkpoints do not match, the roll-forward recovery action

action is initiated as described below. In all the figures in this Chapter, a solid 'X' indicates a fault, whereas a dotted 'X' indicates the possibility of a fault (i.e., the situation remains the same irrespective of whether a fault occurs or not).

## 4.1 Concurrent Retry Mechanism

If the two checkpoints of A and B do not match the concurrent retry mechanism is initiated. A and B proceed to execute the next checkpoint interval while the failed interval is 'retried' on a spare. Depending on the fault scenario four cases may arise, as discussed below. A detailed discussion of these scenarios appear in [15, 24, 16, 25].

**Case 1 - No concurrent retry:** (Fig. 2) Both processing modules A and B are fault-free during the interval $I_j$. Hence, their checkpoints match at time $t_1$ and the checkpoint is committed. Both the processing modules continue to execute the next checkpoint interval $I_{j+1}$ during the time interval $(t_1, t_2)$ without requiring any recovery action.

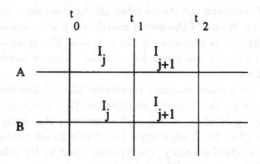

**Fig. 2.** Case 1 - No Concurrent Retry Required

**Case 2 - Concurrent retry without roll-back:** (Fig. 3) Figure 3 depicts the execution of two processing modules, named A and B, executing the same task. Let us assume that B fails during the checkpoint interval $I_j$ and other modules are fault-free. Then, the checkpoints of A and B will mismatch at the end of interval $I_j$. This mismatch will activate "concurrent retry" of checkpoint interval $I_j$ on a spare, as follows.

1. The mismatching checkpoints of the two modules are saved. The previous checkpoint is then loaded into a spare module, say module S. The executable code for the task is also loaded into the spare module. The checkpoint interval in which the fault occurred is then retried on the spare module. Concurrently, A and B continue execution of the next checkpoint interval.

2. After the spare completes interval $I_j$, the checkpoint of spare S is compared with the mismatching checkpoints of modules A and B. The checkpoint of S will mismatch with the checkpoint of B at the end of interval $I_j$, and match with A.

3. When this mismatch and match is detected, B is known to be faulty and A fault-free. Therefore, state of B is made identical to the checkpoint of A. Now, A and B will both be in the correct state (if module A did not fail in the second checkpoint interval named $I_{j+1}$).

4. Concurrent retry mechanism then proceeds to determine if module A failed in interval $I_{j+1}$. Thus, S executes the interval $I_{j+1}$ while A and B execute the interval $I_{j+2}$. Assuming no faults occur during the time interval $(t_2, t_3)$, the checkpoint interval $I_{j+1}$ of the spare S will match that of A and since the checkpoints of A and B match for the checkpoint interval $I_{j+2}$. The checkpoint for the interval $I_{j+2}$ can be committed at $t_3$ without any loss of checkpoint intervals. Thus, the proposed scheme is capable of avoiding any roll-back if there is no more than one fault in two consecutive checkpoint intervals (Fig. 3) in two processing modules or two faults in the consecutive checkpoint intervals of the same module.

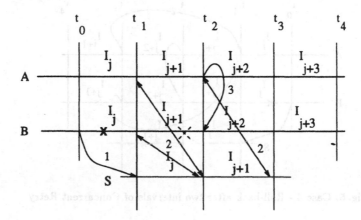

1. Copy State to the spare
2. Compare state of the spare with A and/or B.
3. Copy state from A to B

**Fig. 3.** Case 2 - Concurrent Retry without Roll-back

**Case 3 - Rollback after one interval of concurrent retry:** (Fig. 4) In this situation, the concurrent retry mechanism does not succeed due to multiple faults in processing modules executing the interval $I_j$. Thus, the roll-forward mechanism causes a loss of two checkpoint intervals. One of the possible fault patterns that causes this scenario is demonstrated in Fig. 4.

**Case 4 - Rollback after two intervals of concurrent retry:** (Fig. 5) In this situation also, the system has to roll back due to certain patterns of multiple faults. Fig. 5 demonstrates one such pattern.

Table 1 summarizes the various actions required for the four situations described above. The proposed dynamic scheme avoids rollback if there is a

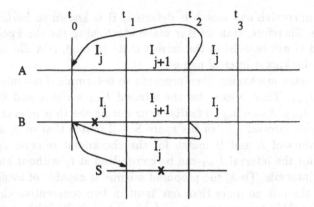

**Fig. 4.** Case 3 - Roll-back after one interval of Concurrent Retry

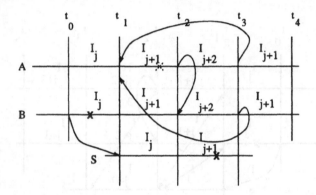

**Fig. 5.** Case 4 - Roll-back after two intervals of Concurrent Retry

single fault in two consecutive checkpoint intervals $I_j$ and $I_{j+1}$. Multiple faults in consecutive checkpoint intervals may cause rollback. Thus, it is applicable to situations where faults are independent. However, for correlated faults, the Static RFCS strategy, described later, is effective in avoiding rollbacks.

## 4.2 Performance Analysis

The performance of the proposed dynamic scheme is compared to that of the duplex roll-back scheme. The various overheads such as the time to checkpoint, the time required for checkpoint comparison, the time required for loading a task in the spare, roll-back, etc. are taken into consideration. The parameters of interest are:

- CDF of the task completion time $F_n(t)$, i.e., denotes the probability that a task will be completed in time $t$, $n$ being the number of checkpoint intervals.

**Table 1.** Actions required in various situations

| Situation | Concurrent retry | Rollback |
|---|---|---|
| (A) | No | No |
| (B) | Yes | No |
| (C) | Yes | Yes |
| (D) | Yes | Yes |

- Average task completion time ($\bar{\tau_n}$).
- Variance of the task completion time ($v_n$).

Analytic expressions have been developed to evaluate these parameters for both the proposed Dynamic RFCS scheme and the duplex roll-back schemes and verified using simulation results. A detailed derivation of the expressions appears in [15, 24, 25].

All the results are presented for a hypothetical task requiring 50 units of useful computation, divided into 10 checkpoint intervals ($n$), a checkpointing cost of 0.5 time units, under an exponential failure rate $\lambda = 10^{-3}$, unless mentioned otherwise. Thus, the task requires 55 units of time for completion, assuming no failures. In the figures, the term 'D-RFCS' denotes the Dynamic RFCS strategy.

Figure 6 plots $(1 - F_n(t))$ for the task. Comparison of the plots for Dynamic RFCS and ROLLBACK schemes indicates that the likelihood that a job will miss a tight deadline is lower with the Dynamic RFCS scheme as compared to the ROLLBACK scheme.

Table 2 shows the relative gain of the dynamic RFCS scheme over the roll-back scheme. The gain is with respect to the mean task completion time assuming the presence of at least one fault. The gain is calculated as the difference in the mean completion times of the two schemes divided by the amount of useful computation per checkpoint interval ($\frac{50}{n}$ units). The gain values are given for various values of $n$ and $\lambda$. Observe that the performance of dynamic RFCS scheme remains better over a wide range of failure rate $\lambda$ and $n$.

**Table 2.** Relative gain achieved by the Dynamic RFCS scheme

| | $n$ | | | | | | | | |
|---|---|---|---|---|---|---|---|---|---|
| $\lambda$ | 3 | 4 | 5 | 6 | 7 | 8 | 10 | 12 | 14 |
| $10^{-3}$ | .325 | .488 | .590 | .660 | .710 | .747 | .800 | .834 | .858 |
| $10^{-6}$ | .331 | .495 | .594 | .658 | .704 | .738 | .784 | .813 | .833 |
| $10^{-9}$ | .331 | .496 | .594 | .658 | .704 | .738 | .784 | .813 | .833 |
| $10^{-12}$ | .331 | .496 | .594 | .658 | .704 | .738 | .784 | .813 | .833 |

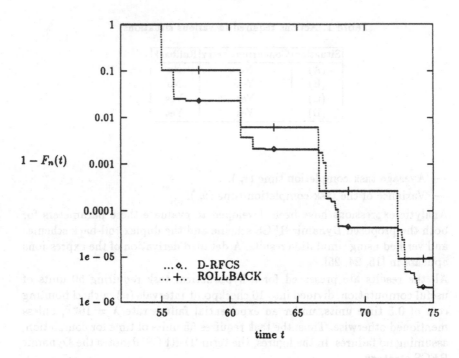

**Fig. 6.** $(1 - F_n(t))$ versus $t$ for task 1 with $n = 10$ and $\lambda = 10^{-3}$.

In Figure 7 variance $v_n$ is plotted versus the mean completion time $\overline{\tau_n}$ for the example task. Each point on the mean-variance plot corresponds to a specific number of checkpoints. By varying the number of checkpoints, different mean and variance can be achieved. Observe that for any mean and variance pair achieved using the ROLLBACK scheme, a pair with lower mean and variance can be achieved using the Dynamic RFCS scheme. For example, in Figure 7, observe that if ROLLBACK scheme with $n = 6$ is used, then one may use the Dynamic RFCS scheme with $n = 5, 6$ or $7$ and achieve lower mean completion time with lower variance. Also, in general, the Dynamic RFCS scheme can achieve a lower minimum average task completion time as compared to the ROLLBACK scheme. Similar results were observed for other values of $\lambda$.

## 5 Static Roll-Forward Checkpointing Scheme

The dynamic roll-forward strategy described above works well if faults occur independently. However, multiple roll-backs may be necessary in the presence of multiple faults over consecutive checkpoint intervals. The static RFCS scheme presented in this Section can achieve a lower mean completion time with a lower variance than the existing schemes by reducing the number

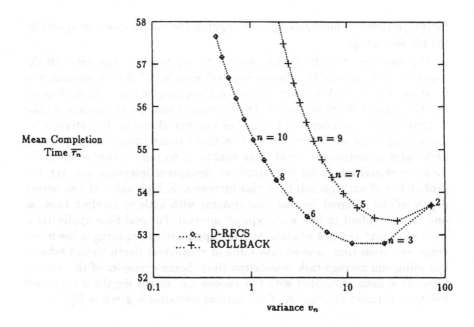

**Fig. 7.** Mean completion time versus variance for task 1 with $\lambda = 10^{-3}$

of rollbacks to be performed in the presence of faults (correlated as well as uncorrelated) under normal as well as hostile environments. In addition, the scheme does not require any task migration over the network, which could slow down the task due to the associated latencies of task migration. Thus, the proposed static scheme can be used for hard real-time systems expecting correlated faults.

The static scheme requires each task to be executed on three processing modules. The checkpoints of these three processing modules are compared at the end of every checkpoint interval. A checkpoint is said to be committed if at least two checkpoints for the same checkpoint interval match. In the absence of any faults, the three checkpoints will match, the checkpoint will be committed and stored in the stable storage and the three processors will continue to execute the next checkpoint interval. In the presence of a single fault, the faulty processor can be detected during checkpoint comparison and the correct checkpoint can be copied to the processor that experienced a fault. Hence, no checkpoint interval is lost and this scheme can tolerate any number of single faults in consecutive checkpoint intervals. The only penalty paid is in copying the committed checkpoint to the faulty processor. This overhead may be minimized by copying the correct checkpoint to the faulty processor simultaneously with logging the committed checkpoint to the stable storage.

In the presence of multiple (i.e., two or three) faults in the same checkpoint interval, none of the checkpoints will match. All the checkpoints will be stored in the stable storage. Various actions may be taken, depending on the *Concurrent Depth* we choose. The concept of concurrent depth is similar to that of validation depth [13]. It is the number of checkpoint intervals we are willing to go ahead (roll-forward) without committing a checkpoint. A high value of concurrent depth may enable us to roll forward even in the presence of multiple faults in consecutive checkpoint intervals; however, the probability of multiple roll-back also increases. A high value of concurrent depth will be required for real-time systems with little or no slack time, as one can not afford to lose a checkpoint interval. For real-time applications with moderate amount of slack and for applications requiring a lower average execution time, a moderate value of concurrent depth should achieve the minimum average task completion time. Some examples of the various recovery actions associated with the various concurrent depths is explained below. A detailed description of the various scenarios is given in [5].

## 5.1 Concurrent Depth 0

This is simply a scheme where checkpoints are majority-voted upon. Thus, in the presence of multiple faults all three processors roll back to the previous committed checkpoint as they can not proceed further without committing one checkpoint (Fig. 8).

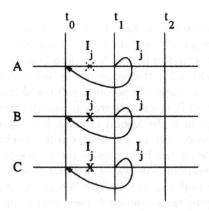

**Fig. 8.** Concurrent Depth 0

## 5.2  Concurrent Depth 1

Consider a situation where none of the checkpoints match due to multiple faults. In this case, one of the three processors is selected at random and rolled back to re-execute the checkpoint interval in which the disagreement had occurred. The other two processors continue with their uncommitted checkpoints. All the three processors store their respective uncommitted checkpoints in the stable storage. For example, as shown in Fig. 9, processor C is rolled back to re-execute the previous checkpoint interval $I_j$ whereas A and B execute the checkpoint interval $I_{j+1}$ based on their (uncommitted) checkpoints of the interval $I_j$. Various cases are possible depending on the fault patterns and we may have no loss of checkpoint intervals or loss of upto two checkpoint intervals. We present three such cases. Detailed description of various other cases appear in [5].

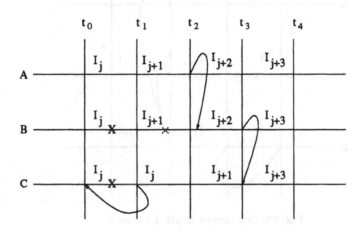

**Fig. 9.** Concurrent Depth 1 : Case 1

**Case 1** (Fig. 9) As described earlier, the processor C rolls back to execute the previous checkpoint interval $I_j$, during the time interval $(t_1, t_2)$, while A and B continue with checkpoint interval $I_{j+1}$ in spite of the disagreement. The checkpoint of C at time $t_2$ matches with that of A at time $t_1$. This establishes the fact that A had executed the checkpoint interval $I_j$ correctly and the checkpoint for $I_j$ can be committed. The checkpoint of A is copied to B after A completes its execution of the checkpoint interval $I_{j+1}$. At this point, the validity of execution of the interval $I_{j+1}$ in processor A has to be established. C continues to execute the interval $I_{j+1}$ during the time interval $(t_2, t_3)$ to validate the execution of A during the checkpoint interval $I_{j+1}$. A and B continue to execute checkpoint interval $I_{j+2}$. At the end of the interval, the checkpoints of A and B are compared for the execution of the checkpoint interval $I_{j+2}$, whereas the checkpoint of A for the interval $I_{j+1}$ is compared with that of C. Given the fault scenarios of Figure 9, both these comparisons will match. Thus, the checkpoint for the checkpoint intervals $I_{j+1}$ and $I_{j+2}$ are committed. Only the committed checkpoint of $I_{j+2}$ is retained. C no longer needs to lag, the checkpoint $I_{j+2}$ can be loaded to C and all three processors can execute the interval $I_{j+3}$ without any loss in checkpoint intervals. This is an example where the system suffers no loss of checkpoint intervals in spite of multiple faults.

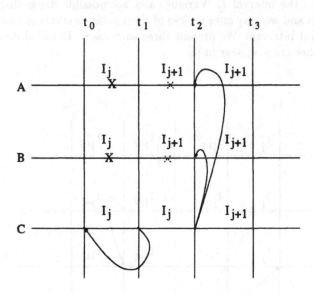

**Fig. 10.** Concurrent Depth 1 : Case 2

**Case 2** (Fig. 10) The checkpoint of C at time $t_2$ matches with the checkpoint of C at $t_1$. Thus, it is established that A and B were erroneous during the checkpoint interval $I_j$. A and B copy the correct checkpoint from C and all three processors execute the checkpoint interval $I_{j+1}$ during the time interval $(t_2, t_3)$. Thus, there is a loss of one checkpoint interval in the presence of two to four faults in two consecutive checkpoint intervals.

**Case 3** (Fig. 11) In this scenario, processor C experiences a second fault during its roll-back and the checkpoint for $I_j$ can not be committed during time $t_2$. Since A and B can not execute the interval $I_{j+2}$ without the checkpoint for $I_j$ being committed (as the concurrent depth is 1), all three processors roll back to execute the interval $I_j$ during the time interval $(t_2, t_3)$. Thus, there is a loss of two checkpoint intervals of computation.

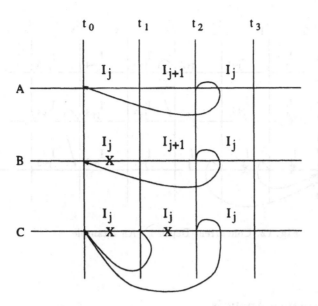

**Fig. 11.** Concurrent Depth 1 : Case 3

## 5.3 Concurrent Depth 2

A value of concurrent depth 2 indicates that the roll-forward operation can be carried forward by 2 checkpoint intervals without committing a checkpoint. Recovery actions in some cases are similar to that of concurrent depth 1 and different in others. The following example illustrates one of the cases in which a concurrent depth of 2 avoids a roll-back whereas a concurrent depth of 1 requires a roll-back by two checkpoint intervals.

Consider the scenario depicted in Fig. 12, where the system does not lose any checkpoint intervals in spite of repeated faults. This is exactly the same scenario described in Fig. 11. The three processors disagree on their results at time $t_1$. A checkpoint for $I_j$ could not be committed at $T_2$ even after rolling back processor C. Since the concurrent depth is 2 we can roll back only processor C during the interval $(t_2, t_3)$ when processors A and B can continue executing the checkpoint interval $I_{j+2}$. This is in contrast to the Case 3 of concurrent depth of 1 where we had to roll back all the three processors and lost 2 checkpoint intervals of computation. The checkpoint for $I_j$ is committed at the end of its re-execution by processor C. Since the execution of processor A for the interval $I_j$ was correct, the checkpoint for interval $I_{j+2}$ is copied from processor A to B. C proceeds to execute the checkpoint intervals $I_{j+2}$ and $I_{j+3}$ in the next two intervals in order to validate the execution of A. Assuming no other faults, the checkpoint for the execution of $I_{j+5}$ will be committed at $t_6$. Thus, any roll-back is avoided in this case, with a concurrent depth of 2. It should be noted that there could be loss of upto 3 checkpoint intervals with a concurrent depth of 2 during the roll-forward action.

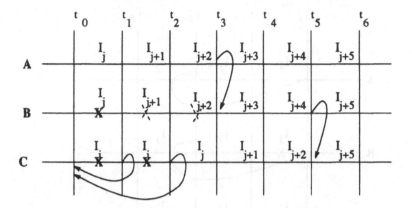

**Fig. 12.** Concurrent Depth 2 : An Example

## 5.4 Performance Analysis

The performance of the proposed static strategy is compared with the proposed dynamic scheme described in the previous Section to demonstrate the effectiveness of the static scheme to avoid roll-backs in the presence of correlated faults. The performance parameters of interest are: the mean task completion time, the variance in task completion time and the probability of missing a deadline (or the CDF of the task completion time). Analytic expressions for evaluating the performance parameters of interest appear in [5]. The various overheads associated with checkpointing, checkpoint comparison, rollback etc. have been accounted for in the simulation results as well as the analytic expressions [5].

The performance of the dynamic and static strategies are compared by performing simulations. In all the graphs, 'D-RFCS' implies the dynamic scheme whereas 'S-RFCS-$i$' denotes the static scheme with a concurrent depth of $i$ ($i = 0, 1, 2$). The following parameters are assumed: amount of useful computation = 500 time units, correlation coefficient (the probability that a processor will have a fault given that another processor has a fault in the same time interval) = 0.5, (exponential) failure rate = $10^{-3}$, number of checkpoint intervals = 10. Each simulation was run for $10^6$ iterations.

In situations where faults exhibit correlation, simulation results demonstrate that the static RFCS scheme outperforms the dynamic scheme in terms of performance parameters such as the mean task completion time, variance in the task completion time and the probability that a task meets a deadline. Figure 13 demonstrates the probability of missing a deadline for various schemes for various amounts of slack. It can be observed that the concurrent

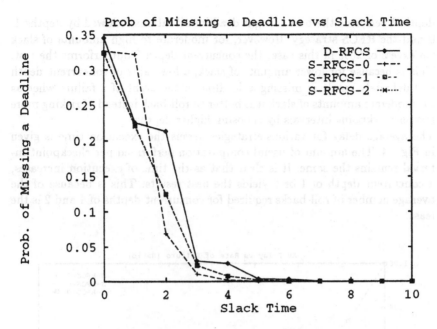

**Fig. 13.** Probability of Failure versus Slack

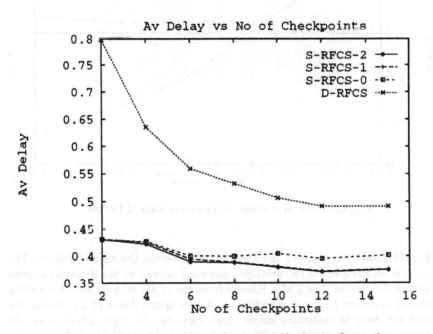

**Fig. 14.** Average Delay versus Number of Checkpoint Intervals

depth 2 performs the best in tight deadline situations followed by depths 1, 0 and the RFCS strategy. However, for moderate to high amounts of slack (in excess of 20% in this case) the concurrent depth 0 outperforms the rest. This is because for lower amounts of slack, a low value of concurrent depth will definitely result in missing a deadline in the event of a failure whereas for moderate amounts of slack it is better to roll-back instead of risking more loss in checkpoint intervals by choosing higher depths.

The average delay for various strategies versus the execution time is given in Fig. 14. The amount of useful computation performed per checkpoint interval remains the same. It is clear that as the time of execution increases, a concurrent depth of 1 or 2 yields the best results. This is because of the average number of roll-backs required for concurrent depths of 1 and 2 is the least.

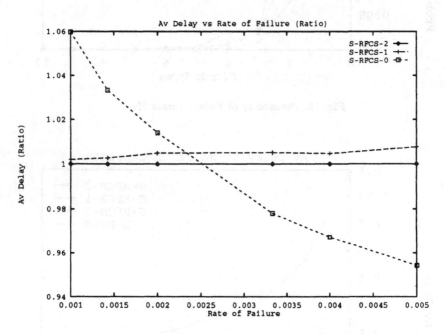

**Fig. 15.** Ratio of Average Delay versus Rate of Failure

Fig. 15 shows the ratio of the average delay versus the rate of failure. The ratio is with respect to the average delay encountered by the dynamic scheme with a concurrent depth of 2. Results from the static scheme have been eliminated to obtain better scaling factors. A concurrent depth of 2 performs the best for lower to moderate failure rates. However, for high failure rates, the concurrent depth 0 wins out. This can be attributed to the high failure rate, coupled with the high correlation coefficient (0.5), which makes it useless to roll back one processor instead of three. Similar trends can be observed if we change the (spatial) correlation coefficient (Fig. 16). As the correlation coefficient increases, the concurrent depth 0 overtakes the concurrent depths of 1 and 2. For lower values of correlation coefficient, implementing a roll-forward scheme (with depth 1 or 2) helps. However, as this value increases, it is more likely that all the processors will be faulty and initiating any roll-forward action will cause more roll-backs. This is the reason why the dynamic scheme and the static scheme with concurrent depths of 1 and 2 exhibit similar performance; inferior to the static scheme with a concurrent depth of 0.

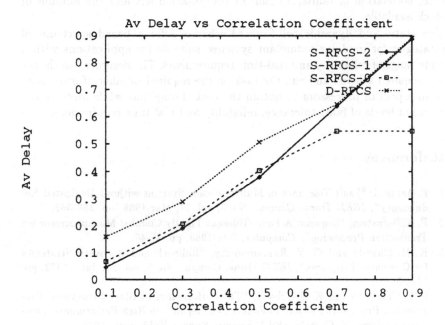

**Fig. 16.** Average Delay versus Correlation Coefficient

The above simulation results suggest that the dynamic scheme outperforms the static scheme in the presence of correlated faults. However, it requires more resources. This illustrates the trade-off between the performance and resource requirements. The choice of concurrent depth may be changed dynamically depending on the (estimated) failure rate, the (estimated) correlation coefficient, the number of checkpoint intervals remaining for completion and the amount of slack available. Such a choice will greatly enhance the performance of the system.

# 6 Conclusions

Dynamic and Static schemes have been proposed to avoid roll-backs in the presence of faults. The dynamic scheme requires only two processors during normal execution and a non-dedicated spare for two checkpoint intervals if a fault is detected. This scheme is shown to be effective in avoiding roll-backs in the presence of independent faults. The static scheme requires three processors during the entire execution and is effective in avoiding roll-backs in the presence of correlated as well as uncorrelated (independent) faults without requiring any task migration. The static scheme offers a choice of concurrent depth which can be changed dynamically depending on the failure rate, correlation of faults, amount of computation left and the amount of slack available.

The static and dynamic roll-forward schemes offer a broad spectrum of strategies for modular redundant systems, suitable for applications with a wide range of reliability and real-time requirements. The designer can choose the required scheme and run the task on the required number of processors from a pool of processors to obtain the best throughput while meeting the required levels of fault-tolerance, reliability and real-time requirements.

# References

1. P. Agrawal, "Fault Tolerance in Multiprocessor Systems without Dedicated Redundancy", *IEEE Trans. Compu.*, No. 3, vol. 37, Mar 1988, pp. 358-362.

2. P. A. Bernstein, "Sequoia: A Fault-Tolerant Tightly Coupled Multiprocessor for Transaction Processing", *Computer*, Feb. 1988, pp. 37-45.

3. K. M. Chandy and C. V. Ramamoorthy, "Rollback and Recovery Strategies for Computer Programs", *IEEE Trans. Compu.*, No. 6, vol. 21, June 1972, pp. 546-556.

4. P. F. Chimento and K. S. Trivedi, "The Performance of Block Structured Programs on Processors Subject to Failure and Repair", in High Performance Computer Systems, E. Gelenbe (Ed.), Elsevier Science Publishers, 1988.

5. D. Das Sharma and D. K. Pradhan, "A Static Roll-Forward Checkpointing Scheme Using Three Processors", *Tech. Rep. TR-93-050*, Dept. of Computer Science, Texas A&M Univ., 1993.

6. C. I. Dimmer, "The Tandem Non-Stop System", in *Resilient Computing Systems*, T. Anderson, ed., vol. 1, John Wiley and Sons, 1985.

7. E. Gelenbe and D. Derochette, "Performance of Rollback Recovery Systems under Intermittent Failures", *Comm. ACM*, No. 6, vol. 21, June 1978, pp. 493-499.

8. S. R. Kane et al., "Impulsive Phase of Solar Flares", in P. A. Sturrock ed., *Solar Flares : A Monograph from Skylab Solar Workshop II*, Univ of Colorado Press, Boulder, CO, 1980.

9. C. M. Krishna and A. D. Singh, "Modeling Correlated Transient Failures in Fault-Tolerant Systems", *Proc. IEEE Intl. Symp. on Fault-Tolerant Computing*, 1989, pp. 374-381.

10. V. G. Kulkarni, V. F. Nicola and K. S. Trivedi, "Effects of Checkpointing and Queuing on Program Performance", *Comm. Stat.-Stochastic Models*, No. 6, vol. 4, 1990, pp. 615-648.

11. P. L'Ecuyer and J. Malenfant, "Computing Optimal Checkpointing Strategies for Rollback and recovery Systems", *IEEE Trans. Comp.*, No. 4, vol. 37, Apr. 1988, pp. 491-496.

12. J. Long, W. K. Fuchs and J. A. Abraham, "Implementing Forward Recovery using Checkpoints in Distributed Systems", *IFIP 2nd Intl. Working Conf. Dependable Computing for Critical Applications*, Feb. 1991.

13. J. Long, W. K. Fuchs and J. A. Abraham, "Forward Recovery using Checkpointing in Parallel Systems", *Proc. Intl. Conf. Parallel Proc.*, Jan 1990, pp. 1272-1275.

14. Y. K. Malaiya, "Linearly Correlated Intermittent Failures", *IEEE Trans. Reliability*, Vol. R-31, No. 2, June 1982, pp. 211-215.

15. D. K. Pradhan and N. H. Vaidya, "Roll-forward Checkpointing Scheme: A Novel Fault-Tolerant Architecture", Submitted to *IEEE Transactions on Computers*, Dec. 1992, Revised Nov. 1993.

16. D. K. Pradhan and N. H. Vaidya, "Roll-Forward Checkpointing Scheme: Concurrent Retry with Nondedicated Spares", *Proc. IEEE Workshop on Fault-Tolerant Parallel and Distributed Systems*, July 1992, pp. 166-174.

17. D. K. Pradhan, "Redundancy Schemes for Recovery", *Tech. Rep. TR-89-CSE-16*, Elect. & Comp. Engg., Univ. of Massachusetts, Amherst, 1989.

18. D. K. Pradhan ed., *"Fault-Tolerant Computing : Theory and Techniques"*, Vol. I & II, Prentice Hall, NJ, 1986.

19. O. Serlin, "Fault-Tolerant Systems in Commercial Applications", *Computer*, Aug. 1984, pp. 19-30.

20. K. G. Shin, T. -H. Lin and Y. -H. Lee, "Optimal Checkpointing of Real-Time Tasks", *IEEE Trans. Comp.*, No. 11, vol. 36, Nov. 1987, pp. 1328-1341.

21. D. P. Siewiorek et al., "A Case Study of C.MMP, CM* and C.VMP. Experiences with Fault-Tolerance in Multiprocessor Systems", *Proc. IEEE*, Oct 1978, pp. 1178-1199.

22. J. J. Stiffler, "Architectural design for near-100coverage", *Proc. Intl. Symp. on Fault Tolerant Computing*, 1976, pp. 134-137.

23. D. Tang, R. Iyer and S. Subramani, "Failure Analysis and Modeling a VAX Cluster System", *Proc. IEEE Intl. Symp. on Fault-Tolerant Computing*, 1990, pp. 244-251.

24. N. H. Vaidya, Ph.D. Dissertation, Elect. & Computer Engg., University of Massachusetts, Amherst, MA 01003, 1993.

25. N. H. Vaidya and D. K. Pradhan, "Concurrent Retry with Nondedicated Spares: A Fault Tolerant Checkpointing Scheme without Rollback", *Tech. Rep. TR-91-CSE-23*, Elect. & Comp. Engg., Univ. of Massachusetts, Amherst, Oct. 1991.

26. N. H. Vaidya and D. K. Pradhan, "A Fault Tolerance Scheme for a System of Duplicated Communicating Processeses", *Proc. IEEE Workshop on Fault-Tolerant Parallel and Distributed Systems*, July 1992, pp. 166-174.

# Fault-Tolerant Architectures -- Past, Present and (?) Future

J.J. Stiffler

*Sequoia Systems, Inc.*
*Marlborough, MA. USA*

*Abstract: It is argued that fault tolerance is a feature that not only is needed in the computer marketplace but that this need is in fact growing, this in spite of the fact that computer hardware has become orders of magnitude more reliable over the last four decades and that, at least by some accountings, most computer outages are due to factors (software bugs, operator errors) other than hardware problems. It is also argued that while techniques for detecting hardware, and to some extent software, faults are well understood, there is still much to be discovered with regard to recovering from detected faults without corrupting data or loosing program continuity.*

## I. Introduction

It is useful periodically to reexamine the premises under which one operates. Those of us who design fault-tolerant computers for the commercial marketplace have no difficulty convincing outselves that such products are needed and that we have something new and useful to offer. But are they? And do we?

The need for fault tolerance has frequently been questioned. Clearly, the technology upon which computers are based has improved immensely in the forty or fifty years since digital computers were first introduced to the commercial world. The mean-time-between-failures of a flip-flop implemented as part of a large-scale integrated circuit is certainly many orders of magnitude greater than that of the same flip-flop implemented using relays or vacuum tubes. Haven't technology advances made fault tolerance unnecessary?

And even if it is necessary, haven't all the techniques for achieving fault tolerance in electronic circuitry been discovered long ago? Von Neumann [1] examined various masking techniques including triple-modular redundancy in the late 1950's and Hamming [2] introduced the error-control coding mechanisms that are by far the most commonly used in computers in 1950. (The other error-control codes that are frequently used in computer applications, Fire codes and Reed-Solomon codes, were introduced in 1959 and 1960, respectively. See, for example, [3].)

The following paragraphs contain some observations on these issues made by an observer who, admittedly, is not entirely disinterested.

## II. Who Needs Fault Tolerance?

While it is obviously true that the reliability of the components from which computers are constructed has improved immensely and is continuing to improve even more, it is equally true that the complexity of computers, measured, for example, in numbers of equivalent gates, has increased almost as rapidly. Programmers used to be able to write useful programs using only four kilobytes of memory; now, even personal computers typically require at least a thousand times as much memory for satisfactory performance. Whereas eight-bit-wide data paths and arithmetic units used to be acceptable, the industry is rapidly moving toward 64 bits, etc.

But even more importantly, computers are becoming much more central to our daily lives. Obviously, in such life-critical applications as computer-controlled avionics systems on passenger aircraft and computer-controlled nuclear power plants, reliability is of the highest importance and fault tolerance is easily justified, at least until the reliability of non-fault-tolerant computers increases another several orders of magnitude. But downtime is expensive even when lives are not threatened. A survey conducted by FIND/SVP Strategic Research Division last year* found that computer downtime cost over $3.8 billion (thousand million) in lost revenue and productivity in 1991 in the United States alone. The problem is not that the frequency of outages is so great (it isn't), but that the cost of a single outage is, on average, over $329,000, reflecting the increased dependence placed by businesses on their computing facilities.

"But", it is often argued, "only a small fraction of these outages are due to hardware failures. Software bugs and operator errors account for the large majority of problems." There are three counter-arguments to this contention.

First, one should be very careful about accepting any statistics reguarding the causes of computer outages. The vast majority of computer hardware faults are transient or intermittent in nature, i.e., momentary glitches, after which the hardware continues to function correctly. It is unlikely that a systems administrator or a field-service engineer is going to blame hardware for a crash when the hardware passes all diagnostics following that crash.

Second, of all the causes of computer outage other than physical damage to the site, hardware faults tend to result in by far the greatest amount of downtime while the problem is being diagnosed and spare parts are being located and installed. Software bugs can be diagnosed, e.g., from a memory dump, after the computer has rebooted and resumed normal operation. Similarly, operator-induced crashes can also generally be recovered from quickly without the need to wait for a service call.

---

* The survey was commissioned by Stratus Computer.

Third, and most important, good fault-tolerant design is not restricted to hardware in any case. In fact, the features designed into a system that enable it to recover from hardware faults, if fully exploited, can also enable it to recover from software bugs and operator errors as well.

## III. But Is There Anything New?

It is often convenient, in discussing fault tolerance, to separate fault coverage (i.e., the ability to survive a fault, given that a sufficient amount of hardware is still operational) into three component parts: detection, isolation and recovery. The remarks concerning the fault-coverage antecedents made in the introduction really apply to the first, and to a somewhat lesser extent, to the second of these steps. And while it is undoubtedly true that new techniques remain to be discovered, the rate of such discoveries does seem to be low. The arsenal of techniques used in commercial fault-tolerant computers for detecting and isolating faults (e.g., error-control coding, triple-modular redundancy, duplication and comparison, watchdog timers, voltage, current and airflow sensors and the like) has, by and large, been around for a long time.

That is not to say that the application of these techniques is routine, however. New technologies, and the resulting higher levels of integration, for example, require that old implementations be constantly revisited. Faults that might have been independent in earlier implementations may no longer be so when the entire circuit in question is implemented on the same chip. Moreover, faults like threshold faults and Byzantine faults that may not have occurred in previous implementations may now pose serious limitations to the efficacy of the fault detection or isolation mechanism previously used.

But it is undoubtedly in the area of fault recovery that the statement that "There is nothing new under the Sun" least applies. This is evidenced by the decidedly different approach to this problem taken by all recent offerings in the fault-tolerant computer market. Since the mid 1970s, at least six companies were formed to address the computer market with fault-tolerant offerings. No two of these offerings used the same, or even very similar, methods for recovering from faults. It is interesting to survey briefly some of these different approaches to the same problem.

Auragen Computers, like most of the others to be discussed here, considered it important that the applications programmer not have to do anything special to take advantage of the fault-tolerant features of their product. There solution was to use a message-based protocol whereby each computer in a network of loosely coupled machines sent messages to a designated companion computer itemizing each of its outputs using a set of parameters that included the identification of the running application and an associated sequence number. The companion computer also received and recorded in sequence copies of all of its companion's inputs. The two computers periodically synchronized their states so that the memory needed to store this information could be purged thereby keeping the storage required for this purpose to within reasonable bounds. In the event of a detected fault, the companion then returned to the last synchronization point and began to execute the programs triggered by the succession of inputs. The sequence number of each new output was compared to the last sequence number received from the failed computer. If the former is less than or equal to the latter, the output is discarded and processing continues; if it is greater, the output is sourced in the normal way. When the companion computer has reached that point for all tasks that were being executing by the failed computer, it has succeeded in taking over its entire function.

Tolerant Computers used a logging approach to enable recovery following a fault. All terminal inputs and all disk writes were logged on disk. Periodic synchronizations were undertaken to keep the logs from becoming arbitrarily large. If a computer in the loosely-coupled network of computers detected an internal fault and ceased to function, another computer used the logged information to back out all disk updates subsequent to the last synchronization and then restarted the tasks that were running on the failed computer using the logged inputs.

Synapse used a transaction model to recover from faults. All operations were treated as transactions controlled through begin_transaction, commit_transaction and abort_transaction primitives. If a module failed in Synapse's tightly-coupled multiprocessor computer, the system underwent a database recovery operation, backing out all uncommitted transactions and completing all committed transactions, before resuming normal operation using the remaining functional modules.

Stratus Computer Corporation uses a "pair-and-spare" technique for masking faults. Each logical processor consists of four physical processors configured as two pairs. All four processors execute the same code in lock step with the outputs of each pair compared. If one of the two pairs encounters a discrepancy, the other pair continues to operate, thereby masking the effect of the fault. Stratus computers, like other computers that use redundant hardware to mask faults, do not require an explicit procedure to recover from faults. (However, when a defective module is replaced, a procedure is needed to bring the new module in synchronism with the existing modules.)

Sequoia Systems, Inc., uses a duplicated memory combined with atomic memory updates to guarantee that main memory always contains a consistent checkpoint to which the system can return following a fault. Each processor in the Sequoia tightly-coupled multiprocessor system uses strictly non-write-through caches that are periodically flushed, first to one of the copies in main memory and then to the other. As a result, at least one of the copies in memory contains a consistent state to which it is possible to return after a fault.

Speakers from both Tandem* and IMP will be making presentations at this workshop so it would be redundant to attempt to describe here the recovery procedures used in their computers. Suffice it to say that those procedures represent still other ways to address the recovery problem.

This brief outline of the recovery procedures used in the various fault-tolerant computers is admittedly highly superficial and omits much of the detail needed to make those procedures work properly. The main purpose here is to point out that there are numerous approaches to fault recovery, all of which work to a greater or lesser degree, and all of which, as a more thorough examination would demonstrate, have their limitations. This indicates that there is no consensus as to the best way to insure fault recovery and suggests that the "best" solution may remain yet to be discovered.

## IV. Conclusions

The criticality of computers to daily commerce is growing even more rapidly than the reliability of the technology with which these computers are built. Consequently, fault tolerance has even more to offer than in the past when the cost of computer downtime was less onerous. But while mechanisms for detecting faults (or, at least, hardware faults) may be well understood, the best mechanism for guaranteeing the ability to recover from them is by no means certain.

## References

1.    J. von Neumann, *Theory of Self-Reproducing Automata*, U. of Illinois Press, 1966.

2.    R.W. Hamming, "Error Detecting and Error Correcting Codes", *Bell System Technical Journal, 29,* 147-160, 1950.

3.    W. Wesley Peterson, *Error-Correcting Codes*, The M.I.T. Press and John Wiley & Sons, Inc., New York, 1961.

---

* As it turned out, there was no presentation by Tandem, so I attempted to describe the Tandem recovery procedure. The Tandem method, as I understood it, involves assigning a backup computer to each computer in a loosely-coupled network. Each computer in the network is capable of acting both as a primary computer for some tasks and as a backup for other tasks. Each computer, in its primary role, periodically sends to its backup certain checkpoint information to be used by the backup to take over the tasks that were being run on the primary in case the latter fails. However, we were informed by Andrea Borr, who previously worked for Tandem, that this recovery technique had not been used by Tandem for some years; that Tandem now uses the undo and redo recovery procedures associated with more conventional transaction processing systems. Since my descriptions of all of the recovery procedures in this section rely largely on memory (references are not readily available in most cases), I may have also misrepresented the recovery techniques used by the other vendors as well and extend my apologies to any vendor so misrepresented. I believe the conclusion remains intact, however, in spite of any inaccuracies of description: there are many ways to attempt to recover from detected faults and the industry has not yet agreed on which is best.

III  Software Architectures for Fault Tolerance

# III Software Architectures for Fault Tolerance

# A Highly Available Application in the Transis Environment

Ofir Amir, Yair Amir and Danny Dolev
Institute of Computer Science
The Hebrew University of Jerusalem,Israel
E-mail: ofiramir, yairamir, dolev @cs.huji.ac.il

**Abstract.** This paper presents a typical replicated application in a distributed system. The application was developed on top of Transis, a reliable and efficient transport layer protocol. The basic properties of the protocol and the advantages of using Transis as the transport layer are discussed. The algorithms used in this application can lead to better solutions in the area of distributed transaction systems and replicated databases.

## 1   Introduction

The reliability and availability of loosely coupled distributed systems is becoming a requirement for many computer systems. One of the main infrastructure services is a distributed database. This paper addresses some aspects of information dissemination within such a service in a dynamic loosely coupled environment.

We chose to tackle this complex problem by studying a particular application. The application we focus on is a Replicated Mail Service. In our design of this service, the database of messages is replicated among several mail servers. Each client can send mail, read it or delete it only when it can connect to one of the servers. A distributed transaction mechanism is used to ensure the eventual consistency of the replicated service.

The Transis project, currently under development at the Hebrew University of Jerusalem, was designed to supply reliable and efficient transport layer services for distributed systems. Transis provides fast and reliable message multicast between all currently connected processors, (despite a possible unreliability of the network). Transis offers several service levels for message ordering, which is a key primitive in managing concurrency in distributed computing. Transis achieves good performance by using the network's basic unreliable broadcast service, it recovers messages that were lost due to omission faults, and it handles processor crashes and dynamic partitions of the network. The Replicated Mail Service presented in this paper utilizes the ability of Transis to keep track of the current membership of connected processors and to efficiently disseminate messages among those processors.

One can approach the consistency problem using the traditional two-phase-commit method. Unfortunately, this will introduce difficulties whenever a connection is unavailable. In many application domains this method is not feasible, since blocking or transaction aborting is not acceptable as a legitimate solution in those domains. Other traditional methods (listed later) impose rigid constraints on the solution.

The main property of our solution is the guarantee that if an eventual path between the source and the target exists, the information will reach the target. By eventual path we don't mean a continuous connection, but rather that pairs of processors along the path were connected at successive periods of time. For each of the processors, the algorithm implicitly builds its knowledge about the status of each message at other processors. This knowledge enables us to efficiently handle all the mail services.

We suggest that the methods used to build this mail service can lead to better solutions in the area of distributed transaction systems and replicated databases.

## Related Work

A lot of work has been done in the area of distributed and replicated databases. Two-phase-commit-like protocols [12] are the main tool for providing a consistent view in a distributed database system over an unreliable network. In a typical protocol [14] of this kind, the transaction coordinator sends a request to prepare to commit to all the participant processors. Each processor answers by a "ready to commit" or an "abort" message. If any processor suggests to abort, all processors abort. The transaction coordinator collects all responses and informs the processors to either commit or abort. Between the two phases, each processor keeps the local database locked, waiting for the final word from the transaction coordinator. The main drawback of such a protocol is that when the transaction coordinator fails, all processors may be left blocked and can't resolve the last transaction. Moreover, when a partition occurs, the lack of dynamic replication forces many distributed transactions to abort.

There are many protocols that optimize specific cases [19]. For example, in a fully replicated database, achieving a quorum is enough to resolve the transaction [21]. Some solutions limit the transactional model to commutative transactions. Others give special weight to a specific processor or to a specific transaction [20]. Explicit use of timestamps enables others [4] to overcome the difficulty.

More advanced solutions define the quorum adaptively. When a partition occurs, if a majority of the previous quorum is connected, a new and smaller quorum is established and updates can be performed within this partition [10, 11]. The advantage of those methods is that in many cases, when faults occur and even if the network splits into two, the larger partition can perform updates. The drawback is that there can be situations where almost all of the processors are connected, but cannot perform updates, because of the potential existence of a previous surviving quorum among the processors that are currently down.

Communication mechanisms are central to any distributed transaction system. Today, distributed and replicated database systems are built using point-to-point communication mechanisms, such as TCP/IP, DECNET, ISO and SNA. These mechanisms provide reliable point-to-point message passing between live and connected processors. These mechanisms do not make efficient use of the hardware capabilities. In particular, the broadcast or multicast mechanisms are not used. A distributed or replicated database system is a classic candidate for using these mechanisms, since each update message is sent to multiple destinations.

In addition, a replicated database system requires a global order on the update transactions. When point-to-point communication mechanisms are used, the message ordering must be determined above the communication layer. Group communication services that utilize broadcast or multicast mechanisms can lead to simpler and more efficient solutions.

One of the leading systems in the area of group communication is the ISIS system [5]. The novelty of ISIS is in the formal and rigorous definition of the service interface. Moreover, ISIS utilizes algorithms that are formally proven to have certain needed properties [6] such as virtual synchrony.

The Trans and Totem protocols [3, 17] for ordered multicast utilize the broadcast capability of the network. These protocols spare the need of separate send operations and acknowledgment management for each of the destinations. Similar approaches can be found in the Psync protocol [18], in the Amoeba system [15], in Delta-4 [22], and in the Chang and Maxemchuk protocol [7].

The above systems and protocols are leading the way for better usage of the hardware capabilities, where certain data replication is needed in an environment which is built as a collection of several local area networks.

Membership maintenance is necessary for developing a broadcast or a multicast protocol for group ordered communication. When a point-to-point communication mechanism is used between two parties, the management of ordering messages and acknowledgments is easy. Each processor knows which messages it received, acknowledged, or sent, and for which messages it received an acknowledgment from the other party. When a broadcast communication mechanism is used, a second level of knowledge is needed to determine which messages were received by which processors, which processors are currently connected, and what is the global message order. A good membership algorithm provides this knowledge, even in the presence of processor crashes, processors recovery, network partitions and merges, and booting of new processors.

It is a known fact [13, 8] that the membership problem in a dynamic asynchronous environment, when faults may exist, is unsolvable. The problem is the inability to distinguish between a slow machine and one that has crashed. A number of approaches to bypassing this obstruction exist [1]. In practical asynchronous systems it is often preferable to give up on a slow machine, rather than get stuck in waiting.

The rest of the paper is organized as follows: The next section describes the Transis environment. The third section describes the Replicated Mail Service application. This section specifies the requirements from the replication protocol and the interface presented to the client. It also describes the conceptual solution. The detailed algorithm of the Replicated Mail Server can be found in Section four. Section five compares the designed solution with other strategies, with and without Transis. Section six concludes the paper.

# 2 The Transis Environment

The Transis System [1, 2] is currently under development at the Hebrew University of Jerusalem. The Transis domain consists of a set of processors that can communicate via multicast messages.

Processes in the Transis environment use group communication mechanisms in order to send and receive ordered messages. The three service levels for group communication in Transis are:

**The *Causal* multicast service** disseminates messages among the process group such that *causal order* of delivery is preserved. Motivated by Lamport's definition of order of events in a distributed system ([16]), the causal order of message delivery is defined as the transitive closure of:

1. $m \overset{cause}{\longrightarrow} m'$ if $\text{receive}_q(m) \rightarrow \text{send}_q(m')$
2. $m \overset{cause}{\longrightarrow} m'$ if $\text{send}_q(m) \rightarrow \text{send}_q(m')$

**The *Agreed* multicast service** disseminates messages among the process group such that *total order* of delivery is achieved. This order is consistent with the causal order. Moreover, it is consistent over overlapping groups. Transis utilizes two different algorithms to implement this service efficiently [3, 9].

**The *Safe* multicast service** delivers the messages in the same order as the Agreed multicast service. A message is delivered only after it was received by all the processors in the currently installed membership.

Transis actually guarantees a stronger property for Safe multicast: a Safe message sent by processor $p$ will be delivered at $q$ that doesn't fail, if at the time of delivery of the message at $p$, $q$ is in $p$'s membership.

The environment is dynamic, processors can crash and restart, and the network can partition and reconnect. The membership protocol of Transis automatically maintains the membership of connected processors, which is necessary for constructing fault-tolerant distributed applications.

The membership protocol guarantees virtual synchrony. It is symmetric and does not disturb the regular flow of messages. The protocol does not allow indefinite blocking of processors, but may rarely remove from the membership live (but inactive) processors unjustly. This is the price that must be paid for maintaining the membership in consensus among all the active processors in an asynchronous environment without blocking. In addition, if a processor is inadvertently taken out of the membership, it can rejoin immediately.

The greatest challenge Transis handles is partitioning and merging. They can be handled because of the symmetric design. All previous membership algorithms deal with the joining of single processors only. Moreover, most systems do not continue execution during network partitioning. However, partitions do occur, especially when the network includes bridging elements. The communication layer must continue to provide service to the application, as well as accurate information about the status of the system, even when the network configuration dynamically changes. The complete merging of partitioned histories is application dependent and therefore is not handled by Transis.

# 3 A Replicated Mail Service

In this Replicated Mail Service application, we make use of the information supplied by the safe messages and the configuration change messages provided by Transis, in order to complete the merging of partitioned histories for our specific needs.

We rely on Transis to efficiently disseminate messages among the currently connected processors and to manage the group membership. Therefore, we do not need to explicitly handle the sending of acknowledgments, message omissions, and processor faults.

## 3.1 The Requirement from the Replication Protocol

An **Eventual Path** exists between servers $S_0$ and $S_n$ within the time frame $[t..t']$ if there is a sequence of servers $S_0$, $S_1$, ..., $S_n$ and a sequence of time indicators $t_0$, $t_1$, ..., $t_n$ such that

- $t \leq t_0$ and $t_n \leq t'$.
- for each $0 \leq i < n$, $t_i < t_{i+1}$.
- for each time $t_i$, a possible message sent by $S_i$ to $S_{i+1}$ at time $t_i$ can be delivered at $S_{i+1}$ by time $t_{i+1}$.

The requirement for the replication protocol is the following: A high priority message sent by a server $S_0$ at time $t$ will reach the server $S_n$ by time $t'$ if there exists an Eventual Path between $S_0$ and $S_n$ within the time frame $[t..t']$. Note that the definition is carefully stated for a specific message, whereas if the connection duration allows, all pending messages will be delivered.

## 3.2 An Interface Specification of the Client

The specifications below define the interface between a mail client and a mail server.

**Connect-to-server** request must be invoked by the client before it can perform any other request. The client must specify one of the working servers in its partition to which it wants to be connected. The client can also invoke this request when it wants to change to another server, if the previous one did not respond.

**Send-mail** request is invoked when the client wants to send a message.

**Query-mail** request is invoked when the client wants to obtain its list of messages. The list also indicates whether each message was already read by that client.

**Read-mail** request is invoked when the client wants to read one of its messages.

**Delete-mail** request is invoked when the client wants to delete one of its messages.

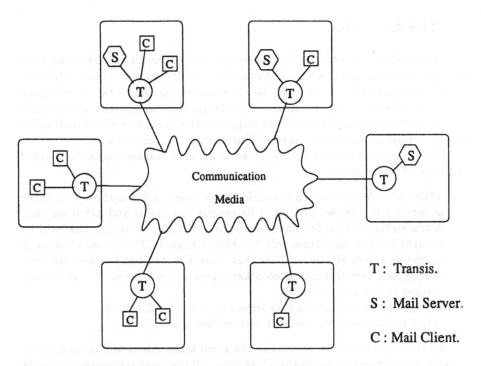

T : Transis.

S : Mail Server.

C : Mail Client.

**Fig. 1.** *The Replicated Mail Service architecture*

### 3.3  A Conceptual Solution

The architecture of the Replicated Mail Service is presented in Figure 1. Each processor runs the Transis demon as a process. In addition, each processor that is part of the Replicated Mail Service runs the mail server as a process. All the client processes (i.e mail users) and all the server processes are connected to the local Transis demon. Each client process can logically connect to one of the mail servers currently running in its partition. The basic concept behind the solution is to have a process group containing all the mail servers.

Each request from a client process to one of the mail servers that changes the message database creates an update message (i.e a transaction). This update message is then multicast via Transis to all the currently connected servers. Since Transis provides a reliable communication service in the sense that omission faults are recovered, there is no need to manage acknowledgments inside the currently connected group of servers. There is a need, however, to transmit those update messages within a configuration after partitioned or failed processors that do not have those messages join the configuration.

It is important to emphasis that after reaching a second level of knowledge about the state of the message database among the servers in the current configuration, knowledge from servers which are not part of the current configuration can be introduced only after a merge occurs.

# 4 The Algorithm

The basic idea is to order update messages (i.e transactions) according to a Lamport timestamp [16] which is stamped by the transaction initiator (i.e one of the Replicated Mail Servers) at the time of creation. When two transactions are stamped with the same Lamport timestamp, they are ordered according to the initiator's server id. The protocol completes this order to a global total order that is consistent among the servers. This order preserves causality.

Each server tags all the received transactions. Each transaction can be marked with one of three colors:

- *white:* A white transaction is stable and ordered. A transaction $T$ is *stable* at server $p$ if $p$ knows that all of its targets received it and put it on disk. A transaction $T$ is *ordered* at $p$ if $p$ knows that no transaction that will be received by $p$ in the future will be ordered prior to $T$. The above order is consistent among all servers. Note that, since $T$ is stable at $p$, $p$ does not need to explicitly keep $T$ because no other server will ask for it. If $T$ is already invoked at $p$, $p$ can discard it.
- *green:* A green transaction is ordered but is not locally stable.
- *red:* A red transaction is neither ordered nor stable (yet).

All the white transactions precede the green transactions and the red transactions in the order and define the white zone. All the green transactions precede the red transactions in the order and define the green zone. Similarly, the red transactions define the red zone. The protocol places the separating lines among the transactions according to their colors consistently. A transaction can be tagged by different colors at different servers.

The stable database contains all the transactions in the white zone and the green zone. The red zone is the zone of uncertainty. All the transactions in the red zone are relatively ordered among themselves. Moreover, there are no causal holes in the red zone. However, there is a possibility that a new transaction, invoked at some other processors, will have to be placed anywhere in this zone. All the transactions in the green zone and in the red zone have to be retained in case of a need for retransmission.

Each transaction contains piggybacked information that helps determine the order and the stability of previous transactions, to the best of the transaction initiator's knowledge. Based on this knowledge, transactions can change colors (i.e from red to green and from green to white). The structure of the three transaction zones is presented in Figure 2.

New transactions are disseminated throughout the currently connected servers (i.e. the membership). Transis assures that all the connected servers will receive those transactions. In case of a membership change in the configuration of connected servers, Transis assures that the Virtual Synchrony property ([6, 1]) will hold. Using this property, the servers of the new membership exchange messages

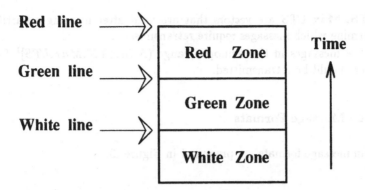

**Fig. 2.** *The Three Transactions Zones.*

containing information about transactions in their local zones. If they remain connected, each processor knows exactly which of the processors have received which transactions. They can now deterministically determine which processor will retransmit which transaction (in case retransmissions are needed).

### 4.1 The Data Structure

Each Replicated Mail Server maintains the following data structures:

**Server_id** is the unique id of this instance of the Replicated Mail Server.

**Servers** is the data structure which contains the current membership of connected servers in the partition of this instance of the Replicated Mail Server.

**List** is the data structure in which all the mail messages and other update messages are stored. The messages are stored according to the structure of the three transaction zones. The *List* has an up-to-date backup on disk.

**Last_LTS** is a vector which contains, for each server, the highest Lamport timestamp of all received messages initiated by that server. The *Last_LTS* vector has an up-to-date backup on disk.

**Last_ARU** is a vector which contains for each of the servers, the highest Lamport timestamp of a message in that server's green zone (i.e the green line in that server). The *Last_ARU* vector has an up-to-date backup on disk. ARU is an acronym meaning "All Received Upto", i.e. this instance knows that that server has, at least, all the messages that are stamped with a Lamport timestamp no greater than the corresponding Last_ARU entry.

Note that the particular entry *Last_ARU[Server_id]* corresponds to the green line in this instance of the Replicated Mail Server.

**LTS** is the highest Lamport timestamp received or initiated by this instance of the Replicated Mail Server. It is also the red line of this instance.

**ARU** is the Lowest entry of *Last_ARU*. This instance of the Replicated Mail Server knows that all the servers have all the messages that are stamped with a Lamport time stamp no greater than *ARU*. This is also the white line of this instance.

**Min_LTS, Max_LTS** are vectors that are used after merging a partition to determine which messages require retransmission.

All the messages in the semiopen range $(Min\_LTS..Max\_LTS]$[1] for each server should be retransmitted.

## 4.2 The Message Formats

The main message formats are presented in Figure 3.

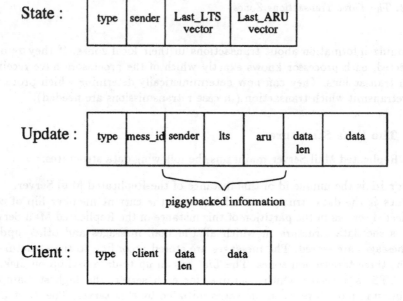

**Fig. 3.** *The Message Formats*

## 4.3 Event Handling

There are seven events that the mail server accepts. The events correspond to the reception of messages of the following seven types : Membership change message from Transis, State message from another server, Update message from another server, Send-mail, Read-mail, Delete-mail and Query-mail messages from a client. The mail server is an event-driven program that invokes an event handling routine.

---

[1] *Max_LTS* is included but *Min_LTS* is not

## Membership change message from Transis

The mail server identifies the other mail servers in its current configuration. If new members joined the servers' group membership, a recovery process is required. If so, the server transmits a State message containing its database state, and sets the recovery vectors as follows:

$$\forall i \in Servers, \quad Min\_LTS[i] = Last\_LTS[i]$$

$$\forall i \in Servers, \quad Max\_LTS[i] = Last\_LTS[i]$$

## State message from another server

The mail server updates its *Last_ARU* status vector and its recovery vectors according to the corresponding vectors in the received State message:

$$\forall i \in Servers, \quad Last\_ARU[i] = \max(Last\_ARU[i], message.Last\_ARU[i])$$

$$\forall i \in Servers, \quad Min\_LTS[i] = \min(Min\_LTS[i], message.Last\_LTS[i])$$

$$\forall i \in Servers, \quad Max\_LTS[i] = \max(Max\_LTS[i], message.Last\_LTS[i])$$

When updating the *Last_ARU* vector, the mail server updates its knowledge about the last message each server has received from every other server. When updating the *Min_LTS* recovery vector, the mail server updates its knowledge about the maximal message from each server, all the servers in the **current** configuration have reported. When updating the *Max_LTS* recovery vector, the mail server updates its knowledge about the message with the highest ordinal from each server that at least one server in the **current** configuration holds.

After receiving a State message from each of the mail servers in the current configuration, the server computes which messages need to be retransmitted. Clearly, those messages are the messages in the range $(Min\_LTS..Max\_LTS]$ For each server.

Since all the servers receive exactly the same messages if they remain connected, they will reach the same conclusion. Based on the fact that they all know the state of each of them prior to the recovery, they can determine, without additional messages, which server will retransmit which messages, and when this retransmission will take place.

The algorithm guarantees that when mail server $p$ receives a message which was initiated by mail server $q$, then $p$ already has all $q$'s previous messages.

## Update message from a server

An update message is triggered by Send-mail, Read-mail and Delete-mail requests, invoked by clients. Upon receiving an Update message from a mail server, the server updates the sender server's entry in the *Last_LTS* and *Last_ARU* vectors as follows:

$$\textbf{if} \quad Last\_LTS[message.sender] < message.lts$$
$$\textbf{then} \; Last\_LTS[message.sender] = message.lts;$$

$$\textbf{if} \quad Last\_ARU[message.sender] < message.aru$$
$$\textbf{then} \; Last\_ARU[message.sender] = message.aru;$$

The server also tries to advance the red, green and white lines.

- The red line is advanced if the *lts* field on this message is higher than the current *LTS* variable. In that case

$$LTS = message.lts.$$

- The green line is advanced if the sending server's entry in $Last\_LTS$ was lower than any other entry in $Last\_LTS$, and was increased. In that case

$$Last\_ARU[Server\_ID] = \min_{i \in Servers} (Last\_LTS[i]).$$

- The white line is advanced if the sending server's entry in $Last\_ARU$ was lower than any other entry in $Last\_ARU$, and was increased. In that case

$$ARU = \min_{i \in Servers} (Last\_ARU[i]).$$

After the white line is advanced, all the update messages in the *List* which are below the white line can be discarded. This can be done because the server knows that all other servers have those update messages and they will never be requested.

The update message is then inserted into the *List* in memory and on disk according to its message id. If it is an update about read-mail or delete-mail requests, the target message's state is also updated in memory and on disk. For example, if an update message is received for a delete-mail request, then that update message is inserted to the *List*. In addition, the mail that was deleted is marked as deleted in the *List*.

**Send-mail, Read-mail and Delete-mail messages from a client**
The server checks the validity and permissions of the request. Only non-deleted messages can be read. If it is the first time a message is read or the first time it is deleted, the server creates an update message which corresponds to the request and transmits it to the servers via Transis. If the request was a valid Read-mail request, it also retrieves the mail message and sends it to the client.

It is important to emphasize that those events do not change the state of the database. Only the corresponding update message will cause a change when invoked.

**Query-mail message from a client**
The server retrieves the identifiers of messages that were sent to the client and reside in the database of this server. The server then sends an answer message containing these identifiers and a field for each message to indicate whether this message is a new message or whether this message was already read by this client.

# 5    A Comparison with Other Methods

We now present a comparison of our solution with other possible strategies. First, we discuss strategies that do not use Transis, and instead use a standard transport layer such as TCP/IP. Next, we discuss several solutions that utilize Transis as a transport layer, with different levels of knowledge about the membership.

**Centralized Server**
This is the usual solution in which one server manages one copy of the mail database. The advantage is that there is no overhead to maintain consistency, the solution is simple and straight forward.

The solution has several drawbacks. If the mail server is not working, or if the computer which hosts the mail server does not function properly or is not connected to the client's computer, then the client can neither send new mail nor read its mail. In some systems this may lead to storing the message in a secondary mail system, where the client is not aware of it.

**One Server With Several NFS Copies**
A way to overcome some of the problems in the centralized solution, is to have a centralized server which manages several copies of the mail database in different computers over the network, using NFS. Here also there is no communication overhead to maintain consistency. The problem is that the server needs to maintain tedious bookkeeping of separate copies, when network partitions may occur. Furthermore, two inconsistent copies can be found in one partition when the server is in another partition or is not working.

In this solution, the client can send mail only if it is connected to the server. The client can read mail if it has a connection to one of the NFS replica.

**Replicated Servers**
A natural way to replicate the service is to use two phase commit as in distributed databases. This is completely unacceptable in a mail application due to the blocking characteristic of two phase commit. Therefore, a nonblocking strategy, similar to the solution presented in this paper may be preferable. The problem is, that without a Transis-like transport layer, upper level protocols need to support three major properties: multicasting, message ordering and membership management. When utilizing a point-to-point transport layer such as TCP/IP, it is difficult to synchronize the membership changes with ordered message delivery

and to ensure that the configuration view is consistent among all the members of the configuration. It is even more resource demanding when done by upper-level protocols.

A way to solve the problem when using point-to-point transport protocols is to implement stable queues between pairs of servers. This scheme is efficient if the responsibility of each server is limited to disseminating its own messages. Thus, a message initiated at server $p$ will reach server $q$, only if server $p$ was connected to server $q$. When the requirements are enhanced (as in this paper), managing stable queues efficiently is even more complicated.

**Using Transis** Transis provides an efficient and reliable multicast service for ordered messages, combined and synchronized with membership services, in an asynchronous environment. By using Transis, we can base our solution on the agreement reached among the processors about the ordering of messages and membership events. The application layer (the mail server in this case) obtains the needed information about membership and message events without going down to the data-link or network levels. The server layer has only to maintain state consistency and to recover histories.

We have investigated several methods of maintaining state consistency and recovering history. The methods differ in the level of knowledge about the membership events. The first method assumes no knowledge about membership events, the second assumes obtaining the membership events without history tracking of membership configurations, and the third method presented in this paper assumes full knowledge about membership events in the system (i.e. each server knows which servers participated in its previous membership and which participate in its current membership).

When there is no information about membership changes, missing messages may be tracked as follows. Messages include piggybacked information about preceding messages. Upon receiving messages that follow missing messages, the server discovers that certain messages are missing, and requests for retransmission. This is similar to other lower-level algorithms such as in the Trans algorithm [17], the Psync algorithm [18],,, and in Transis [2]. Recovery of messages, after partitions are remerged, occurs only if new messages are generated. This is a major drawback because it creates the necessity to initiate new messages from time to time. Long timeouts lead to inconsistent views among servers in the same partition. Short timeouts lead to network flooding.

When there is no history tracking of membership configurations, the algorithm presented in this paper will work with the exception that the server must initiate the recovery process each time the membership is changed. The method fully exploits the available membership information received from Transis. Thus, the recovery process takes place only when new members join the membership.

# 6 Conclusions

The paper presents the development of a highly available and reliable distributed application in the Transis environment. There is an ongoing debate about the usefulness of a reliable membership and message ordering service. The application we chose is a typical application in a distributed system although many other applications exist. The experience we have gained is that having a reliable transport layer drastically simplifies the development process of a replicated application.

The application presented above was assigned as the final project in a Distributed Algorithms course, taught in Fall 1992, at the Hebrew University of Jerusalem. The various solutions presented above cover some of the projects developed during the course. The solution described in the paper was based on a more general replicated transaction tool developed by the authors.

In this solution, Transis takes care of the transport and lower layers responsibilities, such as message dissemination, sending acknowledgments, flow control and membership changes detection. When using Transis, rather than point-to-point mechanisms, it is easy to synchronize the membership changes with ordered message delivery. The only part left to the upper layer protocol is the recovery of the history of events after a join or a processor recovery, and the global ordering of those events. This part is not an integral part of the transport layer and may vary for different applications.

Studying the various alternative solutions to the problem we realized that different teams chose to make different use of the services offered by the lower layer. Some have, unintentionaly, duplicated part of the service offered by the lower layer. We discovered that projects that make better use of the transport layer services tend to be simpler and smaller.

## Acknowledgments

We acknowledge the contribution of Ahmad Khalaila, Rimon Orni and others from the High Availability Lab at the Hebrew University. We thank them and other students for many hours of fruitful discussions, and for developing alternate solutions to the problem.

## References

1. Y. Amir, D. Dolev, S. Kramer, and D. Malki. Membership algorithms for multicast communication groups. In *Intl. Workshop on Distributed Algorithms proceedings (WDAG-6), (LCNS, 647)*, number 6th, pages 292–312, November 1992.

2. Y. Amir, D. Dolev, S. Kramer, and D. Malki. Transis: A communication subsystem for high availability. In *Annual International Symposium on Fault-Tolerant Computing*, number 22, pages 76–84, July 1992.

3. Y. Amir, L. Moser, P. Melliar-Smith, D. Agarwal, and P. Ciarfella. Fast message ordering and membership using a logical token-passing ring. In *International Conference on Distributed Computing Systems*, number 13th, pages 551–560, May 1993.

4. P. Bernstein, D. Shipman, and J. Rothnie, J.B. Concurrency control in a system for distributed databases (sdd-1). *ACM Trans. on Database Systems*, 5(1):18–51, March 1980.

5. K. Birman, R. Cooper, T. A. Joseph, K. Marzullo, M. Makpangou, K. Kane, F. Schmuck, and M. Wood. *The ISIS System Manual*. Dept of Computer Science, Cornell University, Sep 90.

6. K. Birman and T. Joseph. Exploiting virtual synchrony in distributed systems. In *Ann. Symp. Operating Systems Principles*, number 11, pages 123–138. ACM, Nov 87.

7. J. Chang and N. Maxemchuk. Reliable broadcast protocols. *ACM Transactions on Computer systems*, 2(3):251–273, August 1984.

8. D. Dolev, C. Dwork, and L. Stockmeyer. On the minimal synchrony needed for distributed consensus. *J. ACM*, 34(1):77–97, Jan. 1987.

9. D. Dolev, S. Kramer, and D. Malki. Early delivery totally ordered broadcast in asynchronous environments. In *23rd Annual International Symposium on Fault-Tolerant Computing*, pages 544–553, June 1993.

10. A. El Abbadi and N. Dani. A dynamic accessibility protocol for replicated databases. *Data and Knowledge Engineering*, (6):319–332, 1991.

11. A. El Abbadi and S. Toueg. Availability in partitioned replicated databases. In *ACM SIGACT-SIGMOD Symp. on Principles of Database systems*, number 5, pages 240–251, Cambridge, MA, March 1986.

12. K. Eswaran, J. Gray, R. Lorie, and I. Traiger. The notions of consistency and predicate locks in a database system. *Communications of the ACM*, 19(11):624–633, 1976.

13. M. Fischer, N. Lynch, and M. Paterson. Impossibility of distributed consensus with one faulty process. *J. ACM*, 32:374–382, April 1985.

14. J. Gray. Notes on database operating systems. In *Operating Systems: An Advanced Course,Lecture Notes in Computer Science*, volume 60, pages 393–481. Springer-Verlag, Berlin, 1978.

15. M. F. Kaashoek, A. S. Tanenbaum, S. F. Hummel, and H. E. Bal. An efficient reliable broadcast protocol. *Operating Systems Review*, 23(4):5–19, October 1989.

16. L. Lamport. Time, clocks, and the ordering of events in a distributed system. *Comm. ACM*, 21(7):558–565, July 78.

17. P. M. Melliar-Smith, L. E. Moser, and V. Agrawala. Broadcast protocols for distributed systems. *IEEE Trans. Parallel & Distributed Syst.*, (1), Jan 1990.

18. L. L. Peterson, N. C. Buchholz, and R. D. Schlichting. Preserving and using context information in interprocess communication. *ACM Trans. Comput. Syst.*, 7(3):217–246, August 89.

19. C. Pu and A. Leff. Replica control in distributed systems: An asynchronous approach. In *ACM SIGMOD Symp. on Management of Data*, May 1991.

20. M. Stonebraker. Concurrency control and consistency of multiple copies of data in distributed Ingres. *IEEE Trans. on Software Engineering*, 3(3):188–194, May 1979.

21. R. Thomas. A majority consensus approach to concurrency control for multiple copy databases. *ACM Trans. on Database Systems*, 4(2):180–209, June 1979.

22. P. Verissimo, L. Rodrigues, and J. Rufino. The Atomic Multicast Protocol (AMp). In D. Powell, editor, *Delta-4: A Generic Architecture for Dependable Distributed Computing*, pages 267–294. Springer-Verlag, 1991.

# Reliable Enterprise Computing Systems

Kenneth P. Birman*

October 12, 1993

As organizations move to better exploit computing systems, a new class of large–scale distributed applications is emerging. These *enterprise computing systems* offer highly integrated, highly reliable computing to users who may be physically separated by large distances and who interact using a multiplicity of computing devices. They combine large numbers of independently executing programs into an (apparently) seamless whole, and often provide services critical to the organization. The development of software for such systems is difficult, particularly because of the need to dynamically respond to failures and recoveries. This is further complicated by the constraint that such a system behave consistently regardless of where it is accessed.

The basic premise of this paper is that enterprise computing will require advances in the way that we do distributed computing. Specifically, whereas modern distributed systems obtain reliability by running on special purpose high reliability hardware, we conjecture that enterprise systems will not be feasible without substantial changes in the *software* reliability technologies used to develop applications.

## Beyond distributed computing to enterprise computing

Enterprise computing systems differ in significant ways from the types of distributed computing that has been common during the 1970's and 1980's. During this period, a move has occured from mainframe systems to networked *personal computing systems*, with network software providing such functionality as shared data storage and electronic mail. Despite the interconnectivity of such systems, they remain largely independent: each user runs his or her own applications (word-processing, spreadsheets, engineering design tools, etc.), and any interactions between systems are through shared files and mail. Client-server computing has also become common: in such systems, a number of client systems are configured as a sort of ring around a centralized server, which provides database functionality, file management, or other support. Again, the client systems interact indirectly, through shared servers.

Enterprise computing systems, in contrast, are characterized by a close, direct coupling of application programs running on multiple platforms in a networked envi ronment. The programs involved will generally coordinate their actions to present a

*The author is Associate Professor of Computer Science at Cornell University, where he heads the Isis Project. Through this experience, and a company he founded, Dr. Birman has been directly involved in developing highly reliable distributed software systems for financial, telecommunications, factory automation, scientific computing and military applications.

consistent image of the system to users. It is common for a such a system to mimic a single highly reliable program, despite the decentralized nature of the underlying software.

The need for close coupling of this sort arises in many settings. Telecommunications systems that provide services to mobile users are an obvious example. The software involved in providing services to such a user must worry about the handoff of a call from switching node to switching node without disruption of service, and thus the subsystems providing services are enterprise computing systems. Moreover, the trend is to allow easy customization of services and the introduction of new services, suggesting that this problem may need to be solved repeatedly in each of a large number of applications.

Enterprise computing issues are also seen in banking and brokerage settings, and indeed any commercial setting where the trend towards a paperless, information–flow commerce requires coordinated actions at multiple points in a distributed system. Banks and brokerages, for example, are rapidly moving to develop electronic stock and bond trading markets. Moreover, individual institutions must increasingly coordinate trading in multiple markets to hedge against currency fluctuations, manage financial risk associated with the institution's overall position, and to respond to trends in a globalized trading environment. To give just one example, it is common to limit the percentage of financial assets invested in any one currency or trading instrument. In an international firm, this means that trading activity in, say, Tokyo may have important immediate implications for trading in New York or Zurich. The software used to inform traders of the current limits must run close to where they trade – otherwise, a communication outage could cripple trading, since the traders would hesitate to risk exceeding a legal limit or company policy. It follows that a collection of programs running locally to each trading center must somehow coordinate the advice that they are giving to traders, and in a way that is always safe, but that also maximizes the chances of riding out a short communication outage or failure without disruption. This is a typical enterprise computing problem, and additional instances with a similar character are seen throughout modern trading systems.

Enterprise computing issues also arise in scientific computing. For example, modern particle accelerates are increasingly used over networks. In such a situation, experimentalists share the experimental control systems, data acquisition systems, and the supercomputing systems on which data is analyzed. As the scale of such system grow, these problems are shifting from a centralized, batch-style of computing to a decentralized one with multiple computational foci – a type of computing that matches our enterprise model. The computing problems that arise here include resource allocation, facilities for monitoring executions, and mechanisms for dynamically recovering from failures.

Similar issues arise within scientific computing applications. For example, at the Los Alamos Advanced Computing Laboratory, a weather simulation is being developed that combines an atmospheric model specialized for execution on a vector processor with an ocean model developed to exploit a massively parallel processor; output is displaying on a graphics supercomputer. And, all of these resources are dynamically allocated – the machines are shared with large numbers of other users. Taking this one step further, Norwegien researchers are developing a system called StormCast that will integrate a nationwide network of environmental sensors. The data from these will be used to provide local weather prediction and environmental warnings for airports, trawlers at sea, and even public ski trails.

On the factory floor, Sematech has launched a project to increase efficiency and flexibility by automating entire VLSI fabrication lines, linking dozens of specialized computers and devices to a network which may in turn be connected to hundreds of workstations used for engineering design, administration, and other functions. Here, the enterprise revolves around software for coordinating the fabrication process in the presense of dynamic demands. Hospitals look to increased computing support as a way of cutting costs and improving efficiency, and also seek to dedicate substantial computing resources to each patient in order to support realtime monitoring functions. The military seeks to exploit cooperation between distributed computing systems as a way of integrating data from multiple sources, coordinating attacks and improving overall effectiveness of its operations.

As enterprises move to depend more and more heavily on their distributed computing applications and systems, the reliability of these becomes increasingly critical. For this reason, a key issue to ask about this emerging class of software concerns the degree of reliability that systems of this sort can achieve. Strong arguments can be advanced against placing extreme confidence in the reliability of isolated programs (see, for example, Reliable Software, in the Oct. 1992 issue of Scientific American). One must anticipate that both software and hardware failures will occur while an enterprise computing application is running. However, since these are multi–component systems, the question remains of whether redundancy can somehow be exploited to enable the overall system to ride out and recover from all but the most extreme failures. The remainder of this article focuses on this question.

## Reliability in large distributed systems

Reliability is an imprecise term in the context of computing settings. One would expect a reliable distributed system to behave in a predictable, consistent manner regardless of the point(s) through which it is accessed: there should be no contradiction between the actions and state of the system at different locations, the system as a whole should do only what it was designed to do, and the system should operate or "manage" itself, with minimal human intervention.

Beyond consistency, reliability may connote additional properties such as self–management, real–time responsiveness, data recoverability (the ability to restore data that were being manipulated at the time of a crash), security, and the ability of the system to tolerate incorrect input (e.g. from sensors or users). These problems are well known from non–distributed computing systems, and adequate solutions have existed for many years. Were it not for the need to maintain consistency and to tolerate failures, existing technologies could be used to obtain highly reliable distributed software, much as it is possible to develop acceptably reliable non-distributed software using systematic programming techniques and careful testing. Such software may not be *perfectly* reliable, but extremely high levels of reliability are routinely achieved. On the other hand, inconsistent distributed behavior could weaken or violate the reliability properties of a software solution to any of these problems.

Somewhat complicating the picture, even where techniques for making systems reliable are well understood, distributed computing systems have often failed to exploit them. Many readers will recall that in 1987, a highly publicized attack on the "internet" that links tens of thousands of research computers caused some six thousand machines to crash. The "Internet Worm" exploited relatively simple security loopholes that could easily have been plugged. Worse, several of these loopholes were well known and scheduled for repair in future releases of vendor operating systems. The success of the Internet Worm was illustrative more of the low importance that reliability has received in modern computing systems, than of any technical problem. Fortunately, this obstacle to reliability is diminishing through public awareness of the issue, which has created a competitive advantage for vendors able to offer a more reliable computing platform. In the future, the reliability of the basic computing infrastructure should continue to rise.

In contrast, during the same period (1989-1991) there were several major failures of the nationwide telephone system. These problems were tracked to relatively obscure software bugs in the programs used to balance load among the components of a recently introduced switching system, called ESS-5. One bug involved a fairly subtle synchronization problem that was triggered when a switching node was upgraded to a new software release, while a different bug was caused by a minor coding error. In both cases, the problem rippled through the network shutting down large numbers of telecommunication switching nodes. In effect, the system was unable to contain and (correctly) reconfigure itself after certain types of failures occured.

These examples contrast two aspects of the problem. One is social: the developers who build enterprise computing systems and the vendors who provide the platforms on which these will operate must begin to engineer their products to the highest feasible standards of reliability. The second aspect is technical, and concerns maintaining consistency in distributed programs subject to faults. As we will see below, it is impossible to build a system that both reacts to failures in a timely manner, while never making mistakes by classifying an operational component as faulty. Yet, an erroneous failure classification can throw a multi-component system into a chaotic state, in which different components have inconsistent views of the status (operational or faulty) of other components of the system, and hence behave in inconsistent ways. It is only very recently that techniques for tolerating tolerating failures and recoveries while maintaining consistent behavior have been developed.

Problems of this sort are fundamental: they stem from the technical complexity of building distributed software that maintains consistency and dynamically reconfigures itself in the presense of failures and other events. If this issue can be addressed, other aspects of reliability (such as security) follow; lacking adequate solutions to this basic problem, there would be little hope for developing acceptable enterprise computing software.

## Fault-tolerant distributed programs

In developing computing systems, for any purpose, it is useful to separate application-specific issues from the more general ones seen in a wide range of applications. This has been the approach favored by most researchers in the area, and was the one used by the author and his colleagues in developing two *programming environments* that package a collection of software tools for constructing reliable and self–managed distributed software. These environments provide a set of general purpose mechanisms which are then employed in application–specific ways to solve the needs of a particular system. We named the "reliability" environment ISIS, recalling the Egyptian myth of death and resurrection, and the one used for system control and management META. ISIS was developed primarily by the author's research group, and been used widely for building reliable distributed software in both research and industrial settings. META was developed by Keith Marzullo, currently at UCSD, and Mark Wood, using facilities from ISIS, and is now entering into use.

To illustrate the issues confronted in developing these systems, let us ask what can be said about a distributed program without knowledge of the nature of the specific application being solved. Any distributed computer program is just a collection of conventional, non–distributed programs that communicate with one another over a network using messages. No matter how fast the network transfers data and how low communication latency becomes, the round-trip time for a message can equal the time to execute thousands or millions of instructions. The processes in a distributed system invariably have imprecise knowledge of one-another's state and actions: accurate knowledge of past state augmented by inference about current state and actions. One challenge, then, will be to ensure that the "current" states of a set of processes will be mutually consistent, despite the fact that those processes can only be sure of one another's past.

Many kinds of failures can occur in a distributed system. Programs and machines can crash, usually by halting without doing anything disasterously incorrect. (One can protect against more arbitrary failures, and even outright attacks by malicious agents, but only at very high cost.) Messages can also be lost, corrupted, or even delivered in duplicate or delivered out of order – these last cases arising primarily in networks where messages have to be forwarded and where there may be multiple routes between the sender of a message and its destination. However, by including sequence numbers and checksum information in messages, damaged messages can be detected and suppressed, and out-of-order messages put into order. Thus, message loss is the primary communication problem with which a distributed system must cope, typically using an acknowledgement/retransmission strategy.

It is not hard to see that machine failures are effectively indistinguishable from communication outages. Imagine a distributed application consisting of a program $c$ which is a client of a service implemented fault–tolerantly using a primary-backup scheme by $s_1$, the primary, and $s_2$, its backup (figure 1). If a communication outage disrupted communication between $c$ and $s_1$ $c$ might conclude that $s_1$ had failed, and begin sending requests to $s_2$. $s_2$, however, not having observed the outage, would continue to believe $s_1$ operational and hence would not respond to these requests, since it expects $s_1$ to handle them. In the absence of some sort of an exchange of messages between $c$ and $s_2$ to maintain agreement upon the status of $s_1$, the application will have become "inconsistent" and could malfunction. Extrapolating to larger systems, one sees that unless all the programs in a distributed system maintain agreement upon the status,

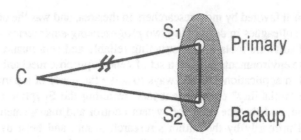

Figure 1: Inconsistent connections after a communication outage

alive or faulty, of the processes comprising the system, it will be hard to build reliable software of any sort.

This leads to one of the fundamental mechanisms that a programming environment like ISIS provides, namely a fault–tolerant service that keeps track of the processes running in a local area network and reports failures and recoveries in a consistent way. As a graduate student in the ISIS group, Aleta Ricciardi studied this problem and showed it to be closely related to other fundamental problems such as reaching agreement or maintaining clock synchronization in distributed settings. The best solution turns out to be approximate: rather than accurately detecting and reporting process failures, which would be impractical, a membership service can instead guarantee timely reporting of process failures by running a small risk of incorrectly classifying a functional (but slow or hard to reach) process as faulty. When such a misclassification does occur, the consistency of the system can be maintained by suppressing messages from the "faulty" process until it has been informed that other processes in the system consider it to have crashed; this permits the excluded process to execute a recovery protocol.

The core of a failure–detection service will be some mechanism that periodically probes processes for liveness. Because this needs to be rapid, failure–detection is generally practical only in local area networks. The basic idea is that when an apparent failure is detected, the members of the failure detection service run a *protocol* – a patterned exchange of messages – to converge upon a new list of system members that excludes the faulty component. The problem would be easy if it were not for the risk of erroneous failure detections, which complicate matters considerably: process $p$ may (incorrectly) consider process $q$ faulty just as process $q$ (incorrectly) concludes that $p$ is faulty. This would fragment the system into two, mutually inconsistent, subsystems. The way to overcome such scenarios is to require a majority consensus before agreeing upon each successive list of system members.

The decision to provide a failure agreement mechanism within a distributed system greatly simplifies all other reliability problems. Using such a mechanism, failure detections can be treated as just another sort of event that a system may need to deal with, and the "consistency" of this layer of the system can be assured.

The ISIS system uses its failure detection service to support two basic distributed programming tools. The first of these offers a way to form processes into *groups*, within which close cooperation between members is facilitated by a diverse collection of standardized mechanisms. The second provides a way to send a message to the members of a group in such a manner that all members receive a copy if any does, despite failures (except, of course, failures that erase all record of the message). If two messages are sent to the same group concurrently, by different senders, the order of message delivery seen at each group member is the same. This type of communication is called an *atomic multicast*, because it offers a way to send a message to multiple destinations without apparent interruption even if failures occur.

Using process groups and atomic multicast as building blocks, ISIS supports a variety of higher–level tools. For example, a group of processes may need to replicate data within an application, so that at least one replica will be likely to survive crashes. The tool for this purpose provides a way to inform group members about updates to the replicated data, to transfer a current replica to a new member of the group when it joins, and to synchronize updates so that if multiple updates occur concurrently, they will be applied in the same order by all group members (any member can query its local copy, so no special tool is needed for this). A typical use of this tool would be to replicate the database of pending trades in a brokerage system, or the state of a service advising traders on prices at which to buy or sell some financial instrument.

Similarly, ISIS includes tools for subdividing a task (such as searching a database) among the members of a group, so as to speed up the task through parallelism. There are also tools for performing a task fault–tolerantly: if the process selected to perform the task fails, another is automatically picked to take over, until the task is completed or no group members remain. ISIS contains tools for security, for example to preserve the secrecy of data, or to ensure that a process group can initiate certain actions be taken if a sufficient number of its members agree. And, all of these tools can be shown to achieve both consistency and fault-tolerance, thereby addressing the basic concerns raised earlier.

The concept of providing reliable programming tools to the developers of enterprise computing systems can also be extended to "higher level" software. For example, computer "bulletin boards" have become extremely popular as a way for humans to interact. ISIS supports a program to program analog of this, in which each news topic corresponds to a process group, and messages posted to a topic become visible to all subscribers (a subscriber that shows up late can request a replay of recent messages). This software tool has a number of desirable features: it is very easy to use, fault-tolerant, and it delivers messages in consistent orders to all subscribers. For example, if two subscribers compare the order in which they receive messages (even on multiple subjects), the orders observed will be the same. Even orders that are inferred indirectly will be consistent. In contrast, human-oriented bulletin boards often suffer from annoying ordering problems, such as a tendency to display messages out of context, particularly when the states of multiple bulletin boards are compared as seen by more than one subscriber. These sorts of anomalous behaviors – inconsistencies – are merely annoying for human users, but represent serious problems when the users are programs that must anticipate and cope with every contingency.

Ideas such as these can also be applied to the development of distributed file systems and database systems, resource managers, and so forth. Moreover, by interconnecting local-area subsystems, highly reliable wide-area computing systems can be developed. Users of such a system would only be aware of its hierarchical structure during communication outages on long–distance links, and since these can often be anticipated, it is frequently possible to conceal their effects for a long enough period to reestablish communication.

Using reliable programming tools, programmers who develop enterprise software are spared the need to repeatedly solve difficult, fundamental problems. Having decided what parts of the data managed by the application must survive failures, and how many failures must be survivable, they employ a process group to replicate the key data. Having decided how to react to a certain type of component failure, they employ a group to track the health of the component; the failure–detector will report any failures to the surviving group members, and this can trigger a coordinated response. Even the coordination can be achieved using tools from the toolkit. Having decided the structure of its enterprise communications "backplane", when an event occurs that should be available throughout the organization, a program simply posts an appropriately formatted message on the news topics to which it applies. Other programs monitoring those topics will be promptly informed of the incoming message, and programs that subscribe later can obtain the message by requesting a replay. The reliability of the overall enterprise system follows from the systematic application of a core collection of mechanisms.

Thus, one sees a hierarchy of software problems and solutions. Given a solution to a core problem – consistent failure detection and reporting – the remaining problems fall one by one. Figure 2 illustrates some of the layers of software needed and their responsibilities. One might worry that even with very fast computers, such a software structure could become inefficient. Our experience suggests that this need not be the case; in the ISIS system many hundreds of atomic multicasts can be exchanged within small groups of processes even over conventional hardware, and these figures will rise with advances in processor and communication speed. Other researchers who have specialized in performance issues have shown that even higher performance is within reach.

## The system management problem

There is a great difference between a program that performs correctly and one that performs *well*. A correct program does not fail or produce incorrect results, but a program that performs well makes efficient use of resources and behaves predictably over a range of environmental and operating parameters. Writing distributed programs that perform well is especially hard. Distributed programs are often expected to run in widely varying configurations, from a single machine to tens or hundreds, and on machines of widely varying performance or from different vendors. Often they must continue operating when some of the machines on which they are running fail.

We call the activity of producing a distributed program that performs well for a given environment *distributed application management*. Distributed application management involves configuring the components of the system for a given hardware and software environment; initializing the application in an orderly way; monitoring the

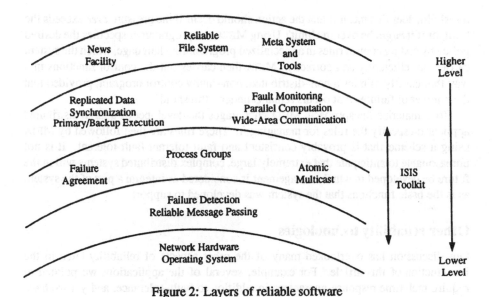

Figure 2: Layers of reliable software

behavior and performance of the application; and scheduling work efficiently among the components of the application. An application must be managed throughout its execution, continually reacting to a varying workload, to changes in the environment, and to failures.

Traditionally, application management is either done manually or hard-wired into the code of the application. A person familiar with the internals of the application must continually monitor and control it, and some adaptations can be made only by extensive reprogramming. In practice, many aspects of application management are ignored, resulting in poorly engineered systems that work most of the time, but often exhibit unpredictable performance, become inconsistent, expose partial failures, and prove fragile when even small changes are made to the hardware or software base. Building over ISIS, Marzullo and Wood have attempted to avoid the deficiencies of this *ad hoc* approach by creating a framework favoring the construction of robust distributed management software and applications, and a set of tools—the META system—which directly supports the approach.

The META model of a distributed application separates the management aspects of an application are from its major functional parts, and the interface between these two layers is well defined. By distinguishing *policy* from *mechanism* in this way, modifying the management of an application is easier, and is less likely to impair the correctness of the program.

Distributed application management raises a number of difficult technical issues. For example, META must deal with imprecision both in the sensors attached to a system and in the clocks used to note the time at which a sensor was sampled. This raises questions about how to interpret a rule; for example, if a rule specifies that a control valve in a chemical plant should be opened if the pressure in a vessel exceeds some threshold, does this mean if that the action should occur if the pressure *ever* exceeds the limit, or if it *might* be over the limit? Using META, the programmer specifies the desired policy by coding control rules in a specialized programming language, which the system carries out efficiently and correctly. META then carries out the control functions in a way that exactly mimics a non–distributed, non–faulty control program, provided that the number of failures that occurs remains under a threshold.

To summarize the approach, META encourages the developer of a large distributed application specify the rules for managing it. These rules are then followed by META using a scheme that is provably consistent and fault-tolerant fault-tolerant. It is not unreasonable to anticipate that extremely large, complex distributed systems will in the future be developed in which management is considered as integral a part of the system as is the basic functions that the system was developed to support.

## Other reliability technologies

Our discussion has overlooked many of the other aspects of reliability cited in the introduction of this article. For example, several of the applications we pointed to require real–time response guarantees in addition to fault–tolerance, and yet we have said little about this issue. Solutions are known in this area too, although they require more analysis of the application than is the case for the other sorts of properties cited above (for example, one must be able to predict the maximum load the application will generate, the maximum delay associated with computations, and the probabilities of various forms of failures). This technique was used successfully by Flaviu Cristan and others in the IBM Advanced Automation System, a next-generation air traffic control system under development for the FAA. Interestingly, the protocols used for group communication in this system are very similar in structure to the ones discussed earlier.

On the other hand, real–time objectives can often be satisfied simply by using a technology that is orders of magnitude faster than the events of interest. For example, in a trading setting, traders may consider a system to give real–time response provided that operations are completed in a small fraction of a second.

Security is an issue of particular importance in many enterprise computing systems. Traditionally, security and reliability have been viewed as being in opposition, since one replicates information and servers to increase availability, but this increases the number of entities that must be secured and complicates the security protocols used by the system. Recently, however, work by Mike Reiter and others has established that security can be provided in systems concerned with consistency and fault-tolerance, and that the cost need not be extreme.

As these technologies are integrated, is not unreasonable to expect that reliability tools spanning all aspects of the problem are increasingly available within a single, coherent framework. Enterprise software developers of the future will find that the computing infrastructure leads them to develop highly reliable systems; today, the converse is often the case.

# The emerging era of large–scale distributed computing

In light of the tremendous potential of reliable enterprise distributed computing systems, it is remarkable that relatively little attention has been paid to developing these sorts of systems and marketing them. The existing technology base, with its many obstacles to reliability, stands as a significant culprit: if a computing system cannot be relied upon, or there appears to be a basic tradeoff between consistency and fault-tolerance, organizations will not think to use computers in settings where reliability is an issue. Indeed, for more than a decade, operatings systems and network research has focused on extreme simplicity and on maximizing performance, even at the expense of consistency and fault-tolerance.

A massive resource has been created by the computing and telecommunications industries, but it is still largely untapped. However, as reliability technologies become increasingly standard, and they surely will, this will inevitably change. Software reliability and consistency technologies will enable a sweeping transformation in how enterprises use computing.

Distributed computing systems are already as critical to society as bridges, airplanes and medical devices. Given distributed software systems that can be relied upon to behave consistently despite the sorts of disruptions and transient outages that any large system experiences, the future holds the promise of a distributed computing technology revolution as far reaching as the computer revolution has already been during its first 3 decades.

## Additional reading

- The process group approach to reliable distributed computing. Birman, accepted for publication, *Communications of the ACM*.

- Tools for distributed application management. Marzullo, Cooper, Wood and Birman. *IEEE Computer*, **24**, 8 (Aug. 1991), 42-51.

- Software Reliability. Scientific American Oct. 1992

- Why do computers stop and what can be done about it? Jim Gray. In *Proc. 5th Symposium on Reliability in Distributed Software and Database Systems*. IEEE Press, Los Angeles, 1986 (3-12).

# Fault Tolerance for Clusters of Workstations

Elmootazbellah N. Elnozahy

School of Computer Science, Carnegie Mellon University, Pittsburgh, PA 15213, USA

**Abstract.** This paper presents a short description of the Manetho system, which provides fault tolerance for parallel application programs that execute on a cluster of workstations. Manetho uses a combination of rollback-recovery and process replication. Both methods are application-transparent, making it possible to automatically provide fault tolerance for existing applications.

## 1 Introduction

Recent technological trends are making it feasible to build loosely coupled multicomputers with workstation clusters. A typical configuration would consist of a number of high performance workstations connected by a high speed network. The workstations offer the compute cycles necessary to run sequential or parallel programs. The multicomputer would also include the servers commonly needed in distributed computing environments, such as name and file servers. Network multicomputers, however, are vulnerable to many failure modes. These modes make it more difficult for a network multicomputer to offer its users the model of a central computing facility that they are accustomed to. Examples of such failures include interprocess communication failures and processor failures. These failure modes are different from those of a central computing facility where no partial failure occurs and the system behaves like a unit that either functions properly or fails entirely. Furthermore, the likelihood of a failure increases with the number of processors, and often a single failure renders the entire system unusable. This paper presents a short description of the Manetho system, which is designed to provide fault tolerance to network multicomputers [7, 8]. Manetho particularly targets long-running parallel applications such as scientific and combinatorial computations that execute on a network multicomputer.

Manetho is an example of techniques that provide fault tolerance in an application-transparent manner [9, 21]. Transparent techniques are attractive for parallel applications in network multicomputer environments, as they can automatically make existing applications fault-tolerant without modifying user programs. Transparent techniques contrast other software approaches for providing fault tolerance, such as techniques based on the process group approach [2, 4, 11, 17, 18, 22, 24], atomic transactions [1, 14], or a combination of both [16]. A comparison among these techniques is, however, meaningless as each is best suited for a certain class of applications.

# 2 Background

Previous techniques for providing transparent fault-tolerance relied on rollback-recovery [9, 10, 20, 21, 23]. However, rollback-recovery is not appropriate for server processes where the lack of service during rollback is intolerable. Furthermore, rollback-recovery protocols assume that a process can be restarted on any available host. As a result, extended downtime cannot be tolerated for example in file servers, which have to run on the host where the disks reside. Manetho solves these problems with an integrated approach by using rollback-recovery for client processes and process replication for server processes. The main features of Manetho are:

- *An integrated approach to providing reliability by rollback-recovery and process replication.* This approach reflects the view that no single recovery method would be sufficient for all applications.
- *Transparency.* Both rollback-recovery and replication are transparent to application programs. Furthermore, if a process fails, the system will use the same recovery protocol regardless of whether the process is checkpointed or replicated.
- *Consistency of the system's behavior despite failures.* If the computation transmits a message outside the system domain (to the outside world), no future failure will cause the system to be in a state that is inconsistent with transmitting this message. This feature of Manetho is similar to the durability property of atomic transactions.
- *Containment of the effects of failures.* The failure in one process does not affect the rest of the computation in the system. The failed process is recovered to a state that is consistent with the functioning processes.

Manetho is based on maintaining an antecedence graph, which describes a history of the nondeterministic events that occur in a distributed computation. The graph allows rollback-recovery to coexist in the same system with process replication. All the processes in the system, replicated or otherwise, cooperate in maintaining the graph. The recovery protocol uses the information in the graph to restore the system to a consistent state, which is also consistent with the observable effects of the computation as perceived by the outside world.

# 3 Assumptions

The computation consists of a number of fail-stop [19] *recovery units* (*RU's*) [21] which communicate only by messages over an asynchronous network. An $RU$ consists of one or more threads that manipulate the $RU$'s internal state. Each $RU$ has access to a stable storage device. A failed $RU$ can be restarted on *any* available machine.

The execution of an $RU$ consists of a sequence of piecewise deterministic state intervals [21], each started by a nondeterministic event. Such an event can be 1) the receipt of a message, 2) an internal nondeterministic event such as a kernel call or a synchronization operation between two threads within the same $RU$, or 3) the creation of the $RU$.

Figure 1 shows the execution of three $RU's$ and their state intervals. A horizontal line represents the execution of each $RU$. An arrow between two horizontal lines denotes a message, and a vertical bar marks the beginning of each state interval. The notation $\sigma_i^p$ denotes the $i^{th}$ state interval of $RU$ $p$, where $i$ is referred to as the *index* of $\sigma_i^p$. Each application message has a system-wide unique identifier.

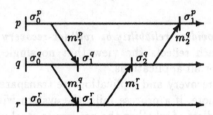

**Fig. 1.** Example Execution

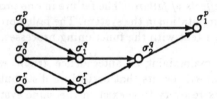

**Fig. 2.** Antecedence Graph of state interval $\sigma_1^p$, $AG(\sigma_1^p)$.

The communication network is not necessarily reliable: messages may be lost, duplicated, delivered out of order, or arbitrarily delayed.

## 4 The Antecedence Graph

The antecedence graph $(AG)$ of a state interval $\sigma_i^p$, $AG(\sigma_i^p)$, is a directed acyclic graph. It contains a node representing $\sigma_i^p$ and a node for each state interval that "happened before" [13] $\sigma_i^p$. Figure 2 shows $AG(\sigma_1^p)$ corresponding to the example of Figure 1.

For a state interval created by the receipt of a message, the corresponding $AG$ node has two incoming edges: one from the node representing the previous state interval in the receiving $RU$, and one from the node representing the state interval from which the message was sent. The node contains: 1) a type field that indicates a message receipt, 2) the identifier of the receiver, 3) the identifier of the sender, 4) the index of the created state interval, and 5) the unique identifier of the message. The $AG$ does *not* contain a copy of the message's data.

For a state interval created by an internal nondeterministic event, the corresponding $AG$ node has one incoming edge from the node representing the previous state interval of the same $RU$. Such a node contains a field that indicates the type of the event and the information necessary to replay the event during recovery.

# 5 Rollback-Recovery

## 5.1 Information in Volatile Storage

Each $RU$ maintains in volatile memory the $AG$ of its current state interval, and a log that contains the data and identifier of each message it *sends*. When an $RU$ sends a message, it (conceptually) piggybacks the $AG$ of its current state interval on the message. The receipt of the message starts a new state interval in the receiving $RU$, and the $AG$ of that state interval is constructed from the $AG$ of the previous state interval and the $AG$ piggybacked on the message, as described in Section 4.

The sender need not include the complete $AG$ of its current state interval in each message. Instead, incremental piggybacking is used. By definition, $AG(\sigma_i^p)$ is a proper subgraph of $AG(\sigma_{i+1}^p)$. Each $RU$ $q$ that communicates with $p$ includes with each message sent to $p$ the maximum state interval index $j$ such that the node representing $\sigma_j^p$ is in $q$'s $AG$. Later, when $p$ sends a message to $q$ from some $\sigma_i^p$, it appends only $AG(\sigma_i^p) - AG(\sigma_j^p)$.

## 5.2 Information on Stable Storage

Periodically, each $RU$ records a checkpoint of its state on stable storage. In principle, the checkpoint need not be coordinated with the other $RU$'s in the computation, though the implementation coordinates the checkpoints to avoid flushing the volatile message log to stable storage, and to simplify garbage collection of recovery information.

Occasionally, each $RU$ asynchronously saves the $AG$ of its current state interval on stable storage. The subgraph on stable storage need not be piggybacked on outgoing messages, avoiding the need to piggyback large $AG$'s. An $AG$ at some $RU$ may be missing one or more subgraphs, but these missing subgraphs are always available on stable storage.

Before sending a message to the outside world, an $RU$ saves the $AG$ of its current state interval on stable storage (output commit). No coordination with other $RU$'s is necessary.

## 5.3 Recovery

The recovery protocol uses the information in the antecedence graph and message logs to recover the system to a consistent state. The protocol tolerates an arbitrary number of process failures, including those that occur during recovery. It also tolerates an arbitrary delay of the message propagation over the network. Details of the protocol and proof of correctness appear elsewhere [8].

# 6 Process Replication

Manetho replicates an application process by a *troupe* that consists of a number of identical processes that execute the same application program [6]. The system transparently translates every application message directed to a replicated process into an *application-multicast* directed to the corresponding troupe. The failure of all but one process in each troupe is tolerated. The communication subsystem delivers multicast messages after an arbitrary delay to all, some, or none of the troupe members.

Manetho uses a *new* negative-acknowledgment, ordered multicast protocol to ensure that the troupe members receive the application-multicasts in the same order. The protocol depends on the combination of *antecedence graph* maintenance [8], a form of sender-based message logging [9], and the fact that all troupe members execute the same deterministic application program. In this protocol, each troupe is structured according to the leader-cohort model [3, 5]. When the troupe receives an application-multicast, the leader defines the receipt order and transmits it in an *unreliable sequence-multicast* to the cohorts. The cohorts do not acknowledge receiving sequence-multicasts or application-multicasts. The protocol delivers the application message to the application program at the leader without waiting for the delivery order information to reach all cohorts. At each cohort, the application message is delivered as soon as its sequence-multicast is received. If both the application-multicast and its sequence-multicast are not lost, the protocol will eliminate the overhead of control messages that would be used to achieve agreement among all troupe members. This works well in an environment in which failures are not frequent. Nevertheless, should a failure occur, the protocol will use the antecedence graph information, piggybacked on every application-multicast and recorded by the receiving troupe, to retrieve the ordering information that might have been lost due to the failure [8].

Manetho's multicast protocol improves on existing negative-acknowledgment multicast protocols in that it does not delay the message delivery to the application program. Existing protocols piggyback the receipt order of an application-multicast on future multicasts [5, 12, 15]. This reduces the number of control messages required by the protocol because the special acknowledgment messages are eliminated. However, an application-multicast cannot be delivered until its receipt order reaches all receivers, which occurs after receiving several subsequent application-multicasts. In Manetho, the application-multicast is delivered without the need for explicit acknowledgment messages or for delay in delivery until all receivers agree on the order. The information propagated in the antecedence graph piggybacked on application messages is used to recover from failures. This has the advantage of requiring a small number of control messages, like existing negative-acknowledgment protocols, while it eliminates the delay in the message delivery.

Consider the following example. Figure 1 shows the execution and state intervals of three application processes $p$, $q$, and $r$. In this example, processes $q$ and $r$ are replicated while process $p$ uses checkpointing and rollback-recovery. For clarity, we do not show the individual members of troupes $q$ and $r$.

Consider the transmission of message $m_1^p$. The system logs a copy of the message data in a volatile log maintained at the sender $p$. The system also appends the antecedence graph of the current state of the sender $p$ on the message. This graph consists of the node $\sigma_0^p$. Since the destination of this message is replicated, the system transmits $m_1^p$ as a multicast to troupe $q$.

When the leader of $q$ receives $m_1^p$, it sends to its cohorts a sequence-multicast that defines the receipt order of $m_1^p$. The graph appended to $m_1^p$ is merged with the local graph at the leader. The system then delivers $m_1^p$ to the application program without waiting for the sequence-multicasts to reach the cohorts.

When a cohort of $q$ receives $m_1^p$, it expects the corresponding sequence-multicast to be sent from the troupe leader within a short period. When the sequence-multicast arrives, the cohort performs the required antecedence graph maintenance as in the leader case, and delivers the message to the application program. The cohort does not acknowledge the receipt of the sequence-multicast.

Now consider the transmission of $m_2^q$. At the leader of $q$, the system adds a copy of $m_2^q$ in a local volatile log. The system then appends the graph of the current state $\sigma_2^q$ of troupe $q$ to $m_2^q$ and transmits it to $p$ in a one-to-one message, since $p$ is not replicated. Only the leader of troupe $q$ transmits the message over the network, the cohorts only add a copy of the message in their local volatile logs.

When $p$ receives $m_2^q$, it merges the appended graph into its own resulting in the graph in Figure 2, and the message is delivered to the application program.

## 6.1 Failures

A cohort may miss either or both of an application-multicast and its corresponding sequence-multicast. To prevent a cohort from "falling behind" the leader by missing both multicasts for several consecutive messages, the leader expects each cohort to periodically send a one-to-one synchronization message that shows the maximum state interval index known by the cohort. The leader's reply to a synchronization message contains the unique identifier, the sender's identifier, and receipt order for each application-multicast that the cohort has missed, if any. These messages are retrieved from the volatile logs of their corresponding senders.

If the leader fails while some sequence-multicasts have been lost, the antecedence graph is used to define the lost order. In the example in Figure 1, if $q$'s leader fails while the sequence-multicasts that carried the receipt orders of

$m_1^p$ and $m_1^r$ to $q$'s cohorts were lost, $p$'s antecedence graph contains these missing orders and the cohorts can retrieve the messages in the correct order from the volatile logs of $p$ and $r$. The recovery protocol ensures that these messages will always be available. If their senders also fail, the messages will be recreated during recovery. The recovery protocol and a complete proof of its correctness as well as the issues of garbage collection and integration after failures appear elsewhere [7, 8].

# 7 Summary

The paper presented a short description of Manetho, a system that provides transparent fault tolerance in network multicomputer environments. Manetho particularly targets long-running, parallel applications that execute on a network multicomputer. For these applications, transparent techniques are more suitable than approaches that require changing the user programs to add fault tolerance. Manetho differs from previous transparent techniques in that it allows processes to use either rollback-recovery or active replication. Thus, client processes tolerate failures by rollback-recovery, while server processes provide high availability by replication. This integrated approach reflects the view that no single method for providing fault tolerance is appropriate for all applications.

# Acknowledgment

I would like to thank David B. Johnson and Willy Zwaenepoel for their comments and support.

# References

1. Ahamad, M., Dasgupta, P., LeBlanc, R.: Fault-tolerant atomic computations in an object-based distributed system. Distributed Computing 4 (1990) 69–80
2. Amir, Y., Dolev, D., Kramer, S., Malki, D.: Transis: A communication subsystem for high availability. Proceedings of the 22nd International Symposium on Fault-Tolerant Computing (1992) 76–84
3. Birman K.: Replication and fault-tolerance in the ISIS system. Proceedings of the 10th ACM Symposium on Operating Systems Principles (1985) 79–86
4. Birman, K., Schiper, A., Stephenson, P.: Fast causal multicast. Technical Report TR-1105, Cornell University (1990)
5. Chang, J., Maxemchuck, N: Reliable broadcast protocols. ACM Transactions on Computer Systems, 2 (1984) 251–273
6. Cooper, E.: Replicated distributed programs. Proceedings of the 10th ACM Symposium on Operating Systems Principles (1985) 63–78
7. Elnozahy, E., Zwaenepoel, W.: Manetho: Transparent rollback-recovery with low overhead, limited rollback, and fast output commit. IEEE Transactions on Computers 41 (1982) 526–531

8. Elnozahy, E., Zwaenepoel, W.: Replicated distributed processes in Manetho. Proceedings of the 22nd International Symposium on Fault-Tolerant Computing (1982) 18–27

9. Johnson, D.: Distributed System Fault Tolerance Using Message Logging and Checkpointing. PhD thesis, Rice University (1989)

10. Juang, T., Venkatesan, S.: Crash recovery with little overhead. Proceedings of the 11th International Conference on Distributed Computing Systems (1991) 454–461

11. Kaashoek, F.: Group Communication in Distributed Computer Systems. PhD thesis, Vrije Universiteit (1992)

12. Kaashoek, F., Tanenbaum, A.: Group communication in the Amoeba distributed operating system. Proceedings of the 11th International Conference on Distributed Computing Systems (1991) 222–230

13. Lamport, L.: Time, clocks, and the ordering of events in a distributed system. Communications of the ACM **21** (1978) 558–565

14. Liskov, B.: Distributed programming in Argus. Communications of the ACM **31** (1988) 300–312

15. Melliar-Smith, P., Moser, L.: Broadcast protocols for distributed systems. IEEE Transactions on Parallel and Distributed Systems, 1 (1990) 17–25

16. Mishra, S., Peterson, L., Schlichting, R.: Implementing fault-tolerant replicated objects using Psync. Proceedings of the 8th Symposium on Reliable Distributed Systems (1989) 42–52

17. Mishra, S., Schlichting, R.: Abstractions for constructing dependable distributed systems. Technical Report TR92-19, University of Arizona (1992)

18. Peterson, L., Bucholz, N., Schlichting, R.: Preserving and using context information in interprocess communication. ACM Transactions on Computer Systems **7** (1989) 217–246

19. Schlichting, R., Schneider, F.: Fail-stop processors: An approach to designing fault-tolerant computing systems. Transactions on Computer Systems 1 (1983) 222–238

20. Sistla, A., Welch, J.: Efficient distributed recovery using message logging. Proceedings of the 8th Annual ACM Symposium on Principles of Distributed Computing (1989) 223–238

21. Strom, R., Yemini, S.: Optimistic recovery in distributed systems. ACM Transactions on Computer Systems **3** (1985) 204–226

22. Veríssimo, P., Rodrigues, L., Baptista, M.: A highly parallel atomic multicast protocol. Proceedings of the SIGCOMM '89 Symposium (1989) 83–93

23. Wang, Y-M., Fuchs, W.: Scheduling message processing for reducing rollback propagation. Proceedings of the 22nd International Symposium on Fault-Tolerant Computing (1992) 204–211

24. Wood, M.: Replicated RPC using Amoeba closed group communication. Proceedings of the Thirteenth International Conference on Distributed Computing Systems (1993) 499–507

# Two Techniques for Transient Software Error Recovery

Yennun Huang

AT&T Bell Laboratories.

Murray Hill, NJ 07974


Pankaj Jalote

Indian Institute of Technology

Kanpur, India 208016


Chandra Kintala

AT&T Bell Laboratories.

Murray Hill, NJ 07974

## Abstract

The traditional approaches for fault tolerance in software - the recovery block approach and the N-version programming - are too expensive, and consequently of limited practical use. Experience has shown that techniques, such as rollback and retry, that do not employ multiple versions of software. are able to mask a range of software faults that exhibit *transient* software failures. These techniques are cost effective as they do not employ design diversity for supporting fault tolerance. In this report we discuss two such techniques that can be used to enhance the reliability of software systems.

## 1   Introduction

A software [1] is written to provide some services satisfying some specifications. Typically a software consists of many components called modules. If some of its modules contain faults, a software can fail to satisfy its specifications. A software is fault tolerant if it can provide the required services even if some of its modules are faulty. Making a software fault tolerant is becoming very important since the current state-of-the-art is such that the hardware on which the software executes is very reliable and software is considered as a weak factor in building highly reliable computing systems.

---

[1] By software, we mean an application program written to compile and execute on a given hardware and operating system platform.

Software faults are inherently different from the faults that are handled by techniques for hardware fault tolerance. In hardware, the failures that most fault tolerance techniques aim to handle are the failures that are caused due to physical phenomenon. The design of the hardware itself is assumed to be correct. Software, on the other hand, has no physical properties. The only faults it has are the design faults, also called "bugs". Since the software has no physical properties, the design faults are permanent. This situation is different from that of hardware, where a vast majority of faults are transient in nature.

Due to the permanent nature of software faults, it has been generally assumed that the failures caused by these faults will also be permanent. That is, if a software module fails, then that module cannot provide the desired service. This belief led to the use of design diversity for supporting fault tolerance. With design diversity, if a module cannot provide the service, then other modules which have different designs are used to provide the required service. The two well known methods for organizing the different versions of a module are the recovery block approach[15], and the N-version programming approach[2].

The main drawback of using design diversity is their high cost. Multiple versions have to be developed to support fault tolerance. Since the bulk of the software cost is the development cost, this diversity becomes very expensive. Furthermore, for design diversity to work, it is important that the different versions of the software should fail on independent inputs. Recent experiments have indicated that failures of independently developed software modules may not actually be independent[14]. It has also been found that if failures are correlated, the effectiveness of design diversity rapidly decreases as correlation increases.

Some observations have also shown that in many systems, the failures caused due to software faults are actually *transient* in nature and do go away if the same software is used after some time (a technique used frequently in hardware to mask transient failures)[5]. This observation has led to work on supporting software fault tolerance without using design diversity to mask the effects of those faults that lead to transient errors.

In this paper we describe two techniques to recover from such software failures. We then discuss the issue of transient software failures, and provide a foundation for the techniques that can be used for masking transient failures.

## 2 Program Input Space

A process executes a given program on some given hardware through some operating system. A given process executes a sequence of instructions. The sequence of instructions is from the code which the process is executing and depends on the inputs the process gets. That is, based on the inputs, a process can execute one of a set of instruction sequences that are possible with the program that the process is executing.

The inputs to a process come largely from (1) user data sources like files, terminal input, etc, (2) environment variables, and (3) messages which include events and signals to the process. The user data is what is traditionally called the "program input", and is often fully in the control of the user. Environment variables capture the state of the operating system and its resources and are generally shared by the different processes in the system. Messages can come to a process from other processes (running on the same node or some other node), operating system (in form of signals etc.), and hardware devices (in form of interrupts, traps).

The behavior of a process depends on *all these inputs*. Even for the same user data input, the behavior of a process may be different at different times depending on the state of the environment variables, or the messages it gets. For example, for printing a file, the behavior of the process will be different depending on whether some other processes have submitted printing jobs before it. For messages, besides the data component, *when* a message is received, and the *interleaving* of the different messages are also significant. In other words, for asynchronous events, besides the events themselves, their timing and ordering also determine the behavior of a process. For example, the behavior of a process when it gets two signals very close in time may be different from its behavior if the two signals are far apart in time. In Unix, for instance, if the signals are the same, in the first case the signal handler may be executed only once, while in the second case it will be handled twice. In other words, the sequence of instructions a process executes depends not only on the user data, but the values the process receives from the environment variables and messages. We say that the user inputs, environment variables, and messages together form the *input space* for a process.

The overall inputs from these sources can also be considered as belonging to two categories - application (or user) dependent inputs and environment dependent inputs. The former consists of user data, messages, etc., while the latter consists of shared variable values, timing of messages, interleaving of messages, etc. While the first category of input is in the control of the user and the application designer, the latter is generally not.

Typically, when a program undergoes verification and validation (V&V) during its development (whether it is testing or some other verification method), its behavior is evaluated mostly for the user inputs. Since the value of the environment inputs depends on events in other processes, and since messages frequently depend on asynchronous events in the system, it is very hard, if not impossible, to create all the different "scenarios" for these environment inputs so that a program can be "verified" or "tested" under all different conditions. In other words, it is practically impossible to verify a program for all possible inputs of environment variables, and for all possible environment inputs and their timing and interleaving. This is especially true if the software is built using modules developed by different groups of people and vendors.

Furthermore, a program that works during testing for most of the "test cases" may still fail due to some unexpected value of environment inputs. That is, a program that has been shown to be "correct" (in practice, however, even ensuring that a program is correct for all possible user data is not within the current state-of-the-art), may have "bugs" in that it may not be able to work for all possible values of environment inputs. In short, most programs will have "bugs" due to which they cannot provide the required service for all the user data under all the environment conditions and messages. The current V&V techniques can (and do) ensure that these bugs are such that the program fails very rarely in some very special situations.

# 3  Techniques for Error Recovery

In this section, we describe two approaches which change the input of a program on-line to recover from those rare errors as described in the previous section. The first approach changes only those inputs that are not in the control of the process or the user. That is, it does not change the user data, but only changes environment data. In the second approach, the user data is modified. Hence, the first approach can be considered as very general that is acceptable to most software systems, while the second approach can be applied only where the application permits user data modification in the manner done in the technique.

The techniques described here are applied when an error is detected. How the error is detected is not of interest to us here - it may be detected by assertion based checks, through hardware checks, signals from the operating systems, or a watchdog process for failure detection[9]. As the method is initiated when an error is detected, error recovery has to be first performed. All the techniques described here use backward error recovery. That is, the process periodically checkpoints its internal state, and if an error occurs it is first rolled back to a previously checkpointed state. Then these techniques are applied. These two techniques have been applied in some telecommunication systems by using the watchd daemon and libft library[9].

## 3.1  Rollback and Restart

In rollback and restart method, the state of the process is periodically checkpointed. If an error is detected, the process is simply rolled back to its most recent checkpoint and reexecuted. No user data is modified. However, since execution, rollback, state restoration and reexecution take time, the state of the environment variables is likely to be different during reexecution as compared to during the first execution in which failure is encountered. Furthermore, any asynchronous events that occurred in the first execution may not occur, or occur in a different order, or at different times during reexecution. It is almost certain that even without changing the user data, the input to the process will change, if the process is reexecuted. If the process had failed because of the environment or messages, then on reexecution the process may not fail.

One of the early use of rollback and restart in commercial systems was in Tandem[3]. The approach uses process pairs with one process being the primary and the other being the backup. The primary periodically checkpoints its state on the backup and if the primary fails the backup restarts the computation from the last checkpoint. The basic approach is rollback and retry, except that with process pairs the retry is done by the backup process. This method of using process pairs and rollback and retry was adopted for coping with the hardware failures. That is, to handle the situation where the primary process fails due to the failure of its processor. However, this rollback and retry has been very successful in coping with software faults as well. This led Gray to categorize software faults as "Heisenbugs" and "Bohrbugs"[5].

More recently, this technique has been implemented in AT&T[9]. The approach here is to have a watchdog monitor process called *watchd*, which periodically monitors the health of the processes and a library called *libft* which can be used to checkpoint application critical data. If a process fails, *watchd* aborts the process and restarts it from its previous checkpoint state. In the simplest form, the restart is from the initial state. This approach has been found to be successful in masking software faults in several systems. One example is a cross-connection system consisting of several processes using shared memory for interprocess communication. One of these processes is a writer process which may modify some data structures in the shared memory and the others are reader processes which only read the data structures. Because of a hideous software bug, there is a slight chance that a reader may be reading a data structure while the writer is modifying it (e.g., manipulating the pointers for inserting a new data node). Consequently, the reader may receive a segmentation violation fault if the reader happens to read the pointer (a byte) while the writer is modifying. In such a case, the reader will be rolled back and restarted by *watchd*. Once the reader is restarted, it will access the same pointer again. This time, however, the read operation will succeed because the writer has finished the modification.

## 3.2 Message Reordering

As stated earlier, the sequence of instructions a process executes depends not only on the data of the messages the process receives, but also on the timing of messages and the order in which the different messages are received. Clearly, changing the order of messages also changes the input of the process. We observe that some reorderings are acceptable in most distributed applications.

In a distributed application with processes communicating with each other over a network, roll back and restart are not as straight forward as with independent processes. The reason for this is that rollback may "nullify" some sending and receiving of messages, and unless the corresponding sender and receiver processes also rollback, the system state may get inconsistent. In other words, rollback of a process may force other processes to rollback, and this rollback propagation may get uncontrolled leading to a domino effect[15].

For handling software failures, we do not want this avalanche of rollbacks; it is preferable to have only one process rollback. This can be done by logging the received messages and properly recovering the messages during reexecution. Various methods for message logging and recovery have been proposed[4, 11, 12, 13, 17]. In these techniques, messages sent to a process are logged by the receiver and if a process rolls back, the messages it had received are recovered from the

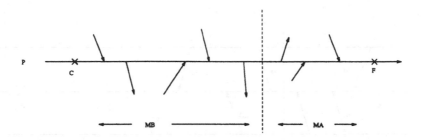

Figure 1: Message Order

log. Due to the properties of communicating systems, this message recovery permits some reordering of messages, without violating system consistency. This reordering can be exploited to support fault tolerance.

In a receiver-based message logging scheme, there is a queue of messages maintained for each process by the system. At any given time the process has consumed some messages, has some messages waiting for it in the queue, and has some messages in transit to it. We will ignore the messages in transit, as they can be easily modeled as part of the queue.

It has been shown in[11] that if a process $P$ rolls back, the requirements for message recovery depend on whether or not the process sent a message between its checkpoint $C$ and the point from where it rolls back, presumably due to an error or failure $F$. The last message sent by $P$ between $C$ and $F$ forms the dividing line. The requirements for recovering messages received before and after the last message sent by $P$ between $C$ and $F$ are different. Let the sequence of messages received by $P$ between $C$ and $F$ be $M = MB\,; MA$ (the ";" is the concatenation operator), where $MB$ is the sequence of messages received by $P$ before the last message sent by it between $C$ and $F$, and $MA$ is the sequence of messages after that together with the messages in the queue for $P$ at time $F$. Together, $MB$ and $MA$ include all the messages that must be recovered; see Figure 1 for an example.

Let $M'$ be a sequence of messages that is recovered on rollback of $P$. That is, $M'$ is the sequence of messages that is added to the queue on restart. It has been shown that the system will reach a valid state if $M' = MB'\,; MA'$ such that $(i) MB' = MB$, $(ii) MA'$ has the same partial order as $MA$[11]. That is, the messages $P$ received before the last message sent must be recovered in the same total order as it received them before. However, the messages it received after the last message sent and the messages in the queue (and in transit) can be received in any total order that preserves the partial order in which the messages were received earlier (partial order of those messages is the order that preserves the sequence of messages from a given process.) The reason for only the partial order is that the communication network only guarantees a partial order. Hence, even in the first execution these messages could have been received

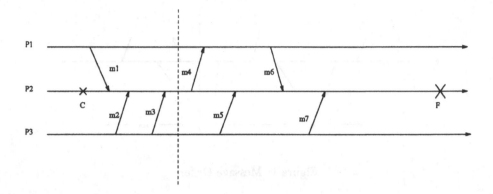

Figure 2: An Example

in any total order that preserves the partial order. So, by having a different total order, which preserves the partial order, the situation is same as some regular execution of the system. However, the earlier messages have to be recovered in the same total order, otherwise other processes will have to be rolled back.

As an example, consider execution of a system consisting of three processes $P_1, P_2, P_3$, as shown in Figure 2 (assume that the message queues are empty and there are no messages in the channels). $P_2$ is the process that establishes a checkpoint at $C$, fails at $F$, and restarts from $C$. In this example, message m4, sent by $P_2$ forms the dividing line. By the message recovery condition, m1, m2, m3 must be received by $P_2$ on restart in the same order as received by $P_2$ in the original execution, i.e., in the order m1;m2;m3. However, messages m5, m6 and m7 can be received in any order that has the same partial order. Hence, besides the order m5;m6;m7, the orders m5;m7;m6 and m6;m5;m7 are also acceptable. However, the order m7;m5;m6 violates the partial order sent by process P3, and hence, is not acceptable. This example shows that, by using message logs, a failed process can restart at a checkpointed state and retry a different message ordering to recover from the failure without violating any user specified consistency of the application.

This message reordering technique has been applied in some telecommunication systems[18]. An example is the nDFS replicated file system[10] in which critical files are replicated from a primary node onto a backup node. All "open", "write" and "close" system calls are trapped by the primary node and passed to an agent process on the backup node. The agent process performs the system calls to replicate files. The agent process opens a file upon receiving an open command and closes a file when a close command is received. There is only one agent process to serve many applications on the primary node. Since the number of available file descriptors for the agent process is limited and each application process could open many files at the same time, the agent process may run out of file descriptors. Therefore, it has to keep track of how many files are open. A boundary condition for the agent process occurs when all file descriptors are used. The agent process then searches for an open file descriptor with the earliest access time and closes that file.

A software bug existed in the search procedure of *nDFS* in such a way that when the agent process entered a certain boundary condition, the search process never finished and the agent process hung up. The agent process implemented the checkpointing and logging mechanism and had an external hang-up detection mechanism. Once the agent process entered the boundary condition, the failure was detected and the agent process was rolled back. When the agent process was restarted, it restored the checkpointed state, reordered and reexecuted the message logs. Once the messages were reexecuted, the agent program was able to continue its operation.

The following example illustrates how message reordering helps in the above description. Let o1 command stand for opening file 1, w1 command stand for writing data to file 1 and c1 command stand for closing file 1. The agent process can open at most 2 files at the same time. The following command sequence will cause the agent program to enter the boundary condition when processing o3 and hang up.

o1 o2 w1 w1 w2 w1 w2 o3 w3 c1 c2

Suppose the logging mechanism had logged all the commands before the failure. When the agent process is restarted, the command log may be reordered with the following sequence:

o1 w1 w1 w1 c1 o2 w2 w2 c2 o3 w3.

In this sequence, the boundary condition never occurs, and therefore the reexecution of the command log succeeds.

## 4   Characterizing Transient Software Errors

Based on our observations about transient software errors and recovery techniques described in the previous two sections, we develop here a characterization or a framework to encapsulate our intuitions about transient software errors or failures.

The behavior of a deterministic program depends entirely on the inputs it gets, and the timing of the inputs. Based on the behavior of the process, the *entire* input space of a process can be divided into two parts - the *standard domain* (SD) and the *exception domain* (ED)[7, 8]. The standard domain consists of all those inputs for which the process behavior is "correct", and the exception domain consists of those inputs for which the process fails and produces erroneous states. We assume that the programs are deterministic and hence SD and ED are disjoint, but together they cover the entire input space for the process, as is shown in Figure 3.

Correct or erroneous behavior of *all* processes executing deterministic programs can be viewed in terms of SD and ED. If the program is blatantly incorrect

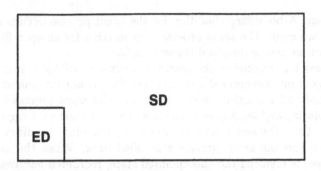

Figure 3: Standard and Exception Domains

(in that it does something totally different than its specifications) then the process may have SD= $\phi$ (i.e. the process does not work correctly on any input). If a program is totally correct then it will have ED= $\phi$ (i.e. the process works correctly on all inputs). In most cases, neither extreme is true.

In most practical situations, the software development methods and testing and verification techniques ensure that the software is of very high reliability before it is put to use. In other words, the standard domain of the process covers most of the input domain, and the exception domain is very small. In addition, the inputs elements in ED are typically very rare values of application inputs, or environment inputs.

If the input to a process is in ED, then the process will produce an error. If this error is detected and the program is reexecuted with a different input which belongs to SD, then the error will not occur, even though the "bug" in the program remains. As the input space also contains environment inputs (shared variable values, message arrival times, ordering of messages etc.) whose values are not in control of the user but can be changed by an external agent such as the operating system. the error may not re-occur if the failed process is restarted with a different environment input but the same application input. It is due to this reason that "transient" failures occur in software even though the faults themselves are permanent. These observations have led Gray to call such faults as "Heisenbugs" and the others as "Bohrbugs" for which rollback and retry methods do not work[5]. This terminology is somewhat misleading in that it implies that the fault themselves are transient or permanent (as is the case in hardware). In reality, the bugs or faults in the software are permanent, but the failures or errors can be transient.

The exception domain of most commercial software is typically very small and comprise of rare inputs. The strategies described in the previous sections change the input (either intentionally as part of recovery, or let time and other activities in the system do it) from ED to SD when an error is observed on those rare inputs. The issue here is not whether this can be done or not. The above characterization clearly shows that we can *always* do this for any program whose

SD is not empty. The main issue with these techniques is whether changing the inputs to avoid a failure is *acceptable* for the software application or not. That is, the method will be useful only if *acceptable transformations* are performed to the input to avoid further failures.

For a given input, many acceptable transformations may be possible. For example, in most applications, if the application (user) inputs are preserved but the environment inputs are modified, then the transformation is acceptable. This is because the environment inputs are not in control of the user or the application process. By performing acceptable transformations to a given input we get a set of alternative inputs, which is a subset of the input space, on which the process can be executed and the results will be acceptable (if the process does not fail). If an input to the process is in ED, then the process will fail. We call a failure of the software as *transient* if the set of inputs obtained by acceptable transformations of the original input is such that some points in that set are in SD.

It is our belief that software in most practical situations is generally well tested before delivery and fails mostly on those rare environment inputs. That is, the software fails if the environment is in some special state which the software designer did not anticipate, or fails for messages that come at unexpected times, or at unexpected speed, or with unexpected interleaving. In such situations many acceptable transformations to the input of the process can be made, which will change that input from ED to SD. We believe that a vast majority of residual faults in software result in transient failures. To tolerate such faults, design diversity is not necessary; more cost-effective techniques such as rollback and restart and message reordering can be used to effectively mask such failures.

## 5  Summary

The traditional approaches for fault tolerance against software design faults - the recovery block approach and the N-version programming - are expensive, as they use design diversity to mask the effects of faults. The assumption behind using design diversity is that since software faults are permanent as they are design faults, their failures will also be permanent. However, observations have shown that the failures caused by software faults are sometimes transient, and go away if the same software is reexecuted perhaps with some message reordering.

We have explained the underlying model behind this phenomenon. The failure of any software can be viewed as occurring because its inputs are in the exceptional domain (ED) for the process. If the process is executed with the input in the standard domain (SD), the process will not fail. As for most software developed using modern methods the standard domain covers most of the input space and the exception domain consists of inputs that can be considered rare or as special cases. A practical way to support fault tolerance which will not require design diversity is to change the input to the process when it fails, such that the changed input is in the standard domain. We described two techniques using this approach.

The "input" to a process needs to be viewed in a more general manner. The input is not only the user data input, but also input from shared environment variables in the system and messages a process gets from other processes, operating system, or hardware devices. For messages, not only their values but also their timing and interleaving determine the process behavior. Any of these can be changed to take a particular input from ED to SD. As environment inputs are not in control of the user or the designer, one way of changing the total input is to change environment inputs without changing the user input or messages. One technique to change the environment input is to simply reexecute the process with the hope that the new timings of the logged events and messages will not recreate the failure. The second technique is to carefully reorder the logged messages during recovery after a failure. These techniques are general but of course can only be used in contexts where such transformations are acceptable.

# References

[1] P. E. Ammann and J. C. Knight. Data diversity: an approach to software fault tolerance. In *Dij. of papers: 17th Int. Conf. on Fault Tolerant Comput. Sys.*, pages 122–126, Pittsburgh, 1987.

[2] A. Avizienis. The n-version approach to fault tolerant software. *IEEE Tran. on Software Engg.*, SE-11(12):1491–1501, Dec 1985.

[3] J. F. Bartlett. A nonstop kernel. In *Proc. of 7th ACM Symp. on Operating Sys.*, pages 22–29, 1981.

[4] A. Borg, J. Baumback, and S. Galzer. A message system supporting fault tolerance. In *9th ACM Symp. on Op. Sys. Principles, Op. Sys. Review, 17:5*, pages 90–99, 1983.

[5] J. Gray. Why do computers stop and what can be done about it? Technical Report 85.7, Tandem Computers, Cupertino, CA, June 1985.

[6] D. Gupta and P. Jalote Increasing system availability through on-line software version change. *23rd Int. Conf. on Fault Tolerance Computing Systems*, Toulouse, France, pages 30-35, June 1993.

[7] F. Cristian. Exception handling and software fault tolerance. *IEEE Tran. on Comput.*, C-31(6):531–540, June 1982.

[8] F. Cristian. Correct and robust programs. *IEEE Tran. on Soft. Engg.*, SE-10(2):163–174, March 1984.

[9] Y. Huang and C. M. R. Kintala. Software implemented fault tolerance: technologies and experience. *23rd Int. Conf. on Fault Tolerance Computing Systems*, Toulouse, France, pages 2-9, June 1993.

[10] G. Fowler and Y. Huang and D. Korn and H. C. Rao, "A User-Level Replicated File System," *Proceedings of Summer USENIX*, pages 279-290, June, 1993.

[11] P. Jalote. Fault tolerant processes. *Distributed Computing*, 3:187–195, 1989.

[12] D. B. Johnson and W. Zwaenepoel. Sender-based message logging. In *Dij. of Papers, 17th Int. Conf. on Fault Tolerant Computing Sys.*, pages 14–19, 1987.

[13] D. B. Johnson and W. Zwaenepoel. Recovery in distributed systems using optimistic message logging an d checkpointing. *Journal of Algorithms*, 11:462–491, 1990.

[14] J. C. Knight and N. G. Leveson. An experimental evaluation of the assumption of independence in multiversion programming. *IEEE Tran. on Soft. Engg.*, SE-12(1):96–109, Jan 1986.

[15] B. Randell. System structure for software fault tolerance. *IEEE Tran. on Software Engg.*, SE-1:220–232, June 1975.

[16] M. E. Segal and O. Frieder. On-the-fly modification: systems for dynamic updating. *IEEE Software*, pp. 53-65, March 1993.

[17] R. E. Strom and S. Yemini. Optimistic recovery: an asynchronous approach to fault tolerance in distributed systems. In *Proc. of 14th Symp. of Fault Tolerant Computing*, pages 374–379, 1984.

[18] Y. Wang, Y. Huang and K. Fuchs, "Progressive retry for software errors," *23rd International Symposium on Fault Tolerant Computer Systems (FTCS-23)*, Toulouse, France, pages 138-144, June 1993.

# Software-Faults:
# The Remaining Problem in Fault Tolerant Systems?

P.A. Lee

Department of Computing Science
University of Newcastle upon Tyne
NE1 7RU, England

**Abstract.** This paper discusses the problems of software-faults in computer systems, and how such faults can be tolerated. After introducing some terminology, the characteristics of software faults and their effects are described. Then four approaches to software-fault tolerance are described. Finally, an architecture for fault tolerant software components is outlined.

## Introduction

Everyone is aware of the need to make computer systems more *dependable*, that is, to minimise the occurrence of *system failures*. Furthermore, everyone is aware that today's complex systems suffer from the effects of faults which, if not tolerated, lead to dependability problems (for some computer uses at least). The principles of fault tolerance are well understood, and in practice have been successfully applied in many systems. Does this mean that there are few remaining problems with providing fault tolerance?

Were this to be true there are several conferences (and workshops!) that could be cancelled. There are, of course, many research areas in fault tolerance remaining to be investigated, as other papers in this book demonstrate. However, the thesis of this paper is that one category of faults, namely *design faults* in general and *software faults* in particular, remains one of the key areas to be tackled. The proposed approaches to software-fault tolerance are discussed briefly in the paper, which concludes with some thoughts on an architecture for fault tolerant software components.

## Terminology

It is useful to define some terminology, since many papers tend to use different terms for what are in fact similar concepts, which makes it difficult to compare and contrast the concepts being discussed in those papers. The following terms will be used in this paper to provide a consistent framework for comparing several approaches to software-fault tolerance.

A system is said to *fail* when it does not provide the behaviour prescribed in that system's specification. System failures are caused by *faults* in a system. When the faulty part of the system is exercised, the fault gives rise to *errors* in the system state which may lead to eventual system failure. (Further detailed discussions of these terms and their definitions, as well as of fault tolerance in general, may be found in [Lee 1990]).

To achieve dependability, two complementary approaches should be followed: fault prevention and fault tolerance. *Fault prevention* is concerned with ensuring that faults are not present in the operational system in the first place, encompassing techniques such as design verification and testing. Facing the inevitable consequence that there will be residual faults in a system, or that faults will develop while the system is in operation, *fault tolerance* techniques are required to provide dependable behaviour in the presence of such faults.

The principles of fault tolerance are straightforward. You have to deal with the *errors* in a system and with the *fault* which caused those errors. Errors have to be detected (*error detection*) and corrected (*error recovery*), actions both involving the state of the system; the fault which gave rise to the errors may have to be identified and treated in some fashion (otherwise it may continue to affect the system's operation), and the system returned to providing its normal service.

It is also convenient to propose a simple model of a "system" to help trying to understand some of the characteristics of fault tolerance. A system can be thought of as being composed of a set of *components* and a *design*. The components are the parts which the system is built up from, and in a computer system can be "real" (e.g. hardware components) or abstract (e.g. the operating system). However, a set of components by itself does not constitute a system, and it is the design of the system which controls how those components interact and produce the desired system behaviour. For example, a bag of hardware components is of little use until those components are interconnected on a printed circuit board to form, say, a computer. The PCB and the interconnections are the physical realisation of the design of the computer. As a software example, a payroll system may be regarded as consisting of a set of components such as a database system, an operating system, a transaction manager etc. together with a design represented by the payroll system software.

Note that the term design here is used to refer to something that is part of the operational system rather than the more abstract concept of design as the blueprints or plans for a system. This is an important point since if the design is in the operational system then it is something that can go wrong and affect the system's behaviour. Since the design of a system has to have a realisation in that system, the term *design-component* will be used subsequently to refer to the part of the operational system that is regarded as being the design.

## Types of Fault

The above model forms a useful basis for discussing several aspects of fault tolerance in computer systems. In particular, one can observe that one reason for a system failing is that one of its components fails (a component is itself a system, and fails when it does not conform to its specification). A component failure is a component fault in the system of which it is a part, and that fault will need to be tolerated if that system's failure has to be averted. With the component model, one can also observe a second reason for a system failing: if all of a system's components work perfectly, yet a system failure still occurs, then it is the *design-component* of the system that has failed - this is regarded as a design fault in the system. For instance, in the payroll system mentioned above, a problem with a disk (a component fault, in the payroll system) might result in the database component failing whereas a bug in the payroll software itself would be a design fault in the payroll system.

It is also interesting to consider the different effects of these two different types of faults, since these effects have a strong bearing on the fault tolerance techniques that have to be adopted. A design fault by its very nature is a fault that cannot be anticipated, and hence will produce *unanticipated* effects. A component fault, however, may or may not be anticipated. If unanticipated, a component fault will have unanticipated effects on the system of which it is a part; if the fault was anticipated then there is the likelihood that the effects of the fault have also been anticipated.

Dealing with the errors arising from anticipated effects can be relatively straightforward, requiring the errors to be fixed up in some appropriate manner. This error recovery technique is called *forward error recovery*. An example is the application of error-correcting codes on memory where single-bit errors have been anticipated and can be fixed if they occur. However, dealing with the errors arising in unanticipated situations is much more difficult, since the specific potential errors cannot be identified a priori (i.e. while the system was being constructed). In this situation a more general error recovery technique is required, and *backward error recovery* is such a technique where the state of the system is (effectively) reversed in time to a prior state which it is hoped is an error-free state which preceded the invocation of the fault.

Dealing with the faults themselves requires there to be some *redundancy* in the system. But the form of that redundancy depends upon the type of fault. Moreover, a further characteristic that has to be taken into account is whether the fault is (or appears to be) *transient* or *permanent*. A transient fault might result in a fault treatment strategy in which no parts of the system are changed. In this case redundancy in time (i.e. retry) is employed to provide continued system service. A permanent fault requires that faulty part of the system is removed from operational use and replaced by an "equivalent" part. A permanent design fault in a system requires the replacement of the design-component with a different but equivalent design-component which meets the same system specification. It is no good replacing the design-component with an exact copy, since that copy will contain an identical fault. Design redundancy (sometimes called design diversity) is what is required. This form of redundancy is important for software-fault tolerance schemes, and will be returned to subsequently.

However, there is a further complication. As mentioned earlier, a design in the real system has to have some representation in that system. A program as a design-component is represented as bits in memory; the design of a chip is represented by the pattern of tracks and wires interconnecting sub-components. An unrecognised memory fault could surreptitiously introduce what appears to be a design fault into a program by changing instructions into other instructions, just as a track which broke would make a chip behave as if that track wasn't there in the first place. In these situations, the system might appear to have a design fault, but replacing the design-component with an identical copy (reload the program, or use a redundant but identical chip) would give the appearance of fixing the design fault!

A permanent component fault requires further elaboration. Regarding the faulty component as a system, it will have failed if either its design-component failed or a sub-component failed, and a sub-component might have failed because its sub-design-component failed or a sub-sub component failed. And so on. Thus treating a permanent component fault by replacing that component with an absolutely identical component may work in some situations, but not in others.

## Faults Affecting Computer Systems

Let us now try to relate the above discussion of faults to computer systems. The traditional view of a computer system separates "hardware" from the "software", and the types of fault can be discussed from these two viewpoints.

Fault tolerance in the hardware of computers has been the prime concern of the majority of fault tolerant systems and research since computers were invented. Hardware systems suffer from physical degradation (they wear out), and hardware component faults occur in both transient and permanent forms. Replacement of a failed component by a physically equivalent copy is commonplace (e.g. duplicated CPUs, disks and networks). Similarly, forward error recovery for anticipated situations is often used (e.g. ECC, mirrored disks). Other papers in this book address the problems of hardware-fault tolerance, particularly those discussing software architectures for tolerating the effects of hardware faults.

Design faults are not often considered in hardware fault tolerant systems, but are by no means unknown. It is commonplace with today's complex ICs to receive bug lists (or "feature" lists!) along with a chip, representing design faults which have been uncovered since the chip was manufactured, and it seems most unlikely that such lists represent the only design faults in such chips. Indeed, it may be that other transient or permanent hardware faults could be caused by design faults, although such an analysis is rarely provided. The design of hardware systems is perhaps sufficiently simple that fault prevention techniques can be effective in removing most design faults from a hardware system. Nevertheless, for safety-critical systems such as transport systems hardware design diversity is employed because of the worries of common-mode failures caused by design faults (examples of rail and air applications are given in [Voges 1988]).

Analyses of computer system failures, such as that by Gray [Gray 1993], suggest that, in general, hardware problems are no longer the key dependability problem in most computer systems, partly because hardware components are becoming increasingly reliably, and partly because of the effectiveness of specific fault tolerance techniques in dealing with anticipated hardware problems. The two major causes of system problems identified by Gray (and others - see [Clem 1987] for instance, as well as the paper by Levendel in this section) are (a) operator mistakes; and (b) software faults. Only the latter of these will be considered further.

# The Nature of Software Faults

Given the complexity in today's software systems and in the (software) components they use (like the operating system, the database manager etc.) it is not surprising that software is a major cause of problems in computer systems.

How do software faults fit into the earlier general discussion of faults and their characteristics? To simplify the picture, let us eliminate one variable from the scene. Earlier, the idea of the representation of a design changing and appearing like a design fault was introduced - e.g. bits in memory changing and hence changing a program. In practice, of course such changes are usually detected by checks in the hardware components and are not permit to go unnoticed; thus the failure of the hardware components which are holding the representation of the software system's design (i.e. the memory holding the program) and those hardware components which cause the program to be executed (i.e. the CPU) can be ignored, and we only need consider the true design faults/bugs in an incorrect program.

Are design faults in software systems transient or permanent? It is often claimed that some software faults are transient (or soft) while others are permanent or hard (as reflected in the use of the terms Heisenbug and Bohrbug by Gray [Gray 1985]- also discussed in Borr's paper in this book). Of course, in practice such faults *are* permanent. However, the effects of software faults, that is, the errors they produce, often make them appear as if they were transient; this aspect will be returned to in the next section.

Dealing with the effects of design faults requires powerful error recovery techniques, since the specific errors generated by an (unanticipated) design fault cannot be anticipated. Thus backward error recovery is an important technique which forms an important part of two of the software-fault tolerance techniques to be discussed in the next section.

What effects do component faults have on software systems? There are two difficulties here: firstly, how you identify components, especially in abstract systems like software systems (should the printf library routine be a component?); and secondly, how do you determine that such components have failed?

Top-down decomposition, object-oriented design and modularisation are recognised as important software engineering concepts and could lead to the identification of software components. What we are really looking for here is some structure in the operational system which can be trusted and upon which we can then base a fault tolerance strategy. Components should therefore be parts of the system which have clean, well defined interfaces and interact in well-defined ways. This is especially important when components fail; if a subroutine is a component which can fail and overwrite the program's memory, then there is little point in regarding that subroutine as a component. If the database manager is a component which only interacts via, say, message passing, then the boundary between the database and the rest of the software is much more "substantial" and allows the fault tolerant system designer to base strategies on firmer assumptions (such as, if the database manager fails it will not corrupt the software).

Determining whether or not a component has failed can be achieved in one of two ways: either the system itself has to check the behaviour of its components to see whether that behaviour conforms to the specification, or the component itself has to check its state and "own up" when it determines it is unlikely to be able to provide its specified service. Of course, ideally a component should never fail and should employ internal fault tolerance to ensure that internal faults are never seen by the system of which it is a part. But even with fully reliable components, design faults can still affect the system, and a system will always require some form of error detection to detect the errors caused by design faults. These topics will be returned to in the final section of this paper.

## Software-Fault Tolerance Approaches

Turning to specific techniques for software fault tolerance, four main schemes can be identified:

1. Recovery Blocks
2. N-Version Programming
3. Recover-and-retry
4. Fix-the-errors

The recovery block scheme was proposed almost 20 years ago (in 1974) and was the first scheme to attack the problem of fault tolerance in software systems. N-version programming was introduced subsequently (1977). Both of these schemes are well known and will not be described further here. The interested reader is referred to [Voges 1988, Lee 1990] for details of these schemes.

Recover-and-retry is the basis of a technique suggested by Gray [Gray 1993] as an effective software-fault tolerance technique. [1] The basic premise of this approach is that many of the errors caused by software faults are caused by transient situations such that if backward error recovery is applied and the erring program is retried on a different machine then the same error is unlikely to recur. [2]

Finally, the Fix-the-errors scheme has been employed for many years in the software systems of the ESS (Electronic Switching Systems). Here there are special programs (called audit programs) the purpose of which are to detect and correct errors in the system's database. No attempt is made to provide full fault tolerance (no attempt is made to deal with the fault which caused those errors).

## Experiences

Recovery blocks and N-version programming have been shown to be successful approaches to software fault tolerance, although neither scheme can guarantee that all software faults will be tolerated [Lee 90]. Since recovery blocks require some

---

[1] Gray actually refers to this technique as "Transactions" but that terminology may be somewhat misleading as in database systems transactions are primarily a unit of recovery and do not address the aspects of dealing with faults.

[2] See also Borr's paper in this book.

hardware assistance in the provision of efficient backward error recovery for the main memory being used by the program, N-version programming has been used more extensively in real systems, primarily in safety-critical systems [Voges 1988]. Here the need for backward error recovery for the main memory is removed by the isolation of the independently executing versions, and by discarding the memory state of a failed version. It is clear that the expense of both of these schemes (in terms of the need to produce multiple but different versions of the software system) is a serious hurdle to the use of the techniques in other than environments where the price of a failure is severe.

The theory behind the recover-and-retry approach is that many software faults produce transient effects, for instance, caused by a timing problem in the program or by transient situations in other software components (such as the operating system or database manager), such that were the program to be recovered (to remove any visible effects of its execution so far) and retried on another system, the likelihood of the fault manifesting itself again is small. As Gray notes, this theory is preposterous but seems to fit practical experience. It was reported [Gray 1990] that in Tandem systems using the process-pairing mechanism (which is a standard part of those systems) "seems to mask more than 99% of all software faults in system processes". The basic process pairing mechanism provides two processes on separate (isolated) systems, which explicitly communicate important state information (from the main process to its backup) to permit the backup to pick up a computation if the primary fails. This assumes that this "important" state information itself does not contain errors, rather that the errors are in the other state which is thrown away and reset by moving the program to another computer.

Extending recover-and-retry to application level software is suggested by using a transaction mechanism together with process-pairs. Transactions provide backward error recovery for some of the effects of a partly completed computation (normally, recovering database updates to their state at the start of the transaction), while the process-pair permits the failed program to be restarted on a separate system with a clean initial state (another part of backward error recovery).

In one important aspect, the recover-and-retry scheme is a less complete software-fault tolerance technique than recovery blocks or N-version programming. This is because while it deals with errors (through the transaction mechanism) there is no design redundancy employed to (try to) deal with a design fault. Recover-and-retry seems successful in coping in a software system with some (software) component faults (e.g. a transient operating system problem) and with some design faults if you are lucky (e.g. coping incorrectly with resource problems or timing problems). Why does it work in these situations? One reason is in the "share-nothing" environment of the Tandem system where the operating systems on different machines have no common state. Hence even though a bug in the operating system component will be common to all systems, the probability of two systems having the same state, and hence showing up the effects of that bug, is small. However, this approach might not be so successful on, say, a shared-memory multiprocessor. Perhaps a second reason for the success is that some software components are being affected by undetected transient hardware problems or rarely encountered hardware design faults. However, it is unlikely that we'll ever know if this is ever the case. (It should also be noted that the recovery blocks and N-version programming schemes could also provide tolerance for these types of component faults.)

It is clear that using recover-and-retry to tolerate design faults in the software system itself (rather than in its components) is possible, but its potential for success is a matter of luck. Gray's experiences as to how often luck is on your side aren't quantified (and probably aren't quantifiable without major effort), but his extensive experiences suggest that the approach does work in practice. It would be interesting to see whether other people's experiences with software systems reinforces the potential effectiveness of recover-and-retry. Certainly, in discussions of this point during the workshop, several people expressed first hand experience of the type of bugs which recover-and-retry would cope with. If this approach might work for other software systems, this would be interesting as it would provide some software-fault tolerance without the expense of multiple software developments as required in N-version programming and recovery blocks. The next section of the paper proposes an architecture for software components which provides some of the attributes of the Tandem environment which contribute to the apparent practical success of recover-and-retry.

Finally, the fix-the-errors scheme is the least complete fault tolerance strategy, since it is concerned only with belatedly detecting errors in the system state and attempting to apply forward error recovery to fix up those errors, in the hope that these belated actions will be successful in preventing system failures. AT&T's pioneering experiences with this technique suggest that it detects and fixes significant numbers of software-caused errors [Connet 1972]. There are no figures to indicate just how many of these errors would have led to system failure. But again, practical experiences suggest that this technique is very effective in practice, and the reader is referred to the papers in this book by Levendel and by Huang, especially the latter in which the techniques used are described in detail.

## A Fault Tolerant Architecture For Software Components

After 20 years of research, it seems that the theory as to how to achieve software-fault tolerance is well understood but the practice is not well established for the majority of fault tolerant systems. If software faults are a major cause of system failures, as most people seem to agree upon, this mismatch between theory and practice seems strange. The question is will this mismatch remain?

Is it the case that hardware systems have the problems of design faults licked? Are their fault prevention techniques sufficiently good and their designs sufficiently simple that all design faults are removed before the (hardware) system is depended upon? Or are design faults really the cause of many supposedly transient hardware (and software) failures, and hence design-fault tolerance is a problem in waiting?

Given the complexity of today's software systems and the lack of success with fault prevention techniques such as program proving, it is inevitable that such systems will contain design faults. If a software system has to be structured not only to deal with such design fault but also to tolerate the many and varied component failures that can affect it, then the likelihood of producing a reliable software system diminishes further. To provide some kind of architecture for structuring software systems to deal with at least the complexities of fault tolerance, in 1981 we suggested the idea of *ideal fault tolerant components*, that is, the architecture for a component which is ideally suited to the coherent provision of fault tolerance (see [Lee 1990]). Many of the features suggested by Gray for the recover-and-retry scheme are in fact a practical implementation of this architecture. Figure 1 shows the main features of an ideal fault tolerant component.

Component C responds to Service Requests emanating from some containing system S which is assumed to be at the top of the figure. Under normal circumstances, Normal Activity in C will invoke sub-components (assumed to be at the bottom of the figure) and will eventually return a Normal Response to the requester (as required by C's specification). Ideally, the activity in C will be encapsulated so that side-effects in the state of S (or of sub-components) cannot occur. This emulates the "share-nothing" aspect of the recover-and-retry technique discussed earlier.

Consider now the abnormal responses (or exceptions) that C can generate for S. First, what if the service request from S was illegal in some fashion. In this situation C can generate an *Interface Exception* to indicate to S that it had attempted to misuse C's interface. There is nothing wrong with C, but there may be some problem in S. Often, an interface exception is caused by a design fault in S.

In contrast, *Failure Exceptions* are generated by C when it determines that it cannot provide its specified service - it is an indication that C has failed - a component fault to be dealt with in the containing system. What might cause C to generate a failure exception? From the earlier discussion, C can be affected by sub-component failures or design faults in C itself, and thus C can receive both interface and failure exceptions from its sub-components. In this model, it is assumed that the receipt of an

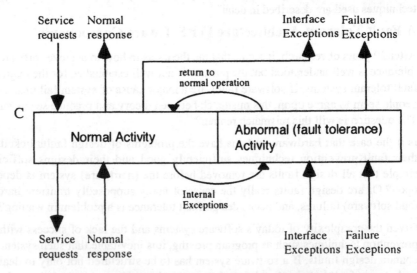

Figure 1. Architecture of Ideal Fault Tolerant Component

exception causes the transfer of control to the exception handling part (Abnormal Activity). Ideally, C will provide fault tolerance measures (to deal with any errors and to deal with the fault) such that the fault can be tolerated and C can be returned to normal service, without any problem being visible to the containing system S. If, however, C cannot provide effective tolerance for the erroneous situation that has arisen, then it should generate a failure exception for S. Fault tolerance actions in S then have to deal with the C-component fault.

Note that the differentiation between interface and failure exceptions permits C to separate the actions it requires for sub-component faults (failure exceptions) and design faults (interface exceptions), since different actions are likely to be necessary, as discussed earlier. This classification of exceptions is an important part of the ideal fault tolerant component model. Indeed, a further characterisation of failure exceptions might permit a failing component to indicate the possible cause of the failure (e.g. whether it was a sub-component or a design fault) since this information could affect the fault treatment strategy - e.g. whether replacing the component with an identical copy might work.

The final class of exceptions indicated in Figure 1, Internal Exceptions, is for the situation when internal error detection checks in C reveal the presence of errors (e.g. errors arising from a design fault which was not revealed by underlying interface exceptions). When an internal exception is raised, the exception handling/fault tolerance actions are invoked.

It is also desirable that an ideal component operates atomically, with the "all-or-nothing" property. in other words when servicing a request, either the normal activity completes and the component is left in an internally consistent state, or the state is reset to some internally consistent state. Components whose state is left internally inconsistent are likely to be the source of further exceptions if invoked again. In the recover-and-retry scheme, the transaction mechanism can provide this atomicity.

A final requirement is that an ideal component such as C can provide backward error recovery for the containing system S. If this form of recovery is provided, then the possibility for tolerating design faults in S is much enhanced. The need here is to permit S to establish, discard or recover to recovery points. These points mark recovery boundaries in S (like the transaction mechanism in the recover-and-retry scheme), such that any operations on C after a recovery point has been established can be undone if recovery is required.

Ideal components are suggested as an architecture for software components and fault tolerance, and the four techniques described above implement this architecture in various forms. The current trend to object-oriented systems perhaps gives a software environment which fits closely with this architecture, allowing the identification of software components (objects) with clean interfaces and without side-effects. However, backward error recovery is also necessary. It may be the case that the clean separation between interface and implementation that is present in object-oriented systems provides a "hook" for design redundancy in that different implementations can be provided for the same interface and possibly combined together to provide design-fault tolerance.

## Conclusions

The title of this paper posed a question: "Software Faults: The Remaining Problem In Fault Tolerant Systems?" The answer to this question still appears to be yes!

## Acknowledgements

This research was in part supported by the ESPRIT FASST Project. Thanks are also due to Andrew Thomas, Ron Kerr and Brian Randell for comments on an earlier draft of this paper.

## References

[Clem 1987]    G.F. Clement and P.K.Giloth, "Evolution of Fault Tolerant Switching Systems in AT&T", pp. 55-76 in *The Evolution of Fault-Tolerant Computing*, (ed. A. Avizienis *et al.*), Springer-Verlag 1987.

[Conn 1972]    J.R.Connet, E.J. Pasternak and B.D. Wagner, "Software Defenses in Real-Time Control Systems", Digest of Papers FTCS-72, June 1972 pp. 94-99.

[Gray 1985]    J. Gray, "Why Do Computers Stop and What Can be Done About It?", 5th Symposium on Reliability in Distributed Software and Database Systems, pp. 3-12.

[Gray 1990]    J. Gray, "A Census of Tandem System Availability Between 1985 and 1990", IEEE Transactions on Reliability, 39(4), Oct. 1990, pp. 409-418.

[Gray 1993]    J. Gray and A. Reuter, *Transaction Processing: Concepts and Techniques*, Morgan Kaufmann, 1993.

[Lee 1990]     P.A. Lee and T. Anderson, *Fault Tolerance: Principles and Practice (second edition)*, Springer-Verlag 1990.

[Voges 1988]   U. Voges (ed.), *Software Diversity in Computerised Control Systems*, Springer-Verlag 1988.

# Fault Tolerance Enablers in the CHORUS Microkernel

*Jim Lipkis*

*Marc Rozier*

Chorus systèmes
6, avenue Gustave Eiffel
78182 Saint-Quentin-En-Yvelines CEDEX
FRANCE
*Email: {lipkis,mr}@chorus.fr*

## 1. Overview

The CHORUS architecture was designed from the outset to facilitate high availability and fault tolerance in both the operating system and user applications. This paper summarizes some of the features of CHORUS that relate to high availability. Where relevant, we briefly describe existing experiences or projects whose purpose is to demonstrate or exploit fault-tolerant aspects of CHORUS. Finally, future directions are outlined.

## 2. Basic Operating System Features for Fault Tolerance

In order to facilitate the design of fault-tolerant systems and applications, the operating system must provide certain fundamental features.

First, the O.S. must provide the building blocks for the system builder to build **well structured, modular** software. Modularity is recognized as a key concept for building fault-tolerant systems. It has a strong impact on:

- Fault avoidance. Modular systems are easier to validate. If the system is built out of small modules, with identified interactions, each module may in principle be individually tested. In addition, small modules are easier to maintain than monolithic software.

- Fault detection and isolation. Small modules, with well-identified interfaces, ease the placing of sanity checks within the system. In particular, such checks are usually placed at module entry/exit points. In addition, when a physical frontier (such as address space protection) may be placed between modules, and when interactions between modules have well defined semantics (message passing for example), modularity is essential for confinement of faults. A fault will be detected earlier, and its consequences limited to the scope of the module into which it occurred.

- Fault recovery. A highly available system is either a system which never fails (high MTBF), or a system which is repaired very easily and quickly (low MTTR). Modularity tends to simplify system repair: If faults have been confined to individual modules, only those modules will have to be repaired or replaced, which is likely to take less time than repairing a full system.

Second, the modularity must be **affordable**. That means that:

- Modularity must be easy to build. The system abstractions used for defining modules must be simple. Interactions among modules must be expressed using uniform, simple invocation primitives.

- Modularity must have minimal impact on software performance. That means in particular that the O.S. must provide very efficient inter-module invocation mechanisms.

Finally, the O.S. must provide the necessary mechanisms for applications of classic fault tolerance techniques:

- Reconfiguration of modules. The O.S. must provide mechanisms allowing modules to be dynamically instantiated, and dynamically reconfigured (i.e., moved and/or replaced). This is essential in providing module-level system repair.

- Replication of modules. Many fault-tolerant applications rely on the ability to replicate some of the software modules. The O.S. must provide basic mechanisms allowing such replication to be easily done.

In summary, the O.S. must provide two classes of enablers:

- Modularity enablers: mechanisms allowing modular software to be efficiently developed and efficiently operated.

- Fault tolerance enablers: mechanisms allowing modules to be reconfigured and/or replicated in order to implement specific fault tolerance policies.

## 3. CHORUS Microkernel Enablers

The CHORUS microkernel technology [Rozier88] has unique characteristics that allow computer system manufacturers, software developers, and system integrators to build highly available and fault tolerant systems. Within the microkernel, emphasis is placed on enablers, as outlined above, rather than on finished or integrated solutions.

### 3.1. Modularity Enablers

Operating systems and user applications in CHORUS are built out of software modules called *actors*, which group together state information concerning local sets of resources and which communicate only via a highly efficient message-passing system.

Actors constitute the basic unit of system and application structuring. An actor is essentially an address space, within which *threads* may execute system or application tasks. Actors are usually protected against each other (by address space and/or machine boundaries). Even when actors can share virtual memory, it is always possible to strictly limit communications between actors to the message passing facility. Such isolation of system modules, together with simple expression of the interactions between modules, provides the necessary modularity enablers described in section 2.

Providing such modularity enablers is not unique to the CHORUS microkernel. In fact, this is one of the main motivations behind all microkernel architectures (see [Accetta86], [Mullender87], [Bomberger92]). What makes CHORUS unique in this area is the fact that the microkernel provides its user with mechanisms that allow very high performance, allowing real modularity to be applied in all components of practical systems and applications.

CHORUS allows the system builder complete flexibility in the mapping of software modules over the protection and privilege features of the hardware. In particular, the software architecture allows the classic tradeoff between protection and performance to be negotiated according to the requirements of a particular target system. By sacrificing a degree of isolation between modules, performance comparable to monolithic O.S. kernels can be achieved while retaining most of the benefits of modularity for high availability.

Actors in CHORUS may run *unprivileged*, in private, protected address spaces, or *privileged*, in which case they share a single memory protection domain (hardware address space) with each other and with the microkernel. Thus each actor is either a *user actor* or a *supervisor actor*, respectively. The programming interface is the same, and any program which runs as a user actor can be loaded instead as a supervisor actor without change and even without recompilation.

Regardless of the type of actor, each one represents a software module which may be loaded and unloaded separately and dynamically.

However, supervisor actors benefit from several specialized features for modularity. First, supervisor actors may "connect" directly to hardware events such as device interrupts, system call traps, and exceptions, with no extra overhead. Thus event-handling software may be located in the appropriate actor; there is never a temptation to violate modularity, by, for example, linking device drivers directly into the microkernel for performance reasons. Second, the architecture provides substantial performance enhancements for interactions involving supervisor actors. In particular, the message passing mechanisms are highly optimized, transparently to sender and receiver, when supervisor actors are involved in a communication. Message buffer copies are avoided in this case, and a very high performance form of *lightweight RPC* is applied, reducing communication overhead to the order of magnitude of the system invocation time.

The advantages of the CHORUS modularity enablers (primitive IPC, actors with different privileges) have been discussed in detail in [Bricker91]. The important observations are that:

- Such enablers have proven to make modular implementations of UNIX systems workable in commercial environments (for example, see [Batlivala92]).

- The fact that modularity can be applied very deeply within the O.S. kernel implementation extends the range of areas where fault tolerance policies may be applied.

### 3.2. Fault Tolerance Enablers

Most of the CHORUS fault tolerance enablers are found in its communication service (IPC).

CHORUS actors have transparent remote access to each others' services so that communication is the same regardless of where the other actors are located, even if the services have moved to another machine. (Communication between actors on the same machine is highly optimized by the microkernel; this is invisible to actors except for performance improvements.) This "late binding" of software components permits *easy dynamic reconfiguration, the ability to migrate services, and resulting disruption-free evolution of the system as it changes.*

The second important enabler is the notion of port group. Groups are becoming more and more popular for implementing fault tolerance in distributed systems. They are very useful when server replication and/or distributed synchronisation is a concern [Birman91].

CHORUS provides the ability to address services in a generic fashion with port groups and migratable ports. Clients of a service do not need to know that a service is distributed or replicated; clients access replicated servers as they do any other server. Ports and port groups provide a *simple, transparent interface to replicated services.*

Such enablers, which are described in more details in the remainder of this section, are sufficient to implement restricted but useful forms of dynamic replacement and fault tolerance. In section 6 we will examine the further ongoing microkernel developments necessary to provide for full and convenient implementation of highly available systems.

**3.2.1. Reliable RPC.** CHORUS supports end-to-end reliable RPC communications through an optimized acknowledgment/retransmission protocol. The protocol provides *at-most-once* failure semantics, which guarantees that a service will not be accidentally executed multiple times because of message retransmission. Experience has shown that the at-most-once policy facilitates deterministic recovery and retry of service requests aborted because of partial server failures.

**3.2.2. Exception Propagation.** The communication service implements *propagation* of software exceptions from the client to the server(s) of an RPC transaction. If an aborted thread happens to be blocked on a pending RPC request, the abort will be *propagated* to the server thread currently processing the request. Thus a server is never prevented from achieving an orderly shutdown because of outstanding activity elsewhere in the system.

**3.2.3. Port Migration.** A service port may be migrated from one server actor to another, transparent to the clients that address service requests to that port. Optionally, queued messages may be moved with the port. This allows online substitution of an active server by a new or upgraded actor that exports the same service.

**3.2.4. Port Groups.** Multiple ports can be collected into a port group, and addressed by group name. Port groups add flexibility, transparency, and persistence by providing a level of indirection and a means for late binding of client programs to system services. Servers can thus be replicated, distributed, reconfigured, and restarted, as needed for fault tolerance, without causing disruption or extra complexity in client applications.

In the current CHORUS microkernel, RPC requests can be addressed to port groups only in *functional* mode, which selects a single port within the group to receive each message. Messages may be broadcast to port groups, but only in unreliable asynchronous mode. Ongoing enhancements include provision for reliable broadcast and broadcast of RPC requests .

## 4. CHORUS/MiX: A Framework for High Availability

CHORUS/MiX, a modular implementation of UNIX based on the CHORUS microkernel, demonstrates a practical application of the microkernel enablers discussed above. Several versions have been developed and employed in commercial products, including CHORUS/MiX V.3.2, a SCO-compatible implementation of UNIX System V release 3.2, and CHORUS/MiX V.4, a compatible implementation of UNIX System V release 4.0. The latter implements full UNIX compatibility, at the source and binary levels, for device drivers and other modules as well as user applications.

The modular design of the CHORUS/MiX system provides the framework for system-level high availability. A monolithic O.S. constitutes a single point of failure, making overall system operation vulnerable to any fault. By contrast, the CHORUS/MiX system segregates individual components so as to localize the effects of failures. If desired, O.S. components can be further isolated into separate protection domains (address spaces). The MiX servers allow for independent replacement, reconfiguration, or replication to provide a highly-available UNIX environment.

A number of studies and prototype implementations have demonstrated the feasibility of online upgrade, component reconfiguration, and resilient services such as mirrored file systems. However, the current CHORUS/MiX products are not fault tolerant.

## 5. Experiences

Several prototype implementations of reliable software systems have been developed under CHORUS.

(1) "SoftWare Replaceable Units" in Ada

In 1988-89, the European Space Agency funded a study of dynamic reconfiguration and software application replacement in a real-time, mission-critical context as part of the Columbus (European Space Station) project. Chorus, with several co-contractors, demonstrated the feasibility of online software upgrade and reconfiguration, without service disruption, under CHORUS/MiX [Guillemont89].

(2) A highly-available CHORUS/MiX server

A prototype dynamic upgrade and fault-tolerant capability has been added to the CHORUS/MiX (V.3.2) system itself. This was intended as a very short-term (90-day) development exercise, performed by individuals unfamiliar with the CHORUS/MiX internals, and hence the implementation was somewhat constrained. The MiX server which provides System V IPC functionality was moved into user space and enhanced for high availability. On-the-fly server replacement is performed using port migration; recovery from server or node failure is accomplished with master/slave replicated servers.

(3)  Persistent file system

Several prototypes of fault-tolerant file systems have been studied within the context of PhD dissertations. In these studies, CHORUS/MiX file servers were replicated, exploiting the benefits of the CHORUS enablers provided by the CHORUS communication services. (For one example, see [Coyote89].)

(4)  Distributed mirroring

The Veritas Volume Manager™ has been integrated within the CHORUS/MiX (V.4) system, in order to provide support for distributed disk mirroring. When moved to the CHORUS architecture, the Volume Manager naturally inherits the benefits of modularity and transparent distribution. Implemented as a CHORUS actor, it is dynamically loaded, and remotely accessible. Moreover, the Volume Manager may access disks located on different nodes of a multicomputer or network of stations.

This integration was initially used for demonstration purposes, and is now being exploited in an ongoing development which will provide system resilience against individual node failures in parallel OLTP machines.

# 6. Ongoing Projects

Upcoming developments in the area of high availability are described in this section.

## 6.1. Invocation Mechanisms

Some of the most important enhancements currently underway in the CHORUS microkernel technology are in the area of invocation mechanisms.

- First, performance of invocation mechanisms is always a very important point of investigation. In particular, the lightweight implementation of remote procedure calls is being extended so as to be more generally applicable, covering for example the case where server actors use protected address spaces.

- Second, we have devoted considerable energy to the definition of an object-oriented interface definition language (IDL) [Gautron92]. This work is partially included within the Ouverture ESPRIT project. We believe that the use of such a language for the expression of server invocations will move a step forward for building fault-tolerant services, by providing better control over servers' interactions. Also, the use of an object-oriented formalism helps in reducing the granularity of system modules. Finally, experiments have already shown that performance enhancements may be obtained using such a language.

## 6.2. Enhanced Communication Service

Within the context of the Ouverture ESPRIT project, we are working with other partners (Alcatel, Siemens) on enhancement of the group communication protocols [Veider92]. The first goal of this project is to provide several atomic broadcast protocol implementations, with various degrees of ordering semantics. Currently, the project uses an adapted version of the HORUS framework from Cornell University.

The second goal of this project is to exploit groups and atomic broadcast protocols in the implementation of fault-tolerant services within telecommunications applications. Fault tolerance strategies such as message logging and master/slave process configurations are being implemented.

## 6.3. Robustness

Providing the necessary features to enable implementation of fault tolerance policies within subsystems and applications is a very important role of the microkernel. However, such features are worth little if the microkernel itself does not strictly obey strong robustness requirements.

First, the basic services provided by the microkernel must incorporate well-defined failure models. For example, the CHORUS IPC is being extended with new protocols for establishing consensus on site or link failures. Another example involves new mechanisms introduced within the basic microkernel services in order to avoid memory exhaustion, especially on distributed configurations. (In a distributed system, guaranteeing that a node will always be able to obtain sufficient physical memory to make forward progress involves distributed algorithms, since its swap devices are located on remote nodes.) Those enhancements are currently being done in collaboration with the Unisys Corporation.

Second, the robustness of the microkernel code itself is of concern. Active work on enhancement of the CHORUS implementation is underway. A systematic analysis of panic situations, and the design of proper recovery actions, is being performed in collaboration with Tandem Computers.

## 6.4. An Enhanced Framework: Transparent Distribution in CHORUS/MiX

The integrated, transparently-distributed CHORUS/MiX V.4 environment will provide the framework for fully reconfigurable and fault-tolerant services. Relevant elements of MiX for high availability include:

- **Distribution within the operating system.** Because MiX itself is modular and distributed, the microkernel enablers discussed above can be applied to create dynamic upgrade capability and fault tolerance at the O.S. level.

- **Process migration.** MiX processes will be dynamically migratable for overall configuration flexibility, and in particular, to shutdown a site for maintenance without disrupting system operation.

- **Checkpoint/restart.** Related to process migration, this facility provides a complement to other fault tolerance approaches such as replication.

- **Single system image.** Distribution transparency over a multicomputer will allow rapid and convenient migration or replication of services on any site.

## 7. Summary

CHORUS/MiX provides the environment and specific capabilities for high availability within both the operating system and critical user applications. Both dynamic reconfiguration/upgrade and fault tolerance rely on CHORUS microkernel enablers and on the modular distributed nature of the MiX implementation. Crucial elements include:

- The underlying communications based architecture, which facilitates a modular and distributed structure for operating system components and user applications;

- Port migration and port group addressing, for configuration flexibility and dynamic replacement of software components;

- Advanced high-availability enablers under development, including atomic ordered broadcast and synchronized port group management;

- Very strong robustness criteria driving the microkernel enhancements.

- Finally, the distributed MiX implementation and single-site semantics, which will provide a comfortable, manageable environment for delivering highly available systems.

# REFERENCES

[Accetta86]
Accetta, M., Baron, R., Bolosky, W., Golub, D., Rashid, R., Tevanian, A., Young, M., "Mach: A New Kernel Foundation for UNIX Development", *Proceedings of Summer Usenix*, July 1986.

[Batlivala92]
Batlivala, N., Gleeson, B., Hamrick, J., Lurndal, S., Price, D., Soddy, J., Abrossimov, V., "Experience with SVR4 Over Chorus" *Proceedings of Usenix Workshop on Microkernels and Other Kernel Architectures*, April 1986.

[Birman91]
Birman, K., "The Process Group Approach to Reliable Distributed Computing", Technical Report, Cornell University, July 1991.

[Bomberger92]
Bomberger, A., Frantz, A., Frantz, W., Hardy, A., Hardy, N., Landau, C., Shapiro, J., "The KeyKOS Nanokernel Architecture" *Proceedings of Usenix Workshop on Microkernels and Other Kernel Architectures*, April 1986.

[Bricker91]
Bricker, A., Gien, M., Guillemont, M., Lipkis, J., Orr, D., Rozier, M., "Architectural Issues in Microkernel-based Operating Systems: the CHORUS Experience" *Computer Communications*, Vol. 14, No. 6, July-August 1991, pp. 347-357.

[Coyote89]
Coyote, H., "Spécification et Réalisation d'un Service de Fichiers Fiable pour le Système d'Exploitation Réparti CHORUS", PhD dissertation, University of Paris VI, June 1989.

[Gautron92]
Gautron, P., Jacquemot, C., Jensen, P.S., "The Ouverture Interface Definition Language Specification" Ouverture Technical Report OU/TR-92-5, Esprit Project 6603, 1992.

[Guillemont89]
Guillemont, M., "Architectural Design Document of the Distributed Operating System for the Columbus DMS", Chorus systèmes Technical Report CS/TR-89-21, March 1989.

[Mullender87]
Mullender, S., et al., *The Amoeba Distributed Operating System: Selected Papers 1984-987*, CWI Tract No. 41, Amsterdam, Netherlands, 1987.

[Rozier88]
Rozier, M., Abrossimov, V., Armand, F., Boule, I., Gien, M., Guillemont, M., Léonard, P., Langlois, S., Neuhauser, W., "CHORUS distributed operating systems" *Computing Systems Journal*, Vol. 1, No. 4, December 1988, pp 305-370.

[Veider92]
Veider, A., Eychenne, Y., Schmitz, J., "Fault Tolerance Enablers Support: Problem Definition and Technical Requirements", Ouverture Technical Report OU/TR-92-4, Esprit Project 6603, 1992.

# A Reliable Client-Server Model on Top of a Micro-Kernel

Gilles Muller

IRISA-INRIA
Campus universitaire de Beaulieu
35042 Rennes Cedex, France
*e-mail : Gilles.Muller@irisa.fr*

**Abstract.** The recently emerged micro-kernel technology is now well recognized as a base mechanism for building distributed systems. This paper addresses the problem of designing a fault tolerant operating system while keeping the advantages of the micro-kernel technology. We introduce a solution based on standard workstations and on global consistent state computation using dynamic atomic actions. The advantages of our solution are that it does not introduce RPC performance degradation and that it avoids complete duplication of workstations, thus offering a satisfactory performance/cost ratio.

## 1 Introduction

The recently emerged micro-kernel technology is now well recognized as a base mechanism for building distributed systems. Its main advantages are modularity and the nice integration of the communication model with distribution. Micro-kernel operating systems are generally based on the client-server model, which means that the system is built from a modular set of servers, each implementing some separate functionalities. One of the main contributions of this technology is that system low-level functionalities such as virtual memory can be tailored without requiring a complete system redesign.

Micro-kernels have been successfully used in the design of general purpose operating systems aimed at local area networks. Such architectures are built from a set of "low-cost" workstations or PCs. Due to the increasing reliability of hardware, failures of such machines are becoming hopefully rare. However, failures have still to be tolerated, as user confidence in its system grows proportionally to hardware reliability. In such an environment, the hardware cost of fault tolerance as well as the resulting execution overhead should be as little as possible. As the cost and the overhead grow with the number of tolerated faults, we think that tolerating a single hardware failure is an appropriate compromise.

This paper addresses the problem of designing a reliable operating system, that provides continuous user and system servicing, while keeping advantages of the micro-kernel technology. Introducing reliability without sacrificing to modularity means that the classical client-sever model has to be modified so as to integrate fault tolerance. One of the critical problems encountered in the design of such a model is related to performance, as the overall system performance is directly related to the cost of communication between clients and servers. In the following, we briefly review existing solutions for implementing fault tolerance in distributed systems and exhibit their limitations with respect to our requirements. Then, we introduce our approach comparing it with the well-known transaction model. Finally, we assess our proposal from the perspective of performance.

## 2  Implementing Fault Tolerance in Distributed Systems

Providing fault tolerance in a distributed system requires ensuring two properties: *availability* and *global system consistency*. Availability means that data can be accessed and modified at any time despite crashes of nodes managing the data. In other words, service availability is necessary to offer continuous operation to users. Global system consistency means that the system is able to deal with either the failure of a server, or the failure of a client calling services shared by several clients. In such a situation, the system must be able either to transparently mask the failure, or to roll-back to a previous consistent state.

A natural approach to provide availability is to replicate data on several nodes having independent failure modes. This solution has been successfully used in systems such as ARJUNA [10], DELTA-4 [12], ARGUS [9] and ISIS [3][4] to build highly available services. However, replication leads to an increased message traffic compared to the one implied by the remote procedure call paradigm used in the client-server model. Moreover, replication techniques (active and process group in a less proportion) consume CPU power. Applying such techniques to a complete local area network may lead to duplicate workstations and hence the hardware cost.

As we assumed that failures are rare and that no hard real-time constraints have to be ensured, backward error recovery model seems to be a better solution. In such an approach, computations are restarted after a crash from a previous consistent state saved in a local persistent storage (e.g., a disk stable storage [8]). After backtracking, it is necessary to restart computations from a global persistent state. Well known solutions that are used to calculate global consistent states rely on distributed transactions or dependencies resulting from information exchange between computations [5]. It should be noticed here that as the persistent state is generally local to a node, no continuous servicing is provided.

Up to now, few proposals have been made to integrate a backward error recovery model within a micro-kernel based operating system. Examples of these systems include ORM [7] and CAMELOT [6]. The message based ORM system is based on asynchronous checkpointing, optimized logging using dependencies maps, and message replay. The main advantage of the ORM approach is that the optimized local logging of messages introduces few performance degradation by backgrounding log copy to disk. Furthermore, ORM offers fault tolerance transparency to user processes by integrating fault tolerance management within the kernel and the communication system. The main drawback of ORM, which restricts its usefulness, is that it enforces determinism due to the replay of messages when restarting after a crash. That makes difficult the design of critical subsystems, such as virtual shared memory, without explicit synchronisation within the application program.

Non determinism solutions imply that, after a crash, no replay is performed and that computations restart from a previously saved global persistent state. Popular distributed transaction systems implement such an approach. For example, the CAMELOT system implemented on top of the Mach micro-kernel, allows the design of reliable services using nested transactions. However, if the concurrency model attached to transactions fits perfectly database management requirements, it is not appropriate for low level servers of an operating system: the programmer has to define static units of work (transactions), and, furthermore, locks prevent resource sharing. Consequently, the transaction model cannot be used to design all the system servers. For instance, the CAMELOT virtual memory management server is programmed using write-ahead logging.

## 2.1 Our Approach

Basically, our approach consists in a transaction-like model, offering non-determinism, though modified to remove locks and static units of work [13][2]. The idea is that the execution of an application process results into dynamic distributed sequences of computations, called recovery units; each recovery unit transforms atomically a local persistent state into a new one.

To achieve fault tolerance, we associate with each process state a persistent state, resilient to any single hardware fault. More precisely, a recovery unit is the sequence of instructions performed by a (user or server) process from the saving of the last persistent state. The commitment of a recovery unit is the atomic saving of a process persistent state and the continuation of this process with a new recovery unit. Aborting a recovery unit leads to restore the process persistent state and to restart the process with a new recovery unit.

To allow computation of a global consistent distributed persistent state, it is necessary to keep track of dependencies arising when a client calls a server operation, i.e, between their respective recovery unit. In fact, two situations may involve a dependency: firstly, when the client updates the server internal state, and secondly, when the client lookups a state modified since the last persistent saving, i.e., the beginning of the server recovery unit. Dependency tracking is performed within the RPC implementation: recovery unit UIDs and the resulting dependency are added to the normal message contents.

## 2.2  Global Consistent State Computation

Unlike standard transactions, the commit decision can be initiated dynamically by any recovery unit. When a such a decision is made, we have to save a global consistent system state [5]. To build and atomically save this global state, we use the dependencies that we have identified above to determine the resulting set of dependent recovery units. This is implemented using a chase protocol [11]. The resulting set, called a *dynamic atomic action*, is then committed (resp. aborted) using a modified version of the popular two-phase commit protocol. We call them dynamic for the following reasons.

In traditional transaction based systems, atomic actions are statically defined by the programmer who writes a "begin" and a "commit" commands. The operations belonging to the distributed transaction depend on the nested calls performed by the top-level (see figure 1). Commitment of all the actions is performed when the top-level transaction commits.

In our model, there is no top-level recovery unit; the commit decision can be initiated by any recovery unit which can be either a server or a user. In practice, decision of committing is undertaken by few servers, i.e., those dealing with I/Os. Consequently, very few programmers write a "commit" order. It should be noticed that the initialization of a new recovery unit (the equivalent of the "begin" command of transaction systems), is performed as part of the commit of the previous recovery unit. As in the transaction model, the operations (i.e., the recovery units) belonging to the current dynamic action result from

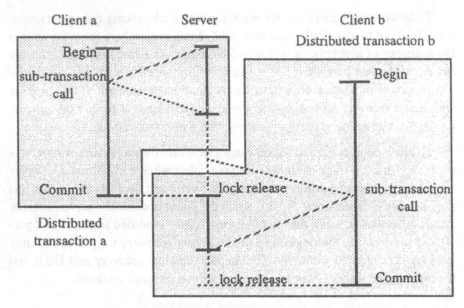

**Fig. 1.** Traditional transaction execution scheme

RPCs. Nevertheless, our model differs in two points: firstly, due to the dependency calculation system, not all the RPCs create a dependency, and secondly, separate client recovery units may be joined as no resource lock is kept. For instance, in figure 2, the first read call from client$_a$ does not create a dependency as the server recovery unit has just started and as the operation reads the server persistent state. On the other hand, the second read call creates a dependency as the server state has been modified by client$_b$. Finally, when the server decides to commit, the dynamic atomic action will contain the recovery units of client$_a$, client$_b$ and the server.

## 2.3 Available Persistent States

Dynamic atomic actions ensure global system consistent state. Providing continuous servicing implies persistent state availability. In a previous study, we have described an efficient RAM implementation of stable storage [1] that provides availability and consistency of data despite machine failure. That work demonstrated the ability to design a low cost fault tolerant distributed system from a network of paired standard machines such as PCs, workstations, upgraded by a fast point to point serial link (200-1000 Mbits). This approach has been undertaken to build the underlaying model architecture.

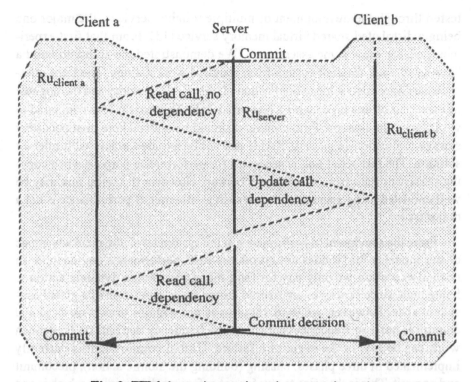

**Fig. 2.** FTM dynamic atomic action execution scheme

In such an architecture each workstation acts as a backup machine for the other workstation of the pair. As for any stable storage implementation, memory has to be duplicated: each workstation memory is divided in a primary bank for its own computation and in a backup bank for the other workstation computation. Commitment of a recovery unit is implemented by copying persistent state through the serial link. As there is no access contention on this type of link and its bandwidth is very high, commit execution takes very few CPU time on the backup workstation. Consequently, all the machines run different jobs in normal operation. However, in the event of a machine failure, the backup has to support the previous load of the two machines.

# 3 Assessments

The proposed reliable client-server model has been experimented within the framework of the FTM project, that aims at building a fault tolerant distributed system on a top of MACH 3.0 micro-kernel. Our system has been successfully tested through the development of multiple reliable services, the major one being a distributed shared virtual memory service [13]. From that first experiment, we can draw some assessments. We demonstrated the ability to build a "low-cost" fault tolerant system from standard workstations. The fault tolerance hardware cost is due to duplication of only RAM memory and the upgrade of each pair of machines with a fast serial link. This cost is low compared to workstation duplication. Furthermore, it should be noticed here, that persistent storage replication (e.g., disk, RAM) can not be avoided in any fault tolerant solution. The fast serial link is necessary for performance purpose when copying persistent state from a bank to its backup. However the serial link may be well emulated using standard network such as ethernet, if performance is not a major issue.

From the standpoint of performance at the system level, the main advantage of our model is that it does not introduces RPC performance degradation. In normal execution we only pay for fault tolerance when a dynamic action is being built, since processes are freezed during the computation of a global consistent state. However, we think that this is not a major drawback as global commit is not a so frequent event where the frequency depends on how much work can be lost in the event of a failure. Global commitment is currently implemented in three phases: chasing (building the atomic action), precommit and commit. This is the price to pay for not enforcing determinism which is one of our major goals. Also, dynamicity of the atomic action introduces the chasing phase that does not exist in transaction systems. In fact, this protocol takes care of complex sharing situations and many optimizations can be implemented. One of our current work is to study new versions of the chasing and commit protocols in order to exhibit better performances in the simple and frequent cases. In the same time, we are pursuing validation of the model implementation through the design of complex reliable services such as a distributed file system.

# References

1. M. Banâtre, G. Muller, B. Rochat, and P. Sanchez. Design Decisions for the FTM: A General Purpose Fault Tolerant Machine. In *Proc. of 21th International Symposium on Fault-Tolerant Computing Systems*, pages 71-78, Montréal, Canada, June 1991.

2.    M. Banâtre, P. Heng, G. Muller, N. Peyrouze and B. Rochat. An Experience in the Design of a Reliable Object Based System. In *Proc of the 2th Conference on Parallel and Distributed Information Systems*, January 1993.

3.    K. P. Birman, Replication and fault-tolerance in the ISIS system. In *Proc. of 10th Symposium on System Principle*, pp. 79-86, December 1985.

4.    K.P. Birman, A. Schiper and P. Stephenson. Lightweight Causal and Atomic Group Multicast. *ACM Transactions on Computer Systems*, vol. 9 (3), August 1991.

5.    K. M. Chandy and L. Lamport. Distributed Snapshots: Determining Global States of Distributed Systems. *ACM Transactions on Computer Systems*, vol 3 (1), pp. 63–75, february 1985.

6.    J. L. Eppinger, L. B. Mummert and A. Z. Spector. Camelot and Avalon: A Distributed Transation Facility. Morgan Kaufmann publishers,inc. San Mateo, 1991.

7.    A. Goldberg, A.Gopal, K. Li, R. Strom and D. F. Bacon. Transparent Recovery of Mach Applications. In USENIX Mach Workshop, pp. 169-183, Burlington, Vermont, October 1990.

8.    B. Lampson. Atomic Transactions. *Distributed Systems and Architecture and Implementation: An Advanced Course*, pp. 246–265, vol. 105, Springer Verlag, Lecture Notes in Computer Science, 1981.

9.    B. Liskov. Implementation of Argus. In *Proc. of the 11th ACM Symposium on Operating Systems Principles*, November 1987.

10.   M. C Little. Object Replication in a Distributed System. Ph. D. Thesis, University of Newcastle, September 1991.

11.   P.M. Merlin and B. Randell. State Restoration in Distributed Systems. In *Proc. of 8th International Symposium on Fault-Tolerant Computing Systems*, pp. 129–134, Toulouse, France, June 1978.

12.   D. Powell. DELTA 4 Overall System Specification. LAAS-CNRS, Toulouse, France, D. Powell editor, 1988.

13.   B. Rochat. Une approche à la construction de services fiables dans les systèmes distribués. Ph. D. Thesis, University of Rennes I, February 1992.

# DISTRIBUTED FAULT TOLERANCE - LESSONS LEARNT FROM DELTA-4*

David Powell

LAAS-CNRS
7 Avenue du Colonel Roche
31077 TOULOUSE Cedex (France)

**Abstract** — Software-implemented approaches to fault-tolerance are very resilient to change since changes in hardware technology do not require extensive re-design of specialized hardware. This paper argues the case for implementing fault-tolerance in a distributed fashion and reports the approach adopted in the European Delta-4 project. Fault-tolerance is achieved by replicating *capsules* (the run-time representation of application objects) on distributed nodes interconnected by a local area network. Capsule groups can be configured to tolerate either stopping failures or arbitrary failures. Multipoint protocols are used for coordinating capsule groups and for error processing and fault treatment. The paper concludes with a critical analysis of the project's results.

## 1. Introduction

Many, if not most, modern computing systems are distributed systems. Distribution is often motivated by organizational reasons (e.g., sharing of data in integrated information systems) or physical constraints (e.g., process control), or it could be simply for economy (e.g., sharing of hardware resources). Lamport, cited in [25], once jokingly defined a distributed system as being "one that stops you getting your work done when a machine you've never heard of crashes". More seriously, but similarly, the *uncertainty* introduced (among other reasons) by the fact that some nodes may be faulty and that communication is unreliable is the main characteristic that enables the class of "distributed" systems to be distinguished from that of "parallel" systems [17]. Lamport's witticism and Fischer's distinction between distribution and parallelism both underline that *dependability* is an inherent concern of distribution. Consequently, *distribution can be a motivation for fault-tolerance* so that users of distributed systems can expect, at worst, a slight degradation in performance should an element "elsewhere" in the system fail.

Of course, fault-tolerance is a necessity, even in non-distributed applications, when extremely high levels of availability or reliability are required. Since it is impossible to achieve fault-tolerance without redundancy, distribution is often regarded as the appropriate paradigm for defining redundancy and managing it to achieve fault-tolerance, i.e., *fault-tolerance can be a motivation for distribution*.

---

\*    This paper is based on an article that is to appear in *IEEE Micro*.

The Delta-4 project investigated this symbiotic relationship between distribution and fault-tolerance in order to define an Open System Architecture (OSA)[1] with distributed fault-tolerance [26]. *Distributed fault-tolerance* is taken here to mean software-implemented fault-tolerance achieved solely by message-passing between the nodes of a distributed system. The nodes constitute the units of hardware redundancy and can communicate (only) by means of a message-passing communication system (in Delta-4, a local area network). The architecture is *open* in that it is (a) based on open distributed processing concepts and, whenever possible, OSI communication standards and (b) uses standard off-the-shelf processors and standard local area network technology with minimum specialized hardware.

The paper is organized as follows. Section 2 discusses fault and failure assumptions that are appropriate for highly dependable distributed fault-tolerant systems in general and Delta-4 in particular. Section 3 introduces the key aspects of the Delta-4 hardware architecture. The Delta-4 software architecture and its communication system are then presented in section 4. Section 5 details the error-processing and fault treatment mechanisms that provide fault-tolerance. Finally, section 6 discusses the lessons that were learnt and the conclusions that can be drawn now that the project has been completed.

## 2. Fault and Failure Assumptions

The two motivations for distributed fault-tolerance outlined in the introduction (viz. distribution-motivated fault-tolerance versus fault-tolerance-motivated distribution) correspond not only to different viewpoints but often also to different application contexts. The reasons for fault-tolerance in each context are quite different and thus so are the relevant assumptions about faults and failures.

### 2.1. Distribution-Motivated Fault-Tolerance

Distribution-motivated fault-tolerance is often the realm of "networked computer systems" where the distributed system is viewed as a collection of autonomous nodes, each under the control of a separate user and/or administrator. The applications in this context are often not really critical. A given user will quite likely be very lenient towards crashes of his own workstation (after all, he is probably the only one to blame) but much less so if he is frequently bothered by "failures" of other nodes. Fault-tolerance mechanisms could be implemented to hide the effects of quite mundane incidents affecting a remote node such as a power outage, a crash of its local operating system (e.g., due to a software bug), a scheduled maintenance intervention, a network incident leading to communication disconnection or quite simply because its user turned it off before going home! All these incidents could be perceived as annoying faults by a user elsewhere if he is prevented from carrying out his work (cf. the Lamport syndrome mentioned in the introduction).

---

[1]  The project also experimented with a variant of this architecture, called the *eXtra-Perfomance Architecture* (XPA), in which openness was sacrificed in the pursuit of higher performance for real-time applications [35]. This paper, however, will focus on OSA.

Consequently, "fault-tolerance" in such systems is often interpreted as meaning the tolerance of the inaccessibility or unavailability of other nodes, where "unavailable" is understood to mean "as if it wasn't there". The designers of distributed fault-tolerance mechanisms under this viewpoint implicitly assume that nodes are "fail-silent" [28], i.e., they either carry out their intended function or, as seen from the rest of the system, they just "disappear".

One final consideration concerning this category of system is the unreliability of the underlying communication network. This network is usually shared with other applications or even other organizations so the designer of a distributed service or application can have little influence on its design. It may therefore be necessary for the application designer to envisage specific fault-tolerance techniques to deal with network partitioning.

## 2.2. Fault-Tolerance-Motivated Distribution

In fault-tolerance-motivated distributed systems, the emphasis is on achieving very high levels of dependability when compared to a fault-intolerant (non-distributed) system. The applications of such systems are typically much more critical than in the previous case. The failure of a distributed application could have very dire economic consequences or even result in the loss of life. Consequently, much attention is paid to the definition of the components that are the elements of distribution (redundant fault containment regions), the faults that the system can tolerate, the way by which components fail and the means by which they are interconnected.

The basic premise of distributed fault-tolerance is that faults affecting processes executed by different nodes are independent, so nodes are natural candidates for defining fault containment regions. This hypothesis is of course quite reasonable for internal accidental faults [21], or *physical faults*. It is also quite fair to assume independence in the manifestations of external accidental faults (or *disasters*) such as fire, floods, etc. if the nodes are sufficiently far apart from one another. Interestingly, it is also quite reasonable for some[2] accidental *design faults* since the differences in local execution environments of processes on different nodes can cause some such faults to manifest themselves in different ways. Gray refers to such faults as "Heisenbugs" because "they go away when you look at them" [18]. Some interesting statistics regarding such faults in the Guardian90[3] operating system are presented in [22]. Now, it is not only necessary to consider the types of faults that the system is to tolerate but also to envisage the admissible effects of these faults on node (or process) behavior, i.e., node failure modes.

In fault-tolerance-motivated distributed systems, the aim is to distribute computation over a collection of redundant nodes, possibly in the same physical box, to provide the illusion of a single virtual machine that never fails. This single virtual machine may have multiple users but is under the control of a single administrator. The nodes in such a machine would not be expected to randomly "disappear" due to users turning

---

[2] Note, however, that high coverage of design faults can only be achieved through diverse design techniques [10, 29].

[3] *Guardian90* is a registered trademark of *Tandem Computers, Inc.*

them off or re-booting them. Since high dependability is the primary aim of distribution in this case, the system is also usually globally protected against power failures and the interconnect network is itself purpose-designed to be fault-tolerant. Overall, the nodes in such a distributed, fault-tolerant machine can be considered as being more reliable than those considered under the "computer network" viewpoint. However, the causes of node failure that we argue as being less relevant in a more tightly coupled, distributed fault-tolerant machine (i.e., shutdowns, re-boots, power outages, network disconnections, OS crashes) are the very ones that largely justify the fail-silent node assumption in a computer network environment. Is it reasonable to assume that the remaining causes of node failure result in nodes failing only by crashing?

The "reasonableness" of any such failure mode assumption is captured by the notion of *assumption coverage* defined as the probability of the assumption being true when a node fails [27] In this case, the coverage of a crash-only assumption is equivalent to the coverage of any self-checking mechanisms built into the nodes aimed at silencing the node should a fault occur. If the self-checking coverage is commensurate with the required application dependability, then it is justifiable to assume that nodes fail only by crashing. Otherwise, it is necessary to make weaker assumptions and devise distributed fault-tolerance techniques that can accommodate more severe modes of failure such as omission failures, timing failures, etc., or even completely arbitrary failures [14, 27]. As described in the next section, Delta-4 follows what could be perceived as a "fence-sitting approach" whereby both strong and weak failure mode assumptions can be adopted according to the criticality of the considered application and to knowledge about the available hardware.

## 3. Hardware Architecture

The Delta-4 architecture is an *open* architecture that can employ *off-the-shelf hardware* to provide fault-tolerance in money-critical (but not life-critical) applications. Fault-tolerance is achieved by the replication of code and data on different computational nodes interconnected by a local area network.

Since the self-checking coverage of off-the-shelf hardware is often insufficient for the crash-only failure assumption to be justified, the architecture allows very critical applications to be configured so that *arbitrary* failures can be tolerated. However, the constraints and the cost of tolerating arbitrary failures are not always warranted, so the Delta-4 architecture also provides simpler mechanisms when stronger failure assumptions are admissible. Both approaches can be followed, even in the same system, for different applications.

Off-the-shelf hardware can be assumed to be either *fail-silent* (crash-only) or *fail-uncontrolled* (admitting arbitrary modes of failure). Unfortunately, if complete nodes can fail arbitrarily then the interconnection scheme must be made much more complex than the single (or possibly, duplex) broadcast channel that would be sufficient for fail-silent nodes. For example, a fail-uncontrolled node connected to multiple channels could fail by saturating all channels, thus bringing down the complete system. Furthermore, protocols for ensuring agreement under such a failure mode assumption are notoriously complex and time consuming. The Delta-4 architecture therefore follows a hybrid approach whereby each node is split into two sub-systems (figure 1):

- an off-the-shelf computation component, called a *host*, that may be fail-uncontrolled;

- a communication component, called a *network attachment controller* (NAC), that is assumed to be fail-silent.

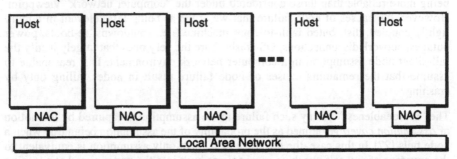

**Figure 1** — Hardware Architecture

The fail-silence assumption for the network attachment controllers alleviates the problems stated earlier regarding the use of broadcast channels and agreement protocol complexity. The NACs of each station are interconnected by a standard LAN (8802.4 or 8802.5). Duplex (or even simplex) channels have been shown to be sufficient for achieving a very low probability of communication system failure in the maintainable environments for which Delta-4 is intended [20]. The communication system is therefore considered as hardcore and no attempt is made at the application level to tolerate physical network partitioning.

The network attachment controller consists of a pair of piggy-backed cards that plugs into the host's back-plane bus and interfaces the node with the physical communication channels. The NAC is very similar to any other standard LAN controller card; the only difference is that it uses built-in hardware self-checking to substantiate the assumption that it is fail-silent. Self-checking is achieved by classic duplication and comparison techniques for the main processing part of the NAC in conjunction with a watchdog timer. A hardware-implemented memory protection scheme is also used to prevent corruption of the NAC memory by some fail-uncontrolled behavior of the host. Duplication could not be carried out in the low-level interface to the network due to the impossibility of synchronizing the specialized LAN-specific VLSI components; coverage of faults in this part of the NAC therefore relies on the built-in error detection capabilities of these components.

## 4. Software Architecture and Communication System

The NACs are the only specialized hardware components in the Delta-4 Open System Architecture; the remainder of the Delta-4 functionality and mechanisms for fault-tolerance is implemented by system software on top of either the hosts' local operating systems or the NACs' real-time kernels. The system software can be split into three main components (figure 2):

- a host-resident infrastructure for supporting distributed applications;

- a computation and communication administration system (executing partly on the hosts and partly on the NACs);

- a multipoint communication protocol stack (executing on the NACs).

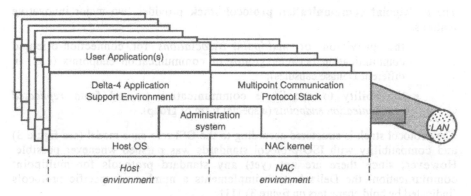

**Figure 2** — Software Architecture

A particular host-resident infrastructure for supporting open *object-oriented* distributed computation was developed for the Delta-4 architecture: the *Delta-4 Application Support Environment* (Deltase) [5]. According to the philosophy of "open" distributed processing, Deltase facilitates the use of heterogeneous languages for implementing the various objects of a distributed application. It provides the means for generating and supporting interactions between run-time software components called "capsules" (executable representations of objects). Deltase provides a run-time environment that allows the differences in underlying local operating systems to be hidden — in practice though, all the implemented Delta-4 prototypes are based on UNIX[4] whereby Deltase capsules map onto UNIX processes.

The **administration system** provides the mechanisms for managing a Delta-4 system: it consists of both support for *network management* in the classic sense as well as support for *computation management*. The three basic tasks carried out by the administration system are:

- configuration management, which provides support for planning and integration of redundancy and distribution;

- performance management, which includes system status monitoring by event counting and polling;

- fault management, including automatic fault treatment and support for maintenance interventions.

The administration system is based on the notions of *managed objects* and *domain managers*. A managed object is a hardware or software component (e.g., a Deltase capsule) that, besides its normal functionality, is formally characterized by *attributes*, *operations* and *events* by which the component can be observed and controlled. A domain manager is a system server that is responsible for managing a set or *domain* of

---

4    *UNIX* is a registered trademark of *UNIX Systems Laboratories, Inc.*

similar or related managed objects. Of particular relevance to fault-tolerance is the notion of a *replication domain manager* for carrying out fault treatment (more on this later).

The **multipoint communication protocol stack** provides two major innovative features:

- the provision of *multipoint associations* for connection-oriented communication between groups of communication endpoints (e.g., in different Deltase capsules);
- the ability to coordinate communication to and from *replicated communication endpoints* (a special form of group).

The protocol stack is structured according to the OSI reference model (see figure 3) and compatibility with ISO protocol standards was pursued whenever possible. However, since there are not (yet) any standard protocols for multipoint communication, the Delta-4 stack implements a number of specific protocols (indicated by bold characters on figure 3) [11].

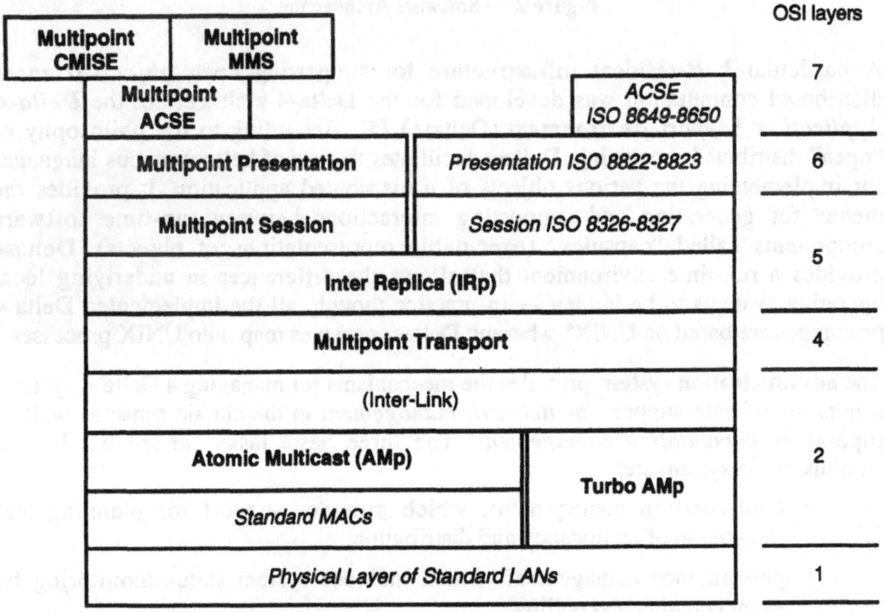

| | | OSI layers |
|---|---|---|
| **Multipoint CMISE** **Multipoint MMS** | | 7 |
| **Multipoint ACSE** | *ACSE ISO 8649-8650* | |
| **Multipoint Presentation** | *Presentation ISO 8822-8823* | 6 |
| **Multipoint Session** | *Session ISO 8326-8327* | 5 |
| **Inter Replica (IRp)** | | |
| **Multipoint Transport** | | 4 |
| **(Inter-Link)** | | |
| **Atomic Multicast (AMp)** | **Turbo AMp** | 2 |
| *Standard MACs* | | |
| *Physical Layer of Standard LANs* | | 1 |

**Figure 3** — The multipoint communication protocol stack

The core of the Delta-4 group communication mechanisms is the *Atomic Multicast protocol* (AMp), which is implemented within layer 2 on top of a standard medium access control protocol.[5] This is a two-phase accept protocol that allows data frames to

---

[5] Another version of this protocol (called "Turbo AMp") was specially targeted at the 8802-5 token ring and was implemented as a hardware and firmware extension of the existing token ring medium access control protocol.

be delivered to a group of logically designated *gates*. The protocol ensures *unanimity*, i.e., that frames are either delivered to all addressed gates on non-faulty nodes or to none of them (this can occur if the sender fails or if a recipient gate cannot accept a frame due to lack of receive credit). The protocol also ensures that frames are delivered to all addressed gates in a consistent *order* and that any changes in *membership* of a gate group (due to node failure or re-insertion) are notified consistently to all members of that group.

All communication entities are executed on the real-time kernels of the fail-silent network attachment controllers (NACs). A communication entity is therefore assumed to react in bounded time in the absence of NAC failure or otherwise crash. If messages are never lost and delivered in bounded time, remote crashes can be reliably detected by time-outs on responses to protocol frames. However, real networks can lose messages so time redundancy by message retry is used to give the illusion of such a perfect network. AMp incorporates a frame retry mechanism that tolerates a pre-defined number (called *omission degree*) of successive omission failures (this in fact also allows a weaker assumption, called *weak fail-silence*, to be made about the NAC failure mode [34]. If a remote entity does not respond after the pre-defined number of retries, it is assumed to have crashed. This triggers the distributed election of an *active monitor* that ensures that any interrupted multicasts are completed (to ensure unanimity) and that all group participants are informed of the new view of the group membership [36].

On top of AMp, the Inter-Link protocol extends the AMp service to interconnections of LANs. The Multipoint Transport protocol is a light connection-oriented protocol that adds segmentation, reassembly and flow control functions to the underlying service. The next sub-layer is the Inter-Replica protocol (IRp) which is at the heart of the Delta-4 fault-tolerance mechanisms. This protocol coordinates communication to and from endpoints that are *replicated* on different nodes such that replication is hidden from the sources and the destinations of messages sent to or by the considered endpoint. This involves not only the transparent delivery of messages to all endpoint replicas (using the underlying multicasting) but also requires arbitration between send events across the set of endpoint replicas such that destinations only receive a single message. This arbitration can optionally include error-detection or error-detection-and-compensation by comparison of replicated messages.

The IRp services can be used either by standard ISO upper-layer protocols or by upper-layer multipoint protocols specific to Delta-4 that allow connection-oriented communication between groups of logically distinct communication endpoints.

## 5. Fault-Tolerance

*Capsules*, the run-time representations of Deltase objects, are the units of replication used in Delta-4 to achieve fault-tolerance. Capsules may be replicated independently so that fault-tolerance can be specified and configured on a flexible, service-by-service basis. The programmer of a Deltase object does not need to know that the capsule corresponding to the object he is programming — or indeed, of any other object with which it communicates — may be replicated[6].

There are two facets to the achievement of fault-tolerance by replicated processing:

(1)     how should the interactions between a replicated capsule and other (possibly-replicated) capsules be managed so that the latter are unaware that some of the former's replicas may be faulty;

(2)     how can the number of capsule replicas be maintained at or restored to the level required to maintain the illusion created in (1) above, despite the occurrence of further failures.

These two issues are respectively related to *error processing* and *fault treatment* [21, 23].

## 5.1.  Error Processing

To achieve fault-tolerance on a capsule-by-capsule basis, error processing is carried out entirely within the scope of each group of replicas without resorting, for example, to the use of transactions or conversations to coordinate error processing over logically distinct capsules. This means that errors must be confined within replica groups — any recovery or compensation action taken within a given group must not require actions to be taken by any other group.

Three different, but complementary, techniques have been investigated and implemented in the Delta-4 architecture: *active*, *passive* and *semi-active* replication.

*Active replication* is a technique in which all replicas process all input messages concurrently so that their internal states are closely synchronized — in the absence of faults, outputs can be taken from any replica. The active replication approach allows quasi-instantaneous recovery from a node failure. Furthermore, it is adapted to both the fail-silent and fail-uncontrolled node assumptions since messages produced by different (active) replicas can be cross-checked (in value and time). However, active replication requires that all replicas be guaranteed to be *deterministic* in the absence of faults, i.e., it must be guaranteed that if non-faulty replicas process identical input message streams, they will produce identical output message streams. One way of achieving this it to oblige the programmer to ensure that capsules behave as state machines [31].

Active replication in Delta-4 is managed directly by means of the Inter-Replica protocol (IRp) briefly described in the previous section [12] The communication endpoints of actively replicated capsules are themselves replicated and configured either according to a fail-silent assumption (only late-timing errors are detected) or a fail-uncontrolled assumption (both timing and value errors are detected). Any detected errors cause the incriminated endpoint replica to be aborted and are reported to the administration system to initiate fault treatment.

---

6   Objects must however be programmed to ensure deterministic execution if active replication is to be used.

Active replication has also been studied (under various names), in the SIFT [24], CIRCUS [13], ISIS [7] and AAS [15] projects. To our knowledge, however, the Delta-4 implementation is the only one that manages replicated output messages at their logical source rather than at their destination and allows arbitrary (host) failures to be tolerated over a general (non-meshed) communication network[7].

*Passive replication* is a technique in which only one of the replicas (the primary replica) processes the input messages and provides output messages — in the absence of faults, the other replicas (the standby replicas) do not process input messages and do not produce output messages; their internal states are however regularly updated by means of checkpoints systematically sent by the primary replica every time that it sends a message. Passive replication can only be envisaged if it is assumed that nodes are fail-silent. Unlike active replication, this technique does not require computation to be deterministic [32]. However, the performance overheads of systematic checkpoints[8] and rolling-back for recovery may not be acceptable in certain applications — especially in real-time applications.

Passive replication in Delta-4 is managed by system code, called a *rep_entity*, included in a capsule when an application object is compiled. The primary rep_entity atomically multicasts all data messages and associated checkpoints to the standby rep_entities. Both the primary and the standby rep_entities then forward data messages to their final destination(s) using the replicated endpoint mechanism of the IRp protocol to ensure that exactly one message is sent, even if the primary fails.

Passive replication is essentially the same approach as the well-known process pair approach used in the Tandem Guardian operating system [4]. In Delta-4, however, as in ISIS [7] and AAS [15], passively replicated groups can include more than just one standby replica, so near-coincident failures can be handled.

*Semi-active replication* can be viewed as a hybrid of both active and passive replication; only one of the replicas (the leader replica) processes all input messages and provides output messages — in the absence of faults, the other replicas (the follower replicas) do not produce output messages; their internal state is updated either by direct processing of input messages or, where appropriate, by means of *notifications* (or "mini-checkpoints") from the leader replica. Semi-active replication seeks to achieve the low recovery overheads of active replication while relaxing the constraints on computation determinism — notifications can be used to force the followers to obey all non-deterministic decisions made by the leader replica.

Semi-active replication, or the *leader-follower* model as it is sometimes known, was initially developed in the context of the Delta-4 eXtra Performance Architecture [3, 35] since it has some interesting real-time properties. First, notifications can be used to inform follower replicas about the order in which messages are consumed by the leader replica. This means that messages no longer need to be sent by the totally

---

7    To be fair, although Cooper [13] assumed that processors only failed by crashing, he did study the concept of a "collator" to vote on multiple replies from "non-deterministic" server replicas.

8    Similar techniques based on *periodic* instead of systematic checkpointing achieve a lower checkpointing overhead (in the absence of faults) but sacrifice the possibility for accommodating non-deterministic computation [9].

ordered atomic multicast protocol but can use a higher performance "reliable" multicast protocol (a protocol ensuring unanimity but not order[9]). It also allows high priority messages to "jump the queue" without introducing inconsistencies across the replica group. Second, notifications can be used to implement consistent preemption of computation across a replica group. This requires the introduction (by a pre-compiler) of *preemption points* that pre-define the points in computation at which execution may be preempted. When a follower replica reaches a preemption point, it awaits a notification from the leader replica that tells it whether to continue (to the next preemption point or to a later one) or to let a specified input message preempt computation at that point.

The semi-active replication technique can also be used for replicating large "off-the-shelf" software components about which no assumption can be made on replica determinism and internal states (e.g., commercially available database management software). However, this cannot be a generic mechanism. It involves either identifying potential sources of non-determinism in the source code (if this is available) or providing a purpose-designed front-end to the replicas that maintain consistency by means of semantic-dependent leader-follower notifications. This technique was used with success to replicate an Oracle[10] database [5].

At first sight, the semi-active replication technique requires nodes to be fail-silent since the notifications from a faulty leader could otherwise propagate errors to the followers. However, this restriction could be relaxed if each notification indicated the choice made by the leader among a pre-defined *finite* set of decisions. If the notification received from a faulty leader indicates a decision inside this finite set then, although the leader may not have taken that decision, the followers can still follow that decision since it a valid one. If the received notification is not in the finite set, then all the followers can detect this and take a default decision. In both cases, errors in the output messages from the leader and follower replicas can be detected and compensated by means of the IRp protocol. Even if the more restrictive fail-silent assumption is adopted (which was the case for the implementations of this technique that were actually carried out), the IRp protocol allows arbitration between messages sent by the leader and follower replicas to ensure that exactly one message is sent, even if the leader fails.

### 5.2. Fault Treatment

The error processing techniques described in the previous section allow capsule interactions to proceed even though a sub-set of replicas of each capsule may be faulty. However, if nothing more is done then subsequent faults could cause a majority or all the replicas in a group to fail, thereby leading to system failure. Such exhaustion of redundancy is avoided by *fault treatment*, which is one of the rôles of the administration system.

---

[9] A multi-primitive extended atomic multicast protocol (xAMp) was developed in the XPA architecture that allowed such a "reliable" multicast option to be selected as a specified *quality of service* [30]

[10] *Oracle* is a registered trademark of *Oracle Corp.*

Fault treatment in Delta-4 is best explained by means of an example. Figure 4 illustrates a simple Delta-4 system with five nodes, each split into its constituent host and NAC components. The figure shows two triplicated application capsules, $P$ and $Q$, whose replicas have been initially allocated to node sets {1, 2, 4} and {2, 3, 5} respectively. The other entities on the figure will be defined during the following explanation of the fault treatment actions that occur following the activation of a fault in node 5. It is assumed in the following that $P$ and $Q$ use active replication (they both have replicated endpoints on any application associations to which they are connected) — the fault treatment actions for the other replication paradigms are similar.

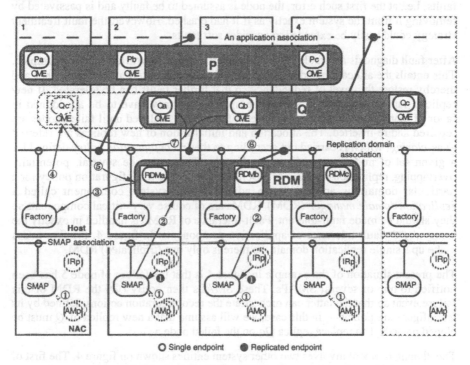

**Figure 4** — Error reporting and fault treatment

Fault treatment involves *fault diagnosis*, *fault passivation* and *system reconfiguration*. *Fault diagnosis* is necessary to localize the fault (i.e., the source of detected errors) and to decide whether *fault passivation* is necessary to prevent the fault from causing further errors. Faults that are judged to not require passivation are called *soft* faults, fault that do are *solid* faults [21].

A fault that results in node crash is automatically "passivated" by the very notion of fail-silence. The location of the fault is made known to all participants of any active AMp group that spans the failed node since it results in a group membership change. Any such AMp group change event is reported (①) to a local system administration component called a *System Management Application Process* (SMAP), of which there is one executing on every NAC in the system. All other SMAPs are then consistently informed of the group change through a multipoint association linking all the SMAPs.

Faults that result in failure other than a node crash, i.e., faults that cause the host to violate the fail-silence assumption, can only be detected if active replication is employed. In this case, discrepancies in the values or the timing of replica output messages are detected by the replicated endpoint entities executing the Inter-Replica protocol (IRp). Any detected errors cause the incriminated endpoint replica to be aborted and are reported locally (❶) to the SMAPs of the stations on which the replicas reside. Any faults revealed by IRp error-detection are considered to be solid faults, i.e., at the first such error, the node is assumed to be faulty and is passivated by removing it from the system exactly as if it had crashed. However, the fault treatment strategy could easily be extended to consider soft faults.

After fault diagnosis and fault passivation, **system reconfiguration** can be attempted. This entails the allocation and initialization of new replicas to replace failed ones and thereby restore the level of redundancy so that further faults can be tolerated. If new replicas cannot be allocated then some applications may have to be abandoned in favor of more critical ones or system reconfiguration is delayed until failed nodes are repaired and re-inserted. The allocation and initialization of new replicas are referred to as *cloning*, which is carried out according to the *reconfiguration policy* defined for a given set of nodes, or *replication domain*. There may be several, potentially overlapping, replication domains in a Delta-4 system. The reconfiguration policy for a particular domain is applied by an administration system component called a *replication domain manager* (RDM). RDMs are of course very critical components so they should be made fault-tolerant. Fault-tolerance of RDMs is handled in exactly the same way as fault-tolerance of application components. In figure 4, the five nodes make up a single replication domain, so there is only one (triplicated) RDM.

The present situation of the example in figure 4 is that the failure of node 5 has been notified to one or several SMAPs. These SMAPs then notify (②) the RDM of this failure event so that the latter can orchestrate the reconfiguration actions defined by its reconfiguration policy — in this case, we will assume that a new replica of $Q$ must be cloned on node 1 to replace replica $Qc$ on the failed node 5.

The cloning protocol involves two other system entities shown on figure 4. The first of these is the *Object Management Entity* (OME) linked to each capsule at compile time. An OME extends the user-defined functionality of a capsule to include management services for initializing and cloning replicas of the capsule. The second entity is a separate administration component, called a *Factory*. A logically distinct factory is installed on every node in the system and is responsible for local instantiation of capsule replicas. The OMEs of each replicated capsule and the RDM have replicated endpoints on a domain-wide multipoint association (called the replication domain association on figure 4). Each factory is also connected to this association through a single (non-replicated) endpoint.

The cloning protocol proceeds as follows:

- the RDM requests (③) the factory on node 1 to create (④) a local "template" of $Q$ (from a local copy of the program file);

- during its initialization phase, the OME of this "fledgling" replica *(Qc')* establishes the communication endpoints necessary for communication with the RDM and confirms (⑤) this to the RDM;

- the RDM then instructs (⑥) the OMEs of *Qa* and *Qb* to transfer (clone) their process context to the new replica;

- the OMEs of *Qa* and *Qb* take a "snapshot" of their local context (data, stack, registers, ...) and initiate the transfer (⑦) of this context to the OME of *Qc'*;

- when all the context data has been transferred, the OME of *Qc'* substitutes the current process context with the received context data and continues execution with that context as a full-fledged replica (after synchronizing with the OMEs of *Qa* and *Qb*).

The actual transfer of context data is subjected to the same IRp error-detection (message comparison) as any other communication from replicated components. This means that near-coincident faults activated during cloning can be confined (or even tolerated if sufficient initial replication is used). However, this means that any location-specific context data must be identified and "equalized" before transfer to avoid the natural differences in such data being perceived as errors [16].

The fault treatment facilities outlined above enable the level of redundancy of replicated capsules to be restored automatically as long as there are sufficient non-failed resources in the system. Nodes that have failed and been disconnected from the system can be tested off-line, repaired if necessary, and then re-inserted into the system. However, such re-inserted nodes are considered by the system to be entirely new nodes with total amnesia regarding their previous "existence". When a node is (re-)inserted into the system, the replication policy can allow for a re-distribution of replicas to balance the overall load.

## 6. Conclusion — Lessons Learnt

The Delta-4 project started in March 1986 and terminated in January 1992. Although the project's results have not been commercially deployed to any great extent, due to the overall economic situation of the computing industry at the time the project drew to an end, the project was technically very successful. Several fully-integrated prototypes were implemented — and extensively validated [19] — that demonstrated the feasibility of distributed fault-tolerance techniques for heterogeneous off-the-shelf hardware. During the project's lifetime, several hardware technology updates occurred with little or no impact on the system software, which strikingly demonstrates one of the major advantages of a software-implemented approach to fault-tolerance. Other advantages of the approach are that it provides a degree of disaster tolerance and design-fault tolerance.

The project successfully demonstrated that active replication can be used to tolerate arbitrary failures in systems seeking to achieve high dependability with off-the-shelf hardware interconnected by standard local area networks. Such tolerance does not come without a price, however, since writers of application software must respect certain rules to achieve deterministic fault-free execution. What, however, is the alternative if off-the-shelf hardware is to be used to implement *highly dependable* systems? If one were to conjecture that the off-the-shelf hardware in question only fails in a less severe fashion, e.g., by crashing, then one could adopt the alternative passive and/or semi-active replication techniques. However, as discussed in section 2, any such assumption should be justified by an estimation of the accompanying coverage and the demonstration that this coverage is commensurate with the overall dependability objective. Estimation of the actual coverage requires failure mode statistics to be gathered either in operational life or by fault injection in prototypes. Note, however, that any upgrade in hardware technology will often require a completely new estimation of the corresponding coverage. Also, it should be noted the error detection coverage achieved with "traditional" (off-the-shelf) computer hardware is often quite low unless extensive self-checking techniques are employed (see for example, the coverage figures given below for the early NAC prototypes used in Delta-4, which can be considered as such "traditional" computer hardware with limited self-checking).

Another aspect that should be taken into account when considering active replication is that of interfacing the actively replicated capsules with the outside world. Whereas active replication is eminently suitable for managing voting on multiple sensors[11], or for driving voting actuators, it is much less so when replication must be entirely hidden from the outside world, for example, when setting up a connection over a public network to a non-Delta-4 site. In such cases, the (necessarily-unique) Delta-4 site that manages the external connection becomes a hardcore. Although (application-specific) procedures can be implemented to tolerate crashes of such an I/O site, any failure of more arbitrary nature could lead to failure of the complete Delta-4 system. Management of such "single-sited" I/O forces adoption of the fail-silence assumption for the I/O site(s) and the overall dependability will be largely determined by the attendant lack of coverage, even if less severe assumptions are made for the other sites in the system.

As discussed in section 3, the key to tolerating arbitrary failures without resorting to costly interconnect hardware and/or agreement protocols is the concept of a fail-silent network attachment controller (NAC) associated with each (off-the-shelf) host computer. A NAC is a single-board 68xxx computer with local memory and a LAN controller. In this component — the only hardware component specific to the Delta-4 architecture — the fail-silence assumption is substantiated by a self-checking implementation and the corresponding error-detection coverage was estimated using fault injection techniques [1]. The early NAC prototypes used in Delta-4 had rather limited self-checking features: bus parity checking and a hardware watchdog. For these early, limited self-checking NACs, the estimated 1-second latency error-detection coverage was only 30%. Even after 100 seconds' latency, the estimated error detection coverage was still only 75% [2]. Consequently, the NAC design was extensively revised to include duplex hardware with cross comparison. This led to a significant improvement since the 1-second and 100-second latency error-detection coverages were then estimated to be 97% and 99%, respectively [2]. Further improvements in NAC error-detection coverage were hampered by the presence of low-level LAN-controller chips, which could not be duplexed and compared due to inaccessible, and therefore non-synchronizable, internal clock circuitry. Higher self-

---

[11] Of course, voting cannot be carried out directly on input values from replicated sensors. For a triplicated sensor, a three-way multicast is required to ensure interactive consistency before applying an averaging function to the resulting vector.

checking coverage would therefore have required re-design of some quite complex VLSI chips.

The Delta-4 approach to distributed fault-tolerance relies heavily on the use of multipoint communication protocols. Such protocols are in fact extremely useful for simplifying distributed computation in general, irrespectively of fault-tolerance. For example, the Delta-4 administration system was significantly simplified due to the availability of multipoint associations that could span all nodes, or all nodes in a particular replication domain (cf. figure 4).

The core group communication protocol, AMp, was implemented at the lowest possible level, at layer 2 in according to the ISO reference model (cf. section 4). One positive consequence of this design decision was that node or NAC crash detection was reliable and usually quite fast. Sometimes, however, a crash can remain undetected by the rest of the system if none of the AMp groups that spans the crashed node are active, i.e., attempting to exchange messages. However, this could easily be improved by imposing an artificial, minimum frequency AMp traffic that spans all nodes. This artificial traffic could be throttled back to save bandwidth if real AMp traffic is sufficiently high to ensure low crash-detection latency.

The low-layer implementation of AMp proved to be somewhat of an impediment to the distribution and uptake of the Delta-4 group communication facilities since it was difficult to envisage porting Delta-4 to an existing networked environment. In contrast, the ISIS team first chose to implement multicasting on top of the widely available UDP [6, 8] which enabled widespread distribution of the ISIS toolkit in the research community and beyond. It is interesting to note, however, that the ISIS team are now considering putting their core mechanisms much closer to the network interface [33].

Finally, although it is difficult for distributed fault-tolerance techniques such as those developed in Delta-4 to compete with the performance that can be obtained using hardware-intensive tightly-synchronized approaches, it is the author's firm belief that the economic and flexibility advantages of software-implemented, distributed fault-tolerance techniques will soon emerge as a major option for highly-dependable systems, especially in distributed workstation environments. In particular, the advent of microkernel technology opens new and exciting possibilities for high-performance, user-transparent, software-implemented fault-tolerance.

## Acknowledgements

The Delta-4 project was partially supported by the Commission of the European Community through the Esprit program (projects 818 and 2252). The consortium for project 2252 consisted of Bull SA (France), Crédit Agricole (France), Ferranti International (UK), IEI-CNR (Italy), IITB-Fraunhofer (Germany), INESC (Portugal), LAAS-CNRS (France), LGI-IMAG (France), MARI (UK), SRD-AEA Technology (UK), Renault (France), SEMA Group (France) and the University of Newcastle (UK).

Many persons contributed to the Delta-4 project over its six-year lifetime. They are far too numerous for me thank individually but I would like to express my gratitude to them all for their professionalism, their enthusiasm and the splendid *esprit de corps* that reigned within the project team. Special and very personal thanks must of course go to "the Davids", Doug, Gottfried, Marc, Pascal, Paulo, Peter and Santosh, as well as all my compeers in the Dependable Computing group at LAAS.

## References

1.  J. Arlat, M. Aguera, Y. Crouzet, J. Fabre, E. Martins, D. Powell: Experimental Evaluation of the Fault Tolerance of an Atomic Multicast Protocol. *IEEE Trans. Reliability*, 39, 455-467, 1990.

2.  J. Arlat, Y. Crouzet, E. Martins, D. Powell: Dependability Testing Report LA3 - Fault-Injection on the Extended Self-Checking NAC. LAAS-CNRS, Report, N°91396, December 1991.

3.  P. A. Barrett, A. M. Hilborne, P. G. Bond, D. T. Seaton, P. Veríssimo, L. Rodrigues, N. A. Speirs: The Delta-4 Extra Performance Architecture (XPA). *Proc. 20th Int. Symp. on Fault-Tolerant Computing Systems (FTCS-20)* (Newcastle upon Tyne, UK). IEEE Computer Society Press, 1990, pp. 481-488 .

4.  J. Bartlett, J. Gray, B. Horst: Fault Tolerance in Tandem Computer Systems. In: A. Avizienis, H. Kopetz, J.-C. Laprie (eds.): *The Evolution of Fault-Tolerant Systems*. Dependable Computing and Fault-Tolerant Systems (1). Vienna: Springer-Verlag, 1987, pp. 55-76.

5.  D. Benson, B. Gilmore, D. Seaton: Delta-4 Application Support Environment. In: D. Powell (ed.): *Delta-4: a Generic Architecture for Dependable Distributed Computing*. Berlin, Germany: Springer Verlag, 1991, pp. 125-163.

6.  K. P. Birman, T. A. Joseph: Reliable Communication in the Presence of Failures. *ACM Trans. Computer Systems*, 5, 47-76, 1987.

7.  K. P. Birman, T. A. Joseph: Exploiting Replication in Distributed Systems. In: S. Mullender (ed.): *Distributed Systems*. New York: ACM Press, 1989, pp. 319-367.

8.  K. P. Birman, A. Schiper, P. Stephenson: Lightweight Causal and Atomic Group Multicast. *ACM Trans. Computer Systems*, 9, 272-314, 1991.

9.  A. Borg, J. Baumbach, S. Glazer: A Message System supporting Fault Tolerance. *Proc. 9th Symp. on Operating System Principles*. ACM, 1983, pp. 90-99 .

10. L. Chen, A. Avizienis: N-Version-Programming: A Fault-Tolerance Approach to Reliability of Software Operation. *Proc. 8th Int. Symp. on Fault-Tolerant Computing (FTCS-8)* (Toulouse, France). IEEE Computer Society Press, 1978, pp. 3-9 .

11. M. Chérèque, G. Bonn, U. Bügel, F. Kaiser, T. Usländer: Open System Architecture (OSA). In: D. Powell (ed.): *Delta-4: a Generic Architecture for Dependable Distributed Computing*. Research Reports ESPRIT. Berlin, Germany: Springer-Verlag, 1991, pp. 165-210.

12. M. Chérèque, D. Powell, P. Reynier, J.-L. Richier, J. Voiron: Active Replication in Delta-4. *Proc. 22nd Int. Conf. on Fault-Tolerant Computing Systems (FTCS-22)* (Boston, MA, USA). IEEE Computer Society Press, 1992, pp. 28-37 .

13. E. C. Cooper: Replicated Procedure Call. *ACM Op. Sys. Review*, 20, 44-56, 1984.

14. F. Cristian, H. Aghali, R. Strong, D. Dolev: Atomic Broadcast: From Simple Message Diffusion to Byzantine Agreement. *Proc. 15th Int. Symp. on Fault-Tolerant Computing (FTCS-15)* (Ann Arbor, MI, USA). IEEE Computer Society Press, 1985, pp. 200-206 .

15. F. Cristian, B. Dancey, J. Dehn: Fault-Tolerance in the Advanced Automation System. *Proc. 20th Int. Symp. on Fault-Tolerant Computing (FTCS-20)* (Newcastle upon Tyne, UK). IEEE Computer Society Press, 1990, pp. 6-17 .

16. Delta-4: Process Replication - The Object Manager Entity (OME). System Administration, Implementation Guide/ Delta-4 Document, N°I90.082/I3/P, December 1992.

17. M. Fischer: A Theoretician's View of Fault Tolerant Distributed Computing. In: B. Simons, A. Spector (eds.): *Fault-Tolerant Distributed Computing*. Lecture Notes on Computer Science (448). Berlin: Springer-Verlag, 1990, pp. 1-9.

18. J. Gray: Why do Computers Stop and What can be done about it? *Proc. 5th Symp. on Reliability in Distributed Software and Database Systems* (Los Angeles, CA, USA). IEEE Computer Society Press, 1986, pp. 3-12 .

19. K. Kanoun, J. Arlat, L. Burrill, Y. Crouzet, S. Graf, E. Martins, A. MacInnes, D. Powell, J.-L. Richier , J. Voiron: Validation. In: D. Powell (ed.): *Delta-4: a Generic Architecture for Dependable Distributed Computing*. Berlin, Germany: Springer Verlag, 1991, pp. 371-406.

20. K. Kanoun, D. Powell: Dependability Evaluation of Bus and Ring Communication Topologies for the Delta-4 Distributed Fault-Tolerant Architecture. *Proc. 10th Symp. on Reliable Distributed Systems (SRDS-10)* (Pisa, Italy). IEEE Computer Society Press, 1991, pp. 130-141 .

21. J.-C. Laprie (ed.): *Dependability: Basic Concepts and Terminology*. Dependable Computing and Fault-Tolerance (5). Vienna, Austria: Springer-Verlag, 1992.

22. I. Lee, R. K. Iyer: Faults, Symptoms and Software Fault Tolerance in the Tandem GUARDIAN90 Operating System. *Proc. 23rd Int. Conf. on Fault-Tolerant Computing (FTCS-23)* (Toulouse, France). IEEE Computer Society Press, 1993, pp. 20-29 .

23. P. A. Lee, T. Anderson: *Fault Tolerance — Principles and Practice*. Dependable Computing and Fault-Tolerant Systems (3). Springer-Verlag, Vienna, Austria, 1990.

24. P. M. Melliar-Smith, R. L. Schwartz: Formal Specification and Mechanical Verification of SIFT: A Fault-Tolerance Flight Control System. *IEEE Trans. Computers*, C-31, 616-630, 1982.

25. S. Mullender (ed.): *Distributed Systems*. New York: ACM Press, Addison-Wesley, 1989.

26. D. Powell (ed.): *Delta-4: a Generic Architecture for Dependable Distributed Computing*. Research Reports ESPRIT. Berlin, Germany: Springer-Verlag, 1991.

27. D. Powell: Failure Mode Assumptions and Assumption Coverage. *Proc. 22nd Int. Symp. on Fault-Tolerant Computing (FTCS-22)* (Boston, MA, USA). IEEE Computer Society Press, 1992, pp. 386-395 .

28. D. Powell, G. Bonn, D. Seaton, P. Veríssimo, F. Waeselynck: The Delta-4 Approach to Dependability in Open Distributed Computing Systems. *Proc. 18th Int. Symp. on Fault-Tolerant Computing Systems (FTCS-18)* (Tokyo, Japan). IEEE Computer Society Press, 1988, pp. 246-251 .

29. B. Randell: System Structure for Software Fault Tolerance. *IEEE Trans. Software Engineering*, SE-1, 220-232, 1975.

30. L. Rodrigues, P. Veríssimo: xAMp: a Multi-Primitive Group Communications Service. *Proc. 11th Symp. on Reliable Distributed Systems (SRDS-11)* (Houston, TX, USA). IEEE Computer Society Press, 1992, pp. 112-121 .

31. F. B. Schneider: Implementing Fault Tolerant Services using the State Machine Approach: a Tutorial. *ACM Comp. Surveys*, 22, 229-319, 1990.

32. N. A. Speirs, P. A. Barrett: Using Passive Replicates in Delta-4 to provide Dependable Distributed Computing. *Proc. 19th Int. Symp. on Fault-Tolerant Computing Systems (FTCS-19)* (Chicago, MI, U.S.A). IEEE Computer Society Press, 1989, pp. 184-190 .

33. R. van Renesse, K. P. Birman, R. Cooper, B. Glade, P. Stephenson: Reliable Multicast between Microkernels. *Proc. Workshop on Microkernels and Other Kernel Architectures* (Seattle, WA, USA). USENIX Assocation, 1992, pp. 269-283 .

34. P. Veríssimo: Redundant Media Mechanisms for Dependable Communication in Token-Bus LANs. *Proc. 13th Local Computer Network Conf.* (Minneapolis, MN, USA). IEEE Computer Society Press, 1988, pp. 453-462 .

35. P. Veríssimo, P. Barrett, P. Bond, A. Hilborne, L. Rodrigues, D. Seaton: Extra Performance Architecture (XPA). In: D. Powell (ed.): *Delta-4: a Generic Architecture for Dependable Distributed Computing*. Research Reports ESPRIT. Berlin, Germany: Springer-Verlag, 1991, pp. 211-266.

36. P. Veríssimo, L. Rodrigues, J. Ruffino: The Atomic Multicast Protocol (AMp). In: D. Powell (ed.): *Delta-4: a Generic Architecture for Dependable Distributed Computing*. Research Reports ESPRIT. Berlin, Germany: Springer-Verlag, 1991, pp. 267-294.

# Arjuna and Voltan: Case Studies in Building Fault-Tolerant Distributed Systems Using Standard Components

*Santosh K. Shrivastava*

*Department of Computing Science*

*University of Newcastle upon Tyne, NE1 7RU, UK*

## 1. Introduction

Designing and building distributed systems that continue to provide specified services in the presence of node and network related failures without appreciable degradation in performance is a challenging task. The main thrust of the research work to be described here is on the development of tools and techniques for constructing fault-tolerant systems by making use of standard, 'off-the-shelf' hardware and software components. Two research systems have been designed and implemented. The first system, *Arjuna*, demonstrates the application of modern object-oriented software technology in building general purpose fault-tolerant distributed applications in workstation environments, whereas the second system, Voltan, demonstrates the application of novel redundancy management techniques in building specialist high availability systems using ordinary hardware components.

## 2. Arjuna

*Arjuna* is an object-oriented system that provides several tools and facilities for the development of fault-tolerant, distributed C++ programs. No changes have made to the programming language (C++) or to the underlying operating system (Unix). This makes *Arjuna* very portable, capable of running on a wide variety of systems and platforms. The *Arjuna* system demonstrates that it is possible to build a persistent object system, containing both user specific and system specific objects (such as name servers), entirely out of user level subsystems. This leads us to state that an operating system kernel should not be concerned with the management of persistent data, other than providing basic support for stable storage (for nodes with disks). This obviates the need for employing any sophisticated fault tolerance techniques within the kernel.

It is assumed that the hardware components of the system are computers (nodes), connected by a communication subsystem. A node is assumed to work either as specified or simply to stop working (crash). After a crash, a node is repaired within a finite amount of time and made active again. A node may have both stable (crash-proof) and non-stable (volatile) storage or just non-stable storage. All of the data stored on volatile storage is assumed to be lost when a crash occurs; any data stored on stable storage remains unaffected by a crash. We assume that processes on functioning nodes are capable of communicating with each other.

We briefly outline the structure of our system. *Arjuna* provides facilities for constructing applications using persistent objects which can be manipulated under the control of atomic actions (atomic transactions). Fault tolerance is necessary primarily for preserving the integrity of persistent objects - that is why atomic actions are required. At the application level, objects are the only visible entities; the client and server processes that do the actual work are hidden. In *Arjuna*, server processes are created dynamically as remote procedure calls (RPCs) are made to objects; these servers are created using the facilities provided by the underlying RPC and persistent object support subsystems. Persistent objects not in use are held in a passive state, residing in object stores or object databases and activated on demand. An object resides on a single node in one object store, however, the availability of an object can be increased by replicating it on several nodes and thus storing it in more than one object store. Object replicas must be managed through appropriate replica-consistency protocols to ensure that the object copies remain mutually consistent. Our basic strategy is to provide support for both active and passive replication, permitting an application to select either at run time.

We have identified the main modules of a distributed programming system, and the services they provide for supporting persistent objects to be the following: (i) *Atomic Action module:* provides atomic action support to application programs in form of operations for starting, committing and aborting atomic actions; (ii) *RPC module:* provides facilities to clients for connecting (disconnecting) to object servers and invoking operations on objects; (iii) *Naming module:* provides a mapping from user-given names of objects to their unique identifiers (UIDs); (iv) *Binding module:* provides a mapping from UIDs to location information such as the identity of the host where the server for the object can be made available; and (v) *Persistent Object Support module:* provides object servers and access to stable storage for objects.

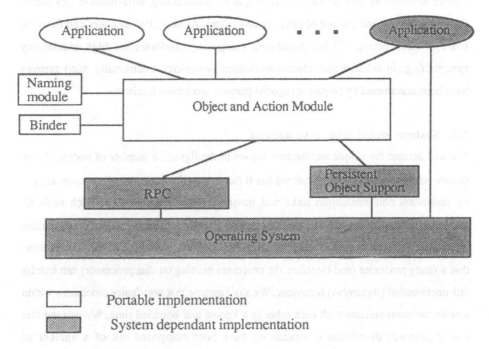

**Fig. 1. Components of a Persistent Object System**

The relationship amongst these modules is depicted in the Figure. Every node in the system will provide RPC and Atomic Action modules. Any node capable of providing object servers and/or (stable) object storage will in addition contain a Persistent Object Support module. A node containing an object store can provide object storage services via its Persistent Object Support module. Nodes without stable storage may access these services via their local RPC module. Naming and Binding modules are not necessary on every node since their services can also be utilised through the services provided by the RPC module. The rationale behind this system structure is discussed in [1], where we discuss how by encapsulating the properties of persistence, recoverability, shareability, serialisability and failure atomicity in an Atomic Action module and defining narrow, well-defined interfaces to the supporting environment, we achieve a significant degree of modularity as well as portability for atomic action based object-oriented systems.

## 3. Voltan

*Voltan* software system provides a technique of constructing ultra-reliable processors (*Voltan nodes*) by making use of ordinary processors. As such, *Voltan* nodes can form the basis of constructing reliable distributed computing platforms for high availability systems (e.g., in avionics and telecommunication switching); traditionally, such systems have been constructed by employing special purpose processing hardware.

### 3.1. System model and assumptions

We will assume the simple architecture shown in the figure:: a number of nodes, $C_i$, are connected by a perfect communications bus B (some specific examples of approximating B by redundant communication links and busses are discussed in [2]). Each node $C_i$ maintains the abstraction of a fail-controlled node by replicated processing of computations over fail-uncontrolled processors $P_{i1},..., P_{in}$, n>1, which make up $C_i$. We will assume, that a faulty processor (and therefore the processes running on that processor) can exhibit fail-uncontrolled (Byzantine) behaviour. We shall assume that non-faulty processors within a node can communicate with each other in a known and bounded time. We assume that (non-replicated) distributed computations have been composed out of a number of processes that interact only via messages. We also assume that if a process with multiple input ports has input messages on those ports then any one of these messages is chosen *non-deterministically* for processing. Message selection is however assumed to be *fair*, that is, the process will eventually select a message present on a port. It is also necessary to assume that the computation performed by a process on a selected message is *deterministic*.

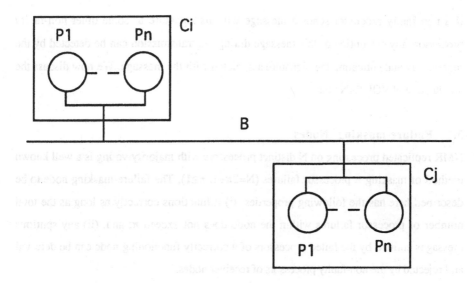

**Fig. 2. Basic architecture**

Given such a model of computation, active replication of a process (with a replica, one each running on the underlying processors of a node) will require the following two conditions to be met:

*Agreement:* All the non-faulty replicas of a process receive identical input messages;

*Order:* all the non-faulty replicas process the messages in an identical order.

So, if all the non-faulty replicas of a process of a node have identical initial states then identical output messages in an identical order will be produced by them. Practical distributed programs often require some additional functionality such as using timeouts when waiting for messages. Timeouts (and other asynchronous events), messages with priority etc. are potential sources of non-determinism during input message selection, making such programs difficult to replicate. We have developed novel techniques for VOLTAN nodes for dealing with such cases [2].

It will be assumed throughout that the messages sent by a non-faulty processor can be authenticated by any non-faulty receiver. Digital signatures implement authentication (with high probability). We therefore assume that each processor has a mechanism to generate a unique unforgeable signature for a given message and further that each processor has an authentication function for verifying the authenticity of a message signature. Thus if a non-faulty processor sends a message with its signature to some other non-faulty processor, any corruption of this message during the transmission can be detected by the receiver by authenticating the signature associated with the message. We now discuss the architecture of VOLTAN nodes.

## 3.2. Failure-masking Nodes

NMR replicated processing on N distinct processors with majority voting is a well known method of masking $\pi$ processor failures ($N=2\pi+1$, $\pi\geq1$). The failure-masking node to be described here has the following properties: (i) it functions correctly as long as the total number of processor failures within the node does not exceed $\pi$; and, (ii) any spurious messages emitted by the failed processors of a correctly functioning node can be detected and rejected by the non-faulty processors of receiver nodes.

As stated earlier, it is necessary that the replicas of computational processes on non-faulty processors of a node select identical messages for processing, to ensure that they produce identical outputs. This can be done by presenting a single input message queue, referred to as a *delivered valid message queue*, *DMQ*, to a process and ensuring that a process picks up the message at the head of its DMQ for processing. An atomic broadcast protocol meeting both the agreement and order property can then be employed to ensure that identical messages are enqueued in an identical order at all the respective DMQs of non-faulty replicas of a node. The broadcast mechanism itself requires that the clocks of all the non-faulty processors of a node be synchronised such that the measurable difference between readings of clocks at any instant is bounded by a known constant. Algorithms for achieving this abstraction exist which require all the non-faulty processors of a node to exchange authenticated messages amongst themselves.

Each non-faulty processor of a node runs the following five 'system' processes:

(i) *Diffuser Process*: this process takes the messages produced by the computational processes of that processor, signs them and sends them to all the other processors of the node for voting.

(ii) *Receiver Process:* this process accepts only authentic messages from the network for processing. Messages with $\pi$ or less number of distinct signatures are sent to the local voter process; messages with $\pi+1$ distinct signatures are sent to the local order process for distribution to the local destination processes.

(iii) *Voter Process*: the voter processes the messages coming from the receiver as follows. If the contents of a message, say m, are identical to its locally produced counterpart, then m is countersigned (by considering the existing signatures on m as part of the message). If the countersigned message m now contains a total of $\pi+1$ distinct signatures, then m is regarded as a *valid* (voted) message and it is sent over the network to its destination. On the other hand, if m contains a total of $\pi$ or less number of distinct signatures, then it is sent to all those processors of the node who have not yet signed m. Messages that cannot be matched at a non-faulty voter are never countersigned and sent out. It follows that any $(\pi+1)$-signed message will be correct (valid).

(iv) *Transmitter Process*: this process transmits valid messages coming from the voter process to their destinations.

(v) *Order Process*: this process atomically broadcasts valid messages coming from the local receiver to all the order processes of that node (including itself). This permits order processes to construct identical queues of valid messages (DMQs) for computational processes.

Note that both clock synchronisation and atomic broadcasts are performed locally within a node. Thus the main "visible" difference between an NMR system and its non-replicated counterpart is that the nodes are required to produce $(\pi+1)$-signed messages and use authentication. Further, under normal conditions, inter-node message traffic is increased by $2\pi+1$ times.

### 3.3. Fail-silent nodes

A $\pi+1$ processor fail-silent node, where, $\pi\geq1$, will be said to exhibit fail-silent behaviour in the following sense: it produces either correct messages which can be verified as such by the non-faulty processors of receiving nodes, or it ceases to produce new correct messages, in which case non-faulty receivers can detect any messages it may produce as invalid. This behaviour is guaranteed so long as no more than $\pi$ processors in the node fail.

The NMR node architecture discussed previously can be modified easily to construct a $\pi+1$ processor fail-silent node. Each non-faulty processor of a node runs the five system processes, with the diffuser, receiver and order processes performing the same functions as their NMR counterparts. The voter process is replaced by a *comparator* process which acts like the voter process, except a disagreement during a comparison is treated as an internal failure. Once a failure is indicated, the comparator process stops, which results in no new $(\pi+1)$-signed messages being produced from that node; any messages coming from this node that are not $(\pi+1)$-signed will be found to be invalid by the non-faulty processors of the receiving nodes.

## 4. Concluding Remarks

Arjuna system has been operational for more than two years. By encapsulating the properties of persistence, recoverability, shareability, serialisability and failure atomicity in an Atomic Action module and defining narrow, well-defined interfaces to the supporting environment, we have shown that it is possible to achieve a significant degree of modularity as well as portability for atomic action based object-oriented systems. The software is available freely and there are users all over the world (email arjuna@newcastle.ac.uk for more information; anonymous ftp: arjuna.ncl.ac.uk (128.240.150.1)).

An instance of the VOLTAN architecture has been implemented on a network of T800 transputers to produce both TMR failure-masking nodes and two processor fail-silent nodes. Several enhancements to the basic architecture described here have been undertaken to obtain very encouraging performance out of these nodes. The main advantages of our approach to building fault-tolerant nodes are that: (i) technology upgrades appear to be easy; since the principles behind the protocols do not change, the protocol software can be reused relatively easily for any type of processor (including the ones expected to be available in future); (ii) we note that by employing different types of processors within a node, a measure of tolerance against design faults in processors can be obtained, again without recourse to any specialised hardware assistance; and (iii) since the replicated computations are loosely synchronised, the architecture should be capable of tolerating common mode transient failures, because transients are less likely to affect the computations on the processors in an identical fashion.

The *Arjuna* system relies on the assumption that the underlying nodes are fail-silent. We are therefore interested in examining whether *Arjuna* can be made to run over *Voltan* fail-silent nodes. Positive results could open up an exciting way forward.

## Acknowledgements

The work reported here has been supported in part by grants from the UK Science and Engineering Research Council, MOD and ESPRIT project BROADCAST (Basic Research Project Number 6360).

# References

(1) Shrivastava, S.K. and D.L. McCue, "Structuring fault-tolerant object systems for modularity in a distributed environment", IEEE Trans. on Parallel and Distributed Systems (to appear). Also available as Tech. Report No. 414.

(2) Shrivastava, S.K, P.D. Ezhilchelvan, N.A. Speirs, S. Tao and A. Tully, "Principle Features of the VOLTAN Family of Reliable Node Architectures for Distributed Systems", IEEE Trans. on Computers, 41 (5), pp. 542-549, May 1992.

# IV   Embedded and Real-Time Systems

# Fault Tolerant Platforms for Emerging Telecommunications Markets

Rod Bark

**Hewlett-Packard Laboratories, Bristol**

With the advent of the Advanced Intelligent Network telecommunication service providers and network equipment manufacturers are increasingly looking to the computer vendors to provide low-cost, scalable fault tolerant platforms. This paper examines the requirements for one such class of system and reviews hardware and software based solutions against them. The paper concludes by discussing some issues in using distributed systems to meet these requirements.

Changes in progress in the telecommunications industry are creating a potentially huge market for vendors of fault tolerant computing platforms. These changes are being driven by the telecoms service providers, particularly the Regional Bell Operating Companies and other operators in the US, who are increasingly finding themselves in competition with one another to provide value added services to their business customers. To differentiate themselves in this competitive marketplace service providers need to be able to offer superior Intelligent Network[1] (IN) services.

To date such services are either supported directly on the telephone switching nodes or require service specific hooks in the switch logic to pass calls off to attached processors. Introduction of new services by service providers therefore requires them first to persuade the manufacturers of their switches to modify the switch software. Due to the complexity of switches, implementation of new services takes around two years, principally because of the volume of regression tests required before modified code can be deployed. To make matters worse, switch manufacturers are in general unwilling to invest in supporting new services unless there is demand from multiple service providers, and this is fundamentally in conflict with the aims of the phone service providers, who want to distinguish themselves from the competition by offering unique services.

Solutions to this issue have been proposed by Bellcore [Bellcore] and CCITT [CCITT], in which a standard model for call processing is supported by the switch manufacturers, with defined points in call processing where control can be handed off to attached processors, based on masks set by these processors. Such architectures allow the service providers to implement the services themselves without

---

1. The 'intelligence' here is the ability to interpret the dialled information as more than a switch routing code

requiring changes to the switch and therefore offer the service providers the potential of rapidly developing differentiating products. The provision of processors to support IN service implementations represents a huge potential market for the computer vendors, with estimates of size of the market of up to $2 billion a year by '96 [Ovum].

This paper addresses the requirements placed on such processors, by describing the requirements placed on a typical telecoms platform - the Service Control Point. We then summarise why hardware fault tolerant solutions are not seen as an acceptable solution by this market and discuss an alternative approach based on a loosely coupled distributed system. Finally we conclude by listing areas of outstanding research issues inhibiting the greater use of distributed systems for implementing fault tolerant platforms for this market.

## 1.0 The Service Control Point

The architectures proposed by Bellcore and others for Advanced·Intelligent Networks include the use of a Service Control Point to support value-added services remote to the switching nodes. An SCP supports a collection of switching nodes, providing a platform for the deployment of proprietary value added services, implemented by the service provider or even the service end-user (figure 1).

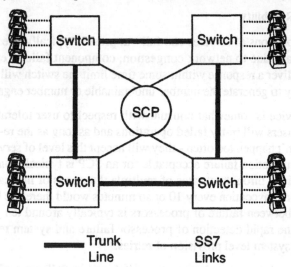

FIGURE 1.SCP connection to a switch network

Call processing in the switching nodes follows a standardised model that allows the SCP to register an interest in user actions (e.g. sequences of dialled digits) at various points in the lifetime of the call, and to intervene in the call processing to modify the call context and thereby its routing and associated billing policy. In this manner services such as freephone numbers, Virtual Private Networks, multi-way calling, call screening and call waiting can be implemented by service providers without modifications to the switch software.

Service Control Points are therefore potentially involved in call setup and management. As such they are required to exhibit performance and fault tolerance characteristics similar to the switches themselves.

## 1.1 Fault Tolerance

There are several aspects to the fault tolerance required for service control points which we term the availability, reliability and integrity of services.

### 1.1.1 Service Availability

The overriding requirement in terms of fault tolerance is that the services supported by the SCP should be continuously available. Outages of elements involved in call set-up and management are not acceptable to telecoms service providers for any reason and they typically demand downtimes of less than one hour in thirty years. This means that all components of an SCP must be upgradable on line - all hardware and software including any inter-processor bus or network.

### 1.1.2 Service Reliability

Individual invocations of services can fail - at present typically one in a thousand call attempts fail (due to network congestion, component failure, etc.). When an SCP fails to deliver a response within some time limit the switch will take a default action, typically to generate the number unobtainable or number engaged tone.

The phone service is somewhat unusual with respect to user toleration of faults. Typically end users will re-try failed operations and as long as the re-try succeeds - and failures don't happen too often - they will accept this level of service. The maximum rate of invocation failure acceptable for an SCP is typically one in a million invocations. Given throughput rates of multiple thousands of invocations per second, a loss of one invocation every 10 or so minutes would therefore be acceptable. As mean time between failure of processors is typically around ten years, the primary issue is the rapid detection of processor failure and system reconfiguration rather than the system level provision of retries.

Having said that, interactions between a switch and an SCP are typically transactional and long lived state should be preserved over these failures. By way of an example consider the IN service that allows billing for calls to credit cards. Typically the user wipes the credit card through the reader on the phone and then is able to make a series of calls based on this single validation. Failures that result in the an individual call setup failing should not result in the loss of the billing information from the previous calls. In addition the user should be able to continue to place further calls without having to wipe the credit card through the card reader again. Some form of persistent storage is therefore required.

### 1.1.3 Service Integrity

The occasional mis-routing of calls, though obviously undesirable, is not catastrophic as phone users historically have tolerated these failures. Consequently value domain errors in the responses to the switch is not an important issue, as long as incorrect results are intermittent (again typically less than one in a million).

## 1.2 Performance

Service Control Points are to some degree centralised solutions, providing services to multiple switches. Busy hour service invocation rates for a single SCP can range from tens of invocations per second through to tens of thousands, as supported services are taken up by the market. Service providers want to be able to deploy SCPs for a small initial investment, and to scale up *on-line* as service demand increases.

## 1.3 Single System Image

For communications and administration purposes the SCP should appear as a single system, with a single network address.

### 1.4 Durability

One further somewhat unique aspect of the telecoms business is the deployment time of equipment. This is currently in the twenty to thirty year timeframe, whereas computer vendors typically roll even their processor architectures on a ten year period. For SCPs this implies that any solution must be plug compatible in particular with future developments in processor technology. Ideally one would want to be able to replace existing processors with new versions without any hardware or software redesign.

## 2.0 Potential Platform Technologies

Network equipment providers and telecom service providers are reluctant to buy custom hardware based solutions for SCPs and the like. There are four main underlying reasons for this:

- the high cost of hardware based solutions
- the non-standard operating systems required for these processors

- requirements for upgrading systems on-line cannot be met. Operating system upgrades and the addition or replacement of processors cannot be achieved on in-service systems.

- the ability to benefit from advances in processor technology is constrained by the time taken to build custom processor boards. This typically causes a two to three year time lag between the incorporation of new technology into hardware fault tolerant systems, compared to workstations and commercial systems[1].

As distributed systems technology is reaching the marketplace and networking technology is evolving to allow gigabit and above LAN connection, solutions based on loosely coupled distributed systems are becoming feasible. This type of approach offers the advantages of:

- price performance in line with workstations and commercial systems through using the same processor boards

- lower development and maintenance costs for the computer vendor and the application developer through the use of a single operating system over the computer vendor's range of workstations, commercial systems and fault tolerant platforms

- easy upgrading to new processor boards as and when they become available in workstations or commercial systems.

- on-line upgrading due to the loose coupling of the system.

The market perceived stumbling blocks though are delivering the performance and the required level of fault tolerance, making transparent to the application programmer of the techniques used to achieve fault tolerance, and providing a single system image to the outside world.

The general purpose fault tolerant distributed-system-in-a-box may well be some way off[2], however for specific applications such as a Service Control Point, their realisation is not so far away.

In the remainder of this section we outline how the requirements listed above can be met using replication of processing over a distributed system.

---

1. For example first versions of RISC based hardware fault tolerant systems will not be available until the '94 -'95 timeframe, whereas the technology is in its third generation in the commercial systems market.

2. Products such as the IBM HACMP/6000, NCR's Lifekeeper and HP Switchover-UX which provide a degree of fault tolerance over a distributed system offer limited support for replication of arbitrary programs. Node failures are detected and processes restarted a surviving node through a user supplied script. The new host node assumes the IP address of the failed one. Typically dual paths are provided to disks to allow access to the application's data, but recovery to a consistent state is left to the application.

## 2.1 Performance

The implementations of individual IN services are typically small programs, consisting of hundreds rather than thousands of lines of code, and easily executable on conventional uniprocessors. The demanding aspects of performance are therefore the number of these programs to be executed in the busy hour.

To achieve the throughput levels required for an SCP requires concurrent execution of multiple requests on multiple processors. Distributed systems provide good platforms for execution of multiple concurrent programs providing these programs do not compete for shared resources, or communicate extensively with one another. Luckily this is the case for SCPs.

## 2.2 Fault Tolerance

Replication of processing over the distributed system offers the potential to provide the required level of fault tolerance. Passive replication is sufficient for even a relatively high performance application such as the SCP, providing failure detection is sufficiently rapid. This avoids the problems of ensuring that system behaviour is deterministic, which is required for active replication.

Passive replication does however have the drawback of requiring periodic checkpointing of processes, to allow a backup to take over after failure of the primary process. Making this checkpointing transparent to the application programmer is difficult for a general purpose application based on a standard operating system. However the call model for interactions between a switch and an SCP defines a stable mid-call point to which one would roll-back on failure. The question remains of what to checkpoint, though the call model also gives some hints here. For Service Control Points it is therefore possible to implement system level checkpointing.

Further, as system level retries are not required, passive replication can be achieved simply by initialising a 'backup' from stable store on failure of the 'primary'. This need only happen when a subsequent invocation is received for this conversation, as we don't need to replay the failed invocation. Costs are therefore minimal, requiring only reliable point-to-point protocols, the provision of stable store and the implementation of fast failure detection. The areas where more sophisticated protocols are required are in the coordination of multiple processes, for instance multiple front-ends distributing incoming requests to a farm of compute processors. Coordination of any such group of processors in the presence of failures is difficult without the provision of group membership protocols, as for instance implemented in Isis [Birman] or Delta-4 [Powell].

A further issue is ensuring that processors are fail-silent, particularly if processes can declare others dead, or if violations of the communication protocols could cause LAN failure. The Network Attachment Controller developed by the Delta-4 project [Powell] offers a hardware based solution to this problem, and results of the

Voltan project [Shrivastava] point to potential software based solutions. Software based solutions with adequate performance for use in applications such as the SCP are however not as yet available.

## 2.3 Single System Image

Providing a single system image is problematic. Unfortunately entities that the SCP communicates with, such as switches and the network management system use standardised protocols (SS7 and $Q_3$ respectively), which do not support indirect addressing, either through group addresses or the use of location brokers. Consequently implementing a transparently fault tolerant front end is difficult. SS7 uses an addressing scheme in which an SCP is connected via a set of links designed to terminate at a single physical machine. Splitting the link set across multiple Signal Interface Units (SIUs) and then cross connecting these SIUs to a collection of front end nodes is the strategy used in all current fault tolerant implementations of SS7. However, to provide fault tolerance all the way up the SS7 protocol stack requires sharing of state between these processes, potentially with checkpointing of state for every message received, at a rate of thousands of messages per second. Achieving this level of throughput requires networking technologies beyond the capabilities of Ethernet or FDDI, though ATM, Fiber Channel and other emerging high throughput networks may support these traffic levels.

## 2.4 Durability

Though a loosely coupled system allows the possibility of on-line upgrading of the operating system and the processor hardware, because it can support heterogeneity, on-line upgrading of the communications protocols is somewhat more problematical. This is akin to modifying the bus arbitration protocols of a hardware fault tolerant system on-line, which is not as far as we know remotely possible. Certain upgrades of the communications protocols for distributed systems may be possible, though we know of no work in this area.

## 3.0 Research Issues

In the preceding section we alluded to several areas where solutions for fault tolerance, based around distributed systems are lacking or even non-existent. We conclude by summarising these problem areas:

- **Communication with alien processes.** Processes external to the fault tolerant 'box' typically use standard communication protocols which expect a single physical machine as the end-point. Replicating this end-point appears to require alteration of the local implementation of the protocol, to allow replication of the protocol stack and implementation of indirect addressing. Currently this process has to be carried out for each protocol on an individual basis, not least for efficiency reasons.

- **Making replication transparent to the application programmer.** Passive replication in general requires the programmer to use a programming paradigm that includes the notion of checkpointing. The only other alternative is the checkpointing of every change in the state of the process, which is not feasible from an efficiency standpoint. Active replication requires that applications (and the operating system) be deterministic, which does not appear feasible given e.g. concurrency and local system calls for timers.

- **Providing fail silence.** Processor fail silence particularly in execution of network and communication protocols needs to be ensured for distributed systems based fault tolerance to be acceptable to the telecoms market.

- **On-line upgrading of communication protocols.** In the lifetimes envisaged for telecoms platforms upgrading of the communication protocols will be inevitably be necessary. Techniques for achieving this are currently unknown for all but simple, special cases.

## Acknowledgments

This paper reports on the work of several HP Laboratories staff, particularly John O'Connell, Paul Harry and Colin Low.

## References

[Bellcore] Bellcore Special Report SR-NPL-001623, Issue 1, June 1990 'Advanced Intelligent Network Release 1 Network and Operations Plan'.

[Birman] 'The Isis distributed Toolkit Version 3.0 User Reference Manual', Isis Distributed Systems, Inc, November 1992.

[CCITT] COM X1-R 163E, CCITT Study Group XI, Report R 163, October 1991.

[Ovum] 'Intelligent Networks' M Li, E. Nichols, Ovum Reports, ISBN 0-903969-74-2.

[Powell] 'Delta-4: A Generic Architecture for Dependable Distributed Computing', D. Powell (Ed.), Springer Verlag, 1991, ISBN 3-540-54985-4.

[Shrivastava] 'Principal Features of the Voltan Family of Reliable node Architectures for distributed Systems.', S. Shrivastava, P. Ezhilchelvan, N. Spiers, S. Tao, A. Tully, IEEE Transactions on Computers, May 1992.

# Fault-Tolerance in Embedded Real-Time Systems

Farnam Jahanian

Department of EECS
University of Michigan
Ann Arbor, MI 48109

farnam@eecs.umich.edu

**Abstract.** Fault-tolerance in real-time systems is defined informally as the ability of the system to deliver correct results in a timely manner even in the presence of faults. Large-scale *embedded real-time systems* are being built in diverse application ranging from avionics to plant automation and process control. These systems often operate under strict dependability and timing requirements that are imposed by the external environment. This paper looks at the misconception that fault-tolerance and real-time requirements are orthogonal and it argues that the traditional approaches to support fault-tolerance must be reexamined for time-critical applications.

## 1 Introduction

With ever–increasing reliance on digital computers in *embedded real-time systems* for diverse applications such as avionics, automated manufacturing and process control, air-traffic control, and patient life–support monitoring, the need for dependable systems that deliver services in a timely manner has become crucial. Embedded systems often interact with the external environment and operate under strict timing and dependability requirements. As shown in Figure 1, an embedded real-time system can be decomposed into three components: the *controlled object*, the *computer system*, and the *operator*. The controlled object and the operator are the *environment* of the system. The interface between the real-time computer system and the controlled object is called the instrumentation interface, consisting of sensors and actuators. The interface between the computer system and the operator is called the man-machine (or the operator) interface. The operator monitors and controls the object via this interface to the computer system. Embedded real-time systems are in essence *responsive*: they often interact with the environment by "reacting to stimuli of external events and producing results, within specified timing constraints" [9]. To guarantee this responsiveness, the system must be able to tolerate failures. Hence, a fundamental requirement of fault-tolerant real-time systems is that they provide the expected service even in the presence of faults.

The above description depicts a real-time computer system as a single entity. In fact, most real-time computer systems are distributed (Figure 2). They consist of a set of nodes interconnected by a real-time communication subsystem.

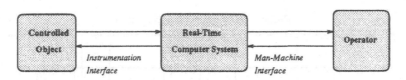

**Fig. 1.** An Embedded Real-Time System.

Conceptually, a real-time computer system is providing a set of well-defined services to the environment. These services must be made fault-tolerant to meet the availability and reliability requirements on the entire system. Therefore, some form of redundancy must be used to detect and to recover from failures. This redundancy can take many forms: it may be a set of replicated hardware or software components that can mask the failure of a component, or it may be a backward error recovery scheme that allows a computation to be restarted from an earlier consistent state after an error is detected.

This paper examines the misconception that real-time and fault-tolerance requirements are orthogonal. It argues that the traditional approaches for providing fault-tolerance in distributed systems is not necessarily appropriate for time-critical applications and it describes some of the challenges that confront the designers of dependable time-critical systems[19]. The motivation for this work is based on three observations:

1. real-time and fault-tolerance are not orthogonal: availability and reliability requirements cannot be addressed independent of timing constraints;
2. the characterization of design methodologies for fault-tolerant systems based on redundancy in space or redundancy in time is inadequate for real-time systems; and
3. establishing a global consistent system state based on the causal ordering of messages among cooperating processes does not consider the temporal consistency requirements imposed on the data in a system.

## 2  Fault-Tolerance vs. Real-Time

Fault–tolerance in real time can be defined informally as the ability of a system to deliver the expected service in a timely manner even in the presence of faults. A common misconception about real–time computing is that fault–tolerance is orthogonal to real–time requirements. It is often assumed that the availability and reliability requirements of a system can be addressed independent of its timing constraints. This assumption, however, does not consider the distinguishing characteristic of real–time computing: *the correctness of a system is dependent not only on the correctness of its result, but also on meeting stringent timing requirements.* In other words, a real–time system may fail to function correctly

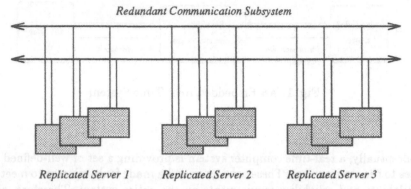

Fig. 2. A Distributed Real-Time Computer System.

either because of errors in hardware / software or because of not meeting the timing requirements that are usually imposed by its environment. A missed deadline can be potentially as disastrous as a system crash or an incorrect behavior of a critical task. When a system specification requires certain service in a timely manner, then the inability of the system to meet the specified timing constraint can be viewed as a failure. However, a simple approach of applying existing fault–tolerant system design methods by treating a missed deadline as a timing fault does not address fully the needs of real–time applications. The fundamental difference is that real–time systems must be predictable, even in the presence of faults.

Fault-tolerance and timing requirements are often derived a high-level requirement specification. Since the logical correctness of a system may be dependent on the timing correctness of other components, the task of separating logical correctness from timing correctness may be very difficult. Furthermore, since fault-tolerance and timeliness may pull each other in opposite directions, actions taken to achieve fault-tolerance may affect the ability of a system to meeting its timing constraints. For example, checkpointing a system state and complex recovery mechanisms will enhance fault-tolerance but may increase the probability of missing a deadline. Hence, one must explicitly consider timing requirements when addressing system fault-tolerance. The challenge is to include the timing and the fault–tolerance requirements in the specification of the system at every level of abstraction and to adopt a design methodology that considers system predictability even during fault detection, isolation, system reconfiguration and recovery phases.

## 3  System State

One can structure a distributed system as a collection of servers that provide services to the outside clients or other servers within the system. A common approach to building fault-tolerant distributed systems is to replicate servers that fail independently. The main approaches for structuring fault-tolerant servers are *passive and active replication*. In passive replication schemes [1, 5], the system state is maintained by a primary and one or more backup servers. The primary communicates its local state to the backups so that a backup can take over when a failure of the primary is detected. This architecture is commonly called the *primary–backup* approach and has been widely used in building commercial fault-tolerant systems. In active replication schemes [7, 17, 2], also known as the *state machine approach*, a collection of identical servers maintain replicated copies of the system state. Updates are applied atomically to all the replicas so that after detecting the failure of a server, the remaining servers continue the service. Schemes based on passive replication tend to require longer recovery time since a backup must execute an explicit recovery algorithm to take over the role of the primary. Schemes based on active replication, however, tend to have more overhead in responding to client requests since an agreement protocol must be performed to ensure atomic ordered delivery of messages to all replicas. Although much work has been done on synchronous and asynchronous protocols for managing replicated servers, the problem of server replication in real-time systems remains an important research problem.

Another widely-studied approach to build fault-tolerant systems is to establish consistent global system states as a computation progresses and to roll back to an earlier system state when a failure is detected. In this approach, one can view a distributed system as a collection of cooperating processes. The global system state is the aggregate set of the local states of the cooperating processes and the set of messages that have been sent by the source, but not yet received by the destination. A consistent global system state is defined to be a state that is reachable from the initial state [6]. Numerous checkpointing/logging-based schemes for establishing a global system state in a distributed environment have been proposed in the past, e.g., [4, 10, 20]. In these approaches, each process checkpoints its state locally, and the messages between processes are logged synchronously or asynchronously. Upon detecting a failure, a global system state is established by a rollback to an earlier point in the computation that could have been reachable from the initial system state. The applicability of this approach to real-time applications is questionable for several reasons. First, checkpoint/logging-based schemes tend to be relatively costly for time-critical systems. More importantly, since the data in real-time applications is perishable, recovering a system to earlier state is useful only if the data is temporally consistent. For example, in an air-traffic control system, recovering a distributed computation to a state that reflects the environment 2 seconds prior to a failure may not be an effective technique. Furthermore, restarting a system from an earlier checkpoint may not be useful if the deadlines on pending time-critical task can not be met when the computation is repeated.

The previous section argued that the real-time and fault-tolerance requirements of a system are not orthogonal. The difficulty in applying traditional approaches for providing fault-tolerance to real-time systems is that time is not explicitly considered in defining a *consistent system state*. In particular, several distinguishing characteristics of distributed real-time systems must be addressed:

1. *Timing Constraints:* The system must provide timely service even in the presence of faults.
2. *Perishable Data:* The data in these systems are perishable in the sense that the usefulness of certain data items, such as a sensor value, decreases with the passage of time.
3. *Interaction with Environment:* A real-time computer system reacts to stimuli from the external environment. Certain responses to the environment can not be recovered.
4. *Redundancy in Data Semantics:* The characterization of fault-tolerance techniques based on redundancy in space or redundancy in time is inadequate. When approximate data values are acceptable, trading *precision* or *quality* for *timeliness* must be considered.
5. *Weaker Consistency:* The semantics of real-time data allows the exploitation of weaker consistency constraints than the classical causal or total ordering on the operations in a system [3].

We will elaborate on the above points by presenting three examples to illustrate why alternative definitions of a system state is needed for real-time system.

For a large class of real-time applications, the system can recover from a server failure even though all servers may not have maintained identical copies of the replicated data. This allows alternative replication protocols that exploit weaker consistency among replicated servers in a real-time system. These protocols may trade off *atomic* or *causal consistency* among replicas for less expensive replication schemes. The following example illustrates this point.

**Example 1: Highly-Available Process Control System**

Consider a primary/backup system for automated manufacturing and process control applications, as shown in 3. The primary and the backup nodes share external devices such as sensors. The primary runs in a tight loop sampling sensors, calculating new values, and sending signal to external I/O under its control. The primary also maintains an in-memory data repository which is updated frequently during each iteration of the tight control-loop. One of the requirements on the system is to be able to switch to the backup in case of the primary failure within a few hundred milliseconds.

The in-memory data repository must be replicated on the backup to meeting the strict timing constraint on the switch-over. Since there can be hundreds of updated to the data repository during each iteration of the control loop, it is impractical (perhaps impossible) to update the backup synchronously each time the primary is updated. An alternative solution is to exploit the data semantics in a process control system by allowing the backup to maintain a less current but an acceptable copy of the data that resides on the primary. If the data on the backup does not fall too far behind the version on the primary, the backup can recover from a primary failure. For example, updates can be sent in batches or selectively to the backup. If the primary fails, the backup can take over even if the last few updates are lost. The objective is, however, to keep the backup data recent such that it can reconstruct a *consistent* system state by extrapolating from previous values and by reading new sensor values. However, one must ensure that the distance between the primary and the backup copies is bounded within a predefined time. In fact, different objects may have distinct tolerances in how far the backup can lag behind before the object state becomes stale. The challenge is to bound the distance between the primary and the backup such that consistency is not compromised while minimizing the overhead in exchanging messages between the primary and its backup. Under transient overload conditions, the system can gracefully degrade by allowing the backup to increase its distance from the primary. □

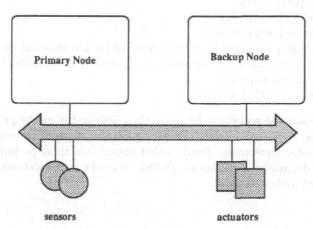

**Fig. 3.** Primary-Backup Process Control System.

In an embedded real-time system, it is often important to use the values of data objects that have existed at approximately the same time. For example, an air traffic controller monitoring the positions of several aircrafts must view the coordinates that are taken within a very short interval. Hence, a set of temporal constraints must be enforced on the data objects in a system. These temporal constraints must be considered when defining a consistent system state in a real-time environment. Consequently, a system state restored after a failure must satisfy these temporal constraints. The following example is intended to illustrate the relationship between temporal consistency and a consistent system state.

## Example 2: Airspace Control

Consider an airplane that is moving from airspace A to an adjacent airspace B.

[1] Different air traffic controllers are responsible for each airspace, as shown in Figure 4. As the airplane is moving from airspace A to airspace B, the control must be passed from one controller system to the other. Two data objects, $O_A$ and $O_B$, reflect which controller is responsible for the airplane. If $O_A = 1$, controller A is in charge of the airplane. If $O_A = 0$, the controller A is not responsible for the airplane. Initially, $O_A = 1 \land O_B = 0$. The hand-off must take place as the airplane is moving from one airspace to the other. A safety property of the system is that there should be a maximum time interval of 500ms during which both data objects are zero, i.e., neither controller is responsible for the airplane. Suppose a process $P_1$ updates both $O_A$ and $O_B$, and $P_2$ and $P_3$ are the displaying processes for controllers $A$ and $B$ respectively. We use the notation $w(O)$ and $r(O)$ to denote a write operation and a read operation to an object $O$, respectively.

$P_1$ :     $w(O_A), w(O_B)$

$P_2$ :     $r(O_A), w(display_A)$

$P_3$ :     $r(O_B), w(display_B)$

If the above safety property (or time constraint) is not imposed on the system, any interleaved execution of the above operations is acceptable. Consider the following execution sequence:

$w(O_A), r(O_A), r(O_B), w(O_B), \ldots$

If the two reads are separated by more than 500ms, the safety property is violated. Thus, the correct relative ordering of operations does not necessarily ensure temporal correctness. Hence, other constraints must be imposed to ensure this performance requirement. In this example, all operations in $P_1$ must be performed within 500ms. □

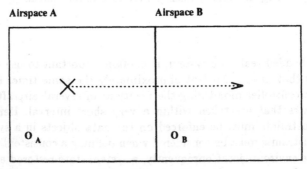

**Fig. 4.** Airspace Control.

Fault-tolerance techniques based on checkpointing and message logging en-

---
[1] This is a variation of an example in [13].

sure that after a failure, a distributed computation recovers to a global state which is reachable from its initial state. There are several problems in applying this approach to real-time systems: First, since a real-time process may include time explicitly in its local state, the definition of a consistent global system state based on partial (or causal) ordering of messages may not be appropriate. For example, consider the data repository in a flight control system. The decision to delay or to land an aircraft is based on the "current" position and status of the aircarfts being monitored. The system state in the data repository is consistent if the timestamps of different data items representing aircraft positions are within an acceptable tolerance. Second, restoring the system to an earlier state may be unnecessary or even incorrect in certain applications. For example, a process may be able to resume its execution at a predefined state and obtain its input directly from a sensor after a failure. Third, since a timing constraint may be imposed on the execution of a process (or a collection of processes), a complex recovery mechanism and resuming execution in an earlier state may result in missing the deadline. The following example illustrates how causal ordering on events may be relaxed when establishing a cut in a distributed real-time computation.

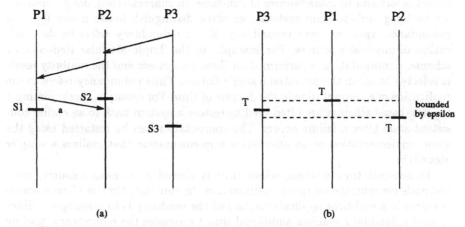

**Fig. 5.** (a) A Distributed Computation. (b) A Time-Based Recovery Line.

## Example 3: Distributed Computation

Figure 5(a) illustrates three cooperating processes $P_1$, $P_2$ and $P_3$ with the corresponding checkpoints $S_1$, $S_2$ and $S_3$. The messages labeled $\alpha$ from process $P_1$ to $P_2$ crosses the recovery line established by the checkpoints. In an asynchronous environment, to establish a consistent cut, message $\alpha$ is logged synchronously or asynchronously by the sender or the receiver. If the processes in Figure 5(a) are real-time processes, several other alternatives for establishing a consistent system state may be possible. If the state variable v updated by $\alpha$ can be extrapolated from its previous values, then it may be unnecessary to log the message to establish a consistent system state. Alternatively, if process $P_2$ is a periodic process and the previous value of v (prior to the checkpoint at $S_2$) is within a predefined distance from the new value of v, this previous value of v can be used in case the process suffers a failure after the checkpoint $T_2$ and before the subsequent checkpoint. Another alternative may be to take checkpoints based on absolute time if the processor clocks are synchronized within a know value $\epsilon$. For example, as shown in Figure 5(b), if each process takes a checkpoint at the local time $T$, then a recovery interval $[T - \epsilon, T + \epsilon]$ can be established. This recovery interval can be used to define a consistent global state to which the system can be restored after a failure. Hence, instead of viewing a global state as a consistent cut of states of processes at some logical instant of time, one can define a system state at an instant of real-time in the same spirit as in [8, 15, 21]. □

## 4 Predictable Redundancy Management

Redundancy (or replication) refers to the additional resources that is required to detect errors and to mask failures at run-time. In characterizing design methods for building fault-tolerant systems, we often distinguish between two types of redundancy: *space* vs. *time* redundancy. Space redundancy refers to the replication of physical resources. For example, in the Triple Modular Redundancy scheme, a computation is performed on three computers and the majority result is selected to mask the potential a single failure. Time redundancy refers to the replication of a computation in the domain of time. For example, checkpointing / logging-based schemes are often used to restore a system back to an earlier consistent state after a failure occurs. The computation can be restarted using the same implementation or an alternative implementation that realizes a simpler algorithm.

In non-real–time systems, where time is viewed as a cheap resource, most methods concentrate on space optimization. In contrast, time is often a scarce resource in a real-time applications, and so the tendency is to trade space. Since spatial redundancy requires additional time to manage the redundancy, trading space for time has potential limits. For example, tolerating transient faults by retrying a computation is an acceptable technique if the timing constraints can be met. The same assertion holds for techniques based on the notion of recovery blocks where a different version of the software module is used in the retry. Although time-space tradeoffs form the basis for most fault-tolerant system design methods, sometimes they may be inappropriate for achieving fault–tolerance in a real–time environment. In particular, redundancy must be considered in the context of achieving both predictability and dependability in a system. When time is scarce and the overhead for managing redundancy is too high, alternative approaches must be considered. An alternative is to consider the quality of the computation or the service as a third dimension in the design space. A fault in a real–time system can result in a (temporary) reduction in the quality of a computation in order to allow the system to meet critical task deadlines. For example, in many real–time control systems, discrete sample values of continuous-time variables are computed. These values can be approximated or estimated if time does not permit more precise computations. The *imprecise computation* approach is one technique that sacrifices accuracy for time in such calculations[14].

Advances in distributed and parallel systems provide the opportunities for achieving real–time performance while satisfying fault–tolerance requirements. However, using the inherent redundancy provided by these systems is not free. The overhead associated with the synchronization of redundant servers, the delay in message communication, and the interaction with the external environment all contribute to the complexity of such protocols. Several recent experimental projects have began to address the problem of replication in distributed hard real-time systems including the MARS [11], the DELTA-4 XPA [22], and the HARTS systems.

The MARS system is a time-triggered distributed real-time system. The architecture of MARS is based on the assumption that the worst-case load is determined apriori at design time. The system is built as a periodic automata and its activities are triggered at environment-independent instants. Hence, the system response to external events is cyclical at pre-specified instants in time. The MARS architecture support active redundancy to handle the occurrence of transient or permanent hardware faults. It also supports time redundancy by executing each task twice and comparing the signatures to detect transient faults. A distributed fault-tolerant clock synchronization protocol and a processor group membership service are provided as part of the MARS operating system. Replica determinism is ensured among active replicas by prohibiting access to local clocks during a task execution and by supporting off-line static schedules. The MARS communication and processor scheduling is done off-line and it is static. The system supports multiple static schedules in different

The DELTA-4 XPA is an event-triggered fault-tolerant real-time system. The objective of XPA is to ensure meeting hard real-time constraints under a "normal operating zone," and change to a best-effort behavior when faced with "unforeseen" operating conditions. Under stress beyond the design-time worst-case load, the system attempts to provide degraded service without falling apart. Distribution and fault-tolerance are supported by a set of group communication services of varying quality. XPA also provides active, semi-active and passive replication of objects. Since XPA architecture assumes components are fail-silent, the semi-active replication scheme allows the decision to be made by a privileged replica who imposes it on the others.

The HARTS system is an experimental distributed real-time systems, consisting of multiprocessor nodes connected by a point-to-point network. Each node in HARTS has several application processors and a network processor. The wrapped-around hexogonal topology of the HARTS interconnection provides reasonably high-connectivity to support hardware routing to detour around nodes and links that may be faulty. The homogeneity of hardware and software components facilitates replication of software and hardware components. An important part of the HARTS architecture is a real-time communication subsystem with several services to support fault-tolerance including a clock synchronization service, a distributed naming service, a reliable broadcast service, and real-time channel with guaranteed delays. Support for group communication, tools for fault-injection and evaulation of the dependability and real-time mechanisms on HARTS, and an implementation of the communication subsystem on a point-to-point switch and a broadcast network are among the ongoing efforts [18].

Although much work has been done on synchronous and asynchronous protocols for managing replicated servers, the problem of server replication in real-time systems requires further research. With the increasing reliance on distributed computing technology in time-critical applications, the need for real-time protocols for failure detection, data replication and distributed management of system-wide resource has become more important. Furthermore, the overhead associated with managing redundancy must be quantified precisely so that certain guarantees about the real-time behavior of the system can be made.

## 5 Scheduling

Managing redundancy in a predictable fashion is related closely to the problem of real-time scheduling. In recent years, significant advances have been made both in distributed systems technologies for building non-real-time applications and in real-time scheduling theory. However, the integration of real-time scheduling theory with techniques for building reliable distributed systems remains an important problem. The requirement of meeting timing constraints in the presence of faults imposes additional demands on the scheduling algorithms. Extension of the real-time scheduling theory that take into account fault-tolerance, redundant resources, and graceful degradation are among the problems being addressed by the researchers in this field. A related problem deals with the scheduling of transient recovery operations with time-critical application tasks [16]. New resource allocation techniques that address the predictability and reliability requirements of complex real-time systems are also being investigated [12].

## 6 Concluding Remarks

Whether the primary motivation for fault-tolerance is to ensure data integrity or to mask failures at run-time, the notion of a consistent system state after a failure defines the correctness criteria for different approaches. The precise definition of a consistent state in a real-time system is complicated by one crucial factor: a system state in time-critical applications changes by the passage of time. This is a key difference from asynchronous systems in which *time* is not considered explicitly in defining a system state. This has several important implications: First, redundancy management must be predictable; meeting stringent timing constraints and achieving fault-tolerance requirements may be contradictory goals in some cases. Second, restoring a system state (by rolling backward or forward) must satisfy certain timing properties imposed on the data in the system. Since usefulness of real-time data diminishes with the passage of time, the definition of a consistent system state must include the temporal relationship between data objects. Third, the ordering constraints, such Lamport's happened-before relation or the total order guaranteed by atomic multicast, may be weakened in managing replicated data in real-time systems. Finally, the inherent non-determinism of time-critical systems can be exploited in developing new fault-tolerance strategies. Instead of characterizing design methodologies by the tradeoff between space and time, new fault-tolerance techniques can exploit data semantics in obtaining timely but acceptable lesser quality results in a computation.

# References

1. J.F. Bartlett. Tandem: A non-stop kernel. *ACM Operating Systems Review*, 15(5), 1991.

2. K. P. Birman. The process group approach to reliable distributed computing. Technical Report TR 91-1216, Department of Computer Science, Cornell University, July 1991.

3. K. P. Birman and T. A. Joseph. Reliable communication in the presence of failures. *ACM Transactions on Computer Systems*, 5(1):47–76, February 1987.

4. A. Borg, J. Baumbach, and S. Glazer. A message system supporting fault-tolerance. In *Proc. of 9th ACM Symposium on Operating Systems Principles*, pages 90–99, October 1983.

5. N. Budhiraja, K. Marzullo, F. B. Schneider, and S. Toueg. Primary-backup protocols: Lower bounds and optimal implementations. Technical Report TR 92-1265, Department of Computer Science, Cornell University, January 1992.

6. M. Chandy and L. Lamport. Distributed snapshot: Determining global states of distributed systems. *ACM Transactions on Computer Systems*, 3(1):63–75, February 1985.

7. F. Cristian and R. Dancey. Fault-tolerance in the advanced automation system. Technical Report RJ7424, IBM Research Laboratory, San Jose, April 1990.

8. F. Cristian and F. Jahanian. A timestamp-based checkpointing protocol for long-lived distributed computations. In *9th Symposiym on Reliable Distributed Systems*, Pisa, Italy, September 1991.

9. H. Hopetz and P. Verissimo. Real time and dependability concepts. In *Distributed Systems, 2nd Edition, S. Mullender(editor)*, pages 411–46 (Chapter 16). Addison-Wesley, 1993.

10. D.B. Johnson. Distributed system fault tolerance using message logging and checkpointing. In *Technical Report COMP TR89-101*. Department of Computer Science, Rice University, December 1989.

11. H. Kopetz, A. Damm, C. Koza, M. Mulazzani, W. Schwabl, C. Senft, and R. Zainlinger. Distributed fault-tolerant real-time systems: The mars approach. *IEEE Micro*, 9(1):25–40, Feb. 1989.

12. C. M. Krishna and K. G. Shin. On scheduling tasks with a quick recovery from faliure. *IEEE Trans. on Comput.*, C–35(5):448–455, May 1986.

13. K-J Lin, F. Jahanian, A. Jhingran, and C. D. Locke. A model of hard real-time transaction systems. Technical Report RC 17515, IBM T.J. Watson Reseach Center, January 1992.

14. J.W.S. Liu, K.-J. Lin, W.-K. Shih, R. Bettati, and J.Y. Chung. Imprecise computations. *to appear in IEEE Proceedings*, January 1994.

15. P. Ramanathan and K.G. Shin. Use of common time base for checkpointing and rollback recovery in a distributed real-time system. *submitted for publication*, 1991.

16. S. Ramos-Thuel and J.K. Strosnider. The transient server approach to scheduling time-critical recover operations. In *Proceedings of 12th Real-Time Systems Symposium*, pages 286–295, San Antonio, December 1991.

17. F. B. Schneider. Implementing fault-tolerant services using the state machine approach: A tutorial. *ACM Computing Surveys*, 22(4), December 1990.

18. K.G. Shin, D.D. Kandlur, D.L. Kiskis, P.S. Dodd, H.A. Rosenberg, and A. Indiresan. A distributed real-time operating system. *IEEE Software*, September 1992.

19. K.G. Shin, G. Koob, and F. Jahanian. Fault-tolerance in real-time systems. In *Panal Session in the Workshop on Real-Time Operating Systems and Software*, Atlanta, May 1991.

20. R.E. Strom and S. Yemini. Optimistic recovery in distributed systems. *ACM Transactions on Computer Systems*, 3(3):204–226, August 1985.

21. Z. Tong, R.Y. Kain, and W.T. Tsai. A low overhead checkpointing and rollback recovery scheme for distributed systems. In *Symposium on Reliable Distributeed Computing*, pages 12–20, 1989.

22. P. Verissimo, P. Barrett, P. Bond, A.Hilborne, L. Rodrigues, and D. Seaton. The extra performance architecture (xpa). In D. Powell, editor, *Delta-4 - A Generic Architecture for Dependable Distributed Computing*, 1991.

# The Systematic Design of Large Real-Time Systems
## or
## Interface Simplicity

H. Kopetz
Technical University of Vienna
Austria

**Abstract:** A key design decision during the development of large real-time systems concerns the decomposition of the system into a set of autonomous subsystem with simple and testable interfaces. In this paper it is argued that time-triggered architectures that eliminate the need for control signals passing subsystem interfaces are better suited for the implementation of large real-time systems than event-triggered architectures, where the control cannot be encapsulated.

## 1. Introduction

The design of large real-time systems is still an engineering challenge with little systematic guidance from the research community. The recently reported difficulty in one of the major ongoing RT system projects--the Advanced Automation System--is a vivid example for the existing situation [1].

We believe that the proper decomposition of a large real-time application into a set of autonomous subsystems is a key activity in the design of any large system. In this paper we investigate the interface complexity between subsystems and come to the conclusion that the elimination of all control signals crossing a subsystem interface should be an explicit design goal. We then show, how such an elimination of the control signals can be achieved with proper architectural support.

The rest of this paper is organized as follows. In the next section we discuss critical design issues and focus on the autonomy of subsystems. In chapter 3 we develop a model of a real-time application that maps naturally into a time-triggered architecture. We propose the introduction of a sparse time base with a proper granularity to eliminate the need for message ordering protocols between subsystem interfaces. Section 4 investigates the difference between temporal control and logical control and sketches a systematic method for the decomposition of a large system into autonomous subsystems. The paper closes with a conclusion in section 5.

## 2. Critical Design issues

In this section we discuss some critical design issues in the development of large real-time systems. The first and in our opinion most important of these design issues concerns the autonomy of subsystems.

### 2.1 Autonomy of Subsystems

We feel that the decomposition of a large real-time application into a set of autonomous subsystems is a key issue in the design of any large system. By autonomy we mean a relative notion: Given two systems A and B that provide a comparable service to their clients, then system A is more autonomous than system B if system A *makes fewer assumptions about the behavior of its environment* than system B.

**2.1.1 Simplicity of Interfaces.** The assumptions a subsystem makes about its environment concern the structure and behavior of the environment at the subsystem interfaces. A small and understandable interface description allows a clear partitioning of the system and increases the comprehensibility of the architecture.

In general, an interface description comprises a data description and a control description. There is a natural limit to the simplification of the data interface: If a subsystem requires a data element from its environment or has to produce a data element for its environment, then this data element must be contained in the interface description.

The situation is different concerning the control part of an interface: At the conceptual level it is possible to eliminate all control signals crossing the interface if the architecture is time-triggered (TT), i.e., all control signals are derived from the progression of the synchronized local clock. If all data elements have state semantics, i.e., a new version of a data element replaces the previous version, then a unidirectional information flow across the interface can be realized and the sender can update an input buffer of the receiver without controlling the receiver or being controlled by the receiver. Sender and receiver can operate under their own control at their own rate independently of each other without exchanging any control information across the interface. (We assume that the low level mutual exclusion problem of accessing the common buffer is solved by a proper synchronization protocol, e.g., the NBW protocol [4]).

It is thus one of our key objectives in the design of large real-time systems to plan the subsystem boundaries such that no control information has to cross them.

In an event-triggered (ET) architecture control signals (interrupts) denoting the occurrence of significant events have to cross the subsystem boundaries. The set of assumptions that relate to the proper behavior of these control signals generated by the environment reduces the autonomy of the subsystem and thus increases the complexity of the architecture.

**2.1.2 Stability of Interfaces.** The stability of the subsystem interfaces over the operational lifetime of the system is another key concern in the design of large real time systems. If changes ripple across subsystem interfaces, then the development and maintenance of large applications is complicated. Interface simplicity and interface stability are non-conflicting goals. If no control signals are crossing an interface then there is no possibility that a change in the control of one subsystem will influence the control in the other subsystem.

**2.3 Timeliness**

The main difference between a real-time application and a non-real-time application is the concern for timeliness. Timeliness is a system property that spans all architectural levels: the structure of the application software, the organization of the operating system and the performance of the hardware. These temporal requirements are concerned with the end-to-end timeliness and not only with some intermediate processing steps, e.g., the posting of interrupts by the hardware or by the operating system. In critical real-time applications the adherence to the temporal requirements should be guaranteed by design.

## 2.4 Testability

Real-time system must be tested in the value domain and in the time domain. Although testing in the value domain has been discussed extensively in the literature, there are relatively few publications that are concerned with testing in the time domain [7]. This is worrying, since fifty percent and more of the development resources of a real-time system project are spent on testing.

Systematic testability of the temporal properties requires architectural support. If the temporal interactions among the subsystem are dependent on the actual load pattern and thus uncontrolled, the temporal system test is not decomposable. If the subsystem are temporally encapsulated and rely on their local control, it is easier to develop a constructive test strategy than in a system with global control.

# 3 A Model of a RT System Application

Any design process starts with building an abstract model of the intended application. The structure and representation of this model has a profound influence on the further design activities. We propose an abstract model of a real-time application that maps naturally into atime-triggered implementation of this application. Let us begin by stating our assumptions about the time base and the error detection coverage.

## 3.1 Assumptions about the Time Base

Any real-time system model must contain a appropriate abstraction of the phenomenon of real time. We propose the introduction of a properly chosen sparse time base into such model.

A timebase is *sparse* if the occurrence of events is restricted to subsections of the timeline, otherwise it is *dense*.

**3.1.1 Sparse Time.** If the occurrence of events is restricted to a specified interval around the lattice points of an abstract space-time lattice with a lattice granularity $g_{lat}$ > 3 $g_{sync}$, the granularity of the synchronized clocks, then the temporal order of events can be recovered from their timestamps. If the events are allowed to occur at the lattice points of the node-local approximation of the space time lattice then the above condition is satisfied. The effect of introducing such a sparse timebase will not be noticeable at the application level, provided the granularity of this lattice is much smaller than the critical timing parameters of the application. In such an architecture it is not necessary to execute agreement protocols to determine a consistent view about the order of event occurrence.

The occurrence of events can only be restricted to a sparse time base if the events are in the sphere of control of the distributed computer system, e.g., the sending of messages, the recognition of message arrival, etc..

**3.1.2 Dense Time.** If events can occur on a dense timebase then it is impossible to recover the temporal order of the events on the basis of the timestamps generated by synchronized clocks. If an event occurring on a dense timebase is observed by two or more nodes (to provide redundancy), then an explicit agreement protocol is needed to establish a consistent view of the temporal point of event occurrence in a distributed system. Such an agreement protocol requires bidirectional communication and thus the exchange of control signals across subsystem boundaries.

The following two event classes are outside the sphere of control of the computer system and can therefore occur at any points in time i.e., on a dense time base:

(1)     External events in the control object

(2)     Faults

The two cases above can be handled as follows: The point of recognition of an external event can be restricted to a sparse timebase. If there is more than one observer, an agreement protocol [1] has to decide what point on the sparse time base is assigned to the event occurrence. To avoid the exchange of control signals across subsystem boundaries, the redundant observers have to be allocated to the same subsystem.

Faults can occur at any point in time. If we assume that an error caused by a fault is detected with a sufficiently high probability before the next output action, i.e., an event on the sparse timebase, then the consequence of the fault is an omission failure on the sparse timebase. This assumption of a sufficiently high error detection coverage is essential for the applicability of this model.

The introduction of a sparse time base reduces the size of the potential input space significantly, since events cannot occur at any time but are restricted to the properly chosen lattice points. A system with a small input space is easier to test than a system with a large input space.

To summarize, if we introduce a properly chosen sparse time base, hide the interface to redundant sensors within a single subsystem, and base our design on self-checking hardware, then a consistent ordering of events is achieved without the execution of agreement protocols, a unidirectional information flow can be maintained across subsystem boundaries, and the testability of the system is improved.

## 3.2 Structure Elements of the Model

The introduction of real-time entities and real-time objects leads to a design description that maps naturally into a an implementation without the need for control signals crossing subsystem boundaries.

### 3.2.1 Real-Time (RT) Entity.
A RT entity is a state variable of interest for the given purpose of the real-time computer application [2]. A RT entity changes its state as a function of real time.

Examples of RT entities are:

    Temperature of a Vessel (continuous)

    Position of a Switch (discrete)

    Setpoint selected by an operator

    Intended position of an actuator

A RT entity has static (e.g., name, type, value domain) and dynamic attributes (e.g., value at a particular point in time). Every RT entity is in the sphere of control of a subsystem that has the authority to set the value of the RT entity. Outside its sphere of control a RT entity can only be observed, but not modified. At the chosen level of abstraction, changes in the representation of a RT entity are not relevant.

**3.2.2 Observation.** The information about the value of a RT entity at a particular point in time is captured in the notion of an observation.

An observation is a triple containing:

-       The name of a RT - entity

-       The point in time when the observation has been made.

-       The information about the RT - entity.

An observation is atomic, i.e., the elements cannot be separated. Observations are transported in messages.

An observation is a state observation, if the information field in the observation contains the full or partial state of the RT - entity. The time of the state observation denotes the point in time when the RT entity was sampled. State observations are idempotent. We call a message that contains a state observation a state message. A new version of a state message overwrites the previous version. State messages do not have to be queued at the receiver, i.e., there is no problem with buffer management requiring a bidirectional informal flow.

An observation is an event observation, if the information field in the observation contains the difference between the "old state" (the last observed state) and the "new state". The time of the event information denotes the point in time of when the "new state" has started. The transport of event information across subsystem boundaries requires the exchange of control signals across the interface for the purpose of explicit flow control.

### 3.2.3 Real-Time (RT) - Object.

A real-time object k is an object that stores observations about RT entities. Every RT object

- has an associated real-time clock which ticks with a granularity $t_k$. This granularity must be in agreement with the dynamics of the RT entity this object is to represent.

- activates an object procedure whenever the object clock ticks.

If there is no other way to activate an object procedure than by the periodic clock tick within the object, we call the RT object a *synchronous* RT object. Otherwise we call the object *asynchronous*.

### 3.3 Relationships between the Structure Elements

We introduce three relationships between the structure elements introduced above: accuracy, stability, and replica determinism

### 3.3.1 Accuracy.

Accuracy is a relation between a RT entity E and an associated RT object O. There is always a delay between the observation of a RT entity and the delivery of this observation to the RT object.

Let us define a recent history $RH_i$ around the present point in time $t_i$ as the ordered set $<t_i, t_{i-1}, \ldots, t_{i-k}>$ of time-points. A RT object O is accurate at the present point $t_i$, if there is a $j \in RH_i$, such that value_O at $t_i$ = value_E at $t_j$, i.e. if the present value in the RT object is the result of a recent observation of the RT entity.

There are three techniques to maintain a given degree of accuracy between a RT entity and a RT object:

(1) Periodically update a RT object by an observation from a RT entity (TT approach).

(2) Update the RT object only when there is a change in the RT entity (ET approach).

(3)     Execute a state estimation model to determine the current state of the RT
        entity by some indirect measurements (either ET or TT).

If it is our goal to eliminate all control signals crossing subsystem boundaries, we have
to exclude alternative (2).

**3.3.2 Stability.** Stability is a relation between a given observation message $M_i$ that
has arrived at a RT object O and all messages $M_{i-1}$, $M_{i-2}$, ... that have been sent to
this object temporally before $M_i$. The message $M_i$ becomes stable at Object O as soon
as all previously sent messages have arrived [6].

The time interval between the send time of $M_i$ and the point in time when $M_i$
becomes stable is called the *action delay*. If a global time-base is available and two or
more processes are observing RT entities, then the action delay amounts to the
maximum protocol execution time + 2 g, where g is the granularity of the global time
base. If a global time-base is not available and two or more processes are observing
RT entities, then the action delay amounts to the maximum protocol execution time
plus the reading error $\varepsilon$, i.e., the difference between the maximum and minimum
protocol execution time. If stability is of interest, then it follows that a system with a
global timebase has a better responsiveness than a system without a global time base.

**3.3.3 Replica Determinism.** Replica Determinism is a relation between a set of
replicated RT objects. It requires that all replicated RT objects must visit the same
states at about the same time (limited by the precision of the clock synchronization). If
fault tolerance is implemented by active redundancy, then replica determinism among
the replicated objects must be provided.

Replica determinism can be destroyed by

-       uncoordinated access to the clock, e.g., in timeouts, time bounds for
        algorithms, etc.,

-       dynamic scheduling decisions in the operating system.

-       algorithms based on random number generators.

It follows that there are major difficulties to implement active redundancy in ET-systems that require dynamic scheduling decisions.

## 4. The Design of the Temporal Control Scheme

The temporal control scheme determines at what point in time the execution of a selected action will start. It has to be distinguished from the logical control that is concerned with the control flow within a program to realize the specified logic or arithmetic functions.

### 4.1 Temporal Control versus Logical Control

Let us demonstrate the difference between temporal control and logical control by the following little example:

Consider an alarm monitoring component that should raise an alarm if the following condition relating pressure $p_1$ and pressure $p_2$ becomes true. Assume that pressure $p_1$ and pressure $p_2$ are observed by another subsystem:

$$\text{WHEN } p_1 < p_2 \text{ THEN raise alarm;}$$

At a first glance, this specification of an alarm condition looks reasonable. However, a closer analysis leads us to the following two open questions:

(1)     What is the maximum allowable temporal interval between the measurement of corresponding values of $p_1$ and $p_2$ ?

(2)     At what points in time must the alarm condition be evaluated?

It is clear that the answers to these rather important questions are not contained in the above specification. The above specification is an example for the obscure mingling of temporal and logical issues into a single specification statement. The temporal issues concern the points in time when $p_1$ and $p_2$ musts be measured and compared, while the logical issues relate to the type of comparison.

The comparison of two *accurate* values of $p_1$ and $p_2$ is an example for logical control. The determination of the point in time when this comparison should take place is an issue of the temporal control. Temporal control is triggered by a *control signal*.

## 4.2 Time-triggered Versus Event-triggered Control

In the example above, there are two possible sources for the control signal to activate the evaluation of the (logical) alarm condition:

(1)    A periodic control signal is derived from the ticks of the local real-time clock of the RT object that stores accurate observations about $p_1$ and $p_2$. This is an example for an autonomous time-triggered (TT) activation.

(2)    A control signal is generated whenever a new value of $p_1$ or $p_2$ is delivered by the communication system. This is an example for an event-triggered (ET) activation.

In the second case the question of how often the control condition has to be evaluated is delegated to the data collection system outside the node performing the comparison, i.e., the control signal has to traverse subsystem boundaries.

The above example shows that in TT-systems the control signal is generated within the subsystem under consideration, whereas in ET-system the control signal traverses a subsystem boundary and thus complicates the subsystem interface.

### 4.3 System Decomposition

Let us now sketch a systematic approach to the decomposition of a large real-time application into a set of autonomous subsystems.

The first step is concerned with the identification of the relevant RT entities within the application. The temporal attributes of the entities (e.g. maximum gradient) must be determined, since these temporal properties are needed for the establishment of the accuracy requirements of the associated real time objects and the deadlines of the real-time (RT) transactions.

Many RT entities will be in the sphere of control of the environment. These RT entities can only be observed, but cannot be modified by the computer system. Some RT entities (e.g., the intended setpoints of the control valves or the alarm indicators to the operator) will be in the sphere of control of the computer system. The algorithms needed to calculate these computer internal RT entities must be contained in the system specification.

After the RT entities have been identified, they must be assigned to distinct subsystems. An analysis of the algorithms that compute the values of computer internal RT entities within a subsystem will reveal the demand for the RT objects in the various subsystems. The end-to-end timing requirements of the RT transactions determine the accuracy requirements of these RT objects. After all the RT entities and RT objects have been identified it is necessary to group them together and establish the subsystem boundaries.

In the next phase it must be decided how the accuracy requirements of the RT objects can be met: either by a periodic update from the RT entity via a state message or by a state estimation model within the subsystem under consideration. The need for any control signal passing a subsystem boundary should be questioned with great scrutiny. The only instance where such a control signal is justified is a requirement for a rapid mode change activation.

## 5. Conclusion

In this position paper it has been argued that the architecture of a complex real-time application is more intelligible if the subsystems have a high degree of autonomy, i.e., make only the absolutely necessary assumptions about the behavior of the subsystem environment.

A set of important assumptions about the subsystem interfaces relates to the number and complexity of the control signals that have to traverse subsystem boundaries. It has been shown that in a properly designed time-triggered architecture no control signals are required to traverse subsystem boundaries. A design based on such an architecture is thus inherently simpler than a design based on an event-triggered architecture. Furthermore the static schedules of TT architectures guarantee timeliness, maintain replica determinism for the implementation of active redundancy, and improve the testability.

# Acknowledgements

This work has been supported, in part, by ESPRIT project PDCS.

# REFERENCES

1. Cristian, F., Aghili, H., Strong R. Dolev,D., Atomic Broadcast: From Simple message diffusion to Byzantine Agreement, Proc. FTCS 15, Ann Arbor, Mich., June 1985, pp.200-206

2. Kopetz, H., Kim, K.,Real-Time Temporal Uncertainties in Interactions among Real-Time Objects, Proc. of the 9th IEEE Symp. on Reliable Distributed Systems, Huntsville, Al, Oct. 1990, pp.165 -174

3. Kopetz, H. Sparse Time versus Dense Time in Distributed Real-Time Systems, Proc. of the 14th Distributed Computing System Conference, Yokohama, Japan, IEEE Press, June 1992

4. Kopetz, H., Reisinger, J, The Non Blocking Write Protocol NBW: A solution to a real-time synchronization problem. Proc. of the Real-Time Systems Symposium 1993, IEEE Press

5. Lewyn, M., Flying in Place: The FAA's Air-Control Fiasco, Business Week, April 26, 1993, p. 64-65

6. Schneider,F.B., Implementing Fault-Tolerant Services Using the State Machine Approach: A Tutorial, ACM Computing Surveys, Vol 22, Nr. 4, December 1990, pp. 299-320

7. Schutz, W., On the Testability of Distributed Real-Time Systems, Proc. of the 10th Symposium on Reliable Distributed Systems, Pisa, Italy, Sept. 1991, pp.52-61.

# Fault Tolerance in Embedded Real-Time Systems: Importance and Treatment of Common Mode Failures[*]

Jaynarayan H. Lala, Richard E. Harper
Advanced Computer Architectures Group
The Charles Stark Draper Laboratory
555 Technology Square, MS 73
Cambridge, MA 02139

## Abstract

Dependable computer architectures used in critical embedded real-time applications have successfully employed Byzantine resilience techniques to tolerate physical, internal, operational faults. The dominant cause of failure of a correctly designed Byzantine resilient computer today is the common-mode failure, i.e., the nearly simultaneously failure of multiple redundant copies, generally due to a single cause. Unlike independent hardware faults, for which theoretically rigorous fault tolerance solutions have been implemented, the sources of common-mode failures are so diverse that numerous disparate techniques are required to predict, avoid, remove, and tolerate them.

This paper describes the technical approach that is being used to reduce the probability of common-mode failure in the Draper Fault Tolerant Parallel Processor which has been designed for critical embedded real-time applications. It begins with placing common-mode failures in the context of overall impairments to dependability to clarify their relative importance with respect to other failure sources. The FTPP's approach to tolerating independent hardware faults is briefly motivated and described. The overall strategy for common-mode failure reduction comprises three major areas: common-mode failure avoidance, removal, and tolerance. For fault avoidance, a novel integrated formal methods and VHDL design methodology has been developed and applied. Common-mode fault tolerance techniques include a combination of on-line checking of timing and functional behavior of operating system and application tasks, use of a formally verified system diagnosis processor to diagnose overall system health, and system-wide recovery actions. Techniques for the reduction of common-mode failure probability due to performance timing faults are also discussed.

Keywords:   Common-mode failure tolerance, formal methods, VHDL, automated design tools, Byzantine resilience

---

[*] This work was supported by NASA Langley Research Center under contract NAS1-18565.

# 1 Introduction

Dependable computer architectures used in critical embedded real-time control applications employ replicated channels executing identical instructions on bit-wise identical inputs; faulty channels are detected and masked via bit-wise comparison of channel outputs. This technique excels in tolerating faults which occur independently in different members of the replicated processing site. For these independent hardware faults theoretically rigorous fault tolerance solutions have been designed, optimized, implemented, evaluated analytically and empirically, and validated. This has been successful to such an extent that the dominant cause of failure of a correctly designed Byzantine resilient (BR) computer today is common-mode failures (CMF). A common-mode failure occurs when multiple copies of a redundant digital system suffer faults nearly simultaneously, generally due to a single cause. Unlike independent hardware faults, the sources of common-mode failures are so diverse that numerous disparate techniques are required to predict, avoid, remove, and tolerate them. There is no silver bullet like the solution to the Byzantine Generals Problem to solve the CMF problem. This paper describes the technical approach that is being used to reduce the probability of common-mode failure in the Draper Fault Tolerant Parallel Processor.

Many of the techniques used to reduce the probability of occurrence of common-mode failures seem like simple common sense. This is because for CMFs common sense is often the best guidance available. In fact, there is nothing novel about any given technique if it is examined all by itself. However, the key to cost-effectively obtaining common-mode failure resilience is to apply appropriate techniques selectively. Employing all available techniques everywhere would not only be too expensive but also be self-defeating by making the system too complex to be validated. For example, it may not be best to formally specify and verify every component of the system. Similarly, design diversity is better applied to application programs rather than redundancy management software. Appropriate use of common-mode failure resilience techniques is very much an engineering judgment issue. What is presented in this paper is the methodical application of an approach to a system where primary emphasis in the past has been on tolerating random hardware faults or physical, operational faults that do not affect multiple fault containment regions simultaneously.

Although the main focus of this paper is on CMF resilience, a discussion of Byzantine resilience (BR) is repeated here from previous publications in order to complete the description of the approach to fault tolerance in FTPP, to clarify the validation and cost-related motivations for BR which have not been understood well in the past (many people think the reason for BR is to tolerate exotic, improbable faults), and to illustrate how CMF tolerance techniques must not violate the theoretical requirements for BR, i.e., CMF tolerance must not be achieved at the expense of coverage of random hardware faults.

# 2 FTPP Overview

The FTPP architecture is described in references [Abl88], [Bab90], [Har87], [Har88a], [Har88b], and [Har91]. It is composed of many Processing Elements (PEs) and a few specially designed hardware components referred to as Network Elements (NEs). A diagram of the FTPP physical architecture is presented in Figure 1. The multiple Processing Elements provide a parallel processing environment as well as components for hardware redundancy. The group of Network Elements acts as the intercomputer communications network and the redundancy management hardware.

265

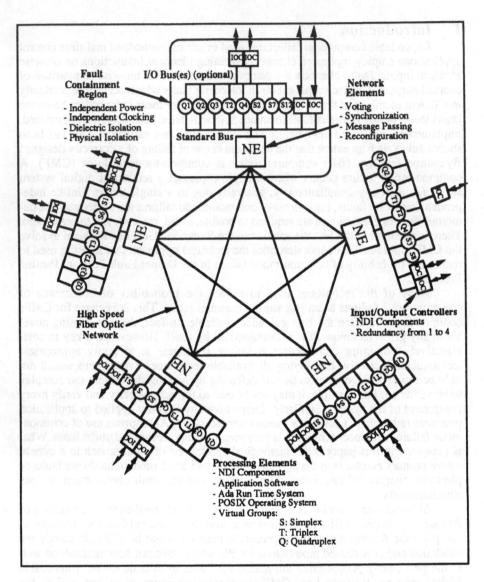

Figure 1. FTPP Physical Architecture

As with most complex computing systems, FTPP is best viewed as a layered system (Figure 2). The top layer consists of the applications programs themselves. Applications are constructed by the applications engineers without regard for the parallel and redundant nature of the FTPP system. In this view, FTPP supports a virtual architecture of a number of tasks which may execute in parallel, subject to preemption, data, and control flow dependencies. The tasks communicate using message passing.

The next lower layer consists of the FTPP System Services. Certain services are visible and may be invoked by the applications programmer; these include input/output, task scheduling, and intertask communication services. This layer is intended to mask the complexity of the FTPP's lower layers from the programmer. Other important functions of the FTPP System Services are not directly accessible by the applications programmer and are performed in a manner which is largely transparent. These include the functions of mapping of tasks to processing sites, arranging of preemption of lower priority tasks by higher priority ones, routing intertask messages to remote tasks, disassembling and reassembling long messages, performing input/output functions, Built-In Testing (BIT) and fault logging, and fielding software exceptions. Other functions are fault detection, identification, and recovery (FDIR); reconfiguration of the parallel resources into redundant computing sites; and interfacing to the interprocessor communication network hardware.

The Sensor redundancy management is partitioned from the FTPP FDIR and is treated as just another application task. Sensor RM does communicate with FDIR task to obtain status of FTPP elements responsible for accessing sensors.

The application tasks and FTPP System Services execute on the FTPP Processing Elements, as indicated in Figure 2.

The next lower layer of the FTPP consists of the interprocessor communication network hardware, known as Network Elements. This hardware implements the interprocessor message passing functions of the FTPP. In addition, it implements throughput-critical fault tolerance-specific functions such as voting of messages emanating from redundant processing sites and providing error indications, assisting in synchronizing redundant processing sites, and assisting in arranging the non-redundant processing resources of the FTPP into redundant processing sites based on the needs of the application, mission mode, and fault state of the FTPP. The inter-Network Element communication links provide high-bandwidth, electrically isolated, optical communication paths between the Network Elements of the FTPP. The data transmissions over the links also keep the Network Elements synchronized to within a small skew using a digital phase-locked loop.

# 3   Overall Approach to Fault Tolerance

## 3.1 Fault Classification

Common-mode failures and their sources are extremely diverse. They can be classified in the same way that all faults are classified in "Dependability: Basic Concepts and Terminology" [Lap92], that is, according to three main viewpoints which are their nature, their origin and their persistence. The three viewpoints are not mutually exclusive.

**Classification by Nature.** Faults may be accidental in nature, i.e., they appear or are created fortuitously, or they may be intentional in nature, i.e., they are created deliberately. For FTPP, intentional faults, e.g. Trojan horses, time bombs, viruses, are not currently considered since they are related primarily to secure systems. Security is currently not a requirement for embedded FTPP applications, although it may be at some future point in time.

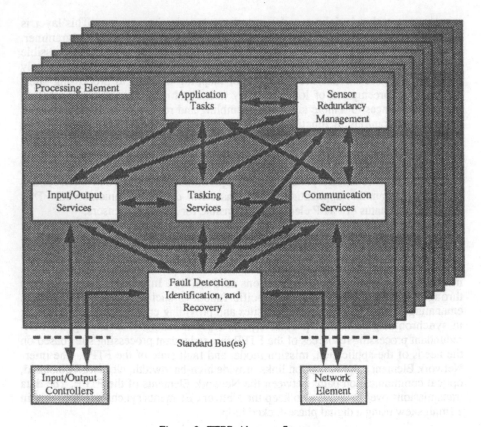

Figure 2. FTPP Abstract Structure

**Classification by Origin.** Classification by origin may be divided into three viewpoints which are not necessarily mutually exclusive: 1. Phenomenological Causes - physical faults, which are due to adverse physical phenomena; - human-made faults, which result from human imperfections. 2. System Boundaries - internal faults, which are those parts of the system's state which, when invoked by the computation activity, will produce an error; - external faults, which result from system interference caused by its physical environment, or from system interaction with its human environment. 3. Phase of Creation - design faults, which result from imperfections that arise during: the development of the system (from requirement specification to implementation), subsequent modifications, or the establishment of procedures for operating or maintaining the system; - operational faults, which appear during the system's exploitation.

**Classification by Persistence.** 1. Permanent Faults - their presence is not related to internal conditions such as computation activity or external conditions such as the environment. 2. Temporary Faults - their presence is related to temporary internal or external conditions and as such they are present for a limited amount of time.

Since intentional faults are excluded from the current scope of work, there are only 16 possible sources of faults that must be considered. These are all the possible combinations of the remaining four viewpoints. Of these the physical, internal, operational faults can be tolerated by using hardware redundancy. This is treated in greater detail in Section 3.2. All other faults can affect multiple fault containment regions simultaneously. These are the sources of common-mode failures. However, only some of these fault classes are meaningful. These are shown in Table 1. Of these, the interaction faults which arise from the interaction of the computer system with its human environment, e.g. an operator, will not be considered here since the man-machine interface is outside the scope of the FTPP's intended use as an embedded control system.

| Phenomenological cause | | System Boundary | | Phase of Creation | | Persistence | | Common Mode Fault Label |
|---|---|---|---|---|---|---|---|---|
| Physical | Human made | Internal | External | Design | Oper-ational | Perm-anent | Temp-orary | |
| X | | | X | | X | | X | Transient (External) CMF |
| X | | | X | | X | X | | Permanent (External) CMF |
| | X | X | | | X | | X | Intermittent (Design) CMF |
| | X | X | | X | | X | | (Permanent) Design CMF |
| | X | | X | | X | | X | Interaction CMF |

Table 1. Classification of Common Mode Faults

Using this taxonomy, then, only 4 sources of common-mode failures need to be considered for FTPP in the context of current applications: 1. Transient (External) Faults which are the result of interference to the system from its physical environment such as lightning, High Energy Radio Frequencies (HERF), heat, etc. 2. Permanent (External) Faults which are the result of system interference caused by its operational environment such as heat, sand, salt water, dust, etc. 3. Intermittent (design) Faults which are introduced due to imperfections in the requirements specifications, detailed design, implementation of design and other phases leading up to the operation of the system. These faults manifest themselves only part of the time. 4. (Permanent) Design Faults are introduced during the same phases as intermittent faults, but manifest themselves permanently.

If the relative likelihoods of these four classes of common-mode failures were known, one could apportion the efforts in dealing with them appropriately. However, the models to predict the occurrence of common-mode failures either do not exist, or are not mature enough to be of any practical value. Similarly, the rates of occurrence of transient faults and permanent external faults are very much dependent upon the operational environment. Thus, while the relative arrival rates of the four classes of common-mode failures cannot be predicted with any accuracy, experience and prudence suggest that all of these are sufficiently likely to be of concern.

## 3.2 Random Hardware Faults or Physical, Internal, Operational Faults

For a computer to be considered adequately reliable for life- or mission-critical applications, it must be capable of surviving a specified number of random component faults with a probability approaching unity. A conservative failure model is to consider faults as consisting of arbitrary behavior on the part of failed components. This type of fault, known as a *Byzantine fault*, may include stopping and then restarting execution at a future time, sending conflicting information to different destinations, and, in short, anything within a failed component's power to attempt to corrupt the system.

Since the concept of Byzantine resilience is central to the theory and operation of the FTPP, it is important to discuss the motivation for this seemingly extreme degree of fault tolerance. Cost-effective validatability and achievement of high reliability are important motivating factors. Validation-based motivation for Byzantine resilience is perhaps best viewed in the context of an example. We suppose that a digital computer system having a maximum allowable probability of failure of $10^{-9}$ per hour is required, and that this system must be constructed of replicated channels each of which has an aggregate failure probability of $10^{-4}$ per hour. In a traditional system Failure Modes and Effects Analysis (FMEA)-based approach to achieving the requisite failure rate: likely failure modes of the system are analyzed, their likely extent and effects are predicted, and suitable fault tolerance techniques are developed for each failure mode which is considered to possess a reasonable chance of occurring. For the system to meet the reliability requirement, the probability that any given fault is not covered must be less than $\approx 10^{-9}/10^{-4} = 10^{-5}$; that is, it is necessary that the likelihood of a failure occurring which was not predicted and planned for must be less than $\approx 10^{-5}$. Viewed another way, it is (or should be) incumbent upon the designer to prove to an aggressive and competent inquisitor such as a certification authority that fewer than one in 100,000 faults which could occur in the field (as opposed to those induced or injected in the laboratory) could conceivably defeat the proposed fault tolerance techniques. If this assertion cannot be demonstrated within a reasonable amount of time and money, then it is not feasible to validate the FMEA assumptions and hence the claimed $10^{-9}$ per hour failure rate.

The FMEA process is tedious, time-consuming, and extremely expensive. This is attested to by the seemingly contradictory trend of increasing costs of digital avionics systems even as the cost of hardware continues to decline. This is at least partially due to the fact that the cost of validating critical systems completely overwhelms the cost of their design and construction. Software validation is a major component of this cost, and inappropriate fault tolerance-related architectural features only aggravate the difficulty.

In contrast consider another fault tolerance technique which guarantees that the system can tolerate faults, <u>without</u> relying upon any *a priori* assumptions about component misbehavior. In effect, a faulty component may misbehave in any manner whatsoever, even to the extreme of displaying seemingly intelligent malicious behavior. A system tolerant of such faults would obviate the expensive and physically intractable problem of convincing a knowledgeable inquisitor of the validity of restrictive hypotheses regarding faulty behavior, in effect permitting faulty behavior to subsume all conceivable FMEAs. Such a system is denoted "Byzantine resilient," that is, capable of tolerating "Byzantine" faults.

One expects a system capable of tolerating such a powerful failure mode to be intrinsically complex and possess numerous inscrutable and exotic characteristics. To the contrary, the requirements levied upon an architecture tolerant of Byzantine faults are relatively straightforward and unambiguous, simply comprising a lower bound on the number of fault containment regions, their connectivity, their synchrony, and the utilization of certain simple information exchange protocols. We assert that a satisfactory demonstration that an architecture possesses these simple attributes is far less expensive and time-consuming than proving that certain uncovered failure modes can occur with a probability of at most $10^{-5}$. Existing critical computing systems are typically designed to be triply or quadruply redundant anyhow; meeting the requirements for Byzantine resilience requires a simple rearrangement of the channels and addition of a few interchannel communication protocols. We think this minor rearrangement of the architecture recovers many times over the cost of an FMEA-based validation. Moreover, it is our experience that the run time overhead required to achieve Byzantine resilience can be substantially less than that required to achieve significantly lower levels of fault coverage using fault tolerant techniques based on restrictive hypothetical models of failure behavior.

By making the system Byzantine resilient, in our opinion we have imparted it some powerful programming attributes which result in a significant reduction in software validation effort and cost. First, the hardware redundancy is largely transparent to the programmer. The applications programs and the operating system are developed, debugged, and validated in a simplex (nonredundant) environment without any regard for the redundant copies of the software executing on redundant hardware. Second, the management of hardware redundancy is transparent to the programmer. The applications programs and the operating system are rigorously separated from the hardware and software that manages redundancy. Redundancy management includes functions for detection and isolation of faults, masking of errors resulting from faults, and reconfiguration and reallocation of resources. This rigorous separation allows independent validation of various software entities such as the applications programs, the operating system, and the redundancy management software. By breaking the destructive synergism that comes from intertwining these entities, significant reduction in software validation effort has resulted for the FTPP's predecessors, including the Fault Tolerant MultiProcessor (FTMP) [Lal86a], the Fault Tolerant Processor (FTP) ([Lal86b]), and the Advanced Information Processing System (AIPS) ([Lal84], [Lal85]). Third, a guarantee is made to the applications programmer and the operating system on interprocessor message ordering and validity which holds in the presence of arbitrary faults, and relieves the programmer from consideration of faulty behavior when designing a distributed application. These guarantees are embodied in the Byzantine Resilient Virtual Circuit (BRVC) abstraction of the FTPP [Har92]. Once again, the practical impact of this abstraction is the reduction of effort required to validate distributed applications software executing on the FTPP.

It has been suggested that Byzantine resilient systems are overdesigned because such strange failure modes cannot occur in real life. On the contrary, we contend that odd unanticipated failure modes occur often enough in practice that their probability of occurrence cannot be dismissed, and that ultra-reliable computing systems must be able to tolerate them. Fortunately, the problem of tolerating such random hardware faults has been solved and optimized. Although incremental refinements continue to be made in areas such as encoded rather than replicated memory, fast realignment of a channel for transient fault recovery, etc. the dominant contributor to failure of correctly designed BR computer is now common-mode failures. This is discussed in the remainder of the paper.

## 3.3 Common-Mode Failures

As of now, no unifying theory has been developed that can treat CMFs the same way that BR treats random hardware faults or physical operational faults. There is no silver bullet to slay the CMF monster. Instead we must rely on three brass bullets: fault avoidance techniques applied primarily during the specification, design and implementation phases, fault removal techniques applied primarily during the test and validation phases, and fault tolerance techniques applied during the operational phases. The next section discusses each of these techniques in detail. One should keep in mind the fact that we do not expect to obtain 100 per cent coverage from any of these techniques individually or even from one group collectively; only that when we have gone through the whole process the likelihood of FTPP failing in operation is reduced significantly.

The coverage of the various CMF resilience techniques is difficult to quantify. However, if one concedes that a modest and quantifiable coverage of, say 99%, is achievable at each of the three layered defenses against CMFs (i.e. avoidance, removal, and tolerance), then this could result in a lack of coverage on the order of $10^{-6}$ for all CMFs, provided no additional sources of CMFs are introduced in the test & validation and the operational phases. Given a fairly pessimistic CMF arrival rate of, say, $10^{-3}$ per hour, one can estimate that the overall probability of a system failure due to CMF would be commensurate with that due to exhaustion of spares or coincident random faults. While this is clearly not a rigorous analysis, the order of magnitude of the parameters involved indicates that the layered CMF defenses constitute a feasible approach, as well as provides certain coverage objectives for each of the three layers of CMF defenses described below.

## 4 Technical Approach to Reducing Probability of CMF in FTPP

### 4.1 Common-Mode Failure Avoidance

The most cost effective phase of the total design and development process for reducing the likelihood of common-mode failures is the earliest part of the program. Avoidance techniques and tools are used from the requirements specifications to the design and implementation phases and result in fewer CMFs being introduced into the computer system.

**Use of Mature and Formally Verified Components.** By using commercial-off-the-shelf (COTS) or non-developmental item (NDI) hardware, software, power supply modules, and formally verified microprocessors and real-time kernels as these come on-line , etc., one can leverage the industry's large investment in the testing and verification of components, essentially having others perform fault removal for free.

The FTPP architecture has been specifically designed to accommodate COTS/NDI components without any modifications required for fault tolerance, synchronization, or parallel processing. This is a major departure from the designs of FTMP and FTP which required that all hardware must be clock-deterministic and which thus inhibited the use of such components. In the FTPP, functional synchronization is employed which is assisted by the Network Element, which is the only hardware development item in the computer.

Reuse of mature software packages is only feasible if the underlying operating system interfaces and services are reasonably consistent from an original system to a reusing system. The FTPP is currently pursuing two operating system development strategies to achieve this consistency. In the first, the FTPP utilizes a vendor-supplied Ada RTS, with some modifications suggested by the Ada Run Time Working Group (ARTWG) having been made to enhance its real time performance [Har92]. It is expected that since the Ada language and many of its underlying RTS support functions are specified in MIL-STD 1815, software components written for one application can be rehosted on the FTPP with minimal effort and consequent introduction of new design faults. In the second avenue of development, a POSIX Open System Environment-compliant (IEEE POSIX OSE Standard P1003.x) operating system is hosted on the FTPP. The goals of the POSIX OSE are to achieve source code portability, interoperability, and user portability. Portability is accomplished through the use of application-system interface standards, to allow a user's application to run on a wide range of hardware and software platforms with no modifications. Interoperability is characterized by the cooperative operation of applications resident on dissimilar computer systems, and a standard user interface allows users to migrate from system to system with a minimum of retraining. These characteristics of the POSIX OSE facilitate code reuse, as well as reduce introduction of new design errors due to unfamiliarity with a new operating system and development environment in a new application.

Use of COTS/NDI hardware and software goes hand-in-hand with conformance of the design to commercial, military and/or de facto standards. Although the primary motivation for the development of standards is ease of interoperability, logistics, maintainability, reduced cost, and so on, one of the side benefits of using standards is the reduction of design errors. Standards usually result in detailed, precise, and stable specifications that can be adhered to in the design phase and, over time, verified against in the verification phase. The design errors that are normally introduced due to ambiguous or changing specifications can be substantially reduced by the use of standards.

The FTPP Network Element has been designed to interface to the VMEbus, allowing us to choose from an extensive selection of COTS/NDI PEs which are available with the VMEbus interface. Furthermore, the NE design has been modularized so that a new application that requires a different backplane bus standard, say Futurebus+, need impact only the bus interface part of the NE circuitry (about 20%), the intent being to minimize the introduction of new design faults into the bus-independent part of the NE.

The combination of the Ada RTS and the VMEbus backplane have allowed us to upgrade the FTPP from a Motorola 68020-based PE from one vendor to a 68030-based PE from another without introducing any new design errors other than those resident in the new PE. The FTPP NE has also been interfaced to a VMEbus-compatible MIPS R3000-based PE from another vendor with no significant effort, and a 68040 upgrade is planned.

As far as the use of formally verified components is concerned, a plan for the insertion of such components into the FTPP was presented at the 2nd Formal Methods Workshop held at the NASA Langley Research Center [Joh92].

**Integrated Formal Methods and VHDL Design Methodology.** Formal methods are mathematically based techniques for specifying, developing, and veri-fying computer systems with strong emphasis on consistency, completeness and correctness of system properties. Formal methods have been applied at various levels of specification and design and to a diverse set of hardware, software and algorithmic parts of fault tolerant computers, in fact, too vast to be enumerated here.

Many of the FTPP components are suitable for the insertion of formal methods technology. Generally speaking, these components are both critical to the correct operation of the machine and are not expected to change significantly from one application to another, thus making the potentially significant effort involved in formal methods a cost-effective means to reduce the introduction of specification, design, and implementation errors. Such components include voters, fault tolerant clocks, synchronization software, task scheduling software, message passing software, and fault detection, identification, and recovery software.

As a step in this technology insertion plan, we provided Odyssey Research Associates (ORA) with a VHSIC Hardware Description Language (VHDL) description of a critical part of the NE called the "Scoreboard." The function of the Scoreboard is to validate all outgoing messages from PEs and assert flow control. For example, if the message emanates from a triply redundant VG, then either all three PEs must have requested the message or a majority, i.e. two PEs, must have requested it and a time-out expired. In addition, the receiving VG's member PEs (a majority of them if the recipient VG is redundant) must have sufficient space in their input buffers to accept the message.

From the VHDL description ORA constructed a formal description of the Scoreboard. At the same time, we interacted with ORA to define critical formal abstract properties that the Scoreboard must satisfy. ORA then constructed formal correspondence proofs intended to show that the formal specification satisfies the abstract properties, and in the process discovered specification inconsistencies and omissions which would have been very difficult to find via testing [Sri92]. One specification omission, if implemented, would have allowed an unlikely but conceivable initialization state of a RAM in the Scoreboard to cause the entire FTPP to halt.

In parallel to this effort, the Scoreboard VHDL description was automatically converted into digital logic using commercially available Synopsis logic synthesis tools. The Scoreboard hardware, consisting of three 8000-gate ACTEL II FPGAs and some RAM chips, to our amazement, worked the first time and passes all tests to date. Only one design error was discovered during testing. This was related to incorrect specification of a part (dual port RAM). This part of the Scoreboard was not described in VHDL, nor was it included in the Scoreboard formalization.

Formalization of critical abstract properties, a specification, and correspondence proofs at an early stage of the Scoreboard design, coupled with the use of VHDL as a common language between the digital engineers and the formal methods organization as well as the use of logic synthesis tools, proved to be a powerful and cost-effective means to identify and correct potentially serious specification and design faults.

Based on this positive experience, we have developed a methodology which integrates the conventional VHDL-based top-down digital design and synthesis methodology with formal specification and verification. We believe that this methodology or one similar in nature is the best way to transition the powerful technology of formal methods into the general digital engineering community.

The participants in the methodology come from two disciplines: engineering and formal methods. A key feature of this methodology is that the engineering participants use the computer-aided design and synthesis to which they are accustomed, and are not expected to become experts in formal methods. The formal methods participants are responsible for extracting and formalizing the key abstract properties of the specification of the design. They are also responsible for verifying that the derived formal descriptions do in fact comply with the formalized version of the specification. They perform this function using formal descriptions and methods which are familiar to them, and which are automatically extracted from the engineers' descriptions of the design.

The methodology is depicted in Figure 3, and is briefly described below.

The design effort usually begins with an informally-defined specification of the intended functionality of the device. Following this, an essentially creative act is performed which results in a number of data bases and functions. In a top-down VHDL-based digital design methodology a hierarchical set of VHDL descriptions of the design is manually constructed. A top-level VHDL model of a design is constructed which is believed to meet the informal specification of the intended functionality. The top-level description is executable in a VHDL Test Bench, as are all VHDL descriptions used in this methodology. A set of functional verification tests is derived from the informal specification for injection into any executable VHDL description, with the objective of empirically demonstrating that the description meets the intent of the informal specification.

Lower level VHDL models are manually constructed, each of which is a more detailed refinement of a model which is higher in the hierarchy. Each VHDL representation in the hierarchy can be tested in the VHDL Test Bench in an attempt to ensure that it is in compli-ance with the informal interpretation of the highest-level informal specification. At a certain level in the hierarchy, a "synthesizeable" description is reached which is suitable for input into an integrated circuit synthesis software package such as Synopses. The synthesis package generates documentation suitable for fabrication of the device, as well as gate-level executable functionality and timing models in both vendor-specific simulation language and in VHDL. The VHDL description of the gate-level circuit can be stimulated and verified with the functional verification tests through the Test Bench. Moreover, the synthesis package provides back-annotated delays which are of use in re-executing higher-level executable models. If the results indicate that critical timing requirements are not met, then the design is modified at one or more hierarchical levels and re-synthesized until all requirements are met.

From the gate-level description of the circuit, Automated Test Pattern Generation software may be used to generate test patterns for use in manufacturing tests. The objective of these tests is to ensure that each node in the circuit can be visibly toggled in order to identify stuck-at manufacturing faults. The test patterns are executed on an integrated circuit tester. Some synthesis software packages include software to automatically design boundary scan paths, boundary scan test patterns, and I/O pads which comply with the IEEE 1149.1 draft standard on scan path testing.

The device's boundary scan capability can be used both for manufacturing quality control tests and for offline testing of the device while in the field.

The formal methods organization also constructs a hierarchical representation of the design. They begin by extracting the salient abstract properties of the informal specification through review of the informal specification, VHDL models, Test Bench, and functional verification tests, and discussions with the engineering team members. The formal methods team transforms these properties into a syntax and semantics which are formally tractable in the language of their own choosing, using automated syntax conversion tools. It is the intent that lower level formal specifications of the design will be rigorously shown to meet this specification by the formal methods practitioners.

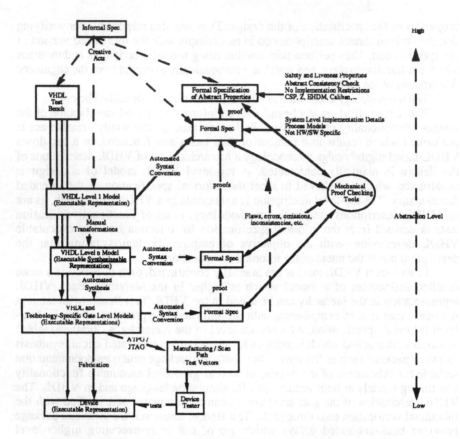

Figure 3. VHDL and Formal Methods Design and Verification Methodology

Lower level formal specifications are generated via an automated process of syntactic transformation to the desired formal specifications using an automated process developed by the formal methods practitioners. Such transformation tools are currently under development by a number of researchers such as ORA, SRI, CLI, and Aerospace Corporation. For this to work, suitable care must be taken by the engineering team to remain reasonably within limitations of the formal semantics used by the formalists. Formal proofs may then be constructed which demonstrate that each level of the hierarchical formal model is a correct representation of the level above it. A complete proof chain may be constructed from the gate-level model which was produced by the synthesis tool all the way up to the formal specification of the abstract properties.

**Design Automation.** Design automation tools and techniques can help automate parts of the hardware and software design cycle. By replacing a labor intensive design process with automated tools, the incidence of human errors can be reduced. In the software arena, more than 75 different CASE (Computer Aided Software Engineering) tools are available that provide different levels of automated software generation. Such a tool, called ASTER, has been developed at Draper to produce Ada source code from high level specifications of control laws and other algorithms. ASTER has been used, among other applications, to produce transport aircraft autoland code in Ada starting from a high level control law specification. The Ada code was compiled and integrated with the existing system software on the FTPP.

In the hardware arena, VHDL is becoming widely available to describe hardware designs at various levels of abstraction, from a high level functional description to all the way down to the gate level. A suite of tools, generally known as Silicon compilers, can be used to convert VHDL or other high level design descriptions through various levels of detailed hardware design, right down to the Silicon implementation with some help from the human designer. The use of such tools for the synthesis of the FTPP Scoreboard has already been described.

**Simplifying Abstractions.** Human errors are more likely when dealing with complex systems and unconventional concepts than when dealing with simple systems and familiar concepts. In a fault tolerant parallel computer, concepts that can add to the design complexity of a conventional Von Neumann uniprocessor computer architecture are redundancy management and distributed and parallel processing. Additional complexities that a designer can face include fault and error containment, synchronization of redundant processes, communication between redundant processes, synchronization of and communication between distributed/parallel processes (all of these in the presence of one or more faults), detection, isolation and recovery from faults, and so on.

If the design complexity can be reduced then the incidence of human errors can be reduced. Some of the fault tolerance concepts can be stated simply and precisely using a mathematical formalism. These include the requirements for synchronization, agreement and validity. Other concepts that can be stated precisely include requirements for fault containment and error containment. Because of their simplicity fault tolerant computers that are based on these concepts and implement these requirements are likely to contain fewer design errors. As discussed above, FTPP has been designed to implement these requirements. There is an added benefit in the design verification and fault removal phases of basing designs on precisely stated requirements.

Another architectural consideration is the hiding of the design complexity. For example, certain architectures implement fault tolerance in such a manner that the virtual architecture apparent to the applications programmer and the operating system programmer appears to be that of a conventional non-redundant computer. The complexities of a redundant architecture are made visible only to the tasks that must deal with detection and isolation of faults and recovery from faults. The FTPP virtual architecture as it appears to the systems programmer is shown in Figure 4. The ensemble of NEs and their interconnections are replaced by a virtual bus. The network communication semantics are that of a Byzantine Resilient Virtual Circuit Abstraction. The messages are guaranteed to arrive in the order sent; all members of a redundant VG receive messages in the same order; all copies of a message are delivered within a fixed small skew. All of these guarantees hold in the presence of a specified set of Byzantine faults. The viewpoint of the applications programmer is even further simplified as shown in Figure 5, which shows how the mapping of tasks to different VGs is transparent to the programmer. The FTPP virtual architecture presented to the applications programmer, for example, is that of a set of communicating Ada tasks with no knowledge of their replication level or mapping to physical processors.

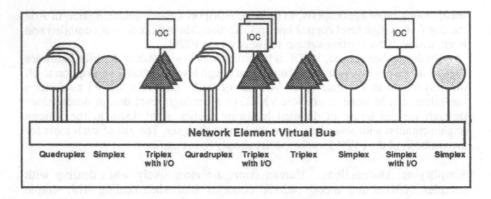

Figure 4. FTPP Virtual Configuration

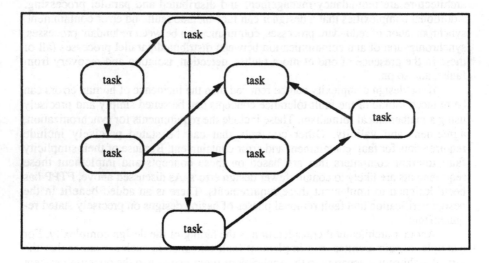

Figure 5. Application Programmer's View of FTPP

**Performance Common-Mode Failure Avoidance.** A frequently encountered source of common-mode failures in hard real-time systems is the inability of the system to deliver the required services by the required deadline under various workload conditions. To avoid this source of CMFs, a complete and accurate performance model is needed, along with the capability to predict *a priori* via static code analysis whether performance timing faults will occur. Such a performance model is only possible with an unambiguously structured and thoroughly benchmarked scheduling system. The scheduler used for hard real-time FTPP applications is a variant of rate monotonic schedule which has been optimized to support task suites having harmonic iteration rates. Tasks are organized into "Rate Groups," that is, tasks which possess identical iteration rates. A concept similar to temporal encapsulation [Kop89] is used to restrict the points in time at which tasks may interact with each other and the outside world to crystal oscillator-generated interrupts. Temporal encapsulation abstracts timing behavior away from (highly variable) task execution times, facilitates predictability and determinism, and provides an unambiguous framework for predicting, detecting, and recovering from performance common-mode failures.

Within this framework, it is necessary to benchmark critical functions such as operating system calls, message passing latencies, task scheduler time, context switches, FDIR, etc. We are in the process of collecting these measurements that relate to the system supplied services, i.e., everything except applications code. This will enable us to predict with accuracy the net processor, bus, NE and other resources that are available to the applications software under various conditions such as normal operating mode, faulted conditions, reduced number of PEs, etc. The performance measurement and analysis apparatus will also be invaluable in determining that application code does not exceed its specified time allotment. These empirical measurements are combined with a static code analysis tool which evaluates the Ada source code to determine the number and frequency of calls to time-consuming functions, and thus compute the overall execution time of each task.

**Software and Hardware Engineering Practice.** Many software and hardware errors can be avoided by following well established engineering design practices. Since these techniques are well known, they will not be discussed here further.

**Design Diversity.** Design diversity is listed here as a fault avoidance rather than a fault tolerance technique since it purports to confine each design fault to a single fault containment region, thereby avoiding a common-mode failure. Design diversity is the concept of implementing different copies in a redundant system using different designs starting from a common set of specifications. The concept can be applied to hardware, software, programming language, design development environment and other design activities. This approach can potentially eliminate many common-mode design faults since each redundant copy uses a different design. Some design faults such as those that result from an incorrect interpretation of ambiguous specifications could still find their way into multiple or all designs. Thus, design diversity can not provide 100 per cent coverage of all design faults.

When attempting to employ design diversity it is critical not to defeat the benefits of bit-wise exact match Byzantine Resilience. It is equally critical not to confuse faults in the diverse redundant application software with faults in the redundant hardware. When redundant hardware and/or software elements are implemented using different designs, bit-wise exact consensus cannot be guaranteed between the outputs of redundant processors. However, it is still possible to provide an exact bit-wise match Byzantine resilient core fault tolerant computer in which design diversity is used for applications programs [Lal88]. We also believe that the core of the fault tolerant computer, including PEs, NEs, OS, can be made error-free or nearly so by the use of many other techniques cited here and then that core can be reused for many different applications. Therefore our approach is to limit the design diversity to applications programs which have the most likelihood of containing residual design errors.

## 4.2 Common-Mode Fault Removal

Faults that slip past the design process can be found and removed at various stages prior to the computer system becoming operational. Fault removal techniques and tools include design reviews, simulations, testing, fault injection, and a rigorous program of discrepancy reporting and closure. Traditionally, these techniques have been relied on almost exclusively to deal with common-mode failures. Most of these techniques, with the exception of fault injection, are well developed and well known. We will, therefore, limit the discussion to the use of fault injection for CMF removal.

Insertion of faults in an otherwise fault-free computer system that is designed to tolerate faults is a powerful technique to exercise redundancy management hardware and software that is specialized, error-prone, difficult to test and not likely to be exercised under normal conditions, i.e., likely to stay dormant until a real fault occurs. Fault insertion techniques can also be used to operate the system in various degraded modes which are expected to be encountered in operational life of the system. Degraded mode operation stresses not only fault handling and redundancy management aspects but also task scheduling, task and frame completion deadlines, workload assignment to processors, inter-task communication, flow control, and other performance-related system aspects. Fault insertion exposes the weaknesses in the hardware and software design, the interactions between hardware and software, and the interactions between redundancy management and system performance. It is an accelerated form of testing the hardware, software and the system, analogous to "shake and bake" testing of hardware devices.

Many researchers, too numerous to be cited here, have developed and used fault/error injection tools. A recent paper [Avr92] attempts to formalize the process of using fault injection for explicitly removing design/implementation faults in fault tolerance algorithms and mechanisms. Fault insertions at higher levels such as module, link, and fault containment region have also been used at Draper for the purposes of design verification. Faults may also be injected into various levels of the executable VHDL design hierarchy, subject to Test Bench simulation time constraints.

## 4.3 Common-Mode Fault Tolerance

Common-mode failures that are not removed prior to operational use of a computer system may eventually manifest themselves in the field as the coincident failure of multiple components of a redundant system. At this point the only recourse is to detect the occurrence of such a failure and take some corrective action. These are fault tolerance techniques and following is an unprioritized list of such methods.

**Common Mode Fault Detection.** Before a recovery procedure can be invoked to deal with common-mode failures in real time, it is necessary to detect the occurrence of such an event. Many ad hoc techniques have been developed over the years to accomplish this objective. Most of these techniques can also be used prior to operational use of the system to eliminate faults. The difference is that in the fault removal phase, detection of a fault leads to some trap in the debugging environment while in the operational phase it will lead to a recovery routine. Similarly, fault removal techniques discussed above can also be used to aid in the task of detecting faults in real time, albeit with a high penalty in performance.

*Watchdog Timers:* Watchdog timers can be used to catch both hardware and software wandering into undesirable states. They are typically used in the Processor Element but can also be employed in the Network Element. Neither hardware watchdog nor task timers unambiguously indicate the occurrence of a common-mode failure. The syndrome in the failed channel of a physical fault is no different from that of a common-mode failure. The syndromes across redundant channels must be compared in real time to determine the cause.

*Hardware Exceptions:* Hardware exceptions such as illegal address, illegal opcode, access violation, privilege violation, etc. are all indications of a malfunction. Again, syndromes across redundant channels must be correlated to distinguish between physical and common-mode failures.

*Ada Run Time Checks:* Ada provides numerous run time checks such as type checks, range constraints, etc. that can detect malfunctions in real time. Additionally, user can define exceptions and exception handlers at various levels to trap abnormal or unexpected program/machine behavior.

*Memory Management Unit:* The Memory Management Unit can be programmed to limit access to memory and control registers by different tasks. Violations can be trapped by the MMU and trigger a recovery action.

*Acceptance Tests:* This is a very broad term and can be applied to applications tasks and various components of the operating system such as the task scheduler and dispatcher. The results of the target task are checked for acceptability using some criteria which may range from a single physical reasonableness check such as pitch command not exceeding a certain rate to an elaborate check of certain control blocks to ascertain whether the operating system scheduled all the tasks in a given frame.

It should be noted again that a physical fault can trigger any of these detection mechanisms just as well as a common-mode failure. Therefore, it is necessary to corroborate the syndrome information across redundant channels to ascertain which recovery mechanism to use.

*Presence Test:* Presence test is normally used in FTPs and FTPPs to detect the loss of synchronization of a single channel due to a physical fault. However, it has also been modified to detect a total loss of synchronization between multiple channels of an AIPS FTP. This is an indication of a common-mode failure. This technique can be extended to the FTPP as well.

*System Virtual Group:* The System VG is a redundant VG composed of formally specified and verified PEs running a small formally specified and verified kernel. It is responsible for detecting random and common-mode failures in itself and other VGs. A typical technique is to require a periodic "heartbeat" message to be sent from each VG in the FTPP to the System VG. Failure of a redundant VG to correctly transmit its heatbeat to the System VG implies that the VG has suffered a common-mode failure. This technique also provides some system-level coverage for faults in simplex VGs.

**Common Mode Fault Recovery.** The recovery from CMF in real time requires that the state of the system be restored to a previously known correct point from which the computation activity can resume. This assumes that the occurrence of the common-mode failure has been detected by one of the techniques discussed earlier and that its source has been identified.

*Exception Handlers:* If a common-mode failure causes an Ada exception or a hardware exception to be raised, then an appropriate exception handler that is written for that abnormal condition can effect recovery. The recovery may involve a local action such as flushing input buffers to clear-up an overflow condition or it may cascade into a more complex set of recovery actions such as restarting a task, a virtual group or the whole system.

*Task Restart:* If the errors from CMF were limited to a single task and did not propagate to the operating system, then only the affected task needs to be restored and/or restarted with new inputs. The state can be rolled back using a checkpointed state from stable storage. Recovery is then effected by invoking an alternate version of the task using the old inputs assuming that the fault was caused by the task software.

This is termed the backward recovery block approach. If the fault is caused by a simultaneous transient in all redundant hardware channels then the same task software can be re-executed using old inputs. This is termed temporal redundancy. Alternatively, forward recovery can be effected by restarting the task at some future point in time, usually the next iteration, using new inputs. This assumes that the fault was caused by an input sensitive software that will not repeat with new and different inputs.

*Virtual Group Restart*: In case the CMF resulted in the loss of synchronization, then redundant channels must be re-synchronized before rollback can begin. Furthermore, the state of the virtual group must be restored before resuming computational activity. This is assisted by system VG concept.

*System Restart*: Finally, if all else fails the whole system can be restarted in real time and a new system state established with current sensor inputs.

## 5 Summary and Conclusions

This paper has described the technical approach that is being used to reduce the probability of common-mode failure in the Draper Fault Tolerant Parallel Processor. The FTPP's approach to tolerating physical, internal, operational faults was also briefly motivated and described. It was noted that the remaining challenge in the design of critical embedded dependable computer architectures is the problem of common-mode failures. A combination of traditional and advanced techniques to avoid, remove and tolerate faults provides a three-pronged, layered defense strategy for reducing the probability of common-mode failures in the FTPP.

One of the advanced fault avoidance techniques is an integrated formal methods and VHDL design methodology that has been developed and applied on a small scale to a key part of the FTPP design, the Network Element. The initial results of this methodology have been very positive. The methodology needs to be developed further and applied on a larger scale.

The last layer of defense against system failure is the detection and tolerance of common-mode faults in real-time. A number of means have been provided in the FTPP to accomplish these goals. We need to collect data on the coverage and effectiveness of these mechanisms.

## 6 References

[Abl88]    Abler, T., *A Network Element Based Fault Tolerant Processor*, MS Thesis, Massachusetts Institute of Technology, Cambridge, MA, May 1988.

[Avr92]    D. Avresky, et al, "Fault Injection for the Formal Testing of Fault Tolerance", 22nd International Symposium on Fault Tolerant Computing, Boston, MA, July 1992.

[Bab90]    Babikyan, C., "The Fault Tolerant Parallel Processor Operating System Concepts and Performance Measurement Overview," *Proceedings of the 9th Digital Avionics Systems Conference*, October 1990, pp. 366-371.

[Har87]    Harper, R., *Critical Issues in Ultra-Reliable Parallel Processing*, PhD Thesis, Massachusetts Institute of Technology, Cambridge, MA, June 1987.

[Har88a]   Harper, R., Lala, J., Deyst, J., "Fault Tolerant Parallel Processor Overview," *18th International Symposium on Fault Tolerant Computing*, June 1988, pp. 252-257.

[Har88b] Harper, R., "Reliability Analysis of Parallel Processing Systems," *Proceedings of the 8th Digital Avionics Systems Conference.*, October 1988, pp. 213-219.

[Har91] Harper, R., Lala, J., *Fault Tolerant Parallel Processor*, J. Guidance, Control, and Dynamics, V. 14, N. 3, May-June 1991, pp. 554-563.

[Har92] R. Harper et. al., "Advanced Information Processing System: Army Fault Tolerant Architecture Conceptual Study Final Report, Volumes I and II", NASA Contractor Report 189632, Langley Research Center, Hampton, VA, July 1992.

[Joh92] Second NASA Formal Methods Workshop, Compiled By S.C. Johnson, C.M. Holloway, and R.W. Butler, Proceedings of a workshop sponsored by NASA, Washington, DC and held at NASA Langley Research Center, August, 1992, NASA Conference Publication 1C110.

[Kop89] Kopetz, H., et. al., "Distributed Fault-Tolerant Real-Time Systems: The MARS Approach," *IEEE Micro*, 9(1):25-40, February 1991.

[Lal84] Lala, J. H., "An Advanced Information Processing System," 6th AIAA-IEEE Digital Avionics Systems Conference, Baltimore, MD, December 1984.

[Lal85] Lala, J. H., "Advanced Information Processing System: Fault Detection and Error Handling," AIAA Guidance, Navigation and Control Conf., Snowmass, CO, Aug. 1985.

[Lal86a] Lala, J.H., "Fault Detection, Isolation, and Reconfiguration in the Fault Tolerant Multiprocessor", Journal of Guidance, Control, and Dynamics, Sept-Oct. 1986, pp 585-592.

[Lal86b] Lala, J. H., "A Byzantine Resilient Fault Tolerant Computer for Nuclear Power Plant Applications," 16th Annual International Symposium on Fault Tolerant Computing Systems, Vienna, Austria, 1-4 July 1986.

[Lal88] Lala, J.H., and L.S. Alger, "Hardware and Software Fault Tolerance: A Unified Architectural Approach", The 18th International Symposium on Fault Tolerant Computing, Tokyo, Japan, June 1988.

[Lap92] Dependability: Basic Concepts and Terminology, Ed: J.C. Laprie, Volume 5 of Dependable Computing and Fault-Tolerant Systems, Springer-Verlag, Wien, New York, 1992, pp.11-16.

[Sri92] M. Srivas and M. Bickford, "Moving Formal Methods into Practice: Verifying the FTPP Scoreboard: Phase 1 Results", NASA Contractor Report 189607, Langley Research Center, Hampton, VA, May 1992.

# V    Data and Databases

# Highly-Available Data Services
# for UNIX Client-Server Networks:
# Why Fault-Tolerant Hardware Isn't the Answer

*Inderpal Bhandari, Tiwari and Computer*
*Carol Kilpatrick - Research, Inc.*

**Abstract.** High-Availability (HA), often tops the feature "wish-list" for customers putting mission-critical applications on-line. The meaning of HA is often
imprecise, however. There is a common perception that HA is actually secondary to "fault-tolerance" — identified with hardware redundancy and perceived
to depend on complex, proprietary, costly technology. The perceived requirement for a "fault-tolerant" machine arises from an erroneous focus on single
machine availability and on hardware faults as the dominant issue for service
availability. On the other hand, empirical studies reveal that software faults and
planned administrative procedures are the dominant issues, and that a customer's real HA requirement comes down to a need for HA data access from a client
network. The issue here is that is available despite software faults, hardware faults,
scheduled maintenance, software upgrade, etc. Recent UNIX-based implementations of an HA configuration based on dual-hosted disks, have demonstrated
that HA data service is achievable using commodity UNIX hardware and software components. We illustrate with a description of a Highly Available Data
Facility prototype we implemented in 1992. We compare our approach to other
contemporary approaches to HA client-server computing.

## 1. Introduction

Availability has traditionally been considered to be a property of computer systems
rather than of computer services. Factors affecting availability — traditionally associated with hardware components — are parameterized in terms of "mean-time-to-failure" and "mean-time-to-repair". Computer system availability is characterized in terms
of "percentage availability".

Faulty hardware has historically been considered to be the leading cause of computer
system failure, and hence unavailability. Consequently, robust or "fault-tolerant" hardware has been viewed as the key to increasing computer system availability.

Two major changes in the computing paradigm motivate a reexamination of common
assumptions concerning both the requirements and techniques for achieving HA computing. The first is the trend toward increasing hardware robustness. The second is the
shift to the client-server model of computing.

In Section 2, we deal with some of the sources of confusion arising from contemporary
usage of the terms "fault-tolerance" and "high-availability". In Section 3, we explain
why the requirements and techniques of HA computing require rethinking as a result

# Highly-Available Data Services
# for UNIX Client-Server Networks:
# Why Fault-Tolerant Hardware Isn't the Answer

*Andrea Borr* - Hewlett-Packard Company
*Carol Wilhelmy* - SunSoft, Inc.

**Abstract.** High-Availability, or *HA*, often tops the feature "wish-list" for customers putting mission-critical applications on-line. The meaning of HA is often imprecise, however. There is a common perception that HA is actually second-best to "fault-tolerance" — identified with hardware redundancy, and perceived to depend on complex, proprietary, costly technology. The perceived requirement for a "fault-tolerant" machine arises from an erroneous focus on single machine availability and on hardware faults as the dominant issues for service availability. On the other hand, empirical studies reveal that software faults and planned administrative procedures are the dominant issues; and that a customer's real HA requirement comes down to a need for HA data access from a client network; i.e. service that is available despite software faults, hardware faults, scheduled maintenance, software upgrade, etc. Recent UNIX-based implementations of an *HA configuration*, based on dual-hosted disks, have demonstrated that HA data service is achievable using commodity UNIX hardware and software components. We illustrate with a description of a *Highly Available Data Facility* prototype we implemented in 1992. We compare our approach to other contemporary approaches to HA client-server computing.

## 1 Introduction

Availability has traditionally been considered to be a property of computer *systems* rather than of computer *services*. Factors affecting availability — traditionally associated with hardware components — are parameterized in terms of "mean-time-to-failure" and "mean-time-to-repair." Computer system availability is characterized in terms of "percentage availability."

Faulty hardware has historically been considered to be the leading cause of computer system failure, and hence unavailability. Consequently, robust or "fault-tolerant" hardware has been viewed as the key to increasing computer system availability.

Two major changes in the computing paradigm motivate a reexamination of common assumptions concerning both the requirements and techniques for achieving HA computing. The first is the trend toward increasing hardware robustness. The second is the shift to the client-server model of computing.

In Section 2, we deal with some of the sources of confusion arising from contemporary usage of the terms "fault-tolerance" and "high-availability." In Section 3, we explain why the requirements and techniques of HA computing require rethinking as a result of the contemporary shift away from proprietary mainframe computing and towards client-server network-based computing. In Section 4, we identify the requirements for a (read-write) data service to be termed *Highly-Available*, or *HA*[1]. In Section 5, we deal with the claim that so-called "fault-tolerant" hardware is not the answer to providing HA data services in a UNIX client-server network environment. In Section 6, we explain how the very same design principles that proprietary vendors use in making systems hardware-fault-tolerant can be applied in the standards-based UNIX client-server environment to achieve the *software fault-tolerance* so crucial to making network data services HA. Section 7 illustrates application of the theory by briefly describing a proof-of-concept prototype that we built in 1992 of a *Highly Available Data Facility, HA-Data*. Section 8 briefly outlines the techniques and issues associated with other approaches to implementing HA client-server data. We conclude with a discussion of problem issues remaining and a description of some items for future work.

## 2 Confusion of Terms: Fault-Tolerance, HA, Data Integrity

Contemporary usage of the terms "fault-tolerance" and "high-availability" is characterized by inconsistency and inexactitude. Some examples are as follows:

- There is confusion between *implementation approaches* (e.g. triple modular redundancy) vs. *functional goals* (e.g. tolerating hardware and software failures).

- There is confusion between the goal of keeping an individual *machine* operational despite a hardware module failure vs. the goal of keeping network *data services* available despite arbitrary combinations of hardware, software, and operational faults.

- There is confusion between the goal of maintaining availability of system services in the presence of *unanticipated failures* vs. the goal of keeping network data services available during *scheduled* system administration operations such as maintenance, software upgrade, and installation change.

What is sometimes overlooked in designs that purport to implement "fault-tolerance" or "high-availability" — *optional* functionality — is that the protection of data integrity — *required* functionality — must not be compromised by the implementation mechanism. Data *integrity* must be preserved even in multi-point failure scenarios that result in loss of data *availability*. Nor can the implementation mechanism permit abrogation of the durability guarantee for data "committed" via the data service protocol.

For example, an NFS[2] *write* request or an RDBMS *commit-work* request is properly acknowledged as "complete" only after its data has been "committed" to stable-storage with the *durability*[3] property. Commit durability is meant to survive arbitrary post-

---

1. For convenience, we abbreviate either High-Availability or Highly-Available as *HA*.

2. NFS (Network File System) is a trademark of Sun Microsystems. For a description of the design and implementation, see [19].

3. Durability is one of the four *ACID* properties of *commitment*, as described in [13]: Atomicity, Consistency, Isolation, and Durability.

commit failures — even multi-point failures (with the possible exceptions of site "disaster" or total disk media failure). Nevertheless, we have seen a commercial file server advertised as "fault-tolerant" despite an implementation that, in lieu of committing file system data updates to disk, acknowledges updates as "committed" by retaining dual memory copies on dual server machines. While this mechanism might well enable continued operation despite single-point failure, it compromises correctness by implementing a version of NFS "commit" that lacks the *durability* property.

## 3 A Client-Server-Centric View of HA Computing

The requirements and techniques of HA computing require rethinking as a result of the shift away from proprietary mainframe computing and towards UNIX-based client-server networking.

With the mainframe paradigm, HA computing required maintaining individual machine availability. The motivation was clear: If the mainframe went "down," all of its services became unavailable. The key to keeping the mainframe "up" was a specially-engineered, proprietary operating system. It relied on techniques such as "hardening"; fault-containment "firewalls"; recovery modules; and facilities for continuous operation during preventive maintenance.

With the advent of the "fault-tolerant" niche vendors, the techniques for maintaining system availability were expanded to include redundant hardware modules and paths; toolkits for constructing resilient applications; and operating systems especially engineered to manage redundancy and hardware fault-tolerance. Due to its complexity and specialization, this technology has tended to remain in the domain of the proprietary vendors.

The requirements and techniques of HA computing require reevaluation as a result of the shift away from mainframes and towards "downsizing" and client-server networks. In the client-server environment, one server machine going "down" does not constitute a total network services failure. Moreover, since the failed node's data service may be made available via an alternate node, node failure need not even imply loss of data service availability. Thus, in a discussion of modern HA computing, the emphasis belongs on *network services availability* rather than on individual *machine availability*.

Another reason for rethinking the requirements for HA computing is the trend toward increasing hardware robustness. It is an outmoded notion that hardware component failures are a leading cause of computer service outages [10, 12]. Recent statistics attribute an order of magnitude more outages today to software faults and operator errors than to hardware faults [12].

We conclude that HA client-server computing requires a network that offers HA services. Since software faults are a leading cause of service outage, software fault-tolerance is a prerequisite for HA network services.

# 4 Data Services, Crash Tolerance, and HA

We define a *data service* as a set of related network services that implement protocol-compliant *read-write* access to disk-based data from clients on a network. The data access model for our definition of a data service is *shared-nothing* client-server. In the shared-nothing model, a disk is owned at any given time by a host that acts as a server for the data resident on it. Even for a disk with physical connectivity to multiple hosts, there is serial mutual exclusion of I/O mastery. This is in contrast to the *shared-disk* model, as exemplified by the VAXcluster™.

Examples of data services are client-server-based RDBMSs and distributed filesystem services such as NFS. Note that an aggregate data service comprises services beyond just the I/O access method. For example, an RDBMS data service typically includes concurrency control and transaction management services. The NFS aggregate data service includes ONC Network Lock Manager.

## 4.1 Data Service Crash Tolerance

Most commercial network data services implement crash-tolerance. Crash-tolerance is the ability to crash-recover the disk and to restart the data service following occurrence on the server machine of a software (OS or application) "crash." It should be noted that crash-tolerance by itself does not provide any tolerance of hardware faults.

Crash-recovery is a data integrity issue. Crash-recovery restores the post-crash disk to a state of physical structural integrity and/or logical transactional consistency. It assures that data "committed" to disk via the write protocol of the data service (whether or not that protocol is transaction-based) survives the crash. Clearly, crash-recovery is only an issue for a read-write data service: If the RDBMS or filesystem data on disk is read-only, its structural and logical integrity is unaffected by a crash.

Restart, on the other hand, is a data service availability issue. Restart restores availability of the service, but the degree of end-user crash-restart transparency, and whether or not clients will be able to seamlessly pick up from where they left off depends on the implementation. A restarted RDBMS will typically roll back uncommitted transactions. However it is implementation-dependent whether the end-user himself needs to detect the crash and rollback, then re-establish his session and resubmit his transaction.

NFS, on the other hand, is architected such that the crash and restart of NFS service proper[1] and Network Lock Manager Service are transparent to the end-user and/or application program. However, the fact that NFS has crash-restart transparency for the end-user does not imply that there is crash-restart transparency for client-side NFS *system* software. While it is true that the crash-restart of NFS service proper does not require the participation of NFS client software (beyond retransmitting unanswered

---

1. Here and elsewhere in the paper we attribute crash-recovery transparency to NFS. Strictly speaking, however, an exception must be noted in the case of a crash that occurs in an interval spanned by retransmissions of non-idempotent operations such as file removals. See discussion of the "duplicate cache" (a.k.a. "nonidempotent reply cache") in [14].

requests), the crash-restart of Network Lock Manager Service requires the participation of all lock-requesting clients in order to reconstruct the pre-crash state of the server Lock Manager's in-core tables.[1]

Crash-tolerance *does* provide an increased degree of availability to a data service. However, the availability features that crash-tolerance alone provides fall short of what we consider to be the requirements for HA. The restoration of service typically requires human intervention for crash-detection, re-boot (if necessary), recovery, and restart. This tends to result in a relatively long mean-time-to-repair. Moreover, crash-tolerance alone does not provide hardware fault-tolerance. Nor does it allow on-line serviceability or on-line software upgradability (defined in the next section).

## 4.2 HA Data Service

In the following, we identify the requirements for a (read-write) data service to be termed *HA*. An HA data service should exhibit, in the face of a single-point hardware or software fault, the *appearance* of "continuous" availability, modulo a "short" hiatus.

The following failure-handling functionality must exist to meet our definition of an HA data service:

- Failures — whether due to operating system software, data service software, application software, or hardware[2] — must be automatically detected.
- *Takeover* — the failure-recovery of an HA data service — must be automatic.
- There must be provisions for running customized recovery and/or restart algorithms.
- There must be a provision for automatically restoring normal service.
- Clients of the disrupted data service must be automatically redirected to an alternate service provider (possibly with loss of transaction or session context).

Additional functionality enabling scheduled system administration operations must be present in order to meet our definition of an HA data service:

- On-line serviceability — the ability to take a server off-line for repair while data service remains available — must be enabled.
- On-line software upgradability — the ability to install a new release of system software on a server while data service remains available — must be enabled.

It is desirable, but not strictly required, that takeover for an HA data service be transparent to end-users. There is no requirement, however, that takeover be transparent to client-side system software.

---

1. There is an excellent and detailed explanation of the crash-recovery algorithm implemented by the ONC Network Lock Manager daemon, *lockd*, and the Status Monitor daemon, *statd*, in [4].

2. Self-checking, FailStop hardware facilitates automated hardware failure detection.

A data service like NFS that already implements end-user-transparent crash-restart will have no problem in exhibiting end-user-transparent takeover (modulo the non-idempotent retry problem that takeover has in common with crash-restart: See [14]). On the other hand, an RDBMS that requires clients to re-login after a crash will need enhancement if it is to approach the goal of end-user-transparent takeover.

Totally end-user-transparent takeover — like totally end-user-transparent crash-restart — may be a relatively unattainable goal for an RDBMS, however. It would require that transactions rolled back due to takeover be transparently resubmitted by system software. (However, at least one proprietary vendor[1] implements this).

## 5 Why FT Hardware Isn't the Answer to HA Data Service

So-called "fault-tolerant" hardware is not the answer to providing HA data services in a UNIX client-server network environment. We concluded earlier that since software faults are a leading cause of service outage, software fault-tolerance is a prerequisite for HA network services. Since hardware faults are also a factor in service outages, the requirements for an HA data service must include both software fault-tolerance and hardware fault-tolerance.

The term "fault-tolerant hardware" is commonly taken to mean a variation on a hardware-redundancy-oriented approach to tolerating single-point hardware component failures. Example implementations are the triple-modular-redundancy approach used in the Tandem Integrity S2™ UNIX system [18] and the "pair-and-spare" approach used by Stratus.

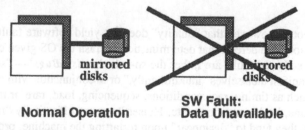

mirrored disks        mirrored disks

**Normal Operation**       **SW Fault: Data Unavailable**

**FIGURE 1.** Redundant HW Approach to 'Fault-Tolerance': No Tolerance of SW Faults

Hardware redundant systems provide a machine that tolerates hardware faults, but fail to provide network data services whose availability survives software faults. The hardware-redundant system is a single logical machine running a single instance of the operating system.[2] That single "OS-instance" manages all the redundant hardware. It

---

1. Tandem's transaction manager and TP monitor work together to provide this functionality for NonStop SQL™.

2. In typical implementations, the operating system runs on redundant processors as multiple lock-step instruction streams with voting.

is a single-point-of-failure: A single software "fault" (e.g. system "panic") can render data services unavailable.

Data services that remain available — despite single-point software faults or single-point hardware faults — can be achieved in a so-called *HA configuration*. The HA configuration consists of two machines, each running an independent instance of the operating system. This configuration of duplicated hardware yields the same protection against hardware faults as classical hardware "redundancy." The term *duality* is more apropos, however, since all components can perform useful work during fault-free operation. Significantly, the dual operating system instances yield tolerance to software crash.

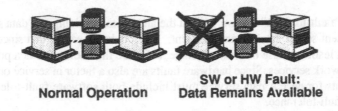

**Normal Operation**

**SW or HW Fault:**
**Data Remains Available**

**FIGURE 2.** High Availability Configuration: Tolerance of SW Faults and HW Faults

It is noteworthy that the redundancy approach requires specialized hardware and an operating system specially engineered to manage the redundancy. By contrast, the duality approach can be configured using commodity hardware and software components.

It should be noted, however, that "duality" does not yield software fault-tolerance of *BohrBugs* — software defects that deterministically crash the OS given certain inputs. The tolerated software faults are rather the so-called *HeisenBugs*[1]— "soft" software defects that manifest themselves "intermittently," or in conjunction with non-deterministic factors such as timing, race conditions, sequencing, load, rare or transient hardware conditions, limit conditions, etc. HeisenBugs are effectively "maskable" by restart; that is, they tend to "disappear" upon restarting the machine, process, or even transaction during which they appeared. Thus, one means of achieving software fault-tolerance for HeisenBugs is by "failover" and automated restart of a crash-recoverable application service (e.g. a database or filesystem) in the environment of the independent OS instance running on the dual node. There is much empirical evidence that most production software defects are of the HeisenBug variety, and that the "failover" strategy is effective in practice as a software fault-tolerance mechanism [11].

---

1. The term *HeisenBug* is attributed to Bruce Lindsay. *BohrBug* was first used by Jim Gray in [9]. BohrBugs, like the Bohr atom, are solid and easily detected. HeisenBugs are elusive under bugcatcher scrutiny, in a manner analogous to the Heisenberg Uncertainty Principle in physics.

By contrast, in an HA configuration based on a Bohr-buggy OS, certain input sequences, sent to each machine in turn, will yield dual crashes rather than "high-availability." BohrBugs must be tested out of an OS that aspires to HA functionality. On the other hand, although there is no hope of testing the HeisenBugs out of an OS, they don't jeopardize availability in an HA configuration, since the probability of a Heisen-Bug reappearing after takeover is infinitesimally small [9].

It is a frequent misconception that a system classified as "highly-available" has less robustness to failure than a system classified as "fault-tolerant" (redundant-hardware interpretation). In reality, the hardware and software fault-tolerant functionality required for an HA data service is a *superset* of the functionality provided by the redundant-hardware approach to "fault-tolerance."

# 6 Using Hardware FT Design Principles to Achieve Software FT

The very same design principles that the vendors of "fault-tolerant" systems use in making systems *hardware fault-tolerant* can be applied in the UNIX client-server network environment in order to achieve the *software fault-tolerance* so crucial to making network data services HA.

The hardware-derived fault-tolerant design principles include the following [9, 12]:

- Modularity.
- FailStop.[1]
- Independent Failure Modes.
- Module Replacement and Repair.
- Request Reroute and Retry.

Tandem Computers Inc., with its Guardian[2] NonStop™ System, was the first vendor to apply these principles to software modules for the purpose of achieving *software fault-tolerance* [2, 9]. The Tandem NonStop System depends on software fault-tolerance as part of its strategy for achieving HA system services within a NonStop *node* (actually a cluster of 2-16 shared-nothing processors).

Significantly, the Tandem Guardian NonStop System does *not* depend on "fault-tolerant" CPU redundancy mechanisms like triple modular redundancy. Instead, it depends on the hardware-software *primary/backup* model in order to achieve HA system services. According to the primary/backup model, for example, a given disk device has

---

1. The model for fault containment is FailStop: the halting, isolation, and removal from service of the bad component before its potentially incorrect operation can spread the damage any further [9].

2. Guardian is a proprietary, message-based, micro-kernel-style, distributed operating system. It uses the client-server model of interaction between modules. Guardian's infrastructure includes a message system with specialized protocols and checkpointing facilities. For more detail, see [2, 6, 7, 9].

hardware connectivity (e.g. via dual-porting) to two CPUs. Only one of those CPUs, at a given time, is its I/O "master"; the other CPU attached to that disk acts as backup with respect to that particular disk (but it may be master with respect to another disk) [15].

In applying the hardware-derived fault-tolerant design principles to software, Tandem chose the software *process*, or more precisely, the *process-pair*, as the unit of FailStop modularity and the unit of repair and replacement.[1] Each disk has an I/O server that is implemented as a process-pair for software fault-tolerance. The disk I/O server consists of a *primary*, I/O master process[2] that runs in the current I/O master CPU and a hot-standby *backup* process that runs in the backup CPU connected to that disk. Changes in software state (such as session establishment) and deltas to data structures that occur during primary process execution are replicated in the memory[3] of the back-up's CPU via primary-to-backup *checkpointing*.[4] In the event of primary CPU failure (software or hardware), Guardian uses the checkpointed data to enable extremely quick restoration of data service availability via the backup CPU. Note, however, that despite Guardian's *availability* mechanism of checkpointing data to battery-backed memory in another CPU, it still relies on disk logging to guarantee *commit durability*.

There is some conceptual commonality between Guardian's achievement of HA via checkpointing and the fast-restart mechanism used for reboot-avoidance in the "Recovery Box" prototype described in [1]. The Recovery Box (really just a designated area of main memory) attempts to preclude lengthy reboot-induced unavailability by serving as a crash-proof fast-restart repository — on the *same machine* — for the type of data that Guardian would have checkpointed to the backup CPU. Unfortunately, this "self-checkpointing" scheme achieves neither software fault-tolerance nor hardware fault-tolerance, since the Recovery Box lacks *failure mode independence*, one of the fault-tolerant design principles. Furthermore, the Recovery Box provides no facilities for either on-line serviceability or on-line software upgradability, both prerequisites to HA data services.

Our challenge was to find a way to apply the fault-tolerant design principles to *commodity* UNIX hardware[5] and software, and yet to avoid the complexity of a proprietary approach like Guardian's. To meet our HA goals, we needed to achieve a combination of software fault-tolerance, hardware fault-tolerance, on-line serviceability, and on-line software upgradability.

---

1. For details, see [2, 9, 6].

2. Actually, the *primary* and the *backup* disk servers are not single processes, but cooperating groups of processes.

3. Main memory in all CPUs has battery-backup.

4. The term *checkpointing* in this context means the sending of a primary-to-backup protocol message that causes the backup to actively update its logical state.

5. This applies to both uniprocessor and shared-memory multiprocessor (SMP) designs.

Guardian's complex infrastructure is geared to making its choice of the process-pair as the software fault-containment unit work [2]. However, a proprietary and highly complex approach like Guardian's is neither desirable nor feasible in a standards-based UNIX environment.

On the other hand, we recognized the virtues of Guardian's shared-nothing primary/ backup model as a data service availability enabler. Our challenge was to find a way to use Guardian's primary/backup model in a standards-based UNIX environment. The key turned out to be the choice of the unit of FailStop modularity, repair and replacement. Guardian chose the software process-pair as the unit. That choice mandated Guardian's complex design. We, on the other hand, chose the *server machine* as the unit. Furthermore, we obviated the need to implement process-pairs and checkpointing, instead relying on disk-based crash-recovery techniques. These choices greatly facilitated design of a standards-based UNIX approach to data service availability.

### 6.1 The Duality Model

We term our approach to implementing HA read-write data services on UNIX the *duality model*. The physical configuration is equivalent to the shared-nothing primary/ backup model. Dual-hosted disks are accessible to both a master and a backup host, with I/O mastery of a particular disk delegated to one host at a time. One logical copy (possibly *mirrored* as two physical copies) of the read-write data is maintained on dual-hosted (possibly mirrored) disk(s). In contrast to the Guardian process-pair model, however, there is no standby backup incarnation of the data service application on the backup host. Nor is there any Guardian-style checkpointing.

## 7 Overview of the *HA-Data* Prototype

We illustrate application of the duality model by briefly describing our prototype of a *Highly Available Data Facility*. We implemented *HA-Data* in 1992 as a research prototype.

Our goal for *HA-Data* was to enable NFS, or a third-party RDBMS, to satisfy the requirements of an HA data service.

*HA-Data* is based on a dual-server *HA-configuration*:

- The configuration is able to provide *server hardware fault-tolerance* because it consists of two complete sets of server hardware.
- Both servers are connected (via dual-port IPI or multi-master SCSI) to each of two *HA-disksets*, one owned by each server in normal operation — the so-called *affinity-disksets*.
- HA-disks are optionally *mirrored*, providing *disk media fault-tolerance*.
- Each server runs an independent instance of operating system, providing *server software fault-tolerance*.

- The dual server configuration has a serial link between the two machines as an alternative to Ethernet as a means of communication.

During normal operation, both servers do useful work. Each acts as I/O master[1] of its affinity-diskset, and runs a data service that exports data resident on that diskset. Concurrently, each server acts as backup for the brother server's data service and diskset. As backup, it uses data-service-customizable *ping-scripts*, run by the *HA-Data Monitor Daemon*, *hadmon*, to monitor the viability of the brother's data service by probing its components at tunable intervals. In addition to monitoring the health of its brother server, *hadmon* also has the task of indirectly monitoring its own health (as seen from the perspective of the outside world) by periodically probing its affinity-diskset to determine whether its disk reservations[2] are still held. Its reservations will remain in force as long as the brother *hadmon* is satisfied with the health of the present machine and its data service.

A customizable *netaddr-takeover-script* enables *HA-Data* to redirect clients from a server to its brother during recovery from machine or data service failure. The default configuration uses one network interface per machine, with both machines on the same Internet-Protocol-based network. The default client redirection mechanism is via the paradigm of the *relocatable IP address*.[3] The latter is an Internet Protocol network address that is used by clients to access data on a diskset. It is thought of as being associated with the diskset rather than with the machine that runs the data service.

In the event that the *hadmon* detects failure of the brother server or its data service, it performs an automatic *takeover* by running a customizable *takeover-script*. The takeover-script performs the following generic functions:

- Assumes I/O mastery (i.e. device reservation ownership) of the superseded server's diskset.
- Assures the halt of the superseded server in accordance with the *FailStop* principle.
- Fires up — in crash-recovery mode — a data service instance to replace the superseded one. The data service instance conditions itself to serve *only* the superseded server's clients by binding to the relocatable IP address that those clients are using — that of the switched diskset.
- Redirects the superseded server's clients by taking over the switched diskset's relocatable IP address.

### 7.1 Avoiding the Split-Brain Syndrome

The process by which *HA-Data* diagnoses failure and initiates takeover is of necessity an heuristic one. The server being superseded may in fact not have crashed. It may be executing correctly but giving slow response; it may be in a "pause failure" (e.g. due to

---

1. I/O mastery is enforced via SCSI or IPI protocol disk reservations.

2. Ibid. footnote 1.

3. This feature is implemented via a kernel networking feature that allows multiple logical Internet addresses per network to be mapped to a single physical interface.

erroneous protracted masking off of interrupts); or it may be executing incorrectly (e.g. it may be in a loop). In either case, it may be unaware that it appears from the outside to be "sick."[1] Should the backup *hadmon* diagnose its brother's failure and initiate takeover, the superseded server's *hadmon*, during one of its periodic disk reservation probes, will find its reservations broken unexpectedly. It then implements the *FailStop* model by immediately halting its machine. This model eliminates any possible window during which both servers might simultaneously consider themselves to be master of the same disk. In a shared-nothing architecture, this so-called *split-brain syndrome* constitutes a liability for data integrity.

FailStop behavior upon detection of lost disk reservation also serves to minimize any possible window during which a superseded server, unaware of takeover by its brother, might try to satisfy a client's pending read request by using a stale cached copy of a data block whose disk copy has since been written by the new master server.

In addition to error-induced takeover, *HA-Data* also implements *switchover*: the graceful switch of a diskset from one running server to the other. Manual switchover can be used to take a server off-line for maintenance. Switchover also occurs during the reintegration reboot of a server that was previously off-line. Administrative procedures utilizing manual switchover enable on-line serviceability and on-line software upgradability of the dual servers.

Use of relocatable IP addresses is the key to executing takeovers and switchovers without disruption of service to clients unaffected by the failure or scheduled administrative operation. *HA-Data* does this by running dual logical environments tied to dual relocatable IP addresses on one physical machine after a takeover or switchover. An example is given in the section describing the HA Lock Manager implementation.

The first implementation using *HA-Data* will be an HA version of NFS. It will include HA implementations of auxiliary services, such as ONC Network Lock Manager. The requirement for a "short" availability hiatus will be met in part by basing the implementation on a logging filesystem.

## 7.2 Consequences of Leveraging Crash-Tolerant Technology to Get HA

*HA-Data* leverages a data service's native crash-recovery capabilities in order to render it HA. The advantage of this approach is that virtually any disk-based client-server application that implements a crash-recovery algorithm can be converted into an HA application. However, the duration of unavailability during takeover is dominated by the application's own crash-recovery time. If crash-recovery is very short, as it is for NFS service proper (as distinguished from Network Lock Manager Service), or for an RDBMS that does frequent database "checkpointing," then takeover time (and hence unavailability time) can be kept to a minimum. If, on the other hand, the crash-recov-

---

1. The general technique used in fault-tolerant systems for diagnosing a malfunctioning component is to detect *externally* a deviation from that component's expected behavior. The fault containment model is *FailStop*.

ery algorithm is long-winded and/or involves interaction with clients on the network, as it does for the Network Lock Manager, then a "short" takeover time may not be achievable.

Another consequence of leveraging a data service's crash-recovery capabilities to yield HA is that a takeover event can only be made as transparent to end-users and application programs as the data service's crash-recovery algorithm makes a crash-restart event transparent. The *HA-Data* framework can help a data service to meet the requirements for HA, but it can do nothing to improve on its end-user-transparency of recovery.

On the other hand, a positive fallout of *HA-Data*'s approach of leveraging the existing implementation of crash-tolerance into a mechanism enabling HA is the resultant backward compatibility with client-side system software. A crash-tolerant version of the server-side software can be replaced with an HA version of the server-side software without upgrading the client software on the network. Using NFS as an example, an HA version of server-side NFS can be installed on server machines in an existing NFS network without any change to the clients. Any client machine running the standard NFS protocol will then be provided with the benefits of HA NFS service.

In the case of NFS service proper, making a crash-restart event (and hence a takeover event) transparent to end-users is trivial because:

1. Server-side NFS is stateless; that is, it retains no "volatile" (in-core) state[1] or "dirty" (un-written-through) buffered data between request-reply cycles.

2. The NFS protocol is "context-free"[2]: No client context is retained between request-reply cycles.

3. The NFS protocol has no "open-file" sessions between client and server. Note that this could be considered a subcase of the "context-free" property.

4. NFS (at least in its usual implementation) runs over a connectionless transport protocol (UDP). Note that this too could be considered a subcase of the "context-free" property.

There are well-known techniques for making a service that does not conform to this model exhibit transparency to the end-user of crash-restart events (and hence of takeover events). The Network Lock Manager Service departs from this model in points 1 and 2, and yet manages to make crash-restart events transparent to the end-user. To this end, *lockd* and *statd*[3] use the strategy of remembering on stable storage the (hostname)

---

1. We are ignoring here the anomaly of the "nonidempotent reply cache."

2. NFS jargon has historically used the term "stateless" for this property of the protocol. We believe "context-free" to be a more precise and descriptive term. It has the further advantage of avoiding confusion with NFS server statelessness as described in point 1.

3. The Network Lock Manager daemon is known as *lockd*. The Status Monitor daemon is known as *statd*.

identities of the clients at the time of their first locking requests.[4] These clients are then re-contacted at crash-recovery time in order to rebuild the server *lockd*'s pre-crash volatile state.

There are other techniques for overcoming the impediments to providing crash-tolerant functionality for data services that don't conform to the NFS model, however. By synchronously writing to stable storage (disk or even battery-backed-up RAM) any change to volatile state that results from processing a request prior to sending the reply, a "stateful" service can be transformed into a "stateless" service. Crash-recovery (as well as takeover) is effected merely by initializing volatile memory from the stable storage copy upon restarting the service. This technique could be applied to implementing an alternate and much faster crash-recovery strategy for *lockd*, thus reducing the period of unavailability of Network Lock Manager Service after a takeover event.

Commercial RDBMSs do not commonly implement end-user crash-restart transparency. That is, they do not implement the (end-user) transparent reestablishment, after a crash-restart event, of sessions and/or transport connections. However, should such functionality be implemented, it would be extensible via *HA-Data* to the takeover case, and would be very desirable for an RDBMS that aspires to HA operation. A well-known technique for achieving this functionality is to log information about existing sessions and/or TCP connections, and to re-establish them after crash-restart by means of a proprietary protocol between RDBMS client and server software. Note that this approach is analogous to the mechanism, used by *lockd/statd*, that "remembers" on disk in the *statd* "database" the existence of client *lockd* "sessions" with the server *lockd*. These "sessions" are reestablished as part of *lockd/statd* crash-recovery.

### 7.3 *HA-Data's* Approach to Implementing an HA Network Lock Manager

*HA-Data's* goal is to avoid disruption of service to clients unaffected by takeover or switchover.[1] In accordance with that goal, an *HA-Data* implementation of an HA Network Lock Manager must have the property that a server superseding its brother be capable of simultaneously supporting two disjoint sets of clients issuing locking requests for two disjoint sets of data, yielding two disjoint sets of in-core tables. Furthermore, the Lock Manager Service may be in crash-recovery mode for one set of clients at the same time that it is functioning in normal mode for the other set of clients.

These requirements are satisfied by arranging for a server that has taken over its brother's affinity-diskset to run two incarnations each of *lockd* and *statd*, bound to two distinct IP addresses — the relocatable IP addresses associated with the two affinity-disksets.

During normal operation (i.e. with each server mastering its "native" affinity-diskset), there would be a single, "native" *lockd/statd* pair of daemons, fired up at boot time. These would bind to the relocatable IP address associated with the "native" affinity-

---

4. In the SunOS implementation, the *statd* client hostname "database" used to implement Lock Manager crash recovery is kept in the directories *sm* and *sm.bak*.

1. Takeover is a failure-induced event. Switchover is a manually-initiated event.

diskset. The "native" *lockd* would also bind to the loopback interface over which communication from the kernel takes place (i.e. in support of the *fcntl()* system call). Normal *lockd*-to-*statd* communication would take place between the "native" *lockd*/*statd* pair, with each addressing the other via the "native" relocatable IP address.

At takeover or switchover time, a "guest" *lockd*/*statd* pair would be launched. These would bind to the relocatable IP address associated with the brother server's affinity-diskset. (The "guest" *lockd* would not bind to the loopback interface, however, since the kernel would not communicate with it). Normal *lockd*-to-*statd* communication would take place between the "guest" *lockd*/*statd* pair, with each addressing the other via the relocatable IP address associated with the brother server's affinity-diskset.

During takeover, the "guest" *lockd*/*statd* pair would execute the crash-recovery algorithm, while the "native" *lockd*/*statd* pair would continue normal operation.

The two-incarnation *lockd*/*statd* solution also requires that the *statd* "database" that remembers on stable storage the hostnames of the clients engaged in "locking sessions" — the *sm* and *sm.bak* directories — be HA-disk-resident, with distinct versions (corresponding to the distinct sets of clients) on HA-disks belonging to the respective affinity-disksets. Although the default execution of *statd* expects to find *sm* and *sm.bak* via a canonical pathname, each *statd* incarnation in the HA version is pointed to its own HA-disk-resident copy.

The fact that the existing *lockd* crash-recovery algorithm is long-winded and involves interaction with all lock-requesting clients may present an impediment to achieving "short" takeover time for the Network Lock Manager Service. With a new crash-tolerance strategy, changes to *lockd*'s in-core tables could be written-through as they occur to a copy on an HA-disk (or, more efficiently, to a dual-ported nonvolatile RAM device). Then, when *lockd* initializes after a crash, takeover, or switchover, it could get its in-core table state from the stable-storage copy, rather than soliciting lock re-sends from the clients.

This radically different approach to server-side *lockd* crash-recovery implies a major re-architecture of *lockd*. The result would be virtually "instantaneous" recovery of the Network Lock Manager Service from a server crash-restart, takeover, or switchover. The cost would be an extra synchronous write to dual-ported stable storage per locking request. (This latency overhead could be alleviated by the use of dual-ported non-volatile RAM).

## 7.4 Comparison with HANFS/6000™

Two recent USENIX papers, [3] and [4], describe the implementation of HANFS/6000™, a Highly Available Network File Server and Highly Available Lock Manager for the IBM RISC System/6000™. The basic duality model is analogous to that used in the *HA-Data* architecture.

There are some significant differences in functionality and approach, however.

- No mention is made in [3] of use of the *FailStop* principle. HANFS/6000 could be vulnerable to the split-brain syndrome.

- *HA-Data* performs takeovers, switchovers, and reintegration reboots without disruption of service to unaffected clients. By contrast, the Highly Available Network File Server implementation described in [4] requires that *all* active Network Lock Manager clients of *both* machines undergo crash recovery during any of these procedures.

- As detailed in [4], HANFS/6000's approach to Network Lock Manager recovery entails a performance impact during normal operation. A latency penalty is paid at the first occurrence of a locking request from a client to a particular server. (The server must contact its twin in order to request monitoring of the client by the twin). The *HA-Data* approach entails no such performance penalty during error-free operation.

- HANFS/6000 relies on the use of two network adaptors per machine in order to effect an *impersonation* by the superseding machine of the failed machine. *HA-Data*, by contrast, relies on the model of the relocatable IP address.[1]

- As detailed in [3], HANFS/6000 preserves the "non-idempotent reply cache" across takeovers by writing it to the AIXv3 file system log. This obviates, for the takeover case[2], the anomaly of a bogus error being returned to the client in case takeover occurs in an interval spanned by retransmissions of a non-idempotent operation. The *HA-Data* team, by contrast, conceptually views takeover as an automatically administered crash-restart event. We consider NFS's non-transparent recovery in this anomalous case to be a protocol design defect. As such, we relegate its solution to the domain of NFS protocol design, rather than to that of HA mechanism design.

# 8 Other Approaches to Implementing HA Client-Server Data

## 8.1 HA Techniques for Read-Only Data Services

In the case of a read-only data service, any node with a data copy can at any time correctly act as a service provider, despite the crash of other service-providing nodes, and despite network partition. There is no crash-recovery problem, no inter-copy consistency problem, and no stale data problem. Thus, read-only data services lend themselves to replica-based availability techniques. Used in conjunction with the replication of the read-only data on multiple server nodes are the following:

- Client-based mechanism for binding to service provider.
- Client-based detection of service failure.

---

1. *HA-Data* can be customized to take advantage of two network interfaces per machine, if present. However, the default requirement is one per machine.

2. It is not clear whether AIXv3 uses this technique to solve the problem for the crash-reboot case.

- Client-based recovery of service availability via rebind to alternate service provider: so-called *client-side failover*.

- A robust distribution mechanism for consistent replica updates.

DCE DFS[1] is an example of a replica-based read-only data service. DCE DFS provides read-only replication, with facilities for automated updates, based on a primary writable copy strategy. A primary writable copy of a fileset (a logical collection of files, and the unit of replication) can be replicated as read-only copies, enhancing availability.

Updates to the single primary writable copy are extracted via a fileset clone operation (yielding a snapshot); changes only are propagated atomically to the read-only replicas. The reader of a replica will see a consistent snapshot. Replicas are tagged with version numbers to enable the client cache manager to detect updates and discard locally cached copies of data. The version numbers also tag replicas which failed to update on a push of the primary copy in the event of network partition. Updates are lazily propagated using a time-based strategy, and replicas are guaranteed to be out of date by no more than a fixed amount of time. Utilities exist to manage and relocate replicas. For a description of the architecture of DCE DFS and the underlying local file system Episode, see [16] and [8].

## 8.2 Replica-Based Techniques for Read-Write Data Services

Remote data replicas have been used as a technique for implementing HA read-write data services. However, the fact that the replicas are writable gives rise to problems of inter-replica consistency, stale data, update propagation latency, protocol complexity, and management of network partition and node crash.

- Most solutions are based on a single real-time-updatable master copy plus one or more slave copies that are kept consistent via a message protocol.

- In the absence of network partition, clients direct all update requests to the node managing the (current) master copy. (Nodes managing slave copies cannot be used for load-balancing of clients requesting updates).

- Complex protocols are required for dealing with network partition. If updates during network partition are permitted, then some method of conflicting update detection and reconciliation is required.

- Real-time inter-copy consistency has a latency penalty for slave updates before commit of the master update.

- Real-time inter-copy consistency presents a challenge for availability: All nodes holding copies must be available in order to commit an update.

- Real-time inter-copy consistency is best maintained with a transaction model.

---

1. DCE DFS is the distributed file system component of the Open Software Foundation's Distributed Computing Environment.

- Delayed inter-copy consistency avoids the latency penalty and the availability challenge, but allows slave copies to get stale with respect to the master copy.
- Complex protocols are required to bring stale replicas up-to-date.
- Quorum protocols can deal with stale copies but are exceedingly complex.
- Examples of remotely-replicated read-write file systems are mostly research prototypes rather than commercial products.[1]
- Proprietary database systems have remote replica facilities based on spooling the log from the master node to the slave node(s).[2] These complex proprietary products allow a choice between transaction-based real-time consistency (at a performance penalty) and delayed consistency (with all of its associated network partition and stale data problems). The issues associated with this approach are discussed in [17].

Thus, it is seen that replica-based mechanisms for implementing HA read-write data services tend to be costly in several aspects:

- Complexity.
- Difficulty of assuring operational correctness in the failure recovery scenario.
- Overhead during normal (error-free) operation.

On the other hand, replica-based mechanisms tolerate a wider variety of faults (including site disaster) than do duality configurations. [3] They also have more flexibility: for example, they can be designed to tolerate disconnected operation. It should be noted that Tandem's Remote Database Facility, RDF™, makes effective use of the two approaches simultaneously.

## 9 Conclusions

We have placed the availability emphasis where it belongs: on *data service availability*, rather than on *individual mainframe* availability. We have seen that a key advantage of using *dual-node configurations* as data service availability enablers is the provision of software *HeisenBug* fault-tolerance (in addition to hardware fault-tolerance) for data services. Both types of fault-tolerance are needed for HA data services.

One of the remaining challenges is the provision of *system administrator fault-tolerance*. Nothing in the duality approach helps deal with the fact that operator or system administrator error is a leading cause of service outage on networks. In fact, the need for correct administration of dual server nodes may even exacerbate exposure to operator-error induced service outages.

---

1. Examples: Coda (CMU), Ficus (UCLA), Deceit (Cornell), Gemini (UCSD), Reliable File System (MIT).

2. Examples are IBM's Remote Replicated Database Facility™ and Tandem's Remote Database Facility, RDF™.

3. For an in-depth comparison of the relative advantages and disadvantages of the duality and replica-based approaches to read-write distributed file systems see [5].

Another area for further work is the previously discussed challenge of making take-over and switchover events (as well as crash-recovery events) totally end-user-transparent for both distributed file systems and RDBMSs.

## 10 Acknowledgments

Thanks are due to Brian Pawlowski, Chris Duke, and John Corbin for editorial suggestions whose implementation improved the presentation of this material.

## 11 References

1. M. Baker, M. Sullivan: "The Recovery Box: Using Fast Recovery to Provide High Availability in the UNIX Environment," Proc. of Summer 1992 USENIX Conference.

2. J. Bartlett: "A NonStop Kernel," Eighth Sigops. ACM, New York, 1981, pp. 22-29.

3. A. Bhide, E. Elnozahy, S. Morgan: "A Highly Available Network File Server," Proc. of Winter 1991 USENIX Conference.

4. A. Bhide, S. Shepler: "A Highly Available Lock Manager for HA-NFS," Proc. of Summer 1992 USENIX Conference.

5. A. Bhide, E. Elnozahy, S. Morgan, A. Siegel: "A Comparison of Two Approaches to Build Reliable Distributed File Servers,"DCS-91, May 1991, pp. 616-623.

6. A. Borr: "Robustness to Crash in a Distributed Database: A Non Shared-Memory Multi-Processor Approach," Tenth International Conference on Very Large Databases, Aug. 1984, pp. 445-453.

7. A. Borr: "Guardian 90: A Distributed Operating System Optimized Simultaneously for High-Performance OLTP, Parallelized Batch/Query, and Mixed Workloads," Tandem TR90.8, Tandem Computers, Cupertino, CA, July 1990.

8. Chutani et al.: "The Episode File System," Proc. of Winter 1992 USENIX Conference.

9. J. Gray: "Why Do Computers Stop and What Can Be Done About It?," Tandem TR85.7, Tandem Computers, Cupertino, CA, June 1985.

10. J. Gray: "A Census of Tandem System Availability, 1985-1990," IEEE Trans. Reliability, Vol. 39, No. 4, Oct. 1990, pp. 409-418.

11. J. Gray, A. Reuter: "Transaction Processing: Concepts and Technology," Morgan Kaufmann Publishers, San Mateo, CA, 1993, pp. 117-152.

12. J. Gray, D. Siewiorek: "High-Availability Computer Systems," Computer, 24:39-48, Sept. 1991.

13. T. Haerder, A. Reuter: "Principles of Transaction-Oriented Database Recovery," ACM Computing Surveys, Vol. 15.4, 1983.

**14.** C. Juszczak: "Improving the Performance and Correctness of an NFS Server," Proc. of Winter 1989 USENIX Conference.

**15.** J. Katzman: "A Fault-Tolerant Computing System," Proc. of the Eleventh Hawaii International Conference on System Sciences, Jan. 1978.

**16.** M. Kazar et al.: "DEcorum File System Architectural Overview," Proc. of Summer 1990 USENIX Conference.

**17.** R. King, et. al.: "Management of a Remote Backup Copy for Disaster Recovery," ACM Transactions on Database Systems, Vol. 16, No. 2, June 1991, pp. 338-368.

**18.** P. Norwood: "Overview of the NonStop-UX Operating System for the Integrity S2," Tandem Systems Review, April 1991, Tandem Computers, Cupertino, CA.

**19.** R. Sandberg, D. Goldberg, S. Kleiman, D. Walsh, B. Lyon: "Design and Implementation of the Sun Network File System," Proc. of Summer 1985 USENIX Conference.

# The Management of Replicated Data

Jehan-François Pâris *

Department of Computer Science, University of Houston
Houston, TX 77204-3475

## 1 Introduction

Fourteen years have passed since Gifford's seminal paper on weighted voting [7]. These years have seen the development of numerous protocols for managing replicated data and a handful of experimental systems implementing replicated files. The time has now come to attempt an inventory of the problems for which we have found solutions and the issues that remain open. One way to structure this inventory is to organize it around general observations reflecting points of agreement and disagreement within the replicated data community.

Our frame of reference will be simple: We will consider systems maintaining multiple copies – or *replicas* – of the same data at distinct nodes of a computer network. We define the *availability* of replicated data for a given operation as the probability that the operation can be successfully carried out at some node within the network. We will focus on the problem of protecting the users of the replicated data from the inconsistencies that may result from node failures and network partitions. This is normally done through a *group communication mechanism* [3,4,22] or a *replication control protocol*. Group communication mechanisms focus on the problem of reliable delivery of messages to the replicas while replication control protocols operate by mediating all accesses to the replicated data. Hence they are more general. An ideal *replication control protocol* should guarantee the consistency of the replicated data in the presence of any arbitrary combination of non-Byzantine failures while providing the highest possible data availability and occasioning the lowest possible overhead.

## 2 What we have learned

**Observation 1.** *Applications that can tolerate slight inconsistencies among replicas should not have to pay the price of maintaining all replicas in a fully consistent state.*

Maintaining replicated data in a fully consistent state is an expensive proposition because all updates must become simultaneously visible to *all* users of the replicated data. Reducing the number of replicas required to obtain a write quorum cannot be achieved without simultaneously increasing the read quorum and vice versa.

---

* Internet Address: paris@cs.uh.edu

Many practical applications can tolerate minor inconsistencies among replicas and operate with data that are slightly out of date. We can provide these applications with replicas that are slightly out of date and even guarantee that these *quasi-copies* will never deviate too far from the true data [1]. For instance, we can guarantee that the quasi-copies will never be more than 10 minutes behind the true data or differ by more than 5%.

Other distributed applications only require *eventual consistency* [10]. Replicas can be in different states but will eventually receive the same set of update messages. Consider, for instance, a mail system where each user is given two mailboxes and incoming messages are guaranteed to be delivered to at least one mailbox. Merging the two mailboxes can be done very easily by sorting their contents according to message arrival time and removing duplicate messages.

**Observation 2.** *Network partitions are much more difficult to handle than node failures.*

In the absence of network partitions, we can guarantee the consistency of replicated data by (a) imposing a total ordering on all writes so that all replicas receive them in the same order, (b) broadcasting these writes to all available replicas, and (c) requiring that replicas residing on nodes recovering from a failure remain unavailable or *comatose* until they are brought up to date. This *available copies* protocol has two major advantages [2,17]. First, read requests never need to access more than one available replica because *all* available replicas are guaranteed to be up to date. Second, the replicated data can be accessed as long as there is at least *one* available replica.

The situation is quite different when network partitions must be taken into account. A first class of replication control protocols takes the approach that network partitions are unlikely to occasion conflicting updates and that many of these conflicts will be easy to resolve. These are known as *optimistic protocols*. They follow the same philosophy as the available copies protocol and trade data consistency for inexpensive reads and high availability. The second class of protocols take the approach that data consistency carries a much more important weight than data availability. These protocols are said to be *pessimistic*. They rely on quorum mechanisms to prevent conflicting updates and provide lower data availabilities than optimistic protocols. For instance, we need *five* replicas managed by the best pessimistic protocol to achieve the same level of data availability as *two* replicas managed by the available copy protocol [17].

Another limitation of pessimistic protocols is the fact that they disallow simultaneous updates in disjoint partitions. Consider for instance a replicated file system like Coda [21] where each user workstation maintains a local copy of the files it currently accesses in addition to the copies maintained by the Coda servers. Some of these workstations are likely to be notebooks and we may expect the owners of these notebooks to disconnect them from time to time from the network. A pessimistic protocol would either disallow all writes to the Coda files stored on the notebook or disallow all accesses to the replicas maintained by the Coda servers.

**Observation 3.** *Witnesses can reduce the storage costs of pessimistic protocols.*

Pessimistic protocols require at least three replicas to implement a robust consensus and improve upon the availability of unreplicated data. However one of these replicas can be replaced by a much smaller *witness* without significantly affecting the availability of the replicated data [16].

Witnesses are very small entities that hold no data but maintain enough information to identify the replicas that contain what it believes to be the most recent version of the data. Conceptually this information could be a *timestamp* containing the time of the latest update. Since it is quite hard to keep clocks synchronized, this timestamp is normally replaced by a *version number*, which is an integer incremented each time the data are updated. Each witness carries a specific number of votes and is allowed to participate in all read and write quorums like a conventional replica.

The small size of witnesses offers two additional advantages. First, witnesses, unlike conventional replicas, can be brought up to date without any significant delay. There is thus no incentive to update witnesses that are not part of a write quorum. As a result, a replicated file consisting of two replicas and one witness will never require more than two replica updates per write while a replicated file consisting of three conventional replica normally requires three replica updates per write. Second, witnesses can be quickly regenerated every time they become unavailable [20,19].

Witnesses are an integral part of the Echo [11] and Harp [14] file systems.

**Observation 4.** *Dynamic voting can improve the availability of replicated data managed by quorum-consensus protocols.*

Dynamic voting protocols adjust read and write quorums whenever they detect a change in the number of available replicas [5,12]. Central to all dynamic voting protocols, is the notion that replicas known to be unreachable should be excluded from all quorum computations. All dynamic voting protocols maintain some record of the set of replicas that are allowed to participate in elections. Because of the distributed nature of the protocol, multiple copies of this set, called the *majority block*, must be maintained. These copies are normally associated with the replicas. Whenever the protocol detects that some replicas in the majority block have become unreachable it checks first that a majority of the replicas in the current majority block can be reached. If this is the case, the unreachable replicas are excluded from the majority block and a new majority block is formed. Otherwise the replicated data remain unavailable until some of the unreachable replicas can be reached again. Finally, the excluded replicas are prevented from participating in voting until they are formally reintegrated into the current majority block.

It has long been known that the best dynamic voting protocol, namely *dynamic-linear voting* [12], provided much better data availabilities than the best static voting protocols whenever there were more than three replicas. It was also widely assumed that dynamic-linear voting did not perform much better than static voting when there were only three replicas. This author has shown more recently that this conclusion does not hold when communication failures are taken into account as static voting provides lower availabilities than dynamic-linear voting even when there are only three replicas [18]. Hence the small overhead of maintaining majority block membership information on each node holding a replica is a very reasonable price to pay for the much better data availabilities afforded by dynamic-linear voting.

**Observation 5.** *There are protocols that can manage efficiently large numbers of replicas.*

The recent years have seen the development of several replication control protocols specially tailored for the management of replicated data that have many replicas.

These protocols have as objective to reduce the number of replicas that need to be accessed to reach a read or a write quorum while distributing these accesses as evenly as possible among the $N$ replicas.

We shall only mention Maekawa's original algorithm [15] because it was the first algorithm to require only $3\sqrt{N}$ messages per access and the *triangular lattice* protocol because it provides a much better data availability than Maekawa's algorithm while keeping the quorum size of $O(\sqrt{N})$ [23].

There are also some wide-area applications, such as the *Archie* FTP location service [8] or the *Refdbms* bibliographic database system [9] , whose users can be distributed at hundreds or thousands of sites around the world. These applications often maintain a very large number of local replicas in order to provide a fast response time and minimize communication costs. Even protocols with $O(\sqrt{N})$ quorums would be too expensive. The only solution is then to relax consistency requirements. Less costly protocols, among which *epidemic* protocols [6,10], can then be used.

# 3 Unresolved Issues

**Observation 6.** *We lack a proper consistency model providing for disconnected – or quasi-disconnected – operation of user workstations.*

Conventional network file systems assume that user workstations are permanently connected to their servers. This assumption is becoming false because of the increasing importance of portable workstations. These portable workstations have enough secondary storage to be fully autonomous and are equally likely to be operated in stand alone mode as to be connected to the network. As we mentioned earlier, pessimistic replication protocols are inadequate because they would unduly restrict the access of data. The Coda file system solves the problem by implementing an optimistic replication control protocol and guaranteeing that the user always sees the most recent accessible version of its data [21]. This solution has the disadvantage of shifting too much burden on the users' shoulders as they become at least partially responsible for the consistency of their data. We need to develop consistency models that provide the users with a more faithful abstraction of the way the replicas are actually managed. We need to take also into account the emergence of new technologies providing portable workstations with more or less reliable low-bandwidth radio links. These links could be used for the exchange of tokens, for the update of witnesses or for the transmission of incremental updates.

**Observation 7.** *We need to develop better methodologies for specifying weak consistency criteria and implementing them.*

Weak consistency protocols allow replicas to diverge temporarily from one another but guarantee that they will eventually reach a single consistent state. Weak consistency protocols incur much lower communication overheads than conventional replication control protocols. They constitute the only practical way to manage very large numbers of replicas scattered over a wide-area network. Unfortunately managing weakly consistent data is a difficult task because it is very data dependent. Hence object-oriented methodologies appear to be the most promising approach [10].

**Observation 8.** *We need to develop tools measuring more accurately the actual performance of replication control protocols.*

Too many studies of replication control protocols still neglect network partitions and assume a perfect coverage of all node failures. These studies provide overoptimistic evaluations of the actual availabilities of the replicated data. As we mentioned earlier, they also fail to notice some behaviors that only occur in the presence of network partitions. The fault-tolerant computing community has an important part to play because of its impressive collective expertise in reliability and availability analysis.

## 4    Final Remarks

This brief inventory of the current state of the art in the field of replicated data management has neglected many interesting problems, among which the optimal allocation of weights to replicas, and failed to discuss many good protocols such as the tree protocol, hierarchical voting, and voting with ghosts to mention only a few ones.

We have also failed to mention the ever growing difference between replicated files and replicated databases. A replicated file is normally a relatively small object often under the control of a single user. As it is in the case for unreplicated files, this owner is quite likely to place a higher priority on faster access times and higher data availability than on data consistency. Hence optimistic replication control protocols are indicated. Replicated databases, on the other hand, need to rely on some formal model of data consistency because they are typically accessed in parallel by many users. As a result, even unreplicated databases require a formal transaction mechanism to guarantee that all updates will leave the database in a consistent state. Hence temporary inconsistencies can only be tolerated if there are formal mechanisms to reconcile them.

# References

1. Alonso, R., Barbara, D., Garcia-Molina, H.: Quasi-copies: efficient data sharing for information retrieval systems. Proc. of the Int. Conf. on Extending Data Base Technology, Lecture Notes in Computer Science # 303, Springer Verlag (1988).
2. Bernstein, P.A., Goodman, N.: An Algorithm for concurrency control and recovery in replicated distributed databases. ACM Trans. on Database Systems, 9, 4 (1984) 596–615.
3. Birman, K.P., Joseph, T.A. : Reliable communication in the presence of failures. ACM Trans. on Computer Systems, 5, 1 (1987) 47–76.
4. Cheriton, D.R., Zwaenepoel, W.: Distributed process groups in the V kernel. ACM Trans. on Computer Systems, 3, 2 ( 1985) 77–107.
5. Davcev, D., Burkhard, W.A.: Consistency and recovery control for replicated files. Proc. 10th ACM Symp. on Operating System Principles, (1985) pp. 87–96.
6. Demers, A., Greene, D., Hauser, C., Irish, W., Lar son, J., Shenker, S., Sturgis, H., Swinehart, D., Terry, D.: Epidemic algorithms for replicated database maintenance. Operating Systems Review, 22, 1, (1988) 8–32.
7. Gifford, D. K.: Weighted voting for replicated data. Proc. 7th ACM Symp. on Operating System Principles, (1979) pp. 150–161.
8. Emtage, A., Deutsch, P.: Archie, an electronic directory service for the Internet. Proc. 1992 Winter USENIX Conf., (1992) pp. 93–110
9. Golding, R.A.: Weak-consi stency group communication and membership. Ph.D. thesis published as Technical Report UCSC–CRL–92–52, Computer and Information Sciences Board, University of California, Santa Cruz (1992).
10. Golding, R.A.: A Weak-consistency architecture for distributed information services. Computing Systems, 5, 4 (1992).
11. Hisgen, A., Birrell, A., Mann, T., Schroeder, M., Swart, G.: Availability and consistency tradeoffs in the Echo distributed file system. Proc. 2nd Workshop on Workstation Operating Systems, (1989) pp. 49–54.
12. Jajodia, S., Mutchler, D.: Dynamic voting algorithms for maintaining the consistency of a replicated database. ACM Trans. on Database Systems, 15, 2 (1990) 230–405.
13. Ladin, R., Liskov, B., Shrira, L.: Lazy replication: exploiting the semantics of distributed services. Proc. 9th ACM Symp. on the Principles of Distributed Computing, (1990).
14. Liskov, B., Ghemawat, S., Gruber, R., Johnson, P., Shrira, L . Williams, M.: Replication in the Harp file system. Proc. 13th ACM Symp. on Operating System Principles, (1991) pp. 226–238.
15. Maekawa, M.: A $\sqrt{N}$ algorithm for mutual exclusion in decentralized systems. ACM Trans. on Computer Sys tems, 3, 2 (1985) 145–159.
16. Pâris, J.-F.: Voting with witnesses: a consistency scheme for replicated files. Proc. 6th Int. Conf. on Distributed Computing Systems, (1986) pp. 606–612.
17. Pâris, J.-F., Long, D. D.E.: On the performance of available copy protocols. Performance Evaluation, 11 (1990) 9–30.
18. Pâris, J.-F.: Evaluating the impact of network partitions on replicated data availability. In Dependable Computing for Critical App lications 2 (J.F. Meyer and R.S. Schlichting eds.), Dependable Computing and Fault-Tolerant Systems #6, Springer Verlag (1992), pp. 49–65.

19. Pâris, J.-F., Long, D.D.E.: Voting with regenerable volatile witnesses. Proc. 7th Int. Conf. on Data Engineering, (1991) 112–119.
20. Pu, C., Noe, J.D., Proudfoot, A.B.: Regeneration of replicated objects, a technique and its Eden implementation. IEEE Trans. on Software Engineering, SE-14, 7 (1988) 936–945.
21. Satyanarayanan, M., Kistler, J.J., Kumar, P., Okasaki, M.E. Siegel, E.H., Steere, D.C.: Coda: a high l y available file system for a workstation environment. IEEE Trans. on Computers, C-39, 4 (1990) 447–459.
22. Schneider, F. B.: Implementing fault-tolerant services using the state machine approach: a tutorial. ACM Computing Surve ys, 22, 4 (1990) 229–319.
23. Wu, C., Belford, G.: The Triangular lattice protocol: a highly fault tolerant and highly efficient protocol for replicated data. Proc. 11th Symp. on Reliable Distributed Systems, (1992) 66–73.

Printing: Weihert-Druck GmbH, Darmstadt
Binding: Buchbinderei Schäffer, Grünstadt

# Lecture Notes in Computer Science

For information about Vols. 1–699
please contact your bookseller or Springer-Verlag

Vol. 736: R. L. Grossman, A. Nerode, A. P. Ravn, H. Rischel (Eds.), Hybrid Systems. VIII, 474 pages. 1993.

Vol. 737: J. Calmet, J. A. Campbell (Eds.), Artificial Intelligence and Symbolic Mathematical Computing. Proceedings, 1992. VIII, 305 pages. 1993.

Vol. 738: M. Weber, M. Simons, Ch. Lafontaine, The Generic Development Language Deva. XI, 246 pages. 1993.

Vol. 739: H. Imai, R. L. Rivest, T. Matsumoto (Eds.), Advances in Cryptology – ASIACRYPT '91. X, 499 pages. 1993.

Vol. 740: E. F. Brickell (Ed.), Advances in Cryptology – CRYPTO '92. Proceedings, 1992. X, 593 pages. 1993.

Vol. 741: B. Preneel, R. Govaerts, J. Vandewalle (Eds.), Computer Security and Industrial Cryptography. Proceedings, 1991. VIII, 275 pages. 1993.

Vol. 742: S. Nishio, A. Yonezawa (Eds.), Object Technologies for Advanced Software. Proceedings, 1993. X, 543 pages. 1993.

Vol. 743: S. Doshita, K. Furukawa, K. P. Jantke, T. Nishida (Eds.), Algorithmic Learning Theory. Proceedings, 1992. X, 260 pages. 1993. (Subseries LNAI)

Vol. 744: K. P. Jantke, T. Yokomori, S. Kobayashi, E. Tomita (Eds.), Algorithmic Learning Theory. Proceedings, 1993. XI, 423 pages. 1993. (Subseries LNAI)

Vol. 745: V. Roberto (Ed.), Intelligent Perceptual Systems. VIII, 378 pages. 1993. (Subseries LNAI)

Vol. 746: A. S. Tanguiane, Artificial Perception and Music Recognition. XV, 210 pages. 1993. (Subseries LNAI).

Vol. 747: M. Clarke, R. Kruse, S. Moral (Eds.), Symbolic and Quantitative Approaches to Reasoning and Uncertainty. Proceedings, 1993. X, 390 pages. 1993.

Vol. 748: R. H. Halstead Jr., T. Ito (Eds.), Parallel Symbolic Computing: Languages, Systems, and Applications. Proceedings, 1992. X, 419 pages. 1993.

Vol. 749: P. A. Fritzson (Ed.), Automated and Algorithmic Debugging. Proceedings, 1993. VIII, 369 pages. 1993.

Vol. 750: J. L. Díaz-Herrera (Ed.), Software Engineering Education. Proceedings, 1994. XII, 601 pages. 1994.

Vol. 751: B. Jähne, Spatio-Temporal Image Processing. XII, 208 pages. 1993.

Vol. 752: T. W. Finin, C. K. Nicholas, Y. Yesha (Eds.), Information and Knowledge Management. Proceedings, 1992. VII, 142 pages. 1993.

Vol. 753: L. J. Bass, J. Gornostaev, C. Unger (Eds.), Human-Computer Interaction. Proceedings, 1993. X, 388 pages. 1993.

Vol. 754: H. D. Pfeiffer, T. E. Nagle (Eds.), Conceptual Structures: Theory and Implementation. Proceedings, 1992. IX, 327 pages. 1993. (Subseries LNAI)

Vol. 755: B. Möller, H. Partsch, S. Schuman (Eds.), Formal Program Development. Proceedings. VII, 371 pages. 1993.

Vol. 756: J. Pieprzyk, B. Sadeghiyan, Design of Hashing Algorithms. XV, 194 pages. 1993.

Vol. 757: U. Banerjee, D. Gelernter, A. Nicolau, D. Padua (Eds.), Languages and Compilers for Parallel Computing. Proceedings, 1992. X, 576 pages. 1993.

Vol. 758: M. Teillaud, Towards Dynamic Randomized Algorithms in Computational Geometry. IX, 157 pages. 1993.

Vol. 759: N. R. Adam, B. K. Bhargava (Eds.), Advanced Database Systems. XV, 451 pages. 1993.

Vol. 760: S. Ceri, K. Tanaka, S. Tsur (Eds.), Deductive and Object-Oriented Databases. Proceedings, 1993. XII, 488 pages. 1993.

Vol. 761: R. K. Shyamasundar (Ed.), Foundations of Software Technology and Theoretical Computer Science. Proceedings, 1993. XIV, 456 pages. 1993.

Vol. 762: K. W. Ng, P. Raghavan, N. V. Balasubramanian, F. Y. L. Chin (Eds.), Algorithms and Computation. Proceedings, 1993. XIII, 542 pages. 1993.

Vol. 763: F. Pichler, R. Moreno Díaz (Eds.), Computer Aided Systems Theory – EUROCAST '93. Proceedings, 1993. IX, 451 pages. 1994.

Vol. 764: G. Wagner, Vivid Logic. XII, 148 pages. 1994. (Subseries LNAI).

Vol. 765: T. Helleseth (Ed.), Advances in Cryptology – EUROCRYPT '93. Proceedings, 1993. X, 467 pages. 1994.

Vol. 766: P. R. Van Loocke, The Dynamics of Concepts. XI, 340 pages. 1994. (Subseries LNAI).

Vol. 767: M. Gogolla, An Extended Entity-Relationship Model. X, 136 pages. 1994.

Vol. 768: U. Banerjee, D. Gelernter, A. Nicolau, D. Padua (Eds.), Languages and Compilers for Parallel Computing. Proceedings, 1993. XI, 655 pages. 1994.

Vol. 769: J. L. Nazareth, The Newton-Cauchy Framework. XII, 101 pages. 1994.

Vol. 770: P. Haddawy (Representing Plans Under Uncertainty. X, 129 pages. 1994. (Subseries LNAI).

Vol. 771: G. Tomas, C. W. Ueberhuber, Visualization of Scientific Parallel Programs. XI, 310 pages. 1994.

Vol. 772: B. C. Warboys (Ed.),Software Process Technology. Proceedings, 1994. IX, 275 pages. 1994.

Vol. 773: D. R. Stinson (Ed.), Advances in Cryptology – CRYPTO '93. Proceedings, 1993. X, 492 pages. 1994.

Vol. 774: M. Banâtre, P. A. Lee (Eds.), Hardware and Software Architectures for Fault Tolerance. XIII, 311 pages. 1994.

Vol. 775: P. Enjalbert, E. W. Mayr, K. W. Wagner (Eds.), STACS 94. Proceedings, 1994. XIV, 782 pages. 1994.